CRITICAL THINKING, WORLD-VIEWS & LOGIC

Paul Catanu

Copyright © BabalonBOOKS 2023
First Edition

All rights reserved under International and Pan-American Copyright Conventions. No part of this book may be reproduced in any form or by any electronic or mechanical means, including information storage and retrieval systems, without permission in writing from the publisher, except by a reviewer, who may quote brief passages in a review.

Published worldwide by 8th House Publishing
www.8thHousePublishing.com
www.BabalonBOOKS.com

Front Cover Design by 8th House Publishing
Front Cover Artwork from 17th Century engraving, Artist Unknown

Set in Raleway, Franklin Gothic, Caslon Pro and Segoe UI Symbols.

ISBN 978-0-9877804-2-3
'Critical Thinking, Worldviews & Logic' by Paul Catanu

BabalonBOOKS is a division of 8th House Publishing, Montreal, Canada.
www.8thHousePublishing.com

8th House Publishing
Montreal, Canada

CRITICAL THINKING, WORLDVIEWS & LOGIC
Paul Catanu

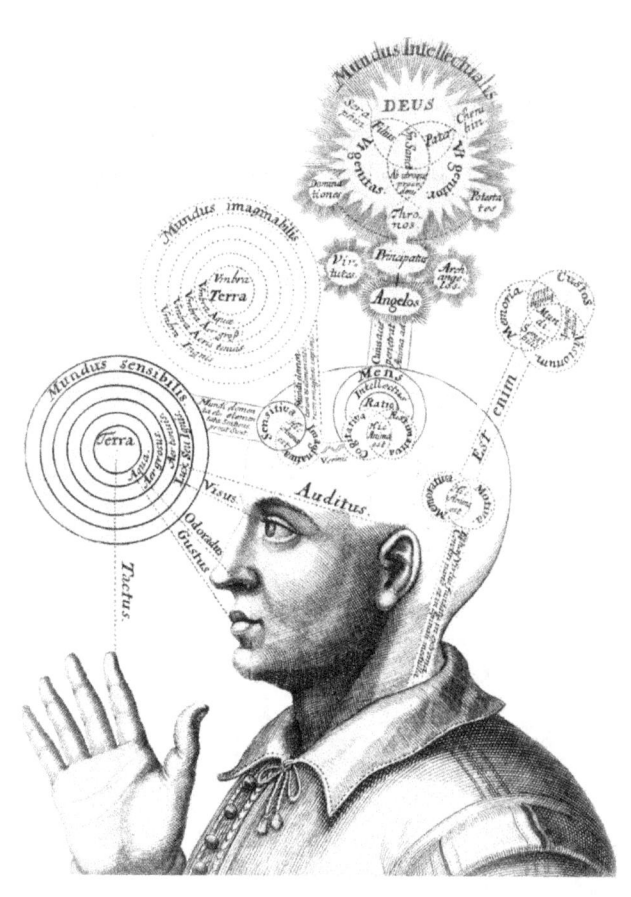

For Raja Vallée-Rai (1975-2004), the friend with whom I first discovered and shared the pleasures and delights of logic and mathematics at McGill and who first explained Russell's paradox to me.

Also, for my beloved mother, Catalina Catanu (1946-) who still can't let go after all these years, and who has put all her soul and heart to make this the best book possible.

AUTHOR'S PREFACE

Critical Thinking and Informal Logic have become disciplines of their own and one could argue that they are as serious and as respectable as formal logic. We will try to recapitulate briefly the history of how critical thinking came to be what it is. We will also review some definitions of critical thinking of the last twenty or thirty years; and finally, propose our own definition of critical thinking.

As Van Eemeren, Grootendorst and Snoeck Henkemans aver, it is the word *critical* in critical thinking that is problematic and most in need of definition (1996, 186). In order to broaden our understanding of what critical means in critical thinking it is necessary to look at the origin of how this word was used in the history of philosophy. Without doubt, the most famous instance of the use of critical comes (at least in modern times) from Kant's use of it in defining his critical project starting with the publication of his famous *Critique of Pure Reason* in 1781. Critique or critical means that Kant wants to set bounds on the use of pure reason and on the use of the word metaphysical which he believes has been used irresponsibly by people like Leibniz and Wolff.

So critique focuses on the dialectical (or erroneous) use of reason in order to clarify when reason and the understanding are properly synchronized and are used reasonably and rationally. Thus critique or critical is not purely negative as sometimes perceived since Kant shows that we can use reason to deduce the categories and there is a positive aspect to the critical project which aims to show how to use our powers and mental faculties well, positively and reasonably.

Another important use of the word critical is the one applied to the critical-historical biblical interpretation tradition (the *kritische-historische* or sometimes known as the *grammatische-historische Schule* in Germany and represented by Johann August Ernesti 1701-1781 and other theologians). These scholars sought to contextualize the Bible and find its historical authors or study Scripture objectively by eliminating superstitious beliefs from Scripture, identifying scientifically its historical authors and studying the text of Scripture philologically with critical attention paid to authorship and textual problems.

In this sense, the critical-historical school is proposing a hermeneutic or an art of interpreting the texts objectively without requiring the theological notion of revelation and divine inspiration.

Here again, critical is not necessarily negative but it does pose itself in the guise of an objective criterion of scientificity or scientism which is opposed to a mere subjective, faith and revelation-laden interpretation of Scripture. Kierkegaard famously claimed that this is misled and that truth is subjectivity, but this school of reading the Bible also influenced Nietzsche and led him to be skeptical about religion and the existence of God (see the famous letter to his sister Elizabeth in this context).

Whichever the right way to read Scripture may be, critical in this context means being attentive to the historical existence of historical authors, the contraposition, comparison and extrapolation of a study of dates and an application of historical method to dates, sources and authors. And yes critical may mean in this context opposed to the positivity of faith and revelation. This context may explain the perceived fact by many teachers teaching critical thinking whose views are also informed by faith and religion that there is an inherent negativity and perhaps darkness or hopelessness associated with the notion of critical thinking.

This contextualization of the word critical in the 18th century is useful, but we need to come closer to the present and look at how this word was used in the 20th century. We may pass over the 19th century by mentioning in passing Marx's ridiculing of some of the Young Hegelians as 'critical criticists'. Marx thought that their attempt to go back to Kant after Hegel was misled and his use of the word critical is purely ironic but little did he know that in the 20th century Marxism would spawn the movement of Critical Theory that was situated at the Social Institute of Frankfurt and that was led at least in part by Horkheimer and Adorno.

Critical Theory sought to resist Nazism and fascism, something it perceived philosophical phenomenology to be either too weak to do or in the worse case complicit with (Martin Heidegger's infamous case). The critical in critical theory seeks to look at social structures, institutions and practices and find the Enlightened and rational elements in order to separate them from the barbaric, regressive, populist and anti-rational ones. In the *Dialectic of Enlightenment*, Horkheimer and Adorno's most pessimist book (written during the second world war when there was a possibility that Hitler could win) the authors claim that Enlightenment cannot extricate itself from myth.

Of course, that was not the position of all of the critical theorists and perhaps a note of optimism may be found at least in the later generations of that school such as Jurgen Habermas and Axel Honneth (both still alive) who believe that modernity is an unfinished project but that critique can show the way forward. Both Adorno and Horkheimer and Habermas were going back to the ideal of the Enlightenment set by Kant where critique was a way for human beings to achieve autonomy and majority from a self-incurred (and other incurred because Kant also blamed subtly the authorities of Church and King) state of minority brought about by simple and crass ignorance and lack of education.

PREFACE

It must be said that these historical preliminaries situate the word 'critical' in the Continental tradition of thinking and philosophizing. But to fully understand critical thinking and not to confuse it with critical theory as some serious and advanced scholars still do sometimes, it is necessary to consider the domain of Analytical philosophy dominated at the beginning of the 20th century by the likes of Russell, GE Moore, Carnap, Whitehead and others.

In fact, the first instance of the use of critical in critical thinking may perhaps be traced to John Dewey who is an American pragmatist (see our summary of his work in Chapter 6). For Dewey critical thinking referred to "Active, persistent and careful consideration of any belief or supposed form of knowledge in the light of the grounds that support it, and the further conclusions to which it tends."[1]

The beginning of the critical thinking and informal fallacy revolution began in the 1950's and we do well to review in this brief preface its main phases and steps. 1958 is an annus mirabilis for informal logic and critical thinking since it marks the publication of both Toulmin's *How to Use Arguments* and *The New Rhetoric; A Treatise on Argumentation* by Chaim Perelman and Lucie Olbrechts-Tyteca. We have already spent quite a bit of time discussing Toulmin and his model of argumentation in Chapter 2. Thus we give a bit more space here to the work of Perelman and Olbrechts-Tyteca.

Perelman earlier adhered to the philosophy of logical empiricism. But according to this philosophy it was not possible to explain the intuitive existence of value judgments. This was due to the fact that logical empiricism (see Chapter 4.5.1 of this textbook for more information on logical empiricism) claims that the fact-value distinction is true following David Hume (this claim was also accepted by Max Weber) and that you cannot derive an is from an ought. The author of this book rejects the fact value distinction or dichotomy and believes that facts are somehow theoretic and value-laden as is reason itself. We distinguish between instrumental reason and value-guided or value-laden reason.

Perelman and Olbrechts-Tyteca did not think that value judgments could be derived out of the logic of argumentation like mathematical or a priori apodictic truths are derived from geometry or analysis and algebra or even set theory. Instead they believed that in common-sense and common, natural language situations people attempted to justify their opinions according to something akin to a juridical model employed around the same time by Toulmin.

After the path-breaking work of Toulmin and Perelman and Olbrechts-Tyteca in 1958, one could argue that a new era begins for critical thinking and informal logic. There are creations of associations for informal logic and there is the development of an entire new industry of publications and associations related to critical thinking. If one were to be

---
1 Dewey, John, *How We Think*, (reissue of the 1909 1st edition), Buffalo, Prometheus Books, 1991, p.6

cynical one could consider perhaps that the emphasis on critical thinking in American and Canadian classrooms at the level of College and University may be a new form of dogmatism. Certainly this is not the position of the author but the quality of publication on Internet websites and within publishing houses on critical thinking is not always met. One does not always distinguish between critical thinking and creative thinking or what some have called parallel thinking or lateral thinking (see the work of Edward de Bono in connection with these principles and ideas).

Traditionally, critical thinking has been defined as a form of fault-finding, but it is the belief of this author that it also has to do with the ability to recognize abstract forms that occur in formal fallacies. Van Eemeren and von Grootendorst distinguish three types of informal logicians depending on whether the logician admits the existence of formal fallacies, believes that formal fallacies are explicable in terms of logical deductive form or analyzable in terms of logical deductive forms. The problems is complex because it involves the description or reference to false logical forms which seems a misnomer since the notion of form in deduction is always positive and hence "false logical forms" seems to lack a proper referent.

My own point of view when faced with logical deductive form and its relationship to critical thinking and informal logic is that informal logicians have gone too far in claiming that critical thinking is only tied to notions of informal logic. Hence my view is that formal fallacies are more than explicable in terms of deductive logical form but are actually analyzable or "resolvable" into deductive logical form. This is the case because form has logical and metaphysical priority over informality and formlessness. This is actually a very involved discussion and even though this is a preface aimed both at the instructor and the student, I prefer to pursue it in a footnote.[2]

---

2 Van Eemeren and Grootendorst (A Handbook of Argumentation, 1996) distinguish between informal fallacy theorists who 1) do not believe that there are such entities as formal fallacies 2) believe that formal fallacies exist but are not relatable in any way to informal fallacies 3) believe that informal fallacies are explainable in terms of formal elements existing in formal fallacies and 4) believe that informal fallacies are analyzable in terms of formal elements existing in formal fallacies. View 4) is attributed to Woods and Walton and it is also the one that this author endorses. The problem is what does analyzable mean in this context. We give Van Eemeren's & Grootendorst's definition from *A Handbook:* "A fallacy F is formally analyzable to the extent that its analysis introduces concepts which are described, in whole or part, by technical vocabulary and/or the formal structures of a system of logic or other sort of formal theory." (p.237) For explicability, Van Eemeren and Grootendorst use the example of an ambiguity or equivocation fallacy (which is informal in principle) which is reducible to a formal fallacy of four terms. In the case of analyzability I refer the reader to the works of Walton and Woods in which they use the notion of Kripke structure (1965) to show that cumulativeness is formally analyzable in terms of Kripke structures and that it allows one to understand and preclude the petitio principii (sometimes called begging the question). Woods and Walton further show that the fallacies of composition and division (also taken to be informal fallacies) are formally analyzable in terms of "aggregate theory" as developed by Tyler Burge (1977). My platonic thesis that informality is always reducible and analyzable in terms of form and formality would require more work to show in detail but I have said enough to show where I situate myself in the debate on the relationship and proximity between informal logic and formal logic and the undisputed importance of formal logic and ability to manipulate abstract forms and structures for critical thinking.

PREFACE

Critical Thinking studies are at a crossroads. They are becoming more scientific and better organized and one can think of developing a research programme on democracy, citizenship, communication and the nature of critical thinking. It is clear to the author of this book that good critical thinkers are better citizens and make up a healthier democracy since they are less prone to be manipulated. More than ever with the appearance of social media and alternative media it is necessary to foster and sustain the development of critical thinkers who can be aware of what some have called fake news or post-factual truth but which is in fact good old propaganda and agitprop. It is the challenge of education for democracy and virtue in the 21st century to enlarge and give a broad toolkit of critical thinking to citizens from all walks of life, regardless of creeds, religion, race, gender or social class. This perhaps is the universal promise of critical thinking and the gift we can give to our students and to future generations. In this sense, perhaps critical thinking should attempt to connect back to its roots in critical theory since one can make the case that there is emancipatory hope in the project of critical thinking for democracy and virtue.

Faced with the challenge of global climate change, overpopulation and other types of problems students will have to use imagination, creativity and what De Bono has called lateral thinking. Critical thinking cannot be a substitute for the creative artistic, humanistic and scientific imagination but an imagination that is not critical and informed can be manipulated and suborned. Imagination and creativity are complements of critical thinking and for this we need to retrieve the contents of our Western tradition. I have done this as well in this book in identifying the notions of ontology and metaphysics which I believe to be the original contribution of Western philosophy to the world and to universal history. The question of Being as Heidegger reminded us at the beginning of the last century is what critique needs to be applied to. But the substance and reality of Being constitutes the content of our Western rational tradition. What Heidegger lost sight of is the necessity of critique, dialectic and logic. For this the student is asked to look at the projects of other great philosophers such as Hegel, Marx and Adorno. It is the thesis of this author that critical thinking has to be value laden. This is the case because reason is value laden and is not a pure fault-finding tool. Reason and its complement faith give substance to the lives of individuals. Nonetheless if we accept Hume's thesis that facts and values constitute a dichotomy we may never find that critical thinking constitutes an intrinsic value which is the belief I am defending in this textbook.

Here are some values that could be shared through critical thinking: equality, hope, solidarity, interdependence, community, love, trust, etc. Here a big challenge is to understand the relationship between value and beliefs. It is the case that through critical thinking we might have to give up some beliefs and come to other beliefs. Thus, critical thinking may also modify our value systems and this is the work that is done through dialectic and critique in the process of sorting ourselves out and realizing what we really believe and what our real values are. But the student needs to understand that once he begins his journey as a critical thinker, he is entering into a community of letters, of excellence and research and that this type of community necessarily places certain positive values at the center of its traditions. No matter how much we criticize our beliefs we will never conclude that selfishness is better than altruism or that evil should be returned with evil. We can analyze our beliefs until the cows come home but hatred will never be better than love, or manipulation better than the search for truth.

Since critical thinking develops the students into atomized, individualized thinkers, the first step is the dawn of a form of relativism in the students but this needs to be overcome by demonstrating that critical thinking can also lead to a form of rational and enlightened community. The students go through a phase of critical relativism (to speak with Alain Leroy Locke) and critical individualism but it is good to make clear to the student from the start that thinking does not happen in a vacuum and that we are always members of an ethical community or what Hegel called the ethical substance (Sittlichkeit). Rather the phase of critical individualism and critical relativism should be seen as a phase in the development of initiates into critical thinking, a phase they overcome when they begin to understand the broader world of culture, reason and universal values.

Still, as critical thinking is at a crossroads, I think some important questions are open for it and any student and advanced educator should bear these questions in mind when attempting to understand and practice critical thinking:

- *Can deep critical thinking be achieved without some understanding of formal methods and so can critical thinking be purely equivalent to informal logic?*
- *What is the relationship between persuasion and conviction?*
- *Does critical thinking aim to persuade or to convince or to express a persuasion versus a conviction?*
- *What role does critical thinking play in changing one's own set of beliefs?*
- *Is critical thinking Western centric or European centric?*
- *Must all individuals think critically and what is relationship of critical thinking to traditional, endogenous or indigenous thought or ecological thought or religious thought?*
- *Are there limits to critical thinking?*
- *What is relationship between critical thinking prejudice and distorted and undistorted communication?*
- *Is critical thinking a new cultural and educational industry, is it reified and has it become the new ideology of Global Capitalism in the 21st century?*
- *What is the difference between lateral thinking and critical thinking?*

- *Can critical thinking be a real agent for social change and modify social relationships so that the Global super-rich class and Capital stop dominating and exploiting the Global middle class and stop making a profit at the expense of the Earth?*

For me the last question is the most urgent to answer by any critical thinking researcher.

In common language "critical" is often used as a negative, "fault-finding" exercise. (e.g.: My sister always criticizes me). This is not the "critical thinking" that we intend to study. In our usage "critical" means "involving and exercising skilled judgement and observation". Critical thinking is the general term given to a wide range of cognitive skills and intellectual dispositions needed to:

- effectively identify, analyze and evaluate arguments and truth claims.
- discover and overcome personal preconceptions, prejudices and biases.
- formulate and present convincing reasons in support of conclusions.
- make reasonable, intelligent decisions about what to believe and what to do.[3]

Some authors such as Bassham, Irwing, Nardone and Wallace have proposed certain standards for critical thinking.[4] I list them below so that this preface may be as complete as possible.

Clarity

In order to understand a problem, an issue, the arguments associated with it and to be able to have a position, the thought and language analyzing and explaining the **issue** need to be clear. **Clear thought** will identify goals, priorities, will help to understand problems and opportunities. To analyze, explain and, communicate well a clear thought, a **clear language** is needed. Lack of language clarity, more often encountered than what we would like, is due to different reasons:

- sloppiness, lack of skill,
- an unfortunate tendency to look learned, to use too much jargon of a specific field.
- We may often find culprits among the following: philosophers, psychologists, pedagogues and many others etc.[5]

---

[3] *Critical Thinking, A Student's Introduction* by G. Bassham, W. Irwin, H. Nardone. J.M.Wallace
[4] *Critical Thinking, A Student's Introduction* by G. Bassham, W. Irwin, H. Nardone. J.M.Wallace
[5] There is a debate among philosophers and other specialists as to whether one need to be clear or be true to the domain of expertise which may require terms of art, specialized language, etc. One could conclude that clarity shows mastery of a subject while lack of clarity does not exclude that some level of mastery difficult to evaluate is nonetheless achieved. When one thinks of the achievements of Heidegger (and other great philosophical masters such as Aristotle or Hegel and Kant) who is notoriously unclear and obscure in expression one may question the fact that clarity is an absolute criterion. But for the beginning student in critical thinking and philosophy, it is important to aim for clarity. Once having mastered this criterion he can transcend it at a later stage much like Wittgenstein's ladder which may be kicked down once one has climbed it.

Precision

Answering precise answers to precise questions, is one of the methods developed by the greatest critical thinkers of all times, starting with Socrates.

-What is the problem?

-What are the alternatives?

-What are the advantages and disadvantages of each alternative?

Accuracy

The computer saying "Garbage In Garbage Out" is valid for a lot of things, including all thought processes. No matter how skilled a critical thinker is, one cannot arrive to a truthful conclusion starting from false information. At least two wars, Vietnam, and Iraq were started based on false and inaccurate information.

Relevance

A clear line of thought means also not to be sidetracked by subjects irrelevant to the issue, problem, position analysed or discussed. This is sometimes a tactic used by debaters or politicians to distract the adversary or the public from the issue on hand. Stay focussed on relevant ideas and information. If one studies Chapter 2 carefully in the section on Fallacies, one will note that this is also a general category of fallacies (fallacies of intrusion or relevance). Thus distinguishing between good arguments and fallacious ones entails looking at what is relevant to achieving a wanted conclusion from the given premises.

Consistence

There are two types of inconsistency to be avoided: Logical inconsistencies: having beliefs or ideas that contradict one each other

- Controversial example: believing in God and in evolution at the same time (Darwin's case)

And practical inconsistencies: saying one thing and doing another.

- Examples: some political promises, some New Year's resolutions

Logical correctness

To reach truthful conclusions you need not only true beliefs but also logical reasoning and a method in order to preserve the truth of your beliefs or of your web of beliefs and to derive new truths or new facts from your original web beliefs once that original web has been subjected to a critical, verification process.

Bertrand Russell's example:

> ... the nuns who never take a bath without a bathrobe... When asked why, since no man can see them, they reply: Oh, but you forget the good God. Apparently, they conceive of the deity as a Peeping Tom. whose omnipotence enables Him to see through the bathroom walls but who is foiled by bathrobes.

Fairness

Ideally the critical thinker is an open minded, impartial, unprejudiced and unbiased thinker. This is a high standard, often difficult to achieve as almost all of us have our own strong beliefs, not easily changed in face of new evidence or ideas. It is a high ideal worth struggling for. Note that fairness unlike the other standards which are purely procedural is normative meaning that it has ethical import. Critical thinking is not to be done or executed in the vacuum by robots or AI's, it presupposes some human ethical engagement that is anti-relativistic. Even though fairness and justice are difficult to define without controversy, critical thinking presupposes some consensus about it that allows one to proceed in good faith, honestly, sincerely and based on a certain amount of trust in others and the world that surrounds us.

So why is this textbook called *Critical Thinking, Worldviews, And Logic*? Part of the title is contingent upon circumstance. I have been teaching in a College in the Province of Quebec since 2008 and part of our curriculum is a class on Worldviews. The worldviews I cover in this book are the idealist worldview, the pragmatist worldview, the scientific worldview, and the humanist worldview. Needless to say, there are many more worldviews, which I do not cover. The notion of worldview goes back to the German philosopher Wilhelm Dilthey. I have identified 4 aspects of worldviews in footnote 1 of Chapter 5. Again there is a certain arbitrariness to this and others such as Apostel see even more sub-aspects of worldviews. (Apostel lists 7 sub-aspects I believe). The main thing in my mind is to clarify that worldviews are relativistic to a certain extent and that this relativistic aspect of worldviews is in tension with the fact that my positions in this textbook criticize knowledge-relativism. In this worldviews are comparable to ideologies and the critique of ideologies. Ideologies can be commonly described as conscious or unconscious systems of representation. Worldviews share this conscious/unconscious aspect with ideologies but they are somehow more fundamental and totalizing. Ideologies are narrower, worldviews are broader. Worldviews can be religious but they do not have to be. We can think of the Islamic or Christian worldview but as I write in the book there is also the Chinese worldview which has a Communist ideology but possesses features in common with the Ancient Greek worldview since it was developed in the what Karl Jaspers calls the Axial Age. Worldviews matter and are important because despite of their fragmentary aspect (tied to the liberal and Neo-liberal atomized subject of knowledge and of citizenship), they have a potential to unify. If treated critically, worldviews with their communal sources have the potential to create a Global polity and inform students about Global citizenship).

Finally, the last aspect of this book is an introduction to inductive and deductive logic. Of course it is my thesis that critical thinking cannot exist without some formal training and some mastery of deductive contents. I define logic as the study of reasoning and intelligence and its relation to structures, models and reality. Thus logic, despite its formal deductive structure, must preserve a connection to induction. To end this preface with an opening, worldviews give us the content of tradition and thought, critical thinking and logic give us the analytical tools to take this content apart and dissect it in order to become aware of what the prejudices of our tradition and origins are. But the highest function of thought is synthesis and for this wisdom and philosophy are required. This wisdom and philosophy lies at the basis of this whole book and it is my hope that I have kindled the interest and wonder of all curious students to go farther and develop their knowledge while understanding their own worldview better, more critically and with analytical-logical discernment. One last word of advice. Critical thinkers of the world, the time has come to understand the world, but above all to change it in the higher interests of social justice and equality. Use this knowledge to change the world and make it a better place.

CRITICAL THINKING, WORLD-VIEWS & LOGIC

CONTENTS

AUTHOR'S PREFACE ii

INTRODUCTION 3
CRITICAL THINKING, LOGIC AND ARGUMENTS 3
Why We Study Critical Thinking 6
What is a presupposition? 7
Some Mistaken Beliefs Regarding Arguments 12
Critical Examination of Prejudices 15
Arguments as Forms of Persuasion 15
Argument Standardization or Formalization 15
CONCLUSION 16
EXERCISES 17

CHAPTER I 23
DEFINITIONS
1.1 SYMBOLIC & MATHEMATICAL LOGIC 24
    Logical Connectives or Operators 28
    Truth Tables 30
    EXERCISES 31
1.2 LOGICAL DEFINITION 34
1.3 VALIDITY & SOUNDNESS 40
    Notions of Deductive Validity and Soundness 40
    What is a syllogism? 41
    Law of Detachment or Modus ponens 41
  1.3.1 Validity & Soundness in Deductive Reasoning 42
    Valid and Unsound Arguments 43
    EXERCISES 44
    Translating INTO Logical Symbolism or Expression 45
    Translating FROM Logical Symbolism or Expression 45
    EXERCISES 47
1.4 CATEGORICAL OR SYLLOGISTIC LOGIC 48
    Categorical Propositions & Classes 48
    Quality, Quantity & Distribution Of Categorical Propositions 49
    Mood And Figures Of Syllogisms 49
    Using Venn Diagrams To Verify The Validity Of Syllogisms 52
    EXERCISES 55
1.5 PROPOSITIONAL or SENTENTIAL (0th Order) LOGIC 57
  1.5.1 RULES OF INFERENCE IN PROPOSITIONAL LOGIC 58
    Derivation Rules in a Propositional Deduction System 58
    BASIC RULES OF INFERENCE 64
    EXERCISES 64
  1.5.2 REPLACEMENT RULES FOR PROPOSITIONAL LOGIC 66
    EXERCISES 68
  1.5.3 Truth Tables and Truth Trees for Propositional Logic 70

    Understanding Truth-Functional Logic   70
    EXERCISES   72
1.6 PREDICATE or FIRST-ORDER LOGIC   73
    First-order logic   73
    Second-order logic   74
  1.6.1 RULES FOR NEGATING QUANTIFIERS   75
    EXERCISES   78
  1.6.2 Free and Bound Variables   79
    EXERCISES   81
  1.6.3 Theory of Inference for Predicate Calculus   82
    Rules for Dropping Quantifiers   82
    EXERCISES   83
  1.6.4 Proving Consistency in Predicate Logic   84
    EXERCISES   84
  1.6.5 PROVING VALIDITY IN PREDICATE LOGIC   85
  1.6.6 Truth Trees as a Proof-Method in Predicate Logic   86
CONCLUSION   87
EXERCISES   89

HISTORICAL INTERLUDE: 91
THE THREE LAWS OF THOUGHT & LEIBNIZ'S LAWS

The Classical Laws of Thought   91
THE THREE LAWS OF THOUGHT   91
The Principle of Identity   92
The Principle of Non-Contradiction   92
The Principle of Excluded Middle   93
The Principle of Bivalence   93
Leibniz's Law (Principle of Identity of Indiscernibles)   94
    THE INDISCERNIBILITY OF INDENTICALS (PRINCIPLE I)   96
    THE IDENTITY OF INDISCERNIBLES (PRINCIPLE II)   96
QUESTIONS   97

CHAPTER 2   99
CRITICAL THINKING, INFORMAL LOGIC AND INDUCTIVE REASONING

2.1 WHAT IS INDUCTION?   101
2.2 STATISTICAL SYLLOGISMS   101
    General form of a Statistical Syllogism   102
    Inductive Analogy as a Form of Inductive Reasoning   103
    EXERCISES   105
2.3 FORMAL AND INFORMAL FALLACIES   106
  2.3.1 Formal Fallacies   106
  EXERCISES   113
  2.3.2 Informal Fallacies   115
    Linguistic fallacies   116
    Fallacies of omission   119
    Fallacies of intrusion (relevance)   122
    Causal fallacies   126
  EXERCISES   131
2.4 NECESSARY AND SUFFICIENT CONDITIONS & INDUCTIVE REASONING   133

2.4.1 Necessary and Sufficient Causes ... 133
2.4.2 Mill's Methods and Inductive Causal Arguments ... 135
    Mill's Method of Direct Agreement ... 136
    Mill's Method of Difference ... 136
2.4.3 Joint Method of Agreement and Difference ... 137
2.4.4 Method of Residue ... 138
2.4.5 Method of Concomitance, Concomitant Variance or Correlation ... 139
EXERCISES ... 140

CHAPTER 3 — 147

THEORIES OF KNOWLEDGE: RATIONALISM

3.1 PARMENIDES ... 148
3.2 SOCRATES AND RATIONALISM ... 149
3.3 DESCARTES AND RATIONALISM ... 150
3.4 SPINOZA: KNOWLEDGE OF THE NECESSITY OF GOD AND THE WORLD ... 155
3.5 LEIBNIZ: LOGIC, MONADS & THE BEST POSSIBLE WORLD ... 160
CONCLUSION ... 166
EXERCISES ... 167

CHAPTER 4 — 169

THEORIES OF KNOWLEDGE: EMPIRICISM

4.1 Empiricism in the Middle Ages ... 170
4.1.1 Francis Bacon ... 172
4.2 British Empiricism ... 177
4.2.1 John Locke: The Founding of British Empiricism ... 177
4.3 Philosophical Skepticism ... 180
4.3.1 Hume: The Radicalization of Empiricism into Philosophical Skepticism ... 180
4.4 Phenomenalistic Empiricism ... 182
4.4.1 MILL: Phenomenalistic Empiricism ... 182
4.5 Logical Empiricism ... 184
  4.5.1 The Vienna and The Berlin Schools ... 184
Conclusion ... 187
EXERCISES ... 189

CHAPTER 5 — 191

WORLDVIEWS: IDEALISM

5.1 ANCIENT & MEDIEVAL IDEALISM ... 193
  5.1.1 Ancient Idealism ... 193
  5.1.2 Medieval (Christian) Idealism ... 196
5.2 Modern Idealism ... 198
  5.2.1 Subjective Idealism ... 198
  5.2.2 Objective Idealism ... 199
  5.2.3 Transcendental Idealism ... 200
  5.2.4 Absolute Idealism ... 202
EXERCISES ... 205

CHAPTER 6 — 207
WORLDVIEWS: PRAGMATISM

6.1 American Idealism — 209
  6.1.2 Ralph Waldo Emerson — 209
6.2 Origins of American Pragmatism — 212
  6.2.1 Charles Peirce: Peirce's Understanding of Logic — 212
6.3 Subjective Pragmatism — 220
  6.3.1 William James: Psychological and Subjective Pragmatism — 220
6.4 End of Classical American Pragmatism — 226
  6.4.1 Dewey — 226
EXERCISES — 231

CHAPTER 7 — 233
SCIENCE, CRITICAL THINKING AND THE SCIENTIFIC WORLDVIEW

7.1 Natural Science, The Human Sciences & The Social Sciences — 234
7.2 The Positivistic Model — 238
  7.2.2 SCIENTIFIC METHOD AND THE ROLE OF EXPLANATION — 240
7.3 Deductive-Nomological Model — 242
  7.3.1 Explanation as a Kind of Argument — 242
7.4 Other Positivistic Models of Science — 246
  7.4.1 The Causal Mechanical Model — 246
  7.4.2 The Unity of Science Thesis — 248
7.5 The Historicist Critics of the Postivist Models of Science — 249
EXERCISES — 253

CHAPTER 8 — 255
KNOWLEDGE AND THE HUMANIST WORLDVIEW

8.1 Ramon Llull — 257
  8.1.1 Ars Magna & the Influence on Calculus and Induction — 257
8.2 Boccaccio — 259
  8.2.1 Naturalization of the Middle-Ages Christian Eros — 259
8.3 Pico de la Mirandola & Marsilio Ficino — 262
  8.3.1 The Dignity of Man and Renaissance Syncretism — 262
8.4 Erasmus's polemic with Luther on free will — 265
8.5 Thomas More's upholding of Catholic Dogma against Henri the VIIIth — 268
8.6 Giordano Bruno's Art of Memory — 271
EXERCISES — 273

CONCLUSION — 275
SELECT BIBLIOGRAPHY — 280
INDEX - IDEAS & NOTIONS — 282
INDEX - PEOPLE & WORKS — 283
Appendix on Syllogistic Logic — 285
Appendix on Informal Argument Diagrams — 287

SOLUTIONS TO EXERCISES — 297

CRITICAL THINKING, LOGIC & ARGUMENTS
INTRODUCTION

Critical thinking is a method we use and apply to various discourses in order to evaluate the veracity or truthfulness of those discourses. We may perhaps have an innate idea of truthfulness and we know now that critical thinking is a way of analyzing discourses; but then what is a discourse? A discourse is something, anything, expressed, most often in language. It can be an article in a paper, but it can also be a cartoon or a work of art. It can be a music video, a movie or a novel. It can be an advertisement or a play. It can be an editorial or a history book. In fact a discourse is anything that can be expressed and that expresses a position or attempts to make a rationally intelligible statement. There are a few terms which we need to define further before we can more fully explore the role of critical thinking in discourse. These terms are: argument, position and issue.

An **argument** is a thought process enunciated in a natural or formal language that attempts to preserve the truth from the premises to the conclusion.

EXAMPLES

1: All men are mortal. Socrates is a man. Therefore Socrates is mortal.
2: My dog is red. Your dog is red. Therefore, all dogs are red.
3: The sun rose yesterday; it rose this morning. Therefore the sun will rise tomorrow.

A **premise** is a sentence or formula enunciated in a natural or formal language which defends or implies the truth of the conclusion.

✓ KEY CONCEPTS & DEFINITIONS - INTRODUCTION

ARGUMENT: A thinking or reasoning process enunciated in a natural or formal language that attempts to preserve the truth from the premises to the conclusion.

PREMISE: A sentence or formula enunciated in a natural or formal language which defends or implies the truth of the conclusion.

CONCLUSION or **THESIS**: The truth or point being defended or asserted in that argument.

POSITION: A point of view or opinion that is defended by rational arguments.

ISSUE: A situation or problem that divides people and on which at least two differing positions can be taken or exist.

PRESUPPOSITION: A belief or *position* that an individual holds about a fundamental question without being aware that he/she holds this belief, or the causes, truthfulness or even desirability of his/her position.

ETHICS: The study of the right, good or virtuous course of action or of the nature of values that inform and authorize action.

ONTOLOGY: The study of being or existence of entities.

EPISTEMOLOGY: The study of the theory of knowledge.

INFERENCE: the process of deriving logical conclusions from premises known or believed to be true.

Three Types of Inference

1. Inductive; 2. Abductive; 3. Deductive

In analyzing arguments, we must ensure that:
- we are cautious in proceeding and keep a lookout for logical traps or fallacies.
- we evaluate an argument at each step or examine each of its parts.
- we produce a global evaluation of an argumentation; and
- we are able to justify this evaluation.

In examples 1, 2 and 3 the premises are respectively, *'All men are mortal', 'Socrates is a man', 'My dog is red', 'Your dog is red', 'The sun rose yesterday; it rose this morning'*.

The **conclusion** or the **thesis** of an argument is the truth or point being defended or asserted in that argument.

In examples 1, 2 and 3, the conclusions or theses are respectively, *'Therefore Socrates is mortal', 'Therefore the sun will rise tomorrow', 'Therefore all dogs are red'*.

A **position** is a point of view or opinion that is defended by rational arguments.

EXAMPLES
*1: Public health care is a good thing and ought to be defended.
2: Time is objective.
3: Marijuana should be legalized.
4: God exists and this can be proved using rational arguments.
5: The right of women to have abortions is based on their ownership of their bodies, which is absolute.
6: There is no personal immortality because the existence of the soul is illusory.*

An **issue** is a situation or problem that divides people and on which at least two differing positions may be taken (e.g. *'for'* or *'against'*).

Examples 1, 2, 3, 4, 5, 6 outline the following issues respectively: (1) The issue of public health care; (2) The issue of the nature of time; (3) The issue of the legal status of marijuana; (4) The issue of the existence of God and its provability or demonstrability; (5) The issue of abortion; (6) The issue of the existence of the soul and of personal immortality.

ⓘ KEY DEFINITIONS

ARGUMENT: A thinking or reasoning process enunciated in a natural or formal language that attempts to preserve the truth from the premises to the conclusion.

PREMISE: A sentence or formula enunciated in a natural or formal language which defends or implies the truth of the conclusion.

CONCLUSION or **THESIS**: The truth or point being defended or asserted in that argument.

POSITION: A point of view or opinion that is defended by rational arguments.

ISSUE: A situation or problem that divides people and on which at least two differing positions can be taken or exist.

Why We Study Critical Thinking

Here is a short survey of why we might choose to study critical thinking. We might do so in order to better:

1. Examine with precision the veracity of beliefs and argued positions and determine how beliefs or positions should be fixed.
2. Throw light on presuppositions, prejudices or inherited beliefs.
3. Determine, after critical deliberation, what the goals for our actions should be.
4. Develop justifiable rules of law and conduct.
5. Understand ethical[1], ontological[2], epistemological[3], political, sociological and historical errors and seek areas of improvement or development.

In examining beliefs and argued positions and determining how beliefs or positions should be fixed, let us examine the following statements:

- *"Reason and the emotions are opposed."*
- *"In our society, people are too individualistic."*
- *"Science and technology are the major sources of actual problems in industrialized societies."*

These are all statements of belief. We might agree with some of the statements and disagree with some others. Reflecting upon these beliefs or opinions and what they mean, if they are true or false, what they imply, what their consequences are, the way in which they are developed and the way in which they could be verified, is the beginning of philosophy.

The fact that we may challenge established beliefs and notions may appear unsettling or threatening to some, but this is the price and the risk of philosophizing. The study of philosophy is like a wonderful adventure which we may choose to engage in, but like any adventure there are risks: the risk is that our beliefs and thus our personality structure, which is dependent on our beliefs may be radically altered, as each belief is brought out of the cupboard and examined in the cold, analytical light of reason.

As regards critical thinking specifically, this subject has a history of many hundreds, if not thousands of years, in what we may call Western civilization. Our study of the subject must take account of this and when we treat the subject of logic our approach must be both theoretical and historical. More generally and with respect to critical thinking we

---

[1] The study of the right, good or virtuous course of action or of the nature of values that inform and authorize action.
[2] The study of Being or existence of entities.
[3] The study of the theory of knowledge.

will be interested in examining how a reliable method for establishing firm beliefs may be arrived at. The second objective of critical thinking is to throw light on presuppositions or prejudices that we may possess. We begin with a cursory examination of these.

ISSUE	POSITIONS
Public health care	Public health care is a good thing and ought to be defended vs. We should have more private health care.
The right to die	Terminally ill suffering people have the right to ask and to receive help to die vs. Assisted suicide is a crime and should stay this way.
The right to wear religious symbols in public space	Wearing religious symbols is part of religious freedom and should be always allowed vs. In a secular society, the people in power positions (judges, police, professors) should not wear religious symbols.
Legal status of marijuana	Marijuana should be legalized vs Marijuana should be criminalized.
The Existence of God	God exists and this can be proven with rational arguments vs. God does not exist—there are no rational arguments to prove its existence.

What is a presupposition?

A **presupposition** is a belief or *position* that an individual holds about a fundamental question without being aware that he/she holds this belief, or the causes, truthfulness or even desirability of their position.

Examples of such fundamental questions are many. All have been attacked, challenged and dissected by philosophers and debate still continues. We have questions and argumentation still about:

- the existence of God.
- what truth is and how we can know;
- the question of what moral values are and whether they are substantially real;
- the meaning of existence;
- the best type of government;
- what a crime is and which forms of punishment are fitting for it;
- what virtue is and what it means to be virtuous;
- the question of what is the meaning of history or life and whether such a meaning exists;
- the continuing and adaptive defining of concepts such as Justice, Goodness, Truth, Knowledge, Science, Fact, Being, Becoming, Existing, Consciousness, and the very word Life.

These fundamental questions though easily stated and understood, are complex. It is sometimes challenging to separate the **ethical** (*the moral, the good*) from the **ontological** (*the actual thing, its existence and essence*) or **epistemological** (*the knowledge and use of a thing*) aspects of a question.

> ### ⓘ KEY DEFINITIONS
>
> **Ethics**: The study of the right, good or virtuous course of action or of the nature of values that inform and authorize action.
>
> **Ontology**: The study of Being or existence of entities.
>
> **Epistemology**: The study of the theory of knowledge.

Thus, one of the goals of philosophy and of critical thinking is to throw light upon those presuppositions so that we may become aware of them and evaluate them; i.e. pass judgment upon them.

Here are some examples of tacit beliefs or presuppositions (not about fundamental questions, but about more common sense concerns) which are incorporated into arguments:

> *There are more juvenile delinquents today.*
>
> *There are also more people who do advanced studies.*
>
> *Therefore, advanced studies encourage delinquency.*

Any argument is made up of premises and conclusions. We will define an argument to be any set of propositions which seeks to convince us of the truth of a state of affairs.[4] The premises of an argument are what defend the truth of its conclusion. The premises and conclusions are usually simple propositions i.e. they possess the grammatical structure of subject, verb, complement (the verb and the complement are sometimes called the predicate, though logic treats the nature of the predicate somewhat differently than grammar does).

Let us return to the previous argument. What is wrong with this argument? We know the leap to the conclusion to be inherently false. But can we explain why? First, what are the premises and what is the conclusion?

The premises are '*There are more juvenile delinquents today*', and '*There are also people who do advanced studies*'. The conclusion is: '*Therefore advanced studies encourage delinquency*'. But the connection between the first premise and the second premise is spurious and does not do enough work to convince us of the truth of the conclusion. We will learn

---

[4] This does not contradict the definition of argument given earlier but complements it. The definition provided is the more generally accepted and therefore is the one we will be referring to.

later that there is an internal connection between the truth of the premises and the truth of the conclusion that allows us to decide whether a deductive argument is valid or not.

Arguments sometimes contain **premise indicators** which qualify the statement. An example list, which is by no means exhaustive, is provided in the table below:

PREMISE INDICATIORS	
• since (non-temporal meaning)	• given that / seeing that
• as indicated by	• for the reason that
• because	• owing to
• in that as / insomuch as / inasmuch as	• may be inferred from
	• the implication that

They may also contain **conclusion indicators** that qualify the conclusion. Again a non-exhaustive example list of such terms might include:

CONCLUSION INDICATORS	
• therefore	• consequently
• wherefore	• it must be that
• accordingly	• whence
• we may conclude / in conclusion	• so
• entails that	• it follows that
• hence / thus / in this way	• implies that
	• as a result we may infer that

The indicators may sometimes be missing and we should be able to tell what the premises and conclusion of an argument are by the general meaning and direction of the series of sentences and propositions.

In argumentation theory it is often asked *whether the conclusion follows from the premises.*

This means we need to ascertain whether there is a logical link of entailment from the premises to the conclusion. Entailment, implication[5] and the 'following relation' are similar though not identical. They all attempt to capture the notion of logical consequence; i.e. the fact that a good argument should preserve the truth from the premises to the

---

5 The term *implicature* was first used by H. P. Grice and since became a technical term denoting what an utterance or expression seeks to convey, even though this 'something' conveyed is neither clearly stated nor entailed by the utterance. For example, the sentence "Paul graduated and got married" strongly suggests that Paul graduated before the wedding, but the sentence would still be true if Paul graduated after he got married. "Implicature" is a term that is used in place of "implication," which has additional meanings in logic and informal language that are not included in the linguistic and pragmatic meaning of implicature.

conclusion. We will make the general claim that all arguments are forms of inference.

Inference is a method or process of deriving logical conclusions from premises known or believed to be true. The laws of valid inference are studied in the field of logic and philosophy.

> ### 🎁 INTERESTING?
>
> The notion of **INFERENCE** is used in more than one field, obviously with different definitions and implications. Here you have some information about Inference as used and defined in other disciplines:
>
> - In *knowledge development* inference is defined as the process of advancing knowledge by analyzing new aspects, meanings or contexts of understanding through patterns of sense-experience. Inference in this case does not necessarily derive conclusions but opens new paths for inquiry and understanding. We will speak more about this type of inference in Chapter 6 of this book.
> - In *philosophy* the notion of Inference is used extensively in its hermeneutic branch. It is defined as the process of understanding and relating the significance of words to articulate meaningful relationships.
> - In *statistics* inference is the ability to extract patterns and general rules from repeated experiences. It is tied to the idea of Bayesiean probabilistic analysis.
> - *Cognitive psychology* uses the concept of "Human Inference" as the act of drawing conclusions from experience as it pertains to humans.
> - In *artificial intelligence*, inference is employed and encoded programmatically to draw conclusions and make decisions independently of human cognition.

We may also define inference as the non-formal, but rational means of indirectly seeing and observing new meanings and contexts of understanding through observation of patterns given in sense-experience. In order to apply this definition of inference and use it, anomalies and symbols observed through sense-experience become of central importance. Inference, in this sense, does not necessarily derive conclusions, but opens new paths for inquiry. This meaning of inference is often used synonymously with the notion of abduction developed by the great American philosopher Charles Peirce, who we study in Chapter 6 of this book. Inductive and Abductive inference are related to the use of our five senses. Deductive inference is a bit of a misnomer since in principle, deduction is thought to be thoroughly *a priori*[6] and independent of experience. Thus deduction would be more generally associated with the former definition of inference since it is effectively a process or method of deriving logical conclusions from premises known or believed to be true.

---

[6] 'A priori 'denotes knowledge or forms of reasoning that do not rely on sense-experience and possess a purely mathematical or logical form that does not depend on observation. The antonym of *a priori* is the term *a posteriori*.

The only problem here is that in principle, deduction should be based on purely formal rules of reasoning and not on belief. The introduction of the notion of belief into the definition of deduction may vitiate its *a priori* element. One could argue that because our beliefs eventually result in knowledge, they contain implicitly that *a priori* element which in turn is submitted to critical thinking in particular and to dialectical and rational critique in general—meaning these beliefs in the end do pass such tests and processes of evaluation and justification.

Unlike the analytical definition of inference we've studied above, the meanings of words are not always forensically tested and publicly scrutinized, but meaningful relationships are articulated. This type of inference and act of understanding is developed in the branch of philosophy called hermenutics[7] and phenomenology,[8] which respectively emphasize interpretation and description.

Human inference (i.e. the act of drawing conclusions from experience as it pertains to humans) has been usually analyzed and studied within cognitive psychology. Also, developments in the domain of artificial intelligence have seen software able to draw inferences automatically and independently of human cognition.

In statistics, inference is connected and tied to the idea of Bayesian probabilistic analysis: that is the ability to extract patterns and general rules from repeated observations.

Here is another example of an argument:

> *Prostitution has always existed and*
> *It will always exist.*
> *We may conclude from this that prostitution is something necessary to society.*

Is this argument credible? Is it valid and sound? What are its premises and what is its conclusion? We can see that this argument commits the fallacy of induction which we will discuss later in connection to the work of David Hume. It makes the assumption that past experience is a guarantor of future experience which may not always be the case. As we know, events and experience are capable of change and development and this is the basis of history and historiography.

Whenever we analyze arguments, we may look at them intuitively or we may analyze them in what we may call a "reflective" mode. This means that we first examine the structure of the argument attentively. We'll make sure that:

---

7 Hermeneutics is the art of interpretation of sacred texts at least in their original meanings. More recently in the 20th century, the German philosopher Gadamer has developed a philosophical hermeneutics. Paul Ricoeur has developed an alternative philosophical hermeneutics to that of Gadamer.

8 Phenomenology is a school of philosophy from Germany that developed around the turn of the 20th century. Its main representatives are Edmund Husserl and Martin Heidegger.

- we are cautious in proceeding and keep a lookout for logical traps or fallacies.[9]
- we evaluate an argument at each step or examine each of its parts.
- we produce a global evaluation of an argument; and
- we are able to justify this evaluation.

> **ⓘ KEY DEFINITIONS**
>
> **INFERENCE**: the process of deriving logical conclusions from premises known or believed to be true.
>
> **Three Types of Inference**
>
> 1. Inductive;   2. Abductive;   3. Deductive

Some Mistaken Beliefs Regarding Arguments

"A good argument is simply an argument that I agree with."

Agreeing with an argument does not make it a good argument. Because we agree with an argument does not necessarily make that argument valid or strong[10]; only the reasoning behind it can do so. In deductive reasoning—a part of symbolic logic—we say that an argument is valid when it formally or *technically* preserves the truth of the premises. We will cover this topic and the additional topic of logical soundness in Chapter 1 of this book.

For now, let us look at some more arguments:

> **Argument A**: *"The law must permit abortion. After all, we allow women to have teeth removed or to have a tumour that exists within their body to be destroyed."*

> **Argument B**: *"The law must allow abortion, since a child that is not wanted or wished for does not come to life in good conditions."*

Now suppose we had the following choices with respect to these arguments:

1. *I agree with this argument.* Yes or No?

2. *I consider that this argument is:*

    1. Very bad; 2. Rather bad; 3. Rather good; 4. Good; 5. Excellent.

---

9 We cover the topic of Formal and Informal Fallacies in Chapter 2 of this book.

10 We would like to say 'valid and true'; but an argument can never be said to be 'true' or 'false'. Its premises or conclusion can be true, but the argument is analyzed strucuturally as we shall see, and its qualities are explained through validity and strength.

What would *your* answer be?

Whatever your answer may be you should at least note that Argument A is a lot more simplistic than Argument B. The analogy between pulling teeth and aborting a fetus is a poor one as there are very little characteristics in common. Argument B is stronger because it is based on reasonable premises even if there could be strong disagreement about the truth of those premises.

Some people are of the opinion that: "We cannot make progress by giving up on our beliefs". However, some philosophers such as Susan Stebbing,[11] have argued that we make progress, moral, or intellectual by relinquishing some of our beliefs in favor of others. Her argument is that we must shed light on our presuppositions by examining not only their 'origin', but also whether they are defendable. The strongest presupposition or conviction that leads Stebbing's argument is that a clear and rational belief is preferable to an unclear and irrational belief or opinion.

> **KEY NOTE**
>
> **In analyzing arguments, we must be sure that:**
> - we are cautious in proceeding and keep a lookout for logical traps or fallacies.
> - we evaluate an argument at each step or examine each of its parts.
> - we produce a global evaluation of an argumentation; and
> - we are able to justify this evaluation.

A standard argument about rationality and emotion is that "Rationality or reason and the emotions are and will always be in conflict". Again this argument is facile and must be debunked. Often a rational argument may be supported by an emotion which is irrational. This means that when we determine whether an argument is rational or not we must 'bracket the emotions', so to speak, in order to determine whether the argument is rational. Nothing prevents us from going back and realizing that what we thought was true for emotional reasons is also true and coincides with our rational beliefs. However, when deciding whether an argument is rational or not, we are looking for a method to arrive at this conclusion that is independent and impartial, and necessarily devoid of emotion or any other quality particular to the individual. This example is also highly loaded as it seems to contradict the notion of emotional and intuitive intelligence that has been developed recently by some psychologists. While emotional intelligence is taken to be a more feminine mode of thought associated with Susan Gilligan's *Ethics of Care,* if we want to craft a science of argument, there must almost be an impartial, ascetic

---

11 See Stebbing's *Thinking To Some Purpose*, London, Penguin Books, 1941.

element to our method. It is dificult to see how that this makes logic a thoroughly male preoccupation as some feminist positions of gender bias have argued. In fact the notion of emotional intelligence may be integrated with logic in the domains of intuitive, hermeneutical forms of inference where symbolism and anomaly play a critical role. These forms of non-linear, a-rational, paralogical cogitations and elucubrations form a foreground and background to our preoccupations and they also explain why science and the humanities have obscure origins in the Age of Renaissance magic (we look at this topic more carefully in Chapter 8: Knowledge And The Humanist Worldview) as much as in the Age of Greek and Roman antiquity. However, origin should not be confused with actuality. When studied as a science, logic and argument do favor a detached and non-emotional approach that has pretentions to universality beyond race, gender and religion.

Here are some examples of questions whose answer would require that we develop an argument:

- What major should I pick in college or in university?
- Which CD should I buy the one by Coldplay or Madonna?
- Which political party should I vote for ?
- Are humans fundamentally violent?
- Is Plato the real author of "The Republic"?
- Does God exist?
- Should war be opposed?
- Do humans possess a soul?
- Should I support or oppose abortion and euthanasia?
- Is Capitalism a good economic system?
- Is democracy a good political system?
- Should we fight to preserve a clean and safe environment?

> ⓘ **KEY NOTE**
>
> **PREMISE INDICATORS:** since (non-temporal meaning) / as indicated by / because / in that as / insomuch as / inasmuch as / given that / seeing that / for the reason that; owing to / may be inferred from / the implication that
>
> **CONCLUSION INDICATORS**: therefore / wherefore / accordingly / we may conclude / in conclusion / entails that / hence / thus / in this way / consequently / it must be that / whence / so / it follows that / implies that / as a result we may infer that

Critical Examination of Prejudices

Arguments also help to submit our prejudices and presuppositions to a critical analysis.

Examples of Arguments:

- *I think that I should do a master's rather than a bachelor's because that will improve my chances of getting a job. What do you think?*
- *I think that there is no point in graduating. After all a diploma does not guarantee that I will get a job. What do you think?*
- *I think that humanity's unhappiness comes from two different causes. Sometimes it comes from people's sheer ignorance but at other times it comes from the fact that they are evil. Thus, ignorance and evil are two different things. Do you agree?*

Arguments as Forms of Persuasion

We sometimes use arguments to attempt to convince others to adopt our points of view.

Examples of Arguments

Argument A: Dear colleagues, as geologists, we have for the longest time held the belief that continents did not move. However, my team of experts and I have discovered that this may not be the case as there are volcanoes that are active in the middle of the oceans and that might explain the movement of continents and their present structure.

Argument B: According to you, there is no more morality these days. But I believe this to be false. These days people no longer tolerate the wrongs and injustices that are committed onto people of different races and onto women.

Argument C: You should not hold the accused guilty of premeditated murder, since he was not responsible for his acts.

Argument Standardization or Formalization

Formalizing or standardizing an argument means rewriting it by clearly identifying its premises and its conclusion. As an example we will standardize the previous three arguments A, B and C.

Argument A:

P1: There are volcanoes that are active in the middle of the Ocean.

P2: These volcanoes explain the movement of continents and their present structure.

C: Therefore continents move.

Argument B:

P1: *People no longer tolerate the wrongs and injustices that are committed onto people of different races and onto women.*

P2: *No longer tolerating wrongs and injustices is a sign of morality.*

C: *Therefore there is morality today.*

Argument C:

P1: *The accused was not responsible for his acts.*

P2: *Someone who is not responsible (in the sense of mentally fit or mentally competent) cannot be held guilty of a crime.*

P3: *Premeditated murder is a crime.*

C: *Therefore the accused cannot be held guilty of premeditated murder.*

CONCLUSION

In this chapter we have briefly introduced the notion of critical thinking and the related notion of arguments. We have looked at the building blocks of arguments and have introduced the notion of argument formalization or standardization. An important distinction that stems from the work of the pure mathematician is the notion of deduction and deductive reasoning. In general, a *deductive argument* is one that is independent of any form of sense-experience and whose conclusion follows with absolute necessity from its premises. By contrast an inductive argument's premises are only probable and depend on some form of generalization from repeated occurrences. This distinction will provide the separation of logic into symbolic or formal logic and into inductive or empirical logic. Though some people, such as Béziau, challenge the notion of a distinction between formal logic and empirical logic and claim that the distinction should be between the structures of a logic and its contents or formulae or expressions, we believe it premature to give up on logical form altogether. The distinction between form and content may be metaphysical in some way, but it also has sound application in logic where abstraction is perhaps more, but not less than a formal operation.

EXERCISES
ARGUMENTS AND CRITICAL THINKING

1. Give an example in which you would use critical thinking to examine an inherited belief.

2. Provide an example in which you would use critical thinking to examine a prejudice or a presupposition.

3. Give one example in which you would use critical thinking to determine your best course of action in a given situation.

4. Give an example in which you would use critical thinking to persuade someone of the truth of something.

5. What are the building blocks of arguments?

6. Define the following terms: *premise, conclusion, issue, position, thesis.*

7. What is the difference between *deductive* reasoning and *inductive* reasoning?

8. In the following passages, determine which passages are arguments. Identify the premises and conclusions for those passages which enunciate an argument and also standardize or formalize the arguments:

   A) And it must not be imagined that in this I commit the fallacy which logicians call arguing in a circle, for since experience renders the greater part of these effects very certain, the causes from which I deduce them do not so much serve to prove their existence as to explain them; on the other hand, the causes are explained by the effects. (Descartes, Discourse On Method, Part VI)

   B) German criticism has, right up to its latest efforts, never quitted the realm of philosophy. Far from examining its general philosophic premises, the whole body of its inquiries has actually sprung from the soil of a definite philosophical system, that of Hegel. Not only in their answers but in their very questions there was a mystification. This dependence on Hegel is the reason why not one of these modern critics has even attempted a comprehensive criticism of the Hegelian system, however much each professes to have advanced beyond Hegel. (Karl Marx, The German Ideology, Part A).

   C) More recent philosophy, as an epistemological scepticism, is, in a concealed or open manner, anti-Christian , although (and this is said for more refined ears) in no way anti-religious. Formerly, that is, people believed in "the soul," as they believed in grammar and the grammatical subject. They said "I" is the condition, "think" is the predicate and conditioned - thinking is an activity for which a subject must be thought of as cause. Now, people tried, with an admirable tenacity and trickery, to see whether they could get out of this net, whether perhaps the opposite might not be true: "think" as the condition, "I" the conditioned - thus "I" is only a synthesis which is itself created by thinking. (Friedrich Nietzsche, Beyond Good And Evil, Aphorism 54)

D) Self-indulgence is more like a voluntary state than cowardice. For the former is actuated by pleasure, the latter by pain, of which the one is to be chosen and the other to be avoided; and pain upsets and destroys the nature of the person who feels it, while pleasure does nothing of the sort. (Aristotle, The Nicomachean Ethics, III.12)

E) But the voice of our age seems by no means favorable to art, at all events to that kind of art to which my inquiry is directed. The course of events has given a direction to the genius of the time that threatens to remove it continually further from the ideal of art. For art has to leave reality, it has to raise itself bodily above necessity and neediness; for art is the daughter of freedom, and it requires its prescriptions and rules to be furnished by the necessity of spirits and not by that of matter. (Friedrich Schiller, Letters On The Aesthetic Education of Man, Letter II)

F) Smart phones have a disastrous impact on children. They appear to be shortening the attention span of the young. They also seem to be eroding their linguistic powers and ability to handle mathematical symbolism. Smart phones also caused them to be increasingly impatient with deferred gratification. Even more serious, smart phones are opening all of society's secrets and taboos, thus erasing the dividing line between childhood and adulthood.

G) In a judgment by which anything is designated simply as great, it is not merely meant that the object has a magnitude, but that this magnitude is superior to that of many other objects of the same kind, without, however, any exact determination of this superiority. Thus there is always at the basis of our judgment a standard which we assume as the same for every one; this, however, is not available for any logical (mathematically definite) judging of magnitude, but only for aesthetical judging of the same, because it is a merely subjective standard.(Immanuel Kant, The Critique of Judgment, 108)

H) There is a painting by Klee called Angelus Novus. An angel is depicted there who looks as though he were about to distance himself from something which he is staring at. His eyes are opened wide, his mouth stands open and his wings are outstretched. The Angel of History must look just so. His face is turned towards the past. Where we see the appearance of a chain of events,he sees one single catastrophe, which unceasingly piles rubble on top of rubble and hurls it before his feet. He would like to pause for a moment so fair [the German verweilen means to stay for a while, to tarry by; it is a reference to Goethe and his masterpiece Faust, in contrast to Nietzsche, the moment can never last or return for Goethe, PC], to awaken the dead and to piece together what has been smashed. But a storm is blowing from Paradise, it has caught itself up in his wings and is so strong that the Angel can no longer close them. The storm drives him irresistibly into the future, to which his back is turned, while the rubble-heap before him grows sky-high. That which we call progress, is this storm. (Walter Benjamin, Theses on History, On the Concept of History, IX)

I) Science, the new nobility! Progress. The world moves!... And why shouldn't it? We have visions of numbers. We are moving toward the Spirit.What I say is oracular and absolutely right. I understand, and since I cannot express myself except in pagan terms, I would rather keep quiet. Pagan blood returns! The Spirit is at hand, why does Christ not help me, and grant my soul nobility and freedom. Ah! but the Gospel belongs to the past! The Gospel! The Gospel. I wait glutinously for God. I have been of an inferior race for ever and ever. (Arthur Rimbaud, A Season in Hell)

J) As far as I am concerned, I resign from humanity. I no longer want to be, nor can still be, a man. What should I do? Work for a social and political system, make a girl miserable? Hunt for weaknesses in philosophical systems, fight for moral and esthetic ideals? It's all too little. I renounce my humanity even though I may find myself alone. But am I not already alone in this world from which I no longer expect anything? (Emil Cioran, On the Heights of Despair)

K) It is in the empiricist development, as we know, that the new psychology, which was required as a correlate to pure natural science when the latter was separated off, is brought to its first concrete execution. Thus it is concerned with investigations of introspective psychology in the field of the soul, which has now been separated from the body, as well as with physiological and psychophysical explanations. On the other hand, this psychology is of service to a theory of knowledge which, compared with the Cartesian one, is completely new and very differently worked out. In Locke's great work this is the actual intent from the start. It offers itself as a new attempt to accomplish precisely what Descartes's Meditations intended to accomplish: an epistemological grounding of the objectivity of the objective sciences. (Edmund Husserl, The Crisis of the European Sciences, 1937, Section 22)

L) As surely as the LORD lives," he said, "the LORD himself will strike him, or his time will come and he will die, or he will go into battle and perish. (1 Samuel 26:10)

M) You never de-territorialize alone but with two terms at least, hand-object of use, hand-breast, face-scenery. And each one of the two terms re-territorializes each itself on the other. Thus one should not confuse re-territorialization with the return of an ancient more primitive territoriality: it (re-territorialization, PC) implicates necessarily a set of artefacts according to which an element, itself de-terrritorialized, serves as a new territoriality that has nonetheless lost its own territoriality. (Gilles Deleuze, A Thousand Plateaus, Theorems of Deterritorialization or Machinistic Propositions)

N) The military is a great matter of the state. It is the ground of death and life. The Tao of survival or extinction. One cannot but examine it. (Sun-Tzu, The Art of War, Part 1, Appraisals)

O) With the pure conceptions of understanding, on the contrary, commences the absolute necessity of seeking a transcendental deduction, not only of these conceptions themselves, but likewise of space, because, inasmuch as they make affirmations concerning objects not by means of the predicates of intuition and sensibility, but of pure thought a priori, they apply to objects without any of the conditions of sensibility. Besides, not being founded on experience, they are not presented with any object in a priori intuition upon which, antecedently to experience, they might base their synthesis. Hence results, not only doubt as to the objective validity and proper limits of their use, but that even our conception of space is rendered equivocal; inasmuch as we are very ready with the aid of the categories, to carry the use of this conception beyond the conditions of sensuous intuition—and, for this reason, we have already found a transcendental deduction of it needful. (Immanuel Kant, The Critique of Pure Reason, Chapter II, Of the Transcendental Deduction of the Pure Concepts of The Understanding)

P) The battle rages, terrifying, fierce,

> *The French still fighting with their burnished lances*
> *There had you seen the sorrow of a nation,*
> *So many men are wounded, bloody, dead.*
> (The Song of Roland, Howard Robertson Translation, cxxva)

Q) *The means whereby to identify dead forms is Mathematical Law. The means whereby to understand living forms is Analogy. By these means we are enabled to distinguish polarity and periodicity in the world.* (Oswald Spengler, The Decline of the West, Chapter 1, Introduction, II)

R) *And how could the Soul lend itself to any admixture? An essential is not mixed. Or of the intrusion of anything alien? If it did, it would be seeking the destruction of its own nature. Pain must be equally far from it. And Grief- how or for what could it grieve? Whatever possesses Existence is supremely free, dwelling, unchangeable, within its own peculiar nature. And can any increase bring joy, where nothing, not even anything good, can accrue? What such an Existent is, it is unchangeably.* (Plotinus, First Ennead, First Tractate, II)

S) *This simple triad of desire-means-end is excluded by the increasing multiplicity and complexity of higher life. Now the complex of means is itself turned into a multiplicity in which the most important means are constituted by means and these by others. So in the practical life of our mature cultures, our pursuits take on the character of chains, the coils of which cannot be grasped in a single vision.* (Georg Simmel, Schopenhauer and Nietzsche, Chapter 1).

T) *What does not kill you makes you stronger.* (Friedrich Nietzsche, Beyond Good And Evil)

U) *The concrete elaboration of the question of the meaning of Being is what is targeted by the treatise that will follow. The interpretation of time as the possible horizon of all understanding of Being in general is from now on its goal.* (Martin Heidegger, Being and Time, 1)

W) *Thus philosophical conscience is unitary, and it appears to us clearly to be: the conscience of Becoming onto Being.* (Constantin Noica, Becoming Onto Being, Bucharest, 1981)

X) *Idiots and geniuses, small and great, sound, soul, light- All are dust-The world is as it is... and we are as She/It is...*(Mihai Eminescu, Epigones)

Y) *Eminescu sings Nature in such a way that it becomes a framework within which one senses the presence of a Voievod even when the Voievod is not mentioned at all. As a deeper alter ego, the Voievod is in a way the lirical, implicit and tacit subject of the poems.* (Lucian Blaga, The Trilogy Of Culture)[12]

Z) *The problem of perception presents itself to theoretical philosophy under a twofold aspect: it may be considered from a psychological and from an epistemological standpoint. Throughout the history of philosophy, the two have been in constant conflict; but the more sharply the oppositions develop, the more evident it seems that here precisely are the two poles around which the whole problem of perception must necessarily move.* (Ernst Cassirer, The Philosophy of Symbolic Forms, Volume 3: The Phenomenology of Knowledge, Part I, Chapter 2)."

AA) *This, yea, this alone is REVENGE itself: the Will's antipathy to time, and its "It was." Verily, a great folly dwelleth in our Will; and it became a curse unto all humanity, that this folly acquired spirit! THE SPIRIT OF REVENGE: my friends, that hath hitherto been man's best contemplation; and where there was suffering, it was claimed there was always penalty.* (Nietzsche, Thus Spoke Zarathustra, On Redemption).

---

12 A Voievod is medieval warlord or regional prince in certain ancient kingdoms that led to the formation of modern day Romania.

9. What is the relationship between critical thinking and logic?

10. What is the relationship between critical thinking and knowledge?

11. Are knowledge and logic the same thing? Why or why not? Justify your answer.

12. Why do we study knowledge and logic in the Humanities? Are these scientific concepts or do the Humanities also play a role in shaping these notions?

13. Make arguments of the following sentences:
    1. Singing is not logical.
    2. The set of all sets that are members of themselves is a member of itself.
    3. Some hard things are boring.
    4. Natural languages are easy.
    5. All logical premises are false.
    6. This statement is a lie.
    7. The previous statement is false.
    8. The set of all sets that are members of themselves is not a member of itself.
    9. The previous statement is a lie.
    10. X is a set that is a member of itself.
    11. Most blue birds are beautiful.
    12. I am singing in the rain.
    13. Formal languages are hard.
    14. All beautiful objects are expensive.
    15. This statement is false.

✓ KEY CONCEPTS & DEFINITIONS - DEFINITIONS

LOGIC is the study of reasoning and intelligence and its relation to structures, models, reality and intuition.

PROPOSITIONAL LOGIC or *sentential* or *statement logic* analyzes the way propositions, statements or sentences are combined, modified and conjoined.

PREDICATE LOGIC studies the relationship between subject and predicate & universal and existential quantification.

VALIDITY: An argument is valid if it is impossible for its premises to be true whenever its conclusion is false.

SOUNDNESS: An argument is sound if it is valid and the premises are true.

CONSISTENCY: A system is said to be consistent when there is no contradiction built into its rules of inference or replacement.

A **THEOREM** in our formal deduction system is *any derivable expression that is non-atomic* (that is not an elementary tautology or contradiction) *and whose negation does not lead to a contradiction*.

Logical Connectives or Operators

Negation ('not P'); Conjunction ('P and Q'); Disjunction ('P or Q'); Material conditionals (If P then Q)

Law of Detachment or Modus Ponens: If P, then Q; P ;Therefore, Q.

REPLACEMENT RULES

1. De Morgan's Laws: (1) $\neg(p \land q) \Leftrightarrow \neg p \lor \neg q$; (2) $\neg(p \lor q) \Leftrightarrow \neg p \land \neg q$
2. Commutativity: (1) $(p \lor q) \Leftrightarrow (q \lor p)$; (2) $(p \land q) \Leftrightarrow (q \land p)$
3. Associativity: (1) $(p \lor q) \lor r \Leftrightarrow p \lor (q \lor r)$; (2) $(p \land q) \land r \Leftrightarrow p \land (q \land r)$
4. Material Implication: $(p \rightarrow q) \Leftrightarrow (\neg p \land q)$
5. Double Negation: $\neg \neg p \Leftrightarrow p$
6. Transposition: $(p \rightarrow q) \Leftrightarrow (\neg q \rightarrow \neg p)$
7. Distribution: (1) $[p \land (q \lor r)] \Leftrightarrow [(p \land q) \lor (p \land r)]$; (2) $[p \lor (q \land r)] \Leftrightarrow [(p \lor q) \land (p \lor r)]$
8.1 Idempotency of disjunction: $(p \lor p) \Leftrightarrow p$
8.2 Idempotency of conjunction: $(p \land p) \Leftrightarrow p$
9. Material Equivalence: $p \Leftrightarrow q$
10. Exportation: $(p \land q) \rightarrow r \Leftrightarrow p \rightarrow (q \rightarrow r)$

IRVING COPI'S 5 TYPES OF DEFINITION:

1. stipulative
2. lexical
3. precising
4. theoretical
5. persuasive

PATRICK SUPPES'S 4 REQUIREMENTS FOR A DEFINITION:

A definition must:

1) give the essence of that which is to be defined.

2) not be circular.

3) not be in the negative when it can be in the positive.

4) not be expressed in figurative or obscure language.

DEFINITION & DEDUCTION

CHAPTER 1

What is deductive logic or the formal analysis of deductive reasoning; and what is its connection to Critical Thinking?

People, mostly philosophers, have been studying logic for thousands of years. Logic began its career in the Western world with Parmenides and Aristotle. More recently logicians have begun focusing on logic using formal methods. Formalism and formals methods means that we treat the language that is used to express critical thoughts and arguments as if it were a mathematical and self-enclosed system.

We define Logic as the study of reasoning and intelligence and its relation to structures, models, reality and intuition.

For instance, premises and conclusions in arguments can be treated in the same way that algebra treats numbers and number systems.[1] Hence a premise or proposition can be represented abstractly and generally as P, and any given predicate (a statement that qualifies an object) Px can be quantified over many objects (all the objects or some of the objects, or one object for which that (object = x) is a true statement) called a class.[2]

---

[1] This insight is due to the great German logician and philosopher Leibniz.
[2] A logical class, not a classroom or a political class. A class in modern logic is a set whose objects share the same properties. Classes and sets are not identical. The set is the more general logical concept. Thus a class may be a set but a set is not necessarily a class as it needs to fulfil additional conditions in order to qualify as a class.

Why is this important for Critical Thinking? Because modern deductive logic (also known as 'formal logic') explains and clarifies universally key notions such as 'validity' and 'soundness', which are useful and applicable to natural language (as opposed to a purely formal language studied by linguistics, computer science or formal logic.)

> **KEY NOTES**
>
> **LOGIC** is the study of reasoning and intelligence and its relation to structures, models, reality and intuition.
>
> **PROPOSITIONAL LOGIC** analyzes and studies how logical relationships and properties can be derived from combining, altering and joining statements.
>
> **TRUTH-FUNCTIONAL PROPOSITIONAL LOGIC** studies logical *operators* and *connectives*.

1.1 SYMBOLIC & MATHEMATICAL LOGIC

Propositional logic, which may also be called *sentential* logic or *statement* logic, is a part of logic that analyzes the way propositions, statements or sentences are combined, modified and conjoined. Complex propositions can be broken down into their elementary components; simple propositions can be analyzed to create and form more complex propositions, statements or sentences. *In short, propositional logic analyzes and studies how logical relationships and properties can be derived from combining, altering and joining statements.*

In sentential or propositional logic, the simplest propositions are taken to be indivisible units, and thus, propositional logic does not study the logical properties and relations connected to parts of statements that do not themselves constitute statements on their own. Typically, these are called the subject and predicate of a statement.

> **KEY DEFINITIONS**
>
> **PROPOSITIONAL LOGIC** or *sentential* or *statement logic* **analyzes the way propositions, statements or sentences are combined, modified and conjoined.**
>
> **PREDICATE LOGIC** studies the relationship between subject and predicate.

A different type of logic called **predicate logic** studies the relationship between subject, predicate and quantification, and is typically a first-order type of logic. In general, Kurt Gödel proved that all single term first-order logics are complete. However there are some non-standard first-order predicate logics that are not complete (an example is Robinson arithmetic, which we outline in section 1.6.6).

Classical truth-functional propositional logic is the most researched branch of logic. This aspect of logic studies logical *operators* and *connectives*. The operators and connectives are put to use to develop complex statements. The truth-value of these complex statements is wholly dependent on the truth-values of the simpler statements out of which they are built. The simple or elementary statements that make up the complex statements are assumed to possess truth-functional value of either true or false. Other types of propositional logic exist besides the binary (true or false only). We have for instance Lukasiewicz's three-valued logic and formal axiomatic system.

> **INTERESTING?**
>
> In Aristotle's logic there were two quantifiers 'All' and 'Some'. Modern logical quantifiers were developed by the philosophers Frege and Peirce. They are used in predicate logic, which we discuss and define later in this chapter. Two common quantifiers are the existential ∃ ("there exists") and universal ∀ ("for all") quantifiers. The variables could be elements in the universe under discussion, or perhaps relations or functions over that universe. For instance, an existential quantifier over a function symbol would be interpreted as "there is a function". However, Aristotle's quantifiers are not formal in the modern sense since they cannot be used to bind variables.

LOGICAL CONNECTIVES OR OPERATORS

There are five main logical connectives or operators. They are:

	OPERATOR	MEANING / USE	SYMBOL
1.	negation	*not*	¬
2.	conjunction	*and*	∧
3.	disjunction	*or*	∨
4.	implication	*if*	→
5.	biconditional	*if and only if*	↔

CRITICAL THINKING, WORLDVIEWS & LOGIC

DEFINITIONS

The logical connective negation has the first priority among connectives. The remaining connectives listed above and defined below, are read and executed as logical operations from left to right. They each have the same priority of operation unless otherwise indicated by parentheses. In the case of parentheses, their contents are always read and operated upon first and then we treat the resulting truth-value as the equivalent of the truth-value of an atomic sentence. In the case of nested paranthesis, the innermost paranthesis are resolved first and one moves outwards successively as one would in mathematics until the atomic expression is reached. An atomic proposition is the basic unit of propositional logic: it is constituted of a single logical symbol which does not include any logical connectives. This logical symbol represents a single unit of meaning: a basic sentence or proposition. For example, consider the following nested operations:

Write "(Blue and (Write "(Write "Hello" and write "Good-bye")"))" would become:

Step 1. Write "(Blue and (Write ("Hello" "Good-bye"))" and then:
Step 2. Write "(Blue and ""Hello" "Good-bye"")" to finally arrive at:
Step 3. "Blue ""Hello" "Good-bye"""

Now, let us assume we have two statements P and Q as follows:
P: "It is sunny outside."
Q: "There are no clouds over Montreal."

The rest of our connectives form a proposition out of two statements. This proposition when evaluated will result in a truth value of True or False depending on:
1. the connective / operator
2. the truth-value of P
3. the truth-value of Q.

For any two propositions, there are four possible assignments of truth values:

Case 1: P is true; Q is true
Case 2: P is true; Q is false
Case 3: P is false: Q is true
Case 4: P is false; Q is false

> 🎁 **INTERESTING?**
>
> For any number of connectives and independent propositions or atomic logical sentences the number of permutations is 2^n in binary logic since there are only two logical possibilities: true or false. One has to build the truth table by making sure that one exhausts and lists all the possible permutations or combinations of true and false for the complex logical expression as we now show for the remaining connectives.

Negation (*not P*)

We write ¬ P to represent the negation of P, which can be thought to be the denial of P or the opposite of P. In the example below, if P represents the statement "It is sunny outside," then ¬ P expresses the statement "It is not sunny outside", or through a more standard reading: "It is not the case that it is sunny outside" or It is false that "It is sunny outside." When P is true, ¬ P is false; and when P is false, ¬ P is true. ¬ (¬ P) always has the same truth-value as P.

LOGICAL NEGATION ('NOT')	
P "It is sunny"	**¬P** "It is not sunny"
T	F
F	T

Conjunction ('*P and Q*')

Conjunction is a truth-functional connective which forms a proposition out of two simpler propositions, for example, 'P *and* Q'. The conjunction of P and Q is written P ∧ Q, and expresses that each are true. Conjunction corresponds to the word 'and' in logical statements.

The conjunction of P and Q is true in case 1 and false in all others. That is, in order for the statement 'P and Q' to be true, both P and Q must be found to be true independently. To continue with our example above, where P is the proposition that "*it is sunny outside*" and Q is the proposition "*there are no clouds over Montreal*". Then P ∧ Q is true only when it is sunny outside and when there are no clouds over Montreal. If it is not sunny outside, or if there are clouds over Montreal, then P ∧ Q is false.

LOGICAL CONJUNCTION ('AND')		
P "It is sunny"	**Q** "There are no clouds"	**P ∧ Q** "It is sunny AND there are no clouds"
T	T	T
T	F	F
F	T	F
F	F	F

Disjunction ('P or Q')

Disjunction is similar to conjunction in that it forms a proposition out of two simpler propositions. The disjunction of P and Q is written P ∨ Q, and read "P or Q". It expresses that either P or Q is true. This means that the statement 'P or Q' is true whenever P is true, or whenever Q is true or both. Thus, in the cases listed above, the disjunction of P and Q is true in all cases except 4. Using the example above, the disjunction expresses that it is either raining outside or there are clouds over Montreal. The statement "*Either it is sunny or there are clouds over Montreal*" becomes true whenever it is raining *or* whenever there are clouds over Montreal. In general, a disjunction of statements becomes true whenever any one of those statements becomes true (at least one). Note that this use of disjunction resembles the use of the English 'or'. Logically, it is like the inclusive "or", which can be used to express the truth of at least one of two propositions; the exclusive "or", which expresses the truth of *only* one of two propositions. That is to say, the exclusive "or" is false when both P and Q are true (case 1). An example of the exclusive "or" is: "*You may take English or Physical Education this term but not both.*" Sometimes the "but not both" is omitted if people readily understand from the context that both possibilities are not available as in "Well, we can go to the concert or go to the movies." In general all "or" are inclusive in mathematics and logic. When we are in the presence of an exclusive or (sometimes symbolized as "xor") it needs to be specified explicitly.

LOGICAL DISJUNCTION ('OR')		
P "It is sunny"	**Q** "There are no clouds"	**P ∨ Q** "It is sunny OR there are no clouds"
T	T	T
T	F	T
F	T	T
F	F	F

Material conditionals *(If P then Q)*

The Material conditional also joins two simpler propositions. When expressing a material conditional in logic, we write P → Q and read "if P then Q". The arrow separates the two propositions, 'P' and 'Q', 'P' is called the antecedent while the 'Q' is called the consequent. In conjunction, we don't need to distinguish between the two since a conjunction is a *commutative* operation—like addition (and unlike division), it doesn't matter which order you place the operands in.

The material conditional expresses that "If P is true, then Q is true". This can also be stated as: "*Q is true whenever P is true*". Thus referring again to Table I, the material conditional P → Q is always true except in case 2, as here P is true when Q is not. Because P implies Q, the material conditional is often confused with the notion of 'cause and effect'. But this error can quickly lead to absurdities. A pertinent example: *Every time the circle of light switches from red to green the giant metal boxes go roaring off.* Here one might naturally assume that the change in the traffic signal is what *causes* the automobiles to move forward. However, our *understanding* of the world, its fundamental laws and traffic signal operations contradicts this belief. We shall argue this point in greater detail later in this book. For now, it is important to keep in mind, that the material conditional merely relates two propositions through their truth-values—which is not the relation of cause and effect (which necessarily presupposes the notion of an event that can be perceived through sense-perception or sense-experience).

LOGICAL IMPLICATION		
P "It is sunny"	**Q** "There are no clouds"	**P → Q** "IF it is sunny THEN there are no clouds"
T	T	T
T	F	F
F	T	T
F	F	T

Here we introduce the material conditional as a syntactic or purely truth functional relation. Later on in this book, when we study the validity of propositions, this process of implication and how it differs from cause and effect will become clear once we show how we can have a false or nonsensical antecedent and a true consequent or a false antecedent and a false consequent, with the resulting conjoined expression possessing a truth-value of true. [3]

LOGICAL BI-CONDITIONAL		
P "It is sunny"	**Q** "There are no clouds"	**P ↔ Q** "It is sunny IF AND ONLY IF there are no clouds"
F	F	T
F	T	F
T	F	F
T	T	T

---

3 See pg. 37, Keynote on Implications and Conditionals.

DEFINITIONS

The bi-conditional or the "if and only if"[4] also joins two simpler propositions, P and Q. We write $P \leftrightarrow Q$, and read "*P if and only if Q*" and expresses that P and Q have the same truth-value. As we can verify from our tables, 'P if and only if Q' is true in cases 1 and 4, and false otherwise. It is called the 'bi-conditional' because to say "P if and only if Q" or $P \leftrightarrow Q$ is equivalent to the two material conditionals, "P if Q" (or $P \rightarrow Q$) and "Q if P" (or $Q \rightarrow P$). (Also, note that $P \rightarrow Q$ is equivalent to $\neg P \vee Q$.)

We show below an equivalence between logical expressions using truth tables. Technically a biconditional is different since it operates between atomic sentences of the language but practically the symbol ⇔ is used interchangeably and there is no truth-functional difference in the definition of a biconditional between individual propositions and an equivalence between complex logical expressions

LOGICAL EQUIVALENCE : $(P \rightarrow Q) = (\neg P \vee Q)$				
P "It is sunny"	**Q** "There are no clouds"	**¬P** "It is not sunny"	**¬P ∨ Q** "It is not sunny OR there are no clouds"	**P → Q** "IF it is sunny THEN there are no clouds"
T	T	F	T	T
T	F	F	F	F
F	T	T	T	T
F	F	T	T	T

We define a **tautology** as a logical expression in propositional logic whose truth table contains only T's in the final column of the truth table.

> **KEY NOTES - ON IMPLICATIONS & CONDITIONALS**
>
> **Distinctions on Material Implication/Conditional & Indicative/Strict Conditional**
>
> The student should understand that a conditional may be discussed and defined syntactically for the purposes of everyday and colloquial language. However, when formalized and treated as a *material conditional, material implication* or *logical implication*, it becomes inherently tied to the notion of *validity* which is a *semantic* notion. Hence the counter-intuitive truth-value or truth-valuation that the conditional combination of a false antecedent with a true or false consequent can yield a positive truth-value within the definition of the *material or logical implication*. There is no necessary relation between the *antecedent* and the *consequent* in the material conditional as there is with the *indicative* (or strict) conditional, which we discuss in Chapter 2 of this book. The notion of *material conditional* involves us in the paradoxes of material implication. In order to deal with these paradoxes, logicians have developed *modal logic* and *counter-factual logic*, which we do not broach in this introductory text, though they remain indispensable topics for the advanced student of logic.

---

4 Often abbreviated to "iff".

EXERCISES

BASIC PROPOSITIONAL LOGIC

1.1 *Construct truth tables for the following expressions:*

- $A \leftrightarrow (B \vee C)$
- $A \leftrightarrow (B \rightarrow C)$
- $(A \rightarrow B) \leftrightarrow (C \wedge \neg D)$
- $(\neg A \vee \neg B) \leftrightarrow \neg (A \wedge B)$
- $\neg (A \vee B) \leftrightarrow (\neg A \wedge \neg B)$

1.2 The last two (iv. and v.) above are called De Morgan's Laws. Prove them using truth tables. Is there any other way of proving DeMorgan's Laws?

2. *Let:*   M = 'Montreal is larger than Quebec'
            Q = 'Quebec is north of Montreal'
            T = 'Montreal is larger than Toronto"
            (Thus, M, Q are true and T is false)

Which of the following sentences are true?

    a) $M \vee T$
    b) $M \wedge T$
    c) $M \vee Q$
    d) $(M \leftrightarrow \neg Q) \vee \neg T$
    e) $\neg M \wedge (\neg T \rightarrow Q)$
    f) $(((M \vee Q) \rightarrow T) \rightarrow Q)$
    g) $\neg M \leftrightarrow (\neg Q \leftrightarrow (\neg T \leftrightarrow \neg Q))$
    h) $((M \rightarrow Q) \rightarrow (M \rightarrow \neg Q)) \rightarrow (\neg Q \rightarrow T)$

3. *Let A, B, and C be three distinct atomic sentences. Decide by truth tables which of the following sentences are tautologies?*

    a) $A \vee B$
    b) $A \vee \neg A$
    c) $A \vee B \rightarrow B \vee A$
    d) $A \vee B \rightarrow (A \vee B) \vee C$
    e) $A \rightarrow (\neg A \rightarrow C)$
    f) $(A \rightarrow B) \rightarrow (C \rightarrow A)$
    g) $[(A \rightarrow B) \leftrightarrow B] \rightarrow A$
    h) $A \rightarrow [B \rightarrow (B \rightarrow A)]$
    i) $A \wedge B \rightarrow A \vee C$
    j) $[A \vee (\neg A \wedge B)] \vee (\neg A \wedge \neg A)$
    k) $[A \wedge B \rightarrow (A \wedge \neg A \rightarrow B \vee \neg B)] \wedge (B \rightarrow B)$

4. Give examples of sentences A and B (not necessarily atomic) such that the following compound sentences are true.

   a) A ∧ ¬B
   b) A ∨ (¬A → B)
   c) A → ¬A ∧ B
   d) A →¬ (A→B)

5. Which of the following statements are true?

   a) ¬ ((Plato was sold as a slave) ∧ (Nietzsche went insane)) → (Heidegger was a Nazi)

   b) (Kant never married) ∨ ((Aristotle taught Alexander the Great) ∧ (Plotinus had many children))

   c) (Philo of Alexandria was a Jew) → ((The Kabbalah influenced Pico of Mirandola) ∧ (Luther was an anti-semite) ∨ (Heidegger was a philo-semite))

   d) ((Socrates was married to Xantippha) → (Saint Paul and Plato never married)) ↔ ((Eminescu is not the Romanian national poet) ∧ (Lord Byron was a fop) ∨ (Blake's genius is as great as that of Nietzsche))

   e) (Lord Byron died in the Greek national revolution) ↔ (¬ (Schelling married Schlegel's wife) ∧ (Women were fascinated by Hitler and Mao) ∨ ((Stalin always had a double walking around for protection in the Kremlin) → (Lenin was partly Mongolian))

   f) (Gichin Funakoshi formalized Shotokan Karate) ↔ ((Ashgosha who went to China from India to teach Buddhism first taught kempo) → ((Moses the Biblical prophet was a stutterer) ∧ (Confucius perfectly embodied the moral law) ∨ (Lao Tze perfectly embodied non-Being)

   g) (Jack Layton believed hope was better than fear) → ((Mackenzie King supported collective bargaining) ∧ (Tommy Douglas, the founder of the NDP, was a great man) ∨ Lester B Pearson won the Nobel Peace Prize)

   h) ¬ (Franklin Delano Roosevelt had four presidential mandates) ∨ (The maximum amount of American Presidential mandates allowed by the constitution is two) ∧ (¬ (Hillary Clinton will not be elected president in 2016)) → (¬ (The next American president will be a Republican))

   i) ¬ (Napoleon took the imperial crown out of the Pope's hands at the last minute and crowned himself) → ((Socrates was the best man in Athens) ∧ ¬ (Napoleon is an ethical egoist) ∧ (¬ (Mandela is an ethical altruist))).

6. Let P = (Plato was not a philosopher)
       B = (Bismarck was the chancellor of the Austro-Hungarian empire)
       N = (Nietzsche was happily married)
       H = (Hegel never divorced)
       K = (Kierkegaard was a Catholic)

   Decide which of the following logical propositions are true or which are false. Exhibit your reasoning.

   (a) ¬ ((¬ P ∧ B) ∨ ¬H) → (N ∧ K))
   (b) (H→K) ∧ ((P ∨ ¬ P) ↔ (H ∨ P))
   (c) [(P↔ B) → ((N ∧ ¬K) → (B ∧ ¬B))] ∧ ((B → H) ∨ P)
   (d) (K ∧ ¬K) ↔ (H ∨ ¬ H)
   (e) (B → (H ∧ P)) ∧ (N → (H ∧ K)) ∨ (H → (P ∨ B))

DEFINITIONS

OPERATOR	USE	SYMBOL	EXAMPLE	RESULT
1. negation	not	¬	¬P	It is NOT sunny outside.
2. conjunction	and	∧	P ∧ Q	It is sunny outside AND there are no clouds over Montreal.
3. disjunction	or	∨	P ∨ Q	It is sunny outside OR there are no clouds over Montreal.
4. implication / conditional	if	→	P → Q	It is sunny outside IF there are no clouds over Montreal.
5. biconditional	if & only if	⇔ or ↔	P ⇔ Q	It is sunny outside IF AND ONLY IF there are no clouds over Montreal.

P: "It is sunny outside."
Q: "There are no clouds over Montreal."

TRUTH TABLES

TRUTH VALUES

p	q	p ∧ q	p ∨ q	p → q	p ⇔ q
T	T	T	T	T	T
T	F	F	T	F	F
F	T	F	T	T	F
F	F	F	F	T	T

1.2 LOGICAL DEFINITION

Definitions are important in logic as they are in mathematics because they set limits to a concept. If we did not have definitions in logic we might leave zones of gray or of vagueness which might affect our ability to think clearly about a topic, issue or concept. So one of the main reasons for providing definitions in logic is to clarify our concepts and avoid vagueness. Another reason which is related to the necessity of avoiding vagueness but is yet different is the problem of ambiguity and equivocation. Sometimes a concept or word or issue has two (or more) distinct meanings and it is used in two (or more) different instances with each one of its distinct meanings. If we are not aware of the different meanings and cannot clearly differentiate them from each other, then we may also fall prey to a misunderstanding and develop inaccurate knowledge about the phenomenon that is being defined. This area of definition is not strictly related to formal or deductive logic but we discuss it here. It could also be developed and explained in Chapter 2 on informal logic. This is because definitions though critical, are often informal. When two people understand the same concept or issue in different ways this can lead to conflict. The conflict can be ethical or political and a logical definition may not easily solve this conflict. But certainly if two parties can agree on a definition this is usually the way forward or one may hope it could lead to further agreement about more substantial issues. This is why definition is not a purely formal issue, but can often emerge out of the practical contexts of dialectical discussion, debate and dialogue. We deal with this issue and the work of Douglas Walton in Chapter 2 of our text. Patrick Suppes, whom we follow here, lists four traditional ideas about the function of definition:[1]

> **KEY NOTES**
>
> Patrick Suppes's **4 REQUIREMENTS FOR A DEFINITION**:
>
> A DEFINITION MUST:
>
> 1) Give the essence of that which is to be defined.
> 2) Not be circular.
> 3) Not be in the negative when it can be in the positive.
> 4) Not be expressed in figurative or obscure language.

We can see that even though these conceptions or ideas about definition have been influential throughout the history of logic and of philosophy some of them are not without controversy. For example some people (whether physicists, mathematicians, or

---

[1] Suppes, Patrick, *Introduction To Logic*, Princeton, N.J. : D. Van Nostrand Co., [1957]

logicians) do not admit that objects possess an essence. The thesis that *what is to be defined* possesses an essence is a metaphysical or ontological thesis and some people associate (unfairly according to us) metaphysics with religion and antiquated ideas. They will only accept a materialist-scientific ontology in which all that really exists are fundamental, material or physical particles. According to them the word essence itself only possesses a verbal reality. It does not refer or denote anything real though it may connote it.

Other more informal logicians like Copi claim other uses for definition such as the increase of vocabulary, theoretical explanation and the influence of attitudes. Copi presupposes like Douglas Walton (see chapter 2 for a discussion of Waltons' theses) that there are no 'absolutely true definitions', at least not in informal logic. Thus there might be a subjective element present within definition, which allows us to influence attitudes and make people change their mind if we provide the right type of definition.

Furthermore Copi[2] distinguishes between five types of definition: stipulative definitions, lexical definitions, precising definitions, theoretical definitions and persuasive definitions.

Stipulative definitions are definitions of novel terms and expressions that need to be explained clearly when they are first introduced. Copi claims that an example of such a definition could be A to the n = B, and could explained or defined to be (A*A*A*...A) n terms = B.

By contrast **a lexical definition** is one that reports the meaning of a word or concept that is already in usage. One could consider the definition of a river or rivulet to be such a lexical definition. To define a rivulet as a series of letters or a series of numbers is wrong or false because this is not how English speakers use this term. According to Copi, neither a stipulative nor a lexical definition can dispel the vagueness of a term though they may point to its ambiguity. This is why another type of definition is required: precising definitions. These definitions go beyond stipulative and lexical definitions insofar as they clarify the intended meaning behind a word, concept, issue or judgment.

Often these types of definitions are used in law where jurists or magistrates clarify the meaning or seek to provide an interpretation of the meaning of a given legal term or judgment. This narrowing of the meaning of term or judgment may go beyond the precedent but still be rational. The criteria for judging or evaluating a precising definition are informal not formal. A simple example of this may be the definition of a student as "anyone enrolled in a college or a university program"; but for the purposes of getting a rebated ticket at the cinema, this definition may become a "precising definition" insofar as a student will be defined as "anyone under the age of 18".

---

2 Copi, Irving, *Introduction To Logic*, New York: McMillan, 1973. Print.

Precising definitions arise in policies or juridical arguments and are intended to reduce vagueness out of which conflicting interpretations may arise. A precising definition is like a stipulative definition in that it may introduce a novel meaning of an old term; but unlike the stipulative definition, the precising definition cannot contradict the lexical definition.

The last two types of definitions are theoretical definitions and persuasive definitions. **Theoretical definitions** are like the famous definitions sought by Socrates in Antiquity. They look for a universal definition that will cover all the particular instances of a given word, concept, notion, idea[3] or term. It is needless to say that theoretical definitions are controversial. The history of philosophy has seen periods of quarrel between idealists and realists, between essentialists and nominalists on the status of theoretical definitions and the status of universals versus individuals or particulars. It is important to know that such a quest for a universal and theoretical definition of concepts, ideas and notions is part of the metaphysical quest of philosophy since its beginnings with Socrates and Plato. Typically one proceeds by asking the definition of virtue or justice which are ethical and political notions but one may also ask what is a table or chair or number in order to acknowledge or reject the thesis that such entities possess a universal nature or essence or do not.

According to Copi, **persuasive definitions** are of a different type than the types of definitions considered above. They belong to the class of discourse called rhetoric in the Ancient world and they possess not only an informative function but also an expressive one. Thus each one of the previous definitions could be applied or used in a rhetorical way in an attempt to persuade an opponent or an audience.

We do not follow Copi fully here. For us theoretical definition belongs to the ancient art of demonstration or dialectic. There could be expressive elements within a demonstration, but in general the dialectic proceeds through processes of analysis and synthesis. In order to provide a theoretical definition no appeal to the emotions is judged a valid one. Dialectic aspires to be a purely rational process and this distinguishes it from the expressive functions of hermeneutic and rhetoric. Thus we accept Copi's view that all other types of definition may be used to influence opinion, but disagree with his opinion that theoretical definitions can be used persuasively.

However, the classical distinction between definitions is between denotative definitions and connotative definitions. This controversy about definition is at least as old as the controversy about universals in the Middle-Ages, which pitted the Scotists and

---

[3] We use the term of idea, notion and concept interchangeably because this is an introductory text but a careful philosophical usage of each of these terms should distinguish between the different meanings that they possess.

Thomists against the Ockhamists. The debate started anew in the 19th century when Frege introduced the distinction between *Sinn* and *Bedeutung* or (Sense and Reference, Sense and Meaning).

> **KEY NOTES**
>
> Copi's **5 TYPES OF DEFINITIONS**:
>
> 1. STIPULATIVE
> 2. LEXICAL
> 3. PRECISING
> 4. THEORETICAL
> 5. PERSUASIVE

Connotation classically is about universals and meaning. It defines by analyzing or dividing an object (this method of division is as old as Plato who called it *diaeresis*) into its respective properties and then listing its essential properties. The method of denotation is a method of definition by example. In order to define an object we begin by indicating it, pointing it out, and picking it out. Each method has strengths and weaknesses. Before we examine these we must mention two more important aspects of each definition. The method of denotation seems to imply something about the nature of signs. Since signs, logical, linguistic or mathematical signs allow us to refer to objects, it seems like the problem of denotation is inherently linked to a theory of signs. The last great theory of signs offered in the history of philosophy, independently of logic is that of Charles Peirce whom we study in Chapter 6.

The problem of formal indication, which is a deep philosophical problem we can only allude to here and which ties into the phenomenological approach to logic, also seems to be connected to the problem of defining or referring by denoting. The problem of individuals or of defining by pointing the individual which comes from Duns Scotus and is referred to as the problem of *haecceity* also seems to belong to the problem of denotation. Denotation is tied to the notion of logical and mathematical extension. When we study functions in mathematics we can list the range of a function according to extension or intension. A simple set in mathematics is the set of primes under 10 or (2, 3, 5, 7). The extension can be listed exhaustively. But the set of all primes has an infinite extension. Thus we can give only a connotative or intensional definition. The set of all primes is the set of all numbers which only possess 1 and themselves as divisors. The previous definition is intensional and bears upon the connotation of the primes.

One further point about connotational definition must be stressed. Classically and in the Middle Ages, one defined individuals and particulars by giving the sub-class to which they belonged and the specific difference of the individual from all the other members in the sub-class called the genus. This so-called method of proximal genus and specific difference (*proximum genus et differentia specifica*) belongs to the connotational aspect of defining because we define an object or an individual by analyzing it into its essential properties and then selecting the closest genus to which they belong and what makes them specifically different from all the members of the genus. Thus this type of definition falls under the method of intension since it is operational and functional to a certain extent. One could think of devising a machine that once given the essential properties would taxonomically and algorithmically classify any object within the right genus or category that it belongs to and identify it or pick it out by its specific difference. This type of definition also fits very well with the type of definitions and constants of modern physics since physicists like Hawking and Einstein admit that the meaning of their theories and the definition of the terms that they employ are not absolute but rather operational and relative to a model.

> **KEY NOTES**
>
> Copi's **5 TYPES OF DEFINITIONS:**
>
> 1. **A STIPULATIVE** definition defines novel terms and expressions when they are first introduced.
> 2. **A LEXICAL** definition reports the meaning of a word or concept that is already in use.
> 3. **A PRECISING** definition is like a stipulative definition in that it may introduce a novel meaning of an old term, but unlike the stipulative definition, the precising definition cannot contradict the lexical definition.
> 4. **A THEORETICAL** definition seeks a universal definition that will cover all the particular instances of a given word, concept, notion, idea or term.
> 5. **A PERSUASIVE** definition belongs to the class of discourse called rhetoric and possess not only an informative function but also an expressive one.

Next we consider the strengths and weaknesses of each type of definition. Denotative definitions have strong psychological and phenomenological import. Logic, without being psychological, still possesses a psychological aspect. If we can point to an object to define it we reduce its features to the features of our conscious perception. This is the famous thesis of Husserl's phenomenological reduction; and even though Husserl rejected psychologism, some of his logical theses maintain a connection to the denotational, indicational and sensible aspect of the individual phenomena. Heidegger also discussed the formal indicative abundantly in his writings. But denotational or phenomenological definitions are not so useful in mathematics where functions and relations are fundamental tools for abstraction. Hence connotation (or intension) makes more sense in this context. Things are defined intensively, functionally and operationally but relative to a model. A model is a subset of the domain of a class that has a relation of logical implication or consequence with the set of all well-formed logical expression in the range of another logical class.

The strength of connotation is also the source of its weakness. Although connotation is very important for logic and mathematics, it is a weak tool to tackle the objects of ontology or metaphysics. Concepts like God, Being, entity, history cannot be captured within one sub-class or category. They are trans-categorical or transcendental. One can hear echoes here of Heidegger's thesis in *Being and Time* that Being is the transcendental pure and simple. It seems like the strength of connotation in other domains of knowledge such as mathematics and logic is precisely its weakness in ontology. Ontological concepts seem to be fundamentally simple and difficult to analyze into their respective parts. Ontological concepts seem to be superstructures, wholes before their parts. Connotational definitions are efficient and effective when they subsume objects or entities under their essential properties and parts and summarize in this way a set of individuals under one larger class or category of objects or functions. Set theory, which may be considered the ambient place that first and second-order (and higher-order) logics inhabit, is generally defined extensionally through the Principle of Extension. This means that a set is defined through the list of its members. However a pure extensional approach to mathematics is insufficient. According to Kurt Gödel, it is the platonic nature of mathematics that is pointed out through the intensional aspect of functions, which in fact mostly connote. There is a great debate here between positivist and nominalist logicians such as Carnap and Tarski (and the structuralists around the French Bourbaki) who see mathematics and logic in a purely definitional manner and Gödel for whom mathematical objects such as sets are both real and ideal and which defend a constituted platonism in the philosophy of mathematics.[4]

What seems to be particular about ontological concepts is that they already are a form of summarized, essential and simple class of objects and they do not suffer further analysis or reduction and simplification. This thesis is not without its difficulties but this is not an ontological treatise: it attempts to be a treatise on logic.

So what are the consequences of this ontological digression on the important concepts of semantics and syntax and how they are viewed in this book? A lot of this will become clearer when we look at specific examples, rules of inference and forms of proof but some preliminary remarks can be made here.

Model theory presupposes that semantics is a process internal to a model. Thus, it can develop the notion of logical and semantic consequence within the model and the classes

---

4 See Tieszen, Richard, After Gödel : Platonism and rationalism in mathematics and logic, Oxford ; New York : Oxford University Press, 2011

that are governed or controlled by the model. (A class has a model if there is a cartesian product and a subset of the first-class logically implies all the well-formed expressions that are true according to a given logical interpretation in the range of the cartesian product of the second class). Thus semantics can allow for proof by defining it in terms of logical consequence. But there is an operational remainder in the concept of proof that is syntactical. This logical, but also ontological remainder, accounts for the fact that proof is also a process that occurs between models and possesses something like an objective reference. Thus the connotational, intensional aspects of the semantics of model-theory cannot account for an external reference that must be both somehow objective and simple. One can think here either of the objectivity of numbers or of the objectivity of God. Obviously in each case an extremely different logical consequence follows. But the main point is that syntax matters. Purely semantic proof without reference to syntactical process aspects of proof which are external to models will become entangled once more in the paradoxes of self-referentiality. Again we hope to clarify this when we consider concrete rules of inference and how syntax and semantics work concretely.

1.3 VALIDITY & SOUNDNESS
Notions of Deductive Validity and Soundness

We need to distinguish between deduction and deductive reasoning.[5] Sherlock Holmes to use a colloquial example, is often depicted as using 'deductive reasoning' to solve crimes or explain apparent mysteries. Deduction on the other hand, is a step or a means within the scientific method (along with other such means or processes as abduction[6] and induction). A related use of deduction or the adjective 'deductive' is when it is applied to reasoning and to evaluations which are produced using natural or formal languages.

A first attempt to explain what deduction is can perhaps be evinced from its etymology (the origin of the word). Deduction comes to us from the early 15th century, via Medieval French *déduction* or directly from Latin *deductionem* (nom. *deductio*), a noun of action from *deducere* (meanding to deduce)[7]; and as a term in logic, from Late Latin use of *deductio* as a loan-translation of Greek *apagoge* or Proof by Contradiction (a.k.a *Reductio ad Absurdum*)"

---

[5] See our discussion of Hempel's Deductive-Nomological model of scientific explanation in Chapter 7 of this book.
[6] See chapter 6, for the notion of abduction
[7] This etymology comes from the Online Etymology Dictionary.

Apagoge is a proof by contradiction. We will see these kinds of proofs later. For now, it is sufficient to know that deductive reasoning is a type of abstract, formal reasoning or logic and that natural deduction is a proof-method. The theory that deals with proof in logic, philosophy and mathematics is called Proof Theory.

What is a syllogism?

We now briefly introduce the deductive syllogism in order to explain the notion of deductive validity. The notion of syllogism is covered more extensively and carefully in the next section of this book. However, syllogisms are an ideal tool to begin understanding what the deductive notion of validity signifies and so we introduce it here.

The major premise is usually the first premise listed in the standard form of a classical syllogism. The minor premise is the second premise in the standard form of the syllogism. Aristotle studied syllogism extensively and as do we in Section 4 of this chapter. He studied not only the general form of the statements such as 'All' and 'Some', but also how the major premise and the minor premise related in terms of an internal logical link or connection. This is the concept of *logical validity* which is sometimes taken to be identical to *logical consequence*.

> **Example of Deductive Syllogism**
>
> *All men are mortal.*
> *Socrates is a man.*
> ___
> *Therefore, Socrates is mortal.*

Deductive reasoning moves from theory to observations or findings or evidence or information or empirical data. All of these words have different meanings, though we overlook their differences at the moment. We will define them more precisely and distinguish between them later. In the example above, the theory is that 'All men are mortal'; and the observation is that 'Socrates is a man.' So, the conclusion can be made that 'Socrates is mortal.'

Law of Detachment or *Modus ponens*

Modus ponens is a very common rule of inference and takes the following form:

> *If P, then Q.*
> *P.*
> ___
> *Therefore, Q.*

The following is an example of an argument using the law of detachment in the form of an If-then statement:

If a geometrical figure has four sides at a 90 degree angle then it is a rectangle.
Figure A has four sides at a 90 degree angle.

Therefore, Figure A is a rectangle.

An aside: Notice that angle A must be measured to verify the first condition or premise. This constitutes an "observation". We should ask whether measurements are perfect and if they depend on our senses; and also whether the act of observing or measuring does not affect the object we are observing. It will be a good question to keep in mind for later in this book. This constitutes what is called the 'measurement problem' in physics and the 'observer effect' of modern science.[1]

> **Example of *Modus Ponens* or Detachment**
>
> *If a geometrical figure has four sides at a 90 degree angle then it is a rectangle.*
> *Figure A has four sides at a 90 degree angle.*
>
> *Therefore, Figure A is a rectangle.*

1.3.1 Validity & Soundness in Deductive Reasoning

Deductive arguments are generally evaluated in terms of their *validity* and *soundness*.

Validity

An argument is **valid if it is impossible for its conclusion to be false whenever the premise or premises are true.** In other words, the conclusion must be true if the premises, whatever they may be, are true. Note that an argument can be valid even though the premises are actually false.

---

[1] The 'observer effect' in modern physical theory can be explained easily by illustration: Because the particles studied are so small, in some cases subatomical, and the observer apparatus so large; the act of introducing the observation or detection apparatus into the particle's environment alters its physical environment (this is Heisenberg's principle of indeterminacy, which claims that the location and the velocity of say an electron may not be known at the same time because at least one photon of light is necessary to observe the electron; the observation then alters the physical characteristics of the electron and renders the act of observation subjective (so to speak) and non-deterministic) and so affects the particle itself and its behavior. Imagine trying to measure the electrostatic or gravitational forces between two subatomic particles: the very act of approaching them with whatever measuring tool whatsoever vitiates any readings you may acquire.

Soundness

An argument is sound *if it is valid and the premises are actually true.*

> ⓘ **KEY DEFINITIONS**
>
> **VALIDITY:** An argument is valid *if it is impossible for its conclusion to be false whenever the premise or premises are true.*
>
> **SOUNDNESS:** An argument is sound *if it is valid and the premises are actually true.*

Valid and Unsound Arguments

The following is an example of an argument that is valid, but not sound; one of the premises of the argument is false:

> *Everyone who has read Thus Spoke Zarathustra is part of the cultural elite.*
> *Joakim has read Thus Spoke Zarathustra.*
>
> *Therefore, Joakim is part of the cultural elite.*

The first premise in the example provided above is false. There are people who have read *Thus Spoke Zarathustra* who are not part of the cultural elite. For example, Donald Trump may have read *Thus Spoke Zarathustra*. Yet he is not part of the cultural elite. The argument therefore is 'unsound'. However, because the premise is false, what follows logically is irrelevant and so the argument as a whole suffers no contradiction. In other words, the only condition that must be met for the argument to satisfy validity requirements is that, if the premises are true, then the conclusion must be true. It is invalid therefore, only when the premises are true and the conclusion false (as we see from our table of Logical Implication under the column $P \rightarrow Q$).

CRITICAL THINKING, WORLDVIEWS & LOGIC

EXERCISES

Elementary Validity & Soundness

1. For each of the following arguments, indicate whether it is:
   (A) valid and sound;
   (B) valid and unsound, or
   (C) invalid and unsound.

   i. If you are married, then you will have children.
   You have children.
   So, you are married.

   ii. Either Princess Diana was assassinated, or she was killed in an accident.
   Princess Diana was not killed in an accident.
   So Princess Diana must have been assassinated.

   iii. December 25th is Christmas.
   December 25th is this Friday.
   So this Friday must be Christmas.

   iv. It is June.
   June is in the summer.
   So it must be summer.

   v. It is June.
   June is in the summer.
   So it must very hot outside.

   vi. Classes at McGill University start on August 20th every year.
   It is August 20th today.
   So classes start today.

   vii. Paul is an adolescent
   All adolescents are grumpy.
   Therefore Paul is grumpy.

   viii. Some Christians are fundamentalists.
   Some fundamentalists are dangerous.
   Hence, some Christians are dangerous.

   ix. All spiders are unfriendly.
   No cats are spiders.
   Therefore, no cats are unfriendly.

   x. Every upright person is believable.
   No woman is believable.
   Therefore, no upright person is a woman.

2. Describe the difference between the following logical terms:
   "*something follows from…*"
   - "*entailment*" and
   - "*inference*"

3. Are deductions forms of inference?

4. Prove through demonstration by listing the steps of your proof that the law of logical contraposition is valid and sound.

Translating INTO Logical Symbolism or Expression

Most expressions or sentences in natural languages such as English have an equivalent symbolic expression in the language of propositional or predicate logic. Since propositional logic totally abstracts from the contents of actual English sentences, the natural candidate to express the equivalent meaning of English sentences in logical language is predicate logic. One may wonder what the use of translating expressions in a natural language into the equivalent expression in symbolic language would be. The reason is as follows.

Reducing statements to their symbolic expression reveals their structure. Sometimes we think that natural-language expressions are clear and unambiguous but we realize this is not the case when we translate them into a symbolic logical expression. Thus the use of this exercise is to realize when we are using clear and unambiguous language in every day expressions and when we are not. A bit like in the previous section on definition where the objective was to clarify our use of everyday language, the objective here is to go between natural language and logical language and to learn something about the difference and similarity between a natural language and a purely logical language.

Let us start with a basic example:
> *"Socrates is brave and Aristotle is a coward."*

We can symbolize this easily if we let the sentence B represent "Socrates is brave" and the sentence C represent "Aristotle is a coward". In logical notation this becomes: $B \land C$.

Now we look at a more intricate example:
> *"We know that either Socrates is brave or Aristotle is a coward; and that it is not the case that Socrates is brave and Aristotle is a coward."*

In logical notation this becomes: $(B \lor C) \land \neg (B \land C)$.

Examples such as these can be made arbitrarily complex and the beginning student should practice translating between English and basic propositional or sentential logic in order to develop his skill and his talent for abstraction.

Translating FROM Logical Symbolism or Expression

The opposite operation to transforming an English sentence into sentential or predicate logic is called that of *fixing an interpretation*.

It is quite easy to find interpretations for sentential logic. We consider a short example:
$$A \land (B \lor \neg C) \to (\neg A \land \neg B)$$

We can fix this logical formula by interpreting it in different ways.

We shall consider two:

- Interpretation 1, A: 2 is an even number, B: 3 is greater than 2, C: 2 and 3 are prime numbers.
- Interpretation 2, A: 2 is an odd number, B: 3 is greater than 2, C: 2 and 3 are prime numbers.

INTERPRETATION 1:

When we translate this into English, the statement becomes: *2 is an even number and (3 is greater than 2) or (2 and 3 are not prime numbers) logically implies (2 is not an even number) and (2 is greater than 3)*.

The conclusion is always false given the meanings or the interpretation we have fixed for this logical formula. Can the expression be valid nonetheless? We know validity is a matter of form and the antecedent has a determinate truth value that is true according to this interpretation. 2 and 3 are not prime numbers ($\neg C$) is false. Therefore ($B \vee \neg C$) has truth-value true for the particular interpretation we have chosen. Furthermore according to this interpretation, A (2 is an even number) has the truth-functional assignment true. Therefore $A \wedge (B \vee \neg C)$ has a truth-functional assignment of true on this interpretation. However, still according to this interpretation we also have ($\neg A \wedge \neg B$) which always has the truth-functional assignment of false. Therefore in this interpretation, the logical formula is always invalid.

Can we find an interpretation according to which this formula would be valid? The answer is 'Yes'. We proceed as follows: We know that whenever the premise of the argument as a whole is fixed as false according to an interpretation then it does not matter whether the conclusion entailed is true or not, since validity is only defined for the case when the premise is true. We apply Interpretation 2.

INTERPRETATION 2:

In this interpretation $A \wedge (B \vee \neg C)$ becomes false and needn't even verify the consequent or conclusion. However we do so here for practice:

($\neg A \wedge \neg B$) is false on this interpretation since ($\neg A$ is true but $\neg B$ (2 is greater than 3) is false. Suppose B were defined otherwise as 2 is greater than 3 and $\neg B$ becomes (3 is greater than 2) which is true. Then the whole consequent or conclusion becomes true, which for our sake however is irrelevant. The formula as a whole remains valid according to Interpretation 2, since whenever the antecedent is false, the truth-functional assignment of the consequent is immaterial to the definition of validity.

EXERCISES

TRANSLATING ENGLISH EXPRESSIONS INTO LOGICAL EXPRESSIONS

1. Translate the following compound sentences into symbolic notation, using letters to stand for atomic sentences.

(a) Either the indigestion was produced by beef or it was produced by noodles.
(b) If there are more horses than zebras, then there are more bulls than goats and there are fewer wolves than horses.
(c) Sasquatch is a fake, and if the same is true of Santa Claus, many children are deceived.
(d) Either jobs are scarce or people like to beg, and if people do not like to beg, then jobs are scarce.
(e) If the weather is clear, then either Henry can see the horizon or he is a nimcompoop.
(f) Either Denise is not there or Jack is, and Mark certainly is.
(g) If Mark testifies and tells the truth, he will be found guilty; and if people do not testify, he will be found guilty.
(h) If either bluejays are lovely or chickens do not have necks, then logic is confusing.
(i) Either Jack must testify and tell the truth, or he does not have to testify.

2. Find proper English sentences and translate the following logical expressions into English

a) $\neg(((\neg A \wedge B) \vee \neg C) \rightarrow (D \wedge E))$
b) $(B \rightarrow C) \wedge ((D \vee \neg E) \leftrightarrow (C \vee A))$
c) $[(A \leftrightarrow B) \rightarrow ((E \wedge \neg F) \rightarrow (A \wedge \neg A))] \wedge ((A \rightarrow B) \vee C)$
d) $(B \wedge \neg B) \leftrightarrow (C \vee \neg C)$
e) $(B \rightarrow (A \wedge B)) \wedge (B \rightarrow (C \wedge D)) \vee (A \rightarrow (E \vee B))$

3. If A denotes that 'Adam wins the first prize', C that 'Chris wins the first prize', and D that 'Dan' wins the first prize', put the following compound statements into logical form:

a) If Adam and Chris both do not win first prize, then Adam and Chris do not both win first prize.
b) If Adam wins first prize then it is not the case that either Chris or Dan wins the first prize.
c) If Adam wins first prize then Chris does not win first prize but if Chris does not win first prize then Dan wins first prize.
d) Either Adam wins first prize and Chris does not win first prize or if Chris wins first prize then Dan does not win first prize.
e) If Adam wins first prize then both Chris and Dan win first prize.

1.4 CATEGORICAL OR SYLLOGISTIC LOGIC[1]
CATEGORICAL PROPOSITIONS & CLASSES

Categorical propositions are statements about classes: claiming that these classes are either included or from other classes in whole or in part. Classes are entities which are described by objects which have certain predicates in common or share certain properties or features. It was shown when Frege tried to apply *quantifiers* to classes (construed generally as sets) that these fall prey to Russell's Paradox[2].

The theory of deductive reasoning known as *categorical* or *term* logic was developed by Aristotle but was eventually supplanted by *propositional (sentential)* logic and *predicate* logic in the modern world. We have defined propositional and predicate logic already. Aristotle's logic is important for historical reasons and we do a short overview of it here.

In categorical logic, propositions are composed of two terms. This is why this type of logic is called *term logic* or *two-term theory* and is distinguished from *sentential* or *propositional* logic (which does not distinguish between terms) and from *predicate* logic which quantifies over logical individuals, variables or constants. The '*term*' in term logic is a part of language which 'stands in' for something. It should be noted that each term is not true or false on its own. A term can be "philosopher", "human", "immortal", etc. In two-term logic the main term or predicate is affirmed or denied of the second term, the subject. It is this combination that forms a proposition and which is capable of being declared 'true' or 'false'. The syllogism consists in how the major premise and middle premise are related together to infer the conclusion. This is the deductive element in syllogistic logic: It consists in the study of the forms of syllogisms which are deductively valid. In order to understand deductive form in this context we must study and classify the permutations of possible syllogistic arguments. This is done by studying the *mood* and *figure* of each argument, as we do below.

---

1 Categorical logic should not be confused with the more advanced category theory which was developed in the late twentieth century and comprised some of the results of abstract geometry and topology developed by the mathematician Grothendieck.

2 Russell's paradox is based on the notion of self-referentiality. It asks whether the set of all sets which are not members of themselves exists. The answer to this question creates a paradox. This is the reason why: if x belongs to the set of sets who are not members of themselves (R) then it is not a member of itself. Therefore it does not belong to the set of sets who are not members of itself. But if it is not a member of itself, it belongs, by definition, to the set of sets who are not members of themselves. This can be expressed symbolically as follows: Let R = $\{x \mid x \notin x\}$, then $R \in R \Leftrightarrow R \notin R$.

> **ⓘ KEY DEFINITIONS**
>
> In **CATEGORICAL LOGIC**, propositions are composed of two terms. This is why this type of logic is called *term logic* or *two-term theory* and is distinguished from **SENTENTIAL** or **PROPOSITIONAL LOGIC** which does not distinguish between terms; and from **PREDICATE LOGIC** which quantifies over logical individuals, variables or constants.

QUALITY, QUANTITY & DISTRIBUTION OF CATEGORICAL PROPOSITIONS

A categorical proposition takes the form of a sentence of the type: S is P where the S gets qualified by a positive or a negative logical type of affirmation and gets quantified in terms of "All" or "Some". Thus we obtain four possible forms:

A-TYPE:
Quantity: Universal and Quality: Affirmative
(E.g.: "*Every philosopher is mortal*")

E-TYPE:
Quantity: Universal and Quality: Negative
(E.g.: "*Every philosopher is immortal*")

I-TYPE:
Quantity: Particular and Quality: Affirmative
(E.g.: "*Some philosophers are mortal*")

O-TYPE:
Quantity: Particular and Quality: Negative
(E.g.: "*Some philosophers are immortal*")

The traditional square of opposition was very influential. Historically it mediated between Aristotle and Leibniz's logics via the *Ars Magna* of Ramon Lull whom we discuss in our Chapter 8. The square embodies the logical relations between the different types of quality and quantity of the categorical propositions:

MOOD AND FIGURES OF SYLLOGISMS

Syllogism may be classified according to mood and figure. We consider first a syllogism of figure 1:

All men are mortal.
Socrates is a man.
―――――――――――――
Socrates is mortal.

If we analyze this typical and famous syllogism, we note that the first or major premise (*All men are mortal*) is an 'A' type of proposition. The second or minor premise (*Socrates is a man*) is an 'I' type (Some person, in this case Socrates, is a man). The conclusion (*Socrates is mortal*) is also an 'I' type.

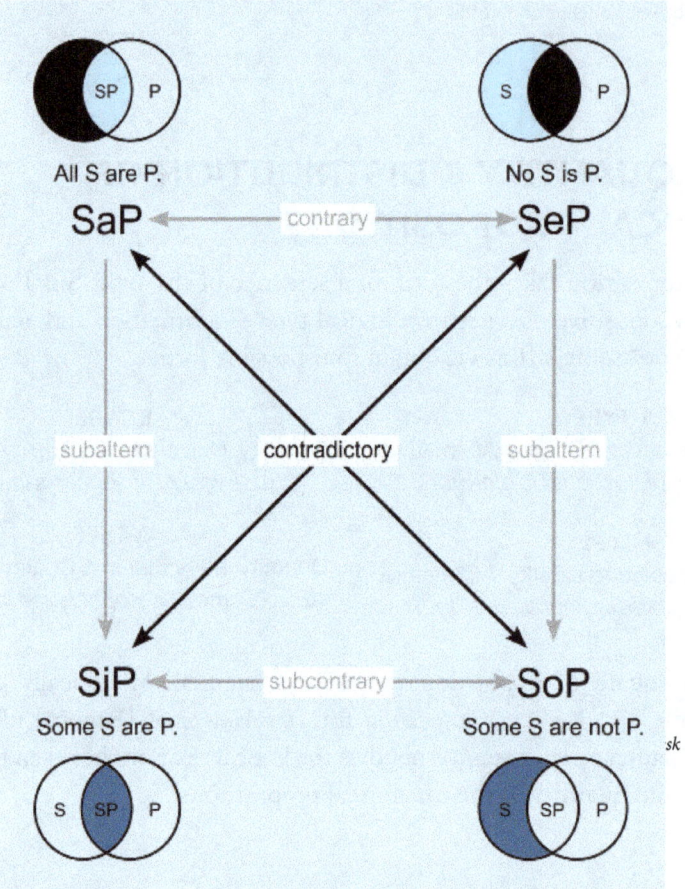

Hence, the form of the mood of this syllogism is AII. There is a connecting middle term (M), which is the term "man". The middle term is defined to be the term that the major premise and the minor premise have in common. In the major premise, the subject is 'man' and the predicate is 'mortal'. In the minor premise, the subject is 'Socrates' and the predicate is 'man'. In the conclusion, the subject is again 'Socrates' and the predicate is 'mortal'.

Let us consider a syllogism of figure 2:

> *All mortals are men.*
> *There is a mortal named Socrates*
> ―――――――――――――――――――
> *Socrates is a man.*

We must consider this in the abstract and even though the apparent truth of the major premise is problematic, what matters here is that essentially this syllogism has the same form AII as the previous one. However, we see quickly that they do not possess the same logical form. It is necessary, therefore, to introduce the notion of *figure* in order to distinguish the many kinds of syllogisms possible of the form AII.

Aristotle distinguished four major figures for syllogisms:

	Figure 1	**Figure 2**	**Figure 3**	**Figure 4**
	M-P	P-M	M-P	P-M
	S-M	S-M	M-S	M-S
Therefore	S-P	S-P	S-P	S-P

Let us compare our two syllogisms of the form AII. We quickly recognize that Syllogism 1, (*All men are mortal. Socrates is a man. Therefore Socrates is mortal.*) represents an instantiation of Figure 1. The second syllogism (2) gives us an AII syllogism with figure 3.

There are specific mnemonic names that were given during the Middle Ages to remember the various figures and moods of syllogisms. We provide a list below which likely originates with some modifications from Peter of Spain's *Summulae Logicales*:

Figure 1	Figure 2	Figure 3	Figure 4
Barbara	Cesare	Datisi	Calemes
Celarent	Camestres	Disamis	Dimatis
Darii	Festino	Ferison	Fresison
Ferio	Baroco	Bocardo	Calemos
Barbari	Cesaro	Felapton	Fesapo
Celaront	Camestros	Darapti	Bamalip

We can see that in our case, the first case under study is *Darii* and the other is *Datisi*. The problem is that many of these syllogisms do not teach us much. They are tools for formalizing existing knowledge and even then, they do so imperfectly. The O forms tend to be more informative, though typically Aristotle did not study the O and I forms very extensively and focused more on the affirmative and universal cases of syllogism.

VENN DIAGRAMS & THE VALIDITY OF SYLLOGISMS

The logical structure of syllogism can be studied and appreciated visually. For example, in the case of *Darii*, this can be represented graphically as follows:

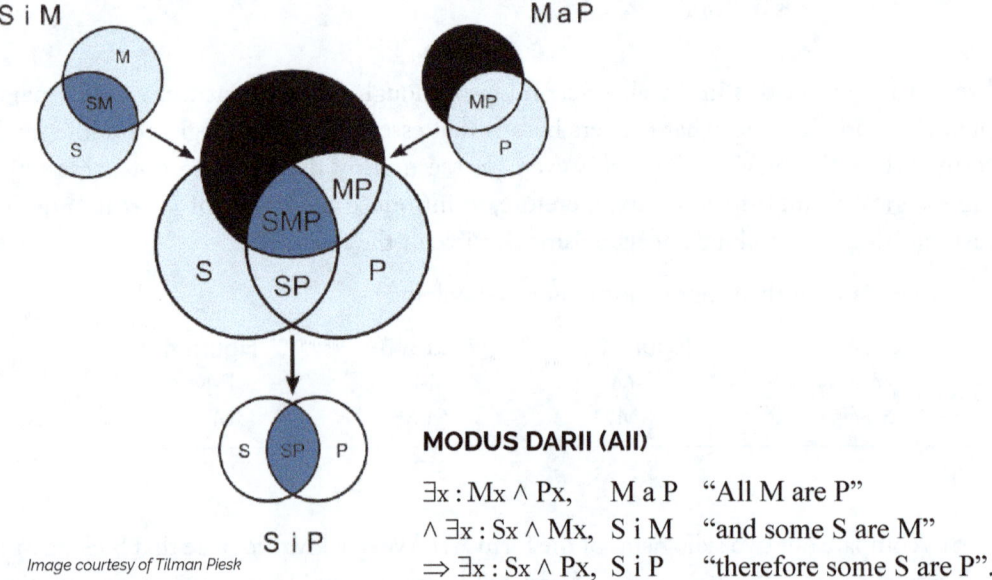

Image courtesy of Tilman Piesk

MODUS DARII (AII)

$\exists x : Mx \wedge Px,$ $\quad M \, a \, P \quad$ "All M are P"

$\wedge \, \exists x : Sx \wedge Mx,$ $\quad S \, i \, M \quad$ "and some S are M"

$\Rightarrow \exists x : Sx \wedge Px,$ $\quad S \, i \, P \quad$ "therefore some S are P".

The general idea is to use three circles one for the subject, one for the predicate and one for the middle term. We show the picture below. We carve the space up additionally with SP' (where this represents the elements or individuals that belong to the class S but do not belong to the class P), S'P and S'P'... This gives us eight sub-classes SP'M, SPM', SP'M', SPM, S'PM', S'PM, S'P'M, and S'P'M'.

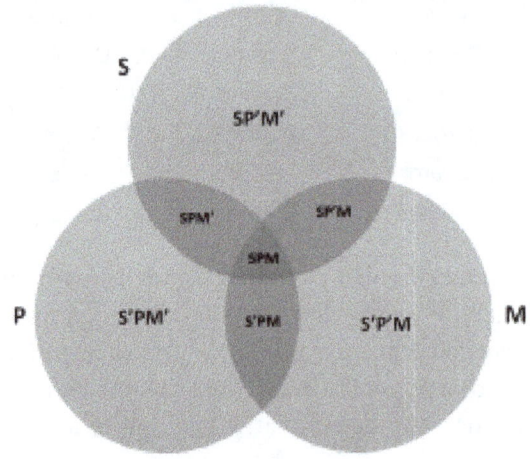

We can then draw the following diagram:

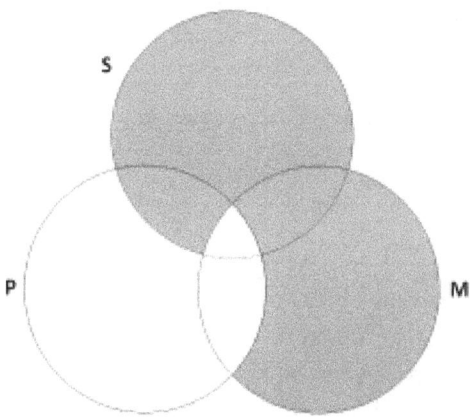

The latter is the diagram of the syllogism AAA-1
All M is P
All S is M
All S is P.

With these examples we encourage students to solve *exercise 7* in order to familiarize themselves with the use of Venn diagrams in clarifying their understanding of syllogisms. The tradition of Aristotelian logic did not study the weak forms of syllogisms and so did not examine all the syllogisms with an O-form conclusion. For this reason, the notion of logical contraposition was opposed by certain logicians like Jean Buridan who did not consider it rational. Some examples given by Buridan in the *Summulae Dialectica* are the following:

> *Every man is a being*
> *Therefore, every non-being is a non-man*
>
> *A chimera is not a human*
> *Therefore, a non-man is not a non-chimera*

The problem with these examples and with syllogisms whose conclusion is an I form such as Darapti and Barbari is that the existential import of the class has to be verified. Existential import typically means that there is at least one individual that belongs to the class that is under study. If no existential import exists, then the statements that are being made about the individuals belonging to the alleged class may be non-sensical or may niether correspond to reality nor to a real domain of discourse.

> **KEY NOTES**
>
> Aristotle's 4 major figures for syllogisms:
>
> | | Figure 1 | Figure 2 | Figure 3 | Figure 4 |
> |---|---|---|---|---|
> | | M-P | P-M | M-P | P-M |
> | | S-M | S-M | M-S | M-S |
> | Therefore | S-P | S-P | S-P | S-P |

One of the interesting features of 20th and 21st century logic is that it does not have to conform to sense-experience. The proof of the validity and soundness of contraposition from principles is left as an exercise in this book. But we can prove its truth precisely because we manipulate propositions of the form $P \rightarrow Q$. In our case P would be "x is a man" and Q would be "x is a being". So that if x is a man this naturally implies that he is also a being. Not-Q is "x is a non-being" and not-P is "x is a non-man". When broken up in this way, the problem becomes clearer: we cannot conclude from x's being a non-being, that it is anything at all whether, a non-man, a non-tree, a non-house, a non-atom...

Formal logic however is about form, not content: it is a perfectly self-enclosed system, at least in its deductive shape which does not require sense-experience of reality to validate it. This is why it is almost unlimited in scope and can tackle problems such as the mathematical infinite. It is true, however, that some results such as Gödel's incompleteness theorem have placed some limitation on the power of formal deductive systems.

> **KEY DEFINITIONS**
>
> A **categorical proposition** takes four possible forms:
>
> **A-TYPE:** Universal and Affirmative (E.g.: "*Every philosopher is mortal*")
> **I-TYPE:** Particular and Affirmative (E.g.: "*Some philosopher is mortal*")
> **E-TYPE:** Universal and Negative (E.g.: "*Every philosopher is immortal*")
> **O-TYPE:** Particular and Negative (E.g.: "*Some philosopher is immortal*")

EXERCISES
CATEGORICAL OR SYLLOGISTIC LOGIC

1. Identify the subject and predicate terms, and name the form of each of the following propositions.

    i) Some actors are extremely gifted and their acting looks like real life.
    ii) Some members of families that are musical and literary are not men of either fame or distinction.
    iii) Some politicians who could not be elected to the most minor positions and have trouble with the English language are appointed officials in our Senate today.

2. Name the *quantity* (universal / particular) and the *quality* (affirmative / negative) of each of the following propositions and state whether their subject and predicate terms are distributed or undistributed.

    i) Some politicians will be unhappy if they leave private life.
    ii) Some advocates of major political, social and economic reforms are not responsible men and women. They are just in it for the money.
    iii) All post-modern writers will be remembered, if at all, as having done a general disservice to the art of literature.

3. What can be inferred about the truth or falsehood of the remaining propositions in each of the following sets if we assume the first to be true? If we assume it to be false?

    i) All successful mathematicians are dupes.
    ii) No successful mathematicians are not dupes.
    iii) Some successful mathematicians are dupes.
    iv) Some successful mathematicians are not dupes

4. If "some bankers are not crooks" is true, what may be inferred about the truth or falsehood of the following propositions?

    i) Some noncrooks are not nonbankers.
    ii) No nonbankers are crooks.
    iii) No crooks are nonbankers.
    iv) All bankers are noncrooks.
    v) All noncrooks are nonbankers.
    vi) No bankers are crooks.
    vii) No nonbankers are noncrooks.
    viii) Some crooks are not nonbankers.
    ix) Some crooks are not bankers.

CRITICAL THINKING, WORLDVIEWS & LOGIC

5. Rewrite each of the following syllogisms in standard form, and name its mood and figure.

   (i) Some animals are objects of worship, because all cows are animals, and some objects of worship are cows.

   ii) All lipids are organic compounds, whence all triglycerides are lipids, as all triglycerides are organic compounds.

   iii) All successful individuals are well-adjusted individuals, and some successful individuals are products of stable homes, hence some well-adjusted individuals are products of stable homes.

6. Refute any of the following arguments that are invalid by the method of constructing logical analogies.

   (i) All artists are active proponents of increased corporation taxes, for all active proponents of increased corporation taxes are members of the Artist's Union, and all members of the Artist's Union are artists.

   (ii) All kittens are pets that can be bought at special rates, so some pets that can be bought special rates are not dogs, since no dogs are kittens.

   (iii) Some orthodontists are not specialists in surgery, some dentists are not orthodontists, since some dentists are not specialists in surgery.

7. Test the validity of each of the following syllogistic forms by means of the Venn diagram method.

   a) AOE-1
   b) AAO-2
   c) AOO-4
   d) EEE-1
   e) AAI-2
   f) EEO-3
   g) OOO-1
   h) OOI-4

1.5 PROPOSITIONAL OR SENTENTIAL (0ᵗʰ Order) LOGIC

We have studied classical syllogistic logic in the previous sections of this chapter and we have looked at the definition of basic logical connectives. We now come to the study of sentential and propositional logic proper. Sentential and propositional logic is considered to be a 0th order logic and as such a complete deduction system of this type of logic can be built. This means that given certain specific rules of inference together with what are known as rules of replacement, any possible true logical formula or sentence within the sentential system of logic can be proven to be valid and sound or to be contradictory. In other words the truth value of any logic formula is fully determined. We will see in the section on predicate logic in this chapter that this is not generally true of all first-order logical systems. (Predicate logic, for instance, is a first-order logical deduction system).

> ⓘ **KEY DEFINITIONS**
>
> **PROPOSITIONAL CALCULUS OR LOGIC** (also called sentential calculus or sentential logic) is a formal system in which formulae of a formal language are interpreted as propositions.

We now move to define a propositional calculus: Mathematical logic defines a propositional calculus or logic (also called sentential calculus or sentential logic) to be a formal system[1] in which formulas[2] of a formal language[3] may be interpreted as propositions. The calculus—or operational method of reasoning—may be taken to be a generalized system of inference rules and axioms, which allows for the derivation of certain formulas. The formulas derived from the inference rules and axioms are called *theorems* and are true propositions since they follow a calculus method of rigorous application of logic. By definition, a built up series or sequence of formulas is called a derivation or proof and the last formula of the series or sequence is called the theorem.

---

1 A *formal system* is a system in which every expression in a given formal language has a definite and determinate truth-functional assignment or assignation. The formal system is usually built from basic axioms or statements whose truth is assumed. Furthermore, every expression in the formal system is either an axiom, a theorem or a well-formed logical expression with a definite and determinate truth-functional assignment. We define formal language below in footnote 3.

2 A *logical formula* is an expression in a formal language that is meaningful or well-defined. This means that anything that does not follow the strict formation (elementary syntactic) rules of formation of expression in a formal language is considered to have no meaning or ruled out as a formula in the formal language and in the formal system under examination.

3 A *formal language* is a set of logical formulas together with logical connectives or operators and clearly defined rules of formation for what is to count as a logical formula in the language.

The derivation is usually given as the proof of the proposition denoted by the theorem.

In truth-functional propositional logic, logical formulas are generally taken to have either a truth-value of true or a truth-value of false. Truth-functional propositional logic and systems isomorphic[4] to it, and can be shown to be equivalent to 0th-order logic (as opposed to first-order and higher-order systems of logic).

1.5.1 RULES OF INFERENCE IN PROPOSTIONAL LOGIC

Derivation Rules in a Propositional Deduction System

In logic, a 'rule of inference', an 'inference rule, or 'transformation rule' or 'derivation rule' is a logical form consisting of a function which takes premises (it substitutes actual premises for logical variables which form the domain of the function), analyzes their syntax (syntax here means the structure that the premises of the argument forms in which variables are substituted) and returns a conclusion or conclusions. For example, the rule of inference called *modus ponens* takes two premises. One in the form "*If p then q*" and another in the form "*p*", and returns the conclusion "*q*". *Modus ponens* is valid in relation to the semantics of classical logic. This rule of inference is also valid in relation to many non-classical logics. This means that if the premises are true (under an interpretation) then by definition so is the conclusion. In principle, any rule of inference should preserve the truth. This is a semantic property. We remind the student that semantics is related to the notions of truth and meaning. There is a debate in modern logic as to whether validity is a semantic or syntactic notion. We have already alluded to this when we discussed *connotation* versus *denotation* in the philosophical theory of definition. In many-valued logic, a rule of inference preserves a general designation. However, a rule of inference's action is purely syntactic[5], and does not need to preserve any semantic property: any function from sets of formulae to other formulae counts as

---

[4] An *isomorphism* is a mathematical notion drawn from the field of algebra in which two structures are deemed to behave in the same way or to be mathematically identical if there is a mapping or function from one of the structures to the other which preserves all the essential properties of each structure.

[5] Logical syntax has two aspects and can be divided into theoretical syntax and practical syntax. Practical syntax has to do with what counts as an acceptable logical formula, logical expression or logical sentence in a given formal language that makes up a formal deduction system. Theoretical syntax ties into proof theory and is related to what can be proved starting from a given clearly defined deduction system. It has been noticed by Tarski and others that some things are a logical consequence from a given formal deduction system and yet cannot be proved to follow from that system. This has led to the development of model theory and to the reduction of syntax to a semantical problem of truth and meaning. It is also related to results on decidability, completeness, compactness and the halting problem of Turing machines.

a rule of inference. Usually only rules that are recursive are important; i.e. rules such that there is an effective procedure for determining whether any given formula is the conclusion of a given set of formulae according to the rule. Recursion occurs when an object, an idea, a thing, replicates itself. For instance, when the surfaces of two mirrors are exactly parallel with each other, the nested images that occur are a form of infinite recursion. The term has a variety of meanings specific to a variety of disciplines ranging from linguistics to logic.

> **INTERESTING?**
>
> The most common application of **RECURSION** is in mathematics and computer science, in which it refers to a method of defining *a function that calls upon itself*.
>
> **Recursion** is prevalent in nature and is typically the means by which nature grows structures (geometric or otherwise):
>
> > The Fibonacci sequence is a good example. It is the formula for all spiral shapes such as are seen on a snail shell, flower growth, etc. The Fibonacci, which calls upon itself, is usually defined as : Fib(n) = Fib(n-1) +Fib(n-2) with Fib(0)=0 and Fib(1)=1.
>
> An example of recursion is the following relation used to define ancestry:
> *"A parent is an ancestor; An ancestor of an ancestor is an ancestor."*

The most common application of recursion is in mathematics and computer science, in which it refers to a method of defining a function that calls upon itself. Recursion is also prevalent in nature and is typically the means by which nature grows structures (geometric or otherwise).[6]

The term is also used more generally to describe a process of repeating objects in a self-similar way. To provide an example of recursion, consider the following relation used to define ancestry:

A parent is an ancestor; An ancestor of an ancestor is an ancestor.

We see a self-referencing 'loop' in the definition ("an ancestor is an ancestor") which can extend itself infinitely. Thus, recursion specifies a non-finite number of functional occurrences using finite expressions in which some occurrences or function values may refer to other occurrences or function values in an apparently circular fashion. However this is done in such fashion that no contradictory, paradoxical loop or chain of references may vitiate the recurring or repeated process through which the definitional instances

---

[6] The Fibonacci sequence is a good example, which is the formula for all spiral shapes such as are seen on a snail shell, flower growth, etc. The Fibonacci which calls upon itself is usually defined as : Fib(n) = Fib(n-1) +Fib(n-2) with Fib(0)=0 and Fib(1)=1.

proceed.

In order to clarify the difference between syntax and semantics we give a brief overview here but this overview will only become clearer when we look at specific deduction systems such as propositional calculus and the predicate calculus which are respectively of 0th and 1st order. Even though an inference form is a logical form, this logical form must be defined with respect to a logical variable and to a notion of logical substitutionality. Any given statement such as G: *"Aristotle was a great philosopher"* becomes fixed when we associate the letter G with the statement. But in order to consider logical form we need to be able to consider logical variables for which we will use lower-case letters. Thus the statement "Aristotle is a great philosopher therefore all logic is syllogistic" may be symbolized as G → S where S stands for "All logic is syllogistic". Now if we write:

$$\frac{G \to S \quad G}{S}$$

then this is simply the logical form of *modus ponens*. The syntax enters into the discussion, when we claim that another statement A → B, and A so therefore B. Here A can state for example that Aristotle was an imbecile and B can stand for "Therefore all logic is intuitionistic".

Now

$$\frac{A \to B \quad A}{B}$$

also possesses the form of *modus ponens* though its conclusion is the not the same at all as that of the other inference. We can substitute both symbolical arguments within the general logical form of *modus ponens*. This insight that logical statements can be treated as variables over a range of statements is due to Leibniz.

This observation of how the method of substitutionality[7] works is crucial, but not uncontroversial. In a way, it abstracts the distinction between logical connotation and logical denotation. (See section on logical definition for the difference between logical denotation and logical connotation). It is true that connotation determines denotation whereas the opposite is not the case. *Connotation* is a semantic notion whereas denotation is a syntactic one, and this dichotomy does not seem to be completely resolvable in a satisfactory way. This is because syntax also governs and controls large portions of proof

---

[7] Some philosophers like Brandom call this the problem of linguistic anaphora.

theory. Semantics has to do with truth and meaning, but syntax has to do with the process and structure or form of proof as such. This is why we cannot follow logicians such as Tarski and Beziault who would reduce syntax to semantics. Surely we can only define and determine validity and thus to a certain extent logical consequence with respect to a given logical model. This may appear reasonable. However, the process aspects of syntax and of proof only work if there exists an objective reference outside of any given model. This objective reference may ultimately be indeterminate or non-determinable, but it does allow us to avoid the paradoxes of self-referentiality to a certain extent.

Modus ponens (affirmation mode), *modus tollens* (negation mode), and the rule of logical *contraposition*[8] are among the most well-known rules of inference of propositional logic though they are also used in predicate logic. First-order predicate logic uses rules of inference to deal with logical quantifiers. Here we merely introduce the general notion of validity without reference to a specific deduction system. It has become a general feature of formal logic that validity seems to be only definable in semantic ways that are relative to a specific deduction system or model.

> ### ⓘ KEY DEFINITIONS
>
> Two important criteria which determine both the **consistency and the completeness of any sentential or propositional deduction system** are that:
> 1. the set of rules of inference of our deduction system must help us to infer ALL conclusions which logically follow from the premises; and
> 2. the set of rules of inference of our deduction system must help us infer or derive ONLY those conclusions which logically follow from the premises.

There is no equivalent concept for quantification in sentential logic and this is why we say it is less expressive. Predicate logic can express mathematical arithmetic (there are different kinds but the standard arithmetic is considered to be that of Peano which is used to construct the real numbers axiomatically), something which sentential logic cannot do. Nonetheless, the study of sentential logic is important as a building step to familiarize ourselves with the basic rules of a deduction system. Once we master sentential logic, we can move to a more complex system such as that of predicate logic.

We outline a typical propositional calculus below. Many different versions of propositional calculi exist and they are more or less identical or equivalent. There is some difference in the details, the symbols for propositions, the logical connectives or operator symbols, the initial axioms and the set of rules of inference but in general if

---

8 *Modus Tollens* and contraposition are equivalent rules of inference.

they are standard, consistent and complete all propositional calculi are of zeroth order and are structurally ismorphic to each other.

All 0th order propositional deduction systems are equivalent as long as they are consistent and complete. Some may be more elegant or more efficient than others from the point of view of economizing rules of inference and replacement rules, but they are all isomorphic[9] to each other. We may represent any given proposition with a letter which we call a propositional constant, analogous to representing a number by a letter in mathematics, for instance, A = 5. We require that all propositions have exactly one of two truth-values: true or false. To take an example, let P be the proposition that it is sunny outside. This will be true if it is sunny outside and false otherwise. Thus we presuppose the law of excluded middle (discussed below) as part of our propositional deduction system.

The first step in any deduction system (and this is true of sentential logic as well) is to define what will count as a well-formed-formula or a well-formed expression. We do this recursively.

In this particular case, recursion works in the following way: First, we define the formula (recursively) by stating that "every atomic formula is a formula". This circular definition is manageable, because the atomic formula is the most basic logical formula that exists in our language.

Expressions such as p, q or z (any lower case letter in the English alphabet can represent an atomic formula in our propositional language). Since our first element in the recursive definition is that every atomic formula is a formula, we know that the smallest unit that a logical formula can be built out of is the atomic formula.

Here is the entire definition of a logical formula in our language:

> **ⓘ DEFINITION OF LOGICAL FORMULAE**
>
> a) Every atomic formula is a formula.
> b) If s is a formula then ¬ (s) is a formula.
> c) If r and s are formulas then r ∧ s, r ∨ s, r → s, and r ↔ s are formulas.
> d) No expression is a formula unless it is built using one of the above rules or unless it satisfies the above conditions.

Besides *modus ponens* there are some other important rules of inference from which a deduction system may be built. We list these in the table on the following page.

---

[9] See footnote 4 for the definition of isomorphism.

THE CLASSICAL RULES OF INFERENCE

NAME	APPLICATON
1. Modus Ponens	$P \rightarrow Q$ P ――― q
2. Modus Tollens (M.T.)	$P \rightarrow Q$ $\neg Q$ ――― $\neg P$
3. Hypothetical Syllogism (H.S.)	$P \rightarrow Q$ $Q \rightarrow R$ ――― $P \rightarrow R$
4. Disjunctive Syllogism (D.S.)	$P \vee Q$ $\neg P$ ――― Q
5. Constructive Dilemma (C.D.)	$(P \rightarrow Q) \wedge (R \rightarrow S)$ $P \vee R$ ――― $Q \vee S$
6. Absorption (Abs.)	$P \rightarrow Q$ ――― $P \rightarrow (P \wedge Q)$
7. Simplification (Simp.)	$(P \wedge Q)$ ――― P
8. Conjunction	P Q ――― $P \wedge Q$
9. Addition (Add.)	P ――― $P \vee Q$

EXERCISES
BASIC RULES OF INFERENCE

1. State the rule of inference for each of the following arguments by which the conclusion follows from the premise or premises. It may help to symbolize the statements prior to doing so.

    i) If it is sunny and I have money, then I am happy. 'Therefore if it is sunny and I have money, then it is sunny and I have money and I am happy.

    Hint: S: It is sunny; M: I have money; H: I am happy.

    (S ∧ M) → H. Therefore (S ∧ M) → ((S ∧ M) ∧ H).

    ii) If emery is abundant, then diamonds can be cut and diamonds can be polished; and if laser cutting technology exists, then diamonds can be cut and diamonds can be stored for later.
    Emery is abundant or laser cutting technology exists, therefore the diamonds can be cut and polished or the diamonds can be cut and stored.

    Hint: E: Emery is abundant, C: Diamonds can be be cut; P: Diamonds can be polished; L: laser technology exists; S: Diamonds can be stored for later.

    [E → (C ∧ P)] ∧ [L → (C ∧ S)]
    [E ∨ L] Therefore (C ∧ P) ∨ (C ∧ S)

    iii) A → ¬C ∧ ¬E
    ¬B → (D ∧ F)
    Therefore (A ∧ ¬B) → (¬C ∧ D)

    iv) (O ∧ M) → N
    Therefore O → M ∧ N

2. Each of the following is a formal proof of validity for the indicated argument. State the justification (in terms of a specific rule of inference outlined in our sentential deduction system) for each line that is not a premise:

    - C → (D → E)
    - E → ¬E
    - (A → C) ∧ (B → D) Therefore A → ¬B
    - (C ∧ D) → E

    - (P ∨ O) ∨ Q Therefore ¬M → [(N → (O ∨ P)]
    - (¬¬M ∨ ¬N) ∨ ¬Q
    - ¬(¬M ∧ N) ∨ ¬Q
    - (¬M ∧ N) → ¬Q

- ¬E ∨ ¬E
- ¬E
- ¬(C ∧ D)
- ¬C ∨ ¬D
- ¬A ∨ ¬B
- A → ¬B

- (M ∨ ¬N) ∨ Q
- Q ∨ (P ∨ O)
- Q ∨ (O ∨ P)
- ¬¬Q ∨ (O ∨ P)
- (¬M ∧ N) → (O ∨ P)
- ¬M → [N → (O ∨ P)]

3. Construct a formal proof of validity for each of the following arguments.

i) (M ∨ N) → (C ∧ D)
(C ∨ D) → A
M Therefore A

ii) A → (¬K ∨ L)
A → K
(¬L ∨ I) Therefore A → D

iii) (N → (P ∧ Q)
(P ∨ R) → S
(R ∨ N) Therefore S

4. Use criterion 2 (that only conclusions which logically follow from the premises be derivable given any single rule of inference) of the criteria we listed for having a complete and consistent set of rules of inference, to determine which of the rules below are valid rules of inference. Where the rules are invalid, provide an example to show how criterion 2 is violated. At this point rules of replacement have not been introduced and you may only use the introduced rules of inference or the method of truth tables to justify the introduction of these new rules of inference.

a) From ¬A and B ∨ C we may derive ¬C.
b) From ¬A and B ∨ A we may derive B.
c) From A and A ∨ B, we may derive B.
d) From A and B, we may derive (A ∧ B).

1.5.2 REPLACEMENT RULES FOR PROPOSITIONAL LOGIC

Replacement rules are additional rules of inference that are derivable and thus provable from the basic rules of inference. Their truth can also be verified through truth-table methods. In fact some propositional deduction systems might not have the same rules of inference and replacement rules (one can drop *modus tollens* for example) and still be complete. Good replacement rules are useful because they increase the ability of a deduction system to easily prove the truth of an expression through a series of transformations operated on the premises and ending through the demonstration of the truth of the conclusion sought.

> **REPLACEMENT RULES**
>
> **1. De Morgan's Laws**
> $\neg(p \land q) \Leftrightarrow \neg p \lor \neg q$
> $\neg(p \lor q) \Leftrightarrow \neg p \land \neg q$
>
> **2. Commutativity**
> $(p \lor q) \Leftrightarrow (q \lor p)$
> $(p \land q) \Leftrightarrow (q \land p)$
>
> **3. Associativity**
> $(p \lor q) \lor r \Leftrightarrow p \lor (q \lor r)$
> $(p \land q) \land r \Leftrightarrow p \land (q \land r)$
>
> **4. Material Implication**
> $(p \to q) \Leftrightarrow (\neg p \lor q)$
>
> **5. Double Negation**
> $\neg\neg p \Leftrightarrow p$
>
> **6. Transposition**
> $(p \to q) \Leftrightarrow (\neg q \to \neg p)$
>
> **7. Distribution**
> $[p \land (q \lor r)] \Leftrightarrow [(p \land q) \lor (p \land r)]$
> $[p \lor (q \land r)] \Leftrightarrow [(p \lor q) \land (p \lor r)]$
>
> **8. Idempotence/Tautology**
> Idempotency of Disjunction:
> $(p \lor p) \Leftrightarrow p$
> Idempotency of Conjunction:
> $(p \land p) \Leftrightarrow p$
>
> **9. Material Equivalence**
> $p \Leftrightarrow q$
>
> **10. Exportation**
> $(p \land q) \to r \Leftrightarrow p \to (q \to r)$

In all these rules the "$\Leftrightarrow$" symbol is a metalogical operator that means "can be replaced with in a proof". A metalogical operator is a logical symbol that belongs to a meta-language. The meta-language expresses certain things that cannot be expressed at the level or at the order of the object language. In our case, it is 0th order propositional or sentential deduction system which the metalogical symbol operates above. However, the mere fact that we have to use a higher language symbol does not mean that our deduction system is not complete, though it does have consequences for the role of syntax and semantics in proof theory.

As mentioned above, the rules of replacement and of inference are used to prove the validity of a logical expression in the sentential deduction system we have presented. We accomplish this through a set of derivations in which the rules of replacement and rules of inference can be assumed to be axiomatic; i.e. the truth of these derivations is guaranteed because we can derive any valid expression that is expressible in our sentential deduction system—a 0th order system. The consistency and completeness of 0th order systems is established. It is the 1st order and higher-order systems like the predicate logical system, that completeness becomes a problem as Gödel's Incompleteness Theorem shows.[10]

Consistency is simply the fact that *there is no contradiction built into the rules of inference or replacement*. If there were, this would imply that any logical expression (valid or not) can be derived from the contradiction. This follows from the properties of material implication whose conclusion or consequent we know to be true even if the premise is false. This is why contradiction must be avoided at all cost when establishing rules of inference and replacement. If not, it would jeopardize the consistency of the deduction system under consideration and the rationality behind most science and reasoning today.

Once we have all our determined rules of inference and replacement rules in place (these can vary from one sentential deduction system to another, since there is nothing forced or necessary behind our choice of rules[11]) we can define **validity in this system** as the fact that *any expression which is derivable from atomic sentences or from other well-formed formulas according to the rules we have listed above is either a theorem, a tautology or a contradiction*. A **theorem** in our deduction system may be defined to be *any derivable expression that is non-atomic* (that is not an elementary tautology or contradiction) *and whose negation does not lead to a contradiction*. The above definitions exhaust the notion of validity within a deduction propositional system. In fact, one of the characteristics of this deduction system and which will be contrasted with the higher-order predicate logical system is that provability and consequence are equivalent. Thus if a well-formed formula follows logically from another, we may say that we have proved its validity. As logic gets more complex and higher orders are reached, we will see that logical consequence and provability appear to move apart and until we are no longer able to equate them or identify them with each other.

---

10 0th-order logical systems are complete in general and this is also owed to Godel (his completeness theorems). But there are specific 0th-order logics that are incomplete. They are referred to as non-standard 0th-order logics
11 Some theorems in the sentential system might not be provable however, if we haven't the sufficient number of rules.

CRITICAL THINKING, WORLDVIEWS & LOGIC

> **ⓘ KEY DEFINITIONS**
>
> **Consistency:** *A system is said to be consistent when there is no contradiction built into its rules of inference or replacement.*
>
> **Validity of a system:** A system is said to be valid when *any expression derivable from atomic sentences or from other well-formed formulas according to the rules of replacement is either a theorem, a tautology or a contradiction under the system.*
>
> A **theorem** in our deduction system is *any derivable expression that is non-atomic* (that is not an elementary tautology or contradiction) *and whose negation does not lead to a contradiction.*

EXERCISES

RULES OF REPLACEMENT

1. Consider the following sets of premises and:

    a) Determine if they are 'consistent' or 'inconsistent'; and

    b) If a set is inconsistent, derive a contradiction; if it is consistent, give a 'true' sentential interpretation to prove it.

    > A) If he is popular, then Justin will be elected. If Justin is elected Canada will not be on the right path. Either Justin will get elected or he will be out of politics. However, he will definitely be out of politics. (P, E, O)
    >
    > B) If Canada bombs Iraq, then the prime minister will not get re-elected. In fact, Canada will bomb Iraq. If the prime minister does not get elected, then the leader of the Official opposition will get elected. But it is not the case either the leader of the opposition will get elected or that Canada will bomb Iraq. (B, R, O).

    c) $(\neg A \lor B)$
        $(B \lor \neg C)$ Therefore $B \to C$

2. Construct the sentential derivation for the following arguments using the letter provided in parentheses. If the argument is invalid, then demonstrate its sentential interpretation identifying the rules of inference or replacement used.

    > A) If a country is a democracy then a single man does not take all the important decisions. If a single man does not take all important decisions, then there are a large number of decision-makers. Moreover, there are a large number of decision-makers.
    > Therefore, the country is a democracy. (D, Id, N)

B) If ethics are neglected, then there are a lot of dishonest people. Ethics are neglected or there are a lot of people found guilty of crimes. Also if there are people found guilty of crimes, then the courts are busy. However, the courts are busy.
Therefore, ethics are neglected. (N, D, C, B)

C) Either aesthetics is difficult or not many students like it. If fine art is easy, then aesthetics is not difficult.
Therefore, if many students like aesthetics, fine art is not easy. (D, A, F)

D) If either the interest rate is raised or retail prices are lowered, there will be deflation. If there is deflation, then either Parliament must regulate it or the people will suffer. If the people suffer, members of parliament will be unpopular. Parliament will not regulate interest rates and retail prices and members of parliament will not be unpopular.
Therefore, the interest rate will not be raised and retail prices will not be lowered (I, P, D, R, U).

3. Prove the validity or invalidity of the following arguments:

(A) $(A \wedge B) \rightarrow (C \rightarrow D)$
$\neg E \rightarrow D$
$\neg (\neg B \wedge E)$
$\neg (A \rightarrow C)$ Therefore $\neg C$

(B) $F \rightarrow (G \wedge H)$
$G \rightarrow (\neg I \rightarrow J)$
$(\neg F \wedge I) \rightarrow (L \leftrightarrow M)$
$(\neg F \wedge G) \rightarrow \neg L$
$\neg L \rightarrow (\neg M \rightarrow J)$ Therefore J

(C) $O \rightarrow (\neg P \rightarrow Q)$
$P \rightarrow (R \wedge S)$
$(\neg O \wedge R) \rightarrow (T \leftrightarrow U)$
$O \rightarrow (\neg P \wedge T)$
$\neg T \rightarrow (\neg U \rightarrow S)$ Therefore S
$\neg F \rightarrow (\neg G \rightarrow E)$ Therefore E

4. For each of the following arguments:
   a) Use the method of truth tables to prove their invalidity;
   b) Use the method of 'proof by contradiction' and the rules of inference and the replacement to prove their validity.

(A) $O \rightarrow P$
$Q \rightarrow R$
$P \vee Q$ Therefore $O \vee R$

(B) $A \rightarrow (B \rightarrow C)$
$D \rightarrow (E \rightarrow F)$
$B \rightarrow (D \wedge E)$
$\neg (B \rightarrow F)$ Therefore $A \wedge C$

(C) $M \rightarrow (N \rightarrow \neg O)$
$(Q \rightarrow N) \wedge (R \rightarrow M)$
$S \wedge O$
$\neg T \rightarrow U$
$(V \rightarrow T) \vee (U \rightarrow W)$
$V \leftrightarrow \neg Q$
$(N \rightarrow U) \wedge (\neg U \rightarrow Q)$ Therefore $R \rightarrow S$

CRITICAL THINKING, WORLDVIEWS & LOGIC

1.5.3 Truth Tables & Truth Trees for Propositional Logic
Understanding Truth-Functional Logic

We now consider a different practical method for checking for the validity of an expression in the propositional logical deduction system. This method is due to Evert Beth and to Jaako Hintikka.

The problem with the method of truth-tables that we have used to introduce logical connectives is that the number of rows in the truth tables grows exponentially with each connective and each term. For $p \wedge q$ we have 2^2 rows; for $p \wedge q \wedge r$ we have 2^3 rows; for $(p \wedge q1 \wedge q2 \wedge q\,n-1)$ (n terms), we have 2^n rows. This is cumbersome and so we introduce the truth-tree method which is more efficient for determining valid expressions and which works for both propositional or sentential logic, as well as for predicate logic.

EXAMPLE OF TREE DIAGRAM FOR BASIC CONNECTIVES

(1) $p \vee q$ — branches to p, q	(2) $p \bullet q$ — stacks p, q	(3) $p \supset q$ — branches to $\neg p$, q
(4) $p = q$ — branches to (p, q) and ($\neg p$, $\neg q$)	(5) $\neg \neg p$ — yields p	(6) $\neg(p \bullet q)$ — branches to $\neg p$, $\neg q$
(7) $\neg(p \vee q)$ — stacks $\neg p$, $\neg q$	(8) $\neg(p \supset q)$ — stacks p, $\neg q$	(9) $\neg(p = q)$ — branches to (p, $\neg q$) and ($\neg p$, q)

∧ or '*and*'

> In the case of ∧ you simply re-write both the propositional terms one under the other.

∨ or '*or*'

> In the case of a logical ∨ you create two separate columns in which you write the two propositional terms (in the examples above there is only one proposition; but in the expression (p → q) ∨ (q → r), the two separate columns will each contain (p → q) and (q → r)).

¬ or '*not*'

> In the case of a negation, we rewrite the result under the original negation without the double negation sign (the negation of a negation is a positive logical proposition).

→ or '*if... then*'

> In the case of a logical implication p → q write in two different columns ¬ p and q (this is because we know and can prove with the help of truth tables that (p → q) ↔ (¬ p ∧ q)).

↔ or '*if and only if*'

> The last connective we consider is p ↔ q. In the truth-tree method this is equivalent to making two separate columns and writing in one column p and q and in the other column ¬ p and ¬ q under each other. This is true because we know that (p ↔ q) ↔ (p ∧ q) ∨ (¬ p ∧ ¬ q) which again can be verified through the truth-table method. Put another way, p ↔ q is true only when either (p ∧ q) is true or (¬ p ∧ ¬ q) is true. Or p ↔ q is false whenever p ∨ ¬ q is false and ¬ p ∨ q is false.

The astute reader will have noticed that we make separate columns because the two different columns capture the 'or' logical nature of the expression: either one of the two columns' truth values will have to be considered independently. On the other hand, when we write two logical expressions one under the other then this is equivalent to asserting the truth of both these expressions together—it results from doing a logical ∧ on the two terms, which are written under each other.

EXERCISES
TRUTH-TREES WITH SENTENTIAL LOGIC

1. *Consistency*: Test the consistency of these sets of statements using the Tree Method. (Note the set is consistent *if and only if* there is at least one open path through the finished tree.)

   i) $X \rightarrow Y, X \rightarrow \neg Y$ ii) $O \rightarrow P, O \leftrightarrow \neg P$ iii) $M \rightarrow M$

2. *Tautology*: Use the Tree Method to determine which of these statements are tautologies. (Note: Construct the tree as though you were testing for validity. If the tree closes, the sentence is a tautology; if not, it isn't.)

   i) $M \rightarrow M$
   ii) $X \rightarrow Y$
   iii) $(N \rightarrow \neg N) \rightarrow N$
   iv) $O \rightarrow (\neg O \rightarrow O)$

3. Build a truth tree-or truth trees- for the following logical sentences and then state whether the tree shows the sentence or proposition to be a contradiction, a contingency or a tautology.

   a) $A \wedge \neg\neg A$ b) $C \vee \neg\neg C$ c) $B \vee (D \vee \neg D)$

4. Build a truth tree (or truth trees) for the set of propositions below and then decide whether the tree demonstrates that the set of propositions is consistent or inconsistent.

   a) $A \rightarrow [(B \vee C) \vee (\neg S \vee M)], (A \vee B) \vee D, (A \rightarrow C) \vee [F \leftrightarrow (\neg G \vee G)], A \rightarrow B, A \wedge \neg C$
   b) $U \vee \neg\neg W, \neg(B \rightarrow C), (U \vee B) \wedge W, Q \rightarrow \neg U, \neg(B \vee C)$

5. Build a truth tree (or trees) for the set of propositions below and then state whether the tree shows the set of propositions to be consistent or inconsistent:

   a) $A \rightarrow B, \neg A \vee B$
   b) $Q, \neg\neg Q$
   c) $A \leftrightarrow B, (A \rightarrow B) \wedge (B \rightarrow A)$
   d) $A \leftrightarrow B, A \rightarrow B, B \rightarrow A$
   e) $\neg(A \wedge B), \neg A \vee \neg B$
   f) $\neg(A \vee B), \neg A \wedge \neg B$

6. Build a truth tree- or truth trees- for the following set of propositions and then state whether the tree shows the set of propositions to be consistent or inconsistent:

   a) $\neg(F \rightarrow Z) \rightarrow \neg(F \rightarrow Z), \neg F \wedge \neg Z$
   b) $P \rightarrow [R \rightarrow (S \wedge W)], (P \wedge \neg W \rightarrow) \neg R$
   c) $S \wedge W, S \vee W, S \leftrightarrow W, S \rightarrow \neg W$
   d) $P \rightarrow (R \vee W), (R \vee W) \rightarrow P, P \rightarrow R, P \rightarrow W$
   e) $\neg(F \rightarrow \neg Z) \rightarrow \neg(F \rightarrow Z) \rightarrow (\neg F \wedge \neg Z), F, Z$

1.6 PREDICATE OR FIRST-ORDER LOGIC

Predicate Logic

Predicate logic is the standard term used in the discipline of mathematical logic for symbolic formal systems like first-order logic and second-order logic. This formal system is different from other logical systems insofar as its logical formulae contain variables that can be quantified. Quantifiers allow one to further refine logical statements and determine how many logical objects the properties of the predicate apply to. Two common quantifiers are the existential $\exists$ ("there exists") and the universal $\forall$ ("for all") quantifiers.

The variables that the quantifiers apply to, could be elements in the logical universe that is described or discussed, or they can be relations or functions over that logical universe. For instance, an existential quantifier applied to a function symbol would be taken to make the claim "there is a function"; whereas the existential quantifier applied to an element would be interpreted as "there is such an element". The foundations of predicate logic were developed independently by the philosophers Gottlob Frege and Charles Sanders Peirce.

Informally, the expression "predicate logic" refers to first-order logic. Some logicians believe that predicate calculus is an axiomatized[1] or formalized type of predicate logic. They believe that predicate logic is an informal, more intuitive development. Predicate logics also include systems of logic that mix modal operators[2] and quantifiers.

First-order logic

First-order logic is a type of formal system that is used in many different disciplines such as mathematics, linguistics, philosophy and computer science. Sometimes first-order logic is called the predicate calculus but there could be first-order logics other than the predicate calculus. The main difference between first-order logic of the predicate brand

---

1 Axiomatized means roughly formalized or standardized according to a given notation and given specifications. An axiom is a foundational truth upon which a mathematical, geometrical or logical system may be built. The first axioms known in the West are those of Euclid's geometry. In the 19th century, mathematicians and logicians attempted to fully axiomatize i.e. formalize and standardize arithmetic. This project failed once Gödel produced his incompleteness theorems in 1931, but was also seriously undermined by the publication of Russell's paradox at the turn of the twentieth century.

2 A modal connective (or modal operator) is a logical connective for modal logic. It is an operator which forms propositions from propositions. In general, a modal operator has the "formal" property of being non-truth-functional, and is "intuitively" characterized by expressing a modal attitude (such as necessity, possibility, belief, or knowledge) about the proposition to which the operator is applied.

and propositional logic is the use of logical quantifiers which we have already introduced above. Also typically propositional logic is considered a 0th order type of logic since it is simpler and less expressive than first-order logic.

EXAMPLE: The first-order sentence

$$\forall P, \forall x, \exists y \ [(Pxy \wedge Pyx) \rightarrow (x*y = y*x = 1)]$$

says that for every P, x and y, if we apply the predicate to P to x and y, there exists an element y which functions as multiplicatory inverse for all elements x to which the predicate P is applied. For all individuals and every individual x, either x is in P or it is not. This statement would not be possible in sentential logic. This is because variables are interpreted as sentences and not as relations as they can be interpreted in first-order second-order predicate logic.

Second-order logic

In second-order logic we may also quantify over sets, classes, functions and relations (we have to be careful with sets and classes because we can create paradoxes of the kind discovered by Bertrand Russell at the beginning of the 20th century). An important notion in both first order, but more so in second-order logic, is the concept of domain of discourse or the universe of discourse.

The universe of discourse is the class of all individuals that our statements may refer to. If the class is empty then non-sensical statements may be trivially true but that does not teach us anything of importance. The universe or domain of discourse is the set of all objects for which our statements are defined. This is important in second-order logic when we introduce the notion of free and bound variables. Thus in order to define a predicate calculus or a predicate deduction system one needs to specify the predicates, the logical individuals, constants or variables and the domain of truth or the universe of discourse that the predicates may apply to.

In order to develop the predicate calculus in this text-book we need to introduce a notion from propositional calculus which we studied in the previous section of this chapter. This notion is the notion of sentential interpretation. We define the notion of **sentential interpretation** following Patrick Suppes[3] in the following manner:

A sentence P is a sentential interpretation of a sentence Q if and only if P can be obtained from Q by replacing the component atomic sentences of Q by other (not necessarily distinct) sentences.

---

3 This definition comes from Patrick Suppes, *Introduction to Logic*, 1957.

In fact, because the predicate calculus is a higher-order logic than the propositional calculus, some of the rules of replacement and of inference can be taken to apply in predicate calculus.

Another important notion in the predicate calculus is that of substitutionality which does tie into the notion of *interpretation*. In the analyses that follow, the letters from 'a' to 'w' will function as logical *constants* in our predicate calculus. The letters x, y and z will function as logical *variables*. Thus the predicate Py will stand for any individual that exists within the universe of discourse, and that can be symbolized through the letters a—w (since as we mentioned the last three letters x, y and z are reserved for use as logical variables). The predicates themselves can be nouns, verbs or adjectives. Our logic does not restrict predicates to adjectives. Thus, the statements "is mortal", "is a mortal" or "dies" are indistinguishable in our system of predicate logic. The uppercase letters will symbolize the predicates. Hence, Ma, Mc, will denote 'a' is mortal, and 'c' is mortal respectively. Mx denotes "all the x's which are mortal".

> **DEFINITION OF LOGICAL FORMULAE (predicate form)**
>
> a) Every atomic formula is a formula.
> b) If S is a formula then ¬ (S) is a formula.
> c) If R and S are formulas then $R \land S$, $R \lor S$, $R \rightarrow S$, and $R \leftrightarrow S$ are formulas.
> d) If R is a formula and v is any variable then (v)(R)—which may also be written as (∀v)(R)—and (∃v) (R) are also formulas.
> e) No expression is a formula unless it is constructed using one of the above rules or unless it satisfies the above conditions.

1.6.1 RULES FOR NEGATING QUANTIFIERS

We have not really introduced quantifiers except through their definitions until now. Before discussing predicate logic further, it is important to understand the crucial role that quantifiers play in this type of logic.

Before explaining the role of quantifiers, we need to define what a logical expression is within our system of predicate logic. Again, just as we did in the section on propositional and sentential logic, we define what a well-formed-formula or expression is in a recursive manner. Here, expressions such as Ux, a + b +c, 'z is red', or 'z is odd' or 'z is a number' are all atomic formulas. Since our first element in the recursive definition will be that every atomic formula is a formula, we know that the smallest unit out of which a logical formula can be built is an atomic formula.

Here is the entire definition of a logical formula in our language:

a) Every atomic formula is a formula.

b) If S is a formula then ¬ (S) is a formula.

c) If R and S are formulas then $R \wedge S$, $R \vee S$, $R \rightarrow S$, and $R \leftrightarrow S$ are formulas.

d) If R is a formula and v is any variable then (v)(R)—which may also be written as ($\forall v$)(R)—and ($\exists v$) (R) are also formulas.

e) No expression is a formula unless it is built using one of the above rules or unless it satisfies the above conditions.

To better familiarize ourselves with the notion of a quantifier, we look at certain general logical equivalences that apply to their respective negations. This will remind the attentive student of the section on syllogistic logic when we considered the Aristotelian square of logical oppositions. We consider a similar square, but one now explained in terms of logical quantifiers.

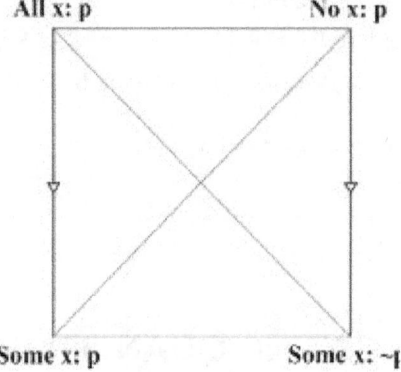

Courtesy of Paul McNamara from the Deontic Logic entry of the Stanford Encyclopedia of Philosophy.

Let us consider the following four logical equivalences the square indicates:

(1) $\neg (\forall x)(Mx) \leftrightarrow \exists x(\neg Mx)$.

(2) These expressions are logically equivalent since to claim that 'not all humans are mortal' (Mx is the claim that humans are mortal) is the same as claiming that 'there exists at least one human that is not mortal', provided that the domain of

the predicate (or what is sometimes called its model) is non-empty.

$(\forall x)(Mx) \leftrightarrow \neg\exists x(\neg Mx)$

Next, we consider the following expression $(\forall x)(Mx) \leftrightarrow \neg\exists x(\neg Mx)$. We can formulate this as the expression that 'all humans are mortal', which is identical to claiming that among the class of humans there does not exist any one individual human who is immortal (the right hand side of the expression).

$\neg(\forall x)(\neg Mx) \leftrightarrow \exists x(Mx)$

We have two more logical equivalences to consider: $\neg(\forall x)(\neg Mx) \leftrightarrow \exists x(Mx)$, this expression can be reformulated as 'no human exists that is not mortal; this is equivalent to saying that there must exist at least one mortal human (given that the set of x's or humans is non-empty).

$(\forall x)(\neg Mx) \leftrightarrow \neg\exists x(Mx)$.

(3) The final expression we consider is the following: $(\forall x)(\neg Mx) \leftrightarrow \neg\exists x(Mx)$. This can be expressed as 'for all humans that exist, no human is mortal', which is identical to stating that 'there that does not exist a human that is mortal'.

EXERCISES

BASIC USAGE OF QUANTIFIERS

1. Rewrite the following statements in logical notation of propositional functions, and quantifiers. Use the abbreviations suggested and have each formula begin with a quantifier, not with a negation symbol.

    1. Rock stars are not always drug addicts. *(Rx: x is a rock star; Dx: x is a drug addict.).*
    2. Ebola is sometimes fatal. *(Ex: x is Ebola ; Fx: x is fatal.).*
    3. Only citizens of Canada can vote in Canadian elections.
       (Cx: x is a citizen of Canada; Vx: x can vote in Canadian elections).
    4. Not a student passed the class. *(Sx: x is a student; Px: x passed the class.)*

2. Rewrite the following statements so that they begin with a quantifier instead of a negation symbol.

    a) $\neg(\forall x)(\neg Tx \lor Ux \lor \neg Vx)$
    b) $\neg(\exists x)(\neg Kx \land Lx \lor \neg Mx)$
    c) $\neg(\forall x)(Cx \rightarrow (Cx \rightarrow Dx))$
    d) $\neg(\exists x)[\neg(\neg Mx \lor \neg Nx \lor Ox)]$
    e) $\neg(\forall x)[(\neg Ux \land \neg Vx \land Wx)]$

3. Symbolize each of the following statements using propositional functions and quantifiers, in each case using the suggested notation.

    a) Men are humans. *(Mx: x is a man. Hx: x is a human)*
    b) Only rich people have chauffeurs. *(Rx: x is rich. Cx: x has a chauffeur).*
    c) All beer and cognac are wholesome and nourishing. *(Bx: x is a beer. Cx: x is a cognac. Wx: x is wholesome, Nx: x is nourishing)*
    d) None but the courageous deserve love. *(Cx: x is courageous, Dx: x deserves love).*

4. A denotes that 'Adam wins the first prize' , 'Chris wins the first prize' as C, and 'Dan' wins the first prize', as D. Put the following compound statements into logical form:

    a) If Adam and Chris both do not win first prize, then Adam and Chris do not both win first prize.
    b) If Adam wins first prize then it is not the case that either Chris or Dan wins its first game.
    c) If Adam wins first prize then Chris does not win first prize but if Chris does not win first prize then Dan wins first prize.
    d) Either Adam wins first prize and Chris does not win first prize or if Chris wins first prize then Dan does not win first prize.
    e) If Adam wins first prize then both Chris and Dan win first prize.

1.6.2 Free and Bound Variables

In sentential or propositional logic, we do not quantify over variables. Hence, we do not have the notion of a bound, or free, variable. This notions appears when we have expressions of a particular kind. Consider the logical sentence:

$$(\exists x\ Fx) \rightarrow (\forall z\ Lzx)$$

According to our rules for defining well-formed formulas or expressions this expression is ambiguous.

A bound variable is one whose scope and logical dependency is clearly defined within an expression. However, in the statement above, we do not know to which x's the predicate Lzx applies—whether it is the subset of x's that satisfy F or otherwise. Thus the truth value of the whole expression or sentence[4] remains undetermined as it cannot take on either of the truth values 'true' or 'false'.

The distinction between *bound* and *free* variables deals with the scope of quantifiers (and thus implicitly with the application of predicates) as they apply to variables.

We will examine the scope of the following expressions: $(\forall z)\ Pz \wedge Bz$. In the first part of the expression $(\forall z)\ Pz$, the variable z is bound therefore the predicate applies to all the z's that are part of the Universe of Discourse, but the second predicate Bz cannot be assumed to apply to the same z's as the first predicate applies to. By definition, z could be any individual or particular within the Universe of Discourse and so what is predicated in the first part of the conjunction will not be automatically true of the second part of the conjunction.

In the following expression $(\forall z)\ (Pz \wedge Bz)$, the universal quantifier ranges over both of the predicates so z is bound for both predicates, whereas it was free in the first example provided. Parentheses are important as they define the scope of assignment for the quantifiers. Let us look at a second example. Here we compare the following two statements:

$((\forall z\ \exists x)(zx = 1) \wedge (z \times x = x \times z))$ and $(\forall z\ \exists\ x)(zx = 1) \wedge (z \times x = x \times z)$.

Note that these two expressions are identical except for the outer parentheses on the first statement. They denote the notion of the mathematical inverse or of the arithmetic reciprocal.

---

[4] It is often referred to as a 'sentence' because the truth-value is assigned in a meta-language and not in the first-level language where the notion of formula or expression applies.

> **ⓘ KEY DEFINITIONS**
>
> **A BOUND VARIABLE** is one whose scope and logical dependency is clearly defined within an expression.

The scope of the two quantifiers ranges only over the first part of the logical expression zx =1 and can be considered to be meaningless for the second part (even if it is true for all those z's and x's in which zx=1). The expression as a whole can be taken to represent both commutativity and the existence of an identity element if the parentheses are written appropriately. In its second form the meaning is not clearly defined or determinate.

The notion of logical sentence is perhaps both a semantical and syntactical notion. We reserve judgment on this issue for now. Carnap the logical empiricist whom we discuss in Chapter 4 would perhaps claim that it is a syntactical notion. Others such as Tarski and Wittgenstein would claim that it is a semantical notion. What both approaches have in common is that the notion of sentence is interpreted in a meta-language (a language about language) in which well-formed-formulas are defined as acceptable. The distinction lies in the fact that the definition of a 'well-formed formula' or 'expression' does not tell us whether a variable is bound or free with respect to the logical quantifiers and thus how it behaves with respect to the Universe of Discourse—that is a semantical notion.

To determine whether a variable is bound or free, we must interpret the formula. Once we have determined that there are no free variables, we can claim the formula is a sentence. By definition in the meta-language there cannot exist expressions from the object-language that have free variables. Thus a sentence receives or is assigned a truth value of true or false when it contains no free variables.

> **KEY NOTES**
>
> **Universal Specification or Instantiation (UI)**
> ($\forall$x) (Rx) to Ra: If for all x, R is true. Then Ra is true, where a is a particular case of x.
>
> **Existential Specification or Existential Instantiation (EI)**
> ($\exists$y) (Py) to Pb : if there exists a y such that Py is true; let us call that y, b.

EXERCISES
FREE AND BOUND VARIABLES

1. Count the free occurrences of variables and how many free variables there are in each of the following formulas. Which of the formulas constitute logical propositions?

    a)   ($\exists$y) ($\exists$z) (x loves y and z is their cat)
    b) ($\exists$x)(x is a square) $\vee$ ($\forall$y) (y is green and x is yellow)
    c) ($\exists$z) (y + y = y)
    d) ($\forall$v)($\forall$w)($\forall$u)(v $\rightarrow$ w $\wedge$ w $\rightarrow$ u) $\rightarrow$ ($\exists$x) (x $\rightarrow$ x)
    e) ($\exists$x) ($\exists$y) (x is married to y and z is their child)
    f) x + y = y + x

2. Look at the formula ($\exists$x)($\exists$y)($\exists$z) [((x = y) $\wedge$ (y = z)) $\rightarrow$ (x = z)]. What is the connection between bound "variable" x and instances of x?

3. Look at the formula ($\forall$x(M(x) $\rightarrow$ N(x))) $\rightarrow$ ($\neg$M(x) $\vee$ N(y)). Which variable instances are free; and which are bound?

4. Analyze the logical forms of the following statements. The universe of discourse is R. What are the free variables in each statement?

    a) Every number that is larger than a is larger than b.

    b) For every number a, the equation $ax^2+6x-12=0$ has at least one solution iff a >= -1.

    c) All solutions of the inequality $x^2-2x < 2$ are smaller than 11.

    d) If there is a number x such that $z^2 + 5z = b$ and there is a number z such that $4-x^2=b$, then b is between -11 and 11.

1.6.3 Theory of Inference for Predicate Calculus
Rules for Dropping Quantifiers

We now proceed to the acceptable usage of quantifiers within our predicate deduction system. These are largely syntactical matters but they are important insofar as they tell us what kind of transformations and substitutions we are allowed to make among logical expressions while preserving the truth of the expression (this last characteristic is a semantic property). If an expression such as $(\forall x)(Rx)$ means that all of the logical constants controlled by the variable x and the universal quantifier satisfy the predicate R. Thus we can arbitrarily replace the expression $(\forall x)(Rx)$ with any constant within the domain of the variable x, say Ra. This is possible because of the rule of Universal Specification or Instantiation (UI), which we posit as necessary for our logical system.

Consider now the expression $(\exists y)(Py)$. According to another syntactical rule that is true in our logic, we may replace $(\exists y)(Py)$ with a specific yet arbitrary logical constant. This expression can thus be replaced by Pb while preserving the truth of the argument or proof it is involved in. This rule is called the rule of existential specification or existential instantiation (EI).

Two more rules of inference are important for our predicate logic deduction system. These are the rules of universal generalization (UG) and existential generalization (EG). We begin by explaining universal generalization. If we have an arbitrary logical variable y to whom a predicate say, V, applies so that the expression is Vy and if Vy appears within a line in a proof of validity that we are attempting within our deduction system, then this Vy can be changed without loss of generality to $(\forall x)(Px)$ where P is our new predicate defined by Vy. However, we must be careful in applying this rule since it can easily lead to logical error. For example, it would be correct to infer from Hy (y an arbitrary object is human) that $(\forall x)(Hx)$. We cannot infer from some arbitrary y that is human, that all individuals in the domain are human. Hy is a free variable and has not been bound in our calculus in any appropriate way. It is only when an arbitrary y is not a free variable and is properly bound, that we can apply the rule of universal generalization.

We now move to consider the rule of existential generalization. This may be stated, following Patrick Suppes's definition in *Introduction to Logic* (1957) as follows:

"If a formula S results from a formula R by substituting a variable v for every occurrence in R of some ambiguous (or proper) name, the $(\exists v)S$ is derivable from R"[5]

---
5 Patrick Suppes, *Introduction to Logic*, p.83. New York: Van Nostrand Reinhold, 1957. Print.

EXERCISES

RULES OF INFERENCES FOR QUANTIFIERS

1. *Write derivations corresponding to the following arguments where possible. The variables used to indicate the predicates are not necessarily the variables you should use in symbolizing the premises.*

    a) All philosophers are eccentrics. No eccentrics are British. Therefore no British are philosophers. (Px, Ex, Bx)

    b) If one man is the boss of a second, then the second is not the boss of the first. Therefore no man is his own boss. (Bxy)

    c) The prime minister is a man with Canadian citizenship, and he is the boss of all Canadian citizens. Therefore he is his own boss. (p, Cx, Bxy)

    d) Given:

    　　i) For any numbers x, y, z, if x = y and y = z then x = z;

    　　ii) For any number x, it is not the case that ¬x = x. Therefore, for any two numbers x and y, if x = y then it is the case that y = x. (¬x, x = y)

    e) Adam is a boy who does not go to Church. Maria dates only boys who go to Church. Therefore Maria does not date Adam. (Cx, Ox, Dxy, a, m)

2. *Using rules of inference for quantifiers, explain why these statements are true.*

    i) $(\exists x)(\exists y) [(x \neq y) \land (Fxy \leftrightarrow Fyx)]$

    ii) $(\exists x)(\exists y)(\exists z) [((x = y) \land (y = z)) \rightarrow (x = z)]$

    iii) $(\exists x)(\exists y)(\forall z) [(x \neq z) \land (y \neq z)]$

3. Verify whether the following arguments are valid or not using the rules of inference governing of quantifiers and predicate logic. If the argument is invalid, produce an interpretation to demonstrate why the argument is not valid.

    a) $(\exists x)(\neg Ax \lor \neg Bx) \lor Cx, \forall x (\neg Bx \lor Cx)$, Therefore $(\forall x) \neg Ax$

    b) $\forall x \forall y (\neg Ax \lor \neg By \lor \neg Cxy), (\exists x)(Ax \land \neg Dx)$, Therefore $\exists x \exists y (Dx \land Cxy)$

    c) $(\exists x) Ax \land (\neg Cx \land \neg Bx), \forall x (\neg Ax \lor Bx)$, Therefore $(\forall x) \neg Cx$

    d) $(\exists x) [Ax \leftrightarrow (Bx \lor Cx)]$ Therefore $\forall x [(\neg Ax \lor \neg Bx) \land (\neg Ax \lor \neg Cx)]$

1.6.4 Proving Consistency in Predicate Logic

To prove the *consistency* of a set of formulas in predicate logic we must be able to show that we cannot select certain truth values for given predicates and a certain arbitrary individual that will lead to a contradiction. *As soon as we have derived a contradiction from a set of expressions in predicate logic, we know that that set of expressions is inconsistent.*

Let us consider the following set of expressions in our predicate logic:

$(\forall x)(Ax \rightarrow \neg Bx)$

1. $(\exists x)(Cx \wedge Ax)$
2. $(\forall x)(\neg Cx \vee Bx)$
3. $Ay \rightarrow \neg By$ By General Instantiation of 1
4. $\neg Cy \vee By$ By General Instantiation of 3
5. $\neg Ay \vee By$ By definition of logical implication and 4
6. $Cy \wedge Ay$ By existential instantiation of 2
7. $\neg Ay$ By simplification of 6
8. Ay By simplification of 7

Since ¬Ay and Ay are in the same column, we have reached a contradiction ('Ay and not Ay'). In lines 8 and 9, we have a logical conjunction between them and so have demonstrated that they system will lead to contradiction for any Ay. Proving consistency necessitates familiarity and the development of skill manipulating the rules of inference.

EXERCISES
CONSISTENCY IN PREDICATE LOGIC

1. *Determine whether the following sets of expressions are consistent or inconsistent using the basic rules of inference of predicate logic (all of the rules of inference of propositional logic, the rules used to negate quantifiers, the rules of Universal and Existential Instantiation and rules of Universal and Existential Generalization) given that the variables are bound correctly in the expressions given.*

a) $(\forall x)(\neg Mx \wedge \neg Nx)$
$(\forall x)(\neg Ox \rightarrow Nx)$
$(\forall x)(\neg Ox \wedge Mx)$

b) $(\exists x)(\neg Bx \rightarrow Cx)$
$(\forall x)(Cx \rightarrow Ax)$
$\neg(\exists x)(\neg Ax \rightarrow Cx)$

c) $(\exists x)(\neg Mx \rightarrow \neg Nx)$
$(\forall x)(\neg Mx \wedge Ox)$
$(\exists x)(\neg Ox \rightarrow \neg Nx)$

1.6.5 PROVING VALIDITY IN PREDICATE LOGIC

We use a similar approach of repeated applications of the rules of inference in order to prove validity with predicate logic. As in the case of showing consistency, all of the rules of inference we have seen in propositional logic may be applied: the rules for negating quantifiers, the rules for Universal and Existential Generalization, and the rules for Universal and Existential Instantiation.

In the case of a logical or quantificational specification, we must make sure that we are not instantiating over a free variable.

Instantiating over a predicate that applies to a free variable will create an error in scope such as deducing or inferring from Mx (x is mortal) that $(\forall y) My$ where y is an arbitrary logical variable. This is obviously not true since there are plenty of things in the universe of discourse or domain that are not mortal or which we cannot assume prematurely that they are until evidence and a general deductive proof to the contrary is provided. For example, the notion of the mortality of a stone, is either not clear, undefined, or simply false seeing as we can postulate that since a rock is not born, it does not die and so cannot be mortal.

We provide an example that shows the proof of the validity of a set of sentences in predicate logic. This will be followed by exercises on this topic.

EXAMPLE

The statements are:

1. $(\forall x)(Mx \rightarrow Nx)$
2. $(\exists x) (Mx \wedge Ox)$
3. Therefore $(\exists x) (Ox \wedge Nx)$

From these we can proceed to the following lines of analysis:

4. $My \rightarrow Ny$	By general instantiation and since both x's are bound
5. $My \wedge Oy$	By general instantiation and since both x's are bound
6. $\neg My \vee Ny$	By 4 and the definition of logical implication
7. Ny	By simplification
8. Oy	By simplification
9. $Ny \wedge Oy$	7, 8 and the rules of conjunction
10. $(\exists x) (Ox \wedge Nx)$	By existential generalization on 9.

1.6.6 Truth Trees as a Proof-Method in Predicate Logic

The truth-tree method is simple and intuitive. It is due to Evert Beth and to the logician Jaako Hintikka.

In the case of ∧ we simply rewrite both the predicate terms one under the other.

In the case of a logical ∨ we create two separate columns in which we write the two predicate terms. In the case of a negation, we re-write the result under the original negation without the double negation sign (the negation of a negation is a positive logical predicate).

In the case of a logical implication Fx → Px we write ¬Fx and Px in two separate columns (because we know and can prove with the help of truth tables that (Fx→ Px) ↔ (¬Fx ∨ Px).

The last connective we consider is Fx ↔ Px. In the truth-tree method, this is equivalent to making two separate columns and writing Fx and Px in one column and ¬Fx and ¬Px in the other column under each other. This is true because we know that (Fx ↔ Px) ↔ (Fx ∧ Px) ∨ (¬Fx ∧ ¬Px)[6]

We summarize:

Fx ∧ Px or 'Fx *and* Px' Re-write both propositional terms, one under the other.	Fx Px
Fx ∨ Px or 'Fx *or* Px' Create two separate columns for the two propositional terms.	Fx Px
¬ or '*not*' Re-write the result under the original negation without the double negation sign.	¬Fx
→ or '*if... then*' Write ¬Fx and Px in two separate columns (because (Fx→ Px) ↔ (¬Fx ∧ Px)).	¬Fx Px
↔ or '*if and only if*' Create two separate columns and write Fx and Px in the first and ¬Fx and ¬Px in the second. under each other. Since 'Fx and Px' and '¬Fx and ¬Px' are conjunctions, we write:	Fx ¬Fx Px ¬Px

---

6 Again, this can be verified through the truth-table method). Put another way: Fx→Px is true only when either both Fx and Px are true or both Fx and Px are false.

The astute reader will have noticed that when we make separate columns, it is because the two different columns capture the 'or' logical nature of the expression: either one of the two columns' truth will have to be considered independently. On the other hand, writing two logical expressions, the one under the other, is equivalent to asserting the truth of both these expressions together—the result of performing a logical $\wedge$ on the two terms written under each other.

We have already considered this method for propositional logic. This method can be used for testing both consistency and the validity of expressions or sets of expressions in predicate logic.

> **KEY NOTES**
>
> Applying the **RULES OF INFERENCE**:
> - Negation of Quantifiers
> - Universal and Existential Generalization
> - Universal and Existential Instantiation.

CONCLUSION

Predicate logic is a first-order type of logic. Whether a predicate has one or two terms might make the logic more flexible and more powerful though this does not change its order. If one could quantify over predicates (which can then be treated as functions) then predicate logic becomes a second-order logic. This concern with orders of logic is tied to our study and understanding of logical syntax and grammar. It can be shown that the propositional deduction system we have studied in the previous section in the book is both consistent and complete. This means that we can devise a logical proof for any well-formed expression in this system. Furthermore, none of its basic rules of inference lead to a contradiction (the consistency requirement). A theorem or an argument constructed in such a system then, would be both valid and consistent.

In first order logic matters grow a bit more complex. Although well-behaved or standard predicate logics such as the arithmetic of Peano are both consistent and complete, this is not the case in general. There are non-standard first-order logics such as Robinson arithmetic[7] and many other types of first-order logics that are not complete. This means that the validity of some statements which may be a logical consequence of the rules of inference of the deduction system may not be provable. This means that there might not be a sequence of steps involving only our assumed rules of inference, which provide a means of arriving at the expression which we wish to prove.

Later in 1931, Gödel proved that first-order logic was incomplete in general. This spelled the end for long-standing projects of many mathematicians. David Hilbert who thought we could formalize or axiomatize all of mathematics had to abandon his work after Gödel demonstrated that this cannot be done in general since most mathematical theories cannot be logically expressed in first-order logic and so can never be complete. This is where semantics or the semantical approach of someone like Tarski took off. Tarski assumed only a formal language, a non-symbolic signature[8], a theory,[9] the logical notion of interpretation and the generalized notion of consequence operator.[10]

It is beyond the scope of this text to discuss the developments of Tarski, Church, Turing[11] and others. However we note that their contributions to the field of logic have yielded developments in computational logic and contributed to the mathematization and algebraization of logic. They have in many ways changed the face of the discipline of formal logic.

---

[7] Robinson arithmetic is a kind of non-standard arithmetic and qualifies as a first-order logic but is not complete. Only standard or well-behaved first logics are complete according to Gödels' completeness theorems for first-order logic. Here are the basic axioms of Robinson arithmetic:

A1: $(\forall x)(\forall y)((x \text{ not} = y) \rightarrow (sx \text{ not} = sy))$
A2: $\forall x (0 \text{ not} = sx)$
A3: $\forall x (x \text{ not} = 0 \rightarrow \exists y(x = sy))$
A4: $(\forall x)((x + 0) = x)$
A5 $(\forall x)(\forall y)((x + sy) = s(x + y))$
A6: $(\forall x)(x * 0) = 0$
A7: $(\forall x)(\forall y)(x * sy) = [(x * y) + x]$. We leave the clever student to discover why this represents an arithmetic. In fact, the axioms outline a system of base 1 addition and multiplication. But this arithmetic is ill-behaved. For example 0 not= s0, s0 not= ss0, ss0 not= sss0, yet $(\forall x)(x \text{ not} = sx)$ is not provable or derivable from a standard set of rules of inference and rules of replacement. There are many similar things which can be verified in particular such as addition commutativity or addition associativity but which cannot be proved in general. One may venture to call this in technical philosophical parlance a nominalistic arithmetic. It only make the mathematician and the logician who are interested in the general and universal frown and nod bitterly.

[8] A signature lists and describes the non-logical symbols of a formal language.

[9] A theory (also called a formal theory) is a set of sentences in a formal language.

[10] The consequence operator theory is a mathematical model that employs basic abstract set-theory to model the most significant aspects of logical discourse.

[11] Church and Turing are very important for the development of the problem of decidability and the halting problem in computational logic, something we can only mention here in passing.

EXERCISES

TRUTH TREES AS PROOF-METHOD IN PREDICATE LOGIC

1. Use the truth tree method to test the following arguments for validity. In each problem, state whether or not the argument is valid; if invalid, give a counterexample.

i) $Bx \to (\Box \forall x)Mx$
    $(\Box \forall x)(Bx \Box \Box \exists Cx) \to \to Nx$
    ─────────────
    $Ba \land \Box Mb$

ii) $(\Box \forall x)(Nx \to \to Px) \Box (\forall \Box x)Bx$
    $Mx \land \Box Cx \land \Box Nx$
    ─────────────
    $Na \lor \Box Ca$

iii) $(\Box \forall x)(Kx \to \to Ax)$
     $(\Box \exists x)(Dx \Box \land Gx)$
     ─────────────
     $Db \to \to Gb$

vi) $\exists \Box x(Bx \to \to Cx) \lor \Box (\Box \forall x)Nx$
    $(\Box \forall x)(Cx \Box \land Nx) \to \to Mx$
    ─────────────
    $Na \to \to Mb$

2. Construct a formal proof of validity for each of the following arguments, in each case using the suggested notation:

   a) No sportsmen are crooks. Carl is a crook. Therefore Carl is not a sportsman. (Sx, Cx, c)
   b) All politicians are knaves. Knaves are lucky. Therefore all politicians are lucky. (Px, Kx, Lx)
   c) No bachelors are happy. Some idealists are happy. Therefore some idealists are not bachelors. (Bx, Hx, Ix)
   d) All peasants are friendly. Some outlaws are peasants. Therefore some outlaws are friendly. (Px, Fx, Ox)
   e) No rock stars are not wealthy. There are no wealthy banjo players. Therefore rock stars are never banjo players. (Rx, Wx, Bx)

3. Construct if possible, a derivation corresponding to the following arguments. If a conclusion does not follow, give an arithmetical interpretation which will prove that it does not.

   a) All Quebeckers speak to anyone whom they know intimately. No Quebecker speaks to anyone who is not a North American. Therefore, Quebeckers know only North Americans intimately. (Qx, Sxy, Kxy, NAx)
   b) No intelligent person who jogs also eats to excess. Some careless persons eat to excess. Therefore, some careless persons are not intelligent. (Ix, Jx, Ex, Cx)
   c) Some foolish people smoke marijuana. Some students do not smoke marijuana. Therefore some students are not foolish. (Fx, Mx, Sx)
   d) No blonde woman uses gel. Some blonde women use peroxide. Therefore, some women use peroxide and not hair gel (Bx, Wx, Hx, Px)
   e) All teachers are clever. Some doctors are clever. Therefore some doctors are teachers. (Tx, Dx, Cx)

✓ KEY CONCEPTS & DEFINITIONS - HISTORICAL INTERLUDE

THE 3 CLASSICAL LAWS OF THOUGHT:
1. The Law of Identity
2. The Principle of Non-Contradiction
3. The Law of Excluded Middle

PRINCIPLE OF NON-CONTRADICTION: contradictory statements cannot both be true with respect to the same object at the same time.

PRINCIPLE OF EXCLUDED MIDDLE: any statement made of a given self-identical object must either be true or false.

PRINCIPLE (OR LAW) OF BIVALENCE: every declarative sentence expressing a proposition (of a theory under inspection) has exactly one truth value—either 'true' or 'false'.

IDENTITY OF INDISCERNIBLES: there cannot be separate objects or entities that have all their properties in common.

THE INDISCERNIBILITY OF IDENTICALS OR PRINCIPLE 1
For any x and y, if x is identical to y, then x and y have all the same properties.
$$\forall x \, \forall y \, [x = y \rightarrow \forall P \, (Px \leftrightarrow Py)]$$

THE IDENTITY OF INDISCERNIBLES OR PRINCIPLE 2
For any x and y, if x and y have all the same properties, then x is identical to y.
$$\forall x \, \forall y \, [\forall P \, (Px \leftrightarrow Py) \rightarrow x = y]$$

INTERESTING ?

Ontological refers to all that is related to the nature of Being or existence.

Ontology is the ancient science of Being.

HISTORICAL INTERLUDE

THE THREE LAWS OF THOUGHT & LEIBNIZ'S LAWS

> **The Classical Laws of Thought**
>
> 1. The Law of Identity
> 2. The Principle of Non-Contradiction
> 3. The Law of Excluded Middle

THE THREE LAWS OF THOUGHT

There are three basic principles or laws of logic that have sometimes been called the laws of thought in the long history of the subject. These principles are important because they connect three apparently disconnected domains of knowledge: psychology, logic and ontology.

Beyond the analytical formalisms of deduction and the experiential and synthetical associationisms of induction, the laws of thought provide a possible integration of psychology, logic and ontology. This was especially visible during the period of the history of philosophy called German Idealism (and German thought seems to be in general more favorable to this approach compared to their empirically minded British and Scottish counterparts). One could approach this subject by saying that in general German logicians have stressed the connection of logic to metaphysics and ontology (and an ontologized version of the philosophical psychology or consciousness philosophy). We have here in mind Fichte's *Wissenschaftslehre* (Doctrine of Science), Schelling's *System of Transcendental Idealism* and Hegel's *Greater Logic*. In Britain psychology and nominalism usually undercut the study of logic but this has also been fruitful, as the work of Hume and John Stuart Mill have shown.

In German Idealism, to which this section is perhaps more directly relevant (even though the formulation The Laws of Thought is actually the title of a work by the deductive logical formalist George Boole), the principle of identity (A = A or I = I as it was sometimes formulated, I = I places the emphasis on the thinking ego or subject or consciousness and was especially used by Fichte) stands at the foundation of all knowledge and ontological scientific systems.

The systems of the German idealists were also psychological or consciousness based systems but psychology was conceived in an ideal, ontological and historical way that was in marked contrast with the empiricism of Hume and Mill. Their logics were accordingly radically different and in some ways eluded the turn to formalism of the late 19th century by going back to Aristotle and (especially in the case of Hegel) to Plato's understanding and concept of logic. For the German logicians, thought or consciousness was conceived as coeval with reality. Thus the principle of identity and self-identity functioned as a synthetic principle of knowledge, of self and of the world.

The Principle of Identity

If we examine the principle of identity more closely and leave aside these more historical considerations we may notice that it separates reality into two sets: that of whatever is taken or understood to be identical with a given object A or I and a second set to which belong all objects different from A or I.

The Principle of Non-Contradiction

The remaining two principles, (of contradiction and of the excluded middle) may be partially derived from the principle of Identity. *No two opposed or contradictory statements can be made at the same time and with respect to the same aspect or same attribute by a given self-identical object A or I.*

Notice that the principle of non-contradiction seems to require a notion of language and of time which was not explicitly required by the principle of identity which only required self-perception, self-consciousness, self-cognition or self-sentience.

We take the ontological position in this text that identity is more fundamental than contradiction; thus time merely works to solve the contradiction and to remove it not to make it possible. (This would be a first or lower order contradiction. As mind or consciousness progresses it recognizes a higher-order contradiction between time and eternity. Finally it comes to the realization that there is an underlying ontological identity between time and eternity, which is presupposed by the apparent contradiction between time and eternity.) Also non-contradiction presupposes the notion of statement and attribute or aspect which was not explicit in the principle of identity. Thus for non-contradiction we need a notion of language: whether this is a natural language or whether a formal language is not determined in advance.

> **THE PRINCIPLE OF NON-CONTRADICTION**
>
> The **principle of non-contradiction**: *contradictory statements cannot both be true with respect to the same object at the same time.*

The earliest known formulation is Aristotle's principle of non-contradiction, first proposed in *On Interpretation*[1], where he says that of two contradictory propositions (i.e. where one proposition is the negation of the other) one must be true and the other, false.

The Principle of Excluded Middle

Finally the principle of excluded middle claims that any statement made of a given self-identical object must either be true or false. Excluded middle does not presuppose or at least does not seem to presuppose explicitly a notion of time. It does presuppose a notion of statement and a notion of truth in which only two distinct logical possibilities are given: either it is true that there is a sea-battle (Aristotle's famous example) or it is false that there is a sea-battle. However, when we need to validate the truth of a given statement we seem to need to introduce a notion of definite or determinate time. Is there a sea-battle tomorrow, today or yesterday (and where in Sparta, Athens or Persia?). This means that the future is determinate, not that the thesis of determinism is true as some philosopher's have argued unconvincingly.[2]

> **THE PRINCIPLE OF EXCLUDED MIDDLE**
>
> The **principle of excluded middle**: *any statement made of a given self-identical object must either be true or false.*

The Principle of Bivalence

The *principle of bivalence* is often confused with the principle of excluded middle. Bivalence states that any statement in a language (natural or formal, though it is more commonly used to develop formal logics) has either a true or a false value. Two contradictory state of affairs could both be true at the same time as long as the condition that any given statement has only one of two possible truth-functional values (true or false).

Bivalence was studied more intensively in the twentieth century because logicians like Ian Lukasiewicz develped three-valued logics (the three values are true, false, possible)

1 Aristotle, *The categories: On Interpretation,* Cambridge, Mass. :Harvard University Press, 2002. Print.
2 See Taylor, Richard, *Fate*, from Metaphysics, New Jersey: Prentice Hall, 1992, 4th edition. Print.

which were then developed by intuitionist mathematicians and logicians. The student should note that bivalence is a semantic notion[3] whereas the excluded middle, without being an explicitly syntactic notion, does make a substantive claim about the way the world is (that it is determinately in one way which is not to say that it is set up or functions in a deterministic fashion).

> **THE PRINCIPLE OF BIVALENCE**
>
> The **semantic principle (or law) of bivalence**: *every declarative sentence expressing a proposition (of a theory under inspection) has exactly one truth value—either 'true' or 'false'.*

Leibniz's Law (Principle of Identity of Indiscernibles)

The *identity of indiscernibles* states that there cannot be separate objects or entities that have all their properties or attributes or true predicates in common. This principle is controversial as we discuss below.[4] It makes a claim about the relation of the world to our cognitive apparatus. The claim is that if we cannot discern two objects minutely enough (*les petites perceptions* which was a favorite topic of Leibniz's), then they must be identical. Of course one could claim that our sense-apparatus was somehow imperfect or fallible and that the objects were not in themselves identical but only for our sensory apparatus. However, Leibniz did not possess the later Hegelian distinction of the in itself and the for itself. The identity of indiscernibles is thus both an ontological[5] and an

---

3 Intuitionistic Logics of the type developed by Brouwer reject the law of excluded middle and proofs by contradiction.

4 Max Black has argued against the identity of indiscernibles by counterexample (in *Identity of Indiscernibles, MIND, A Quarterly Review of Psychology and Philosophy*, Vol. LXI. No. 242 April, 1952). Notice that to show that the identity of indiscernibles is false, it is sufficient that one provide a model in which there are two distinct (numerically nonidentical) things that have all the same properties. Black claimed that in a symmetric universe wherein only two symmetrical spheres exist, the two spheres are two distinct objects even though they have all their properties in common. Black's argument is significant because it shows that even relational properties (properties specifying distances between objects in space-time) fail to distinguish two identical objects in a symmetrical universe. The two objects are, and will remain, equidistant from the universe's line of symmetry and each other. Even bringing in an external observer to label the two spheres distinctly does not solve the problem because it violates the symmetry of the universe. The same problem has been raised by Robert Brandom with respect to the discernibility of Complex Numbers in Frege's philosophy of numbers in Brandom's *Tales of the Mighty Dead*. Leibniz's laws may bee seen as test cases for whether one is a logical rationalist or a logical empiricist. Certainly identicals may be indiscernible, this is reasonable but that indiscernibles may be identical makes a claim about the ability to discern, differentiate and distinguish of the human intellect and even perhaps of the divine intellect. If there are limits to the abilities of the human intellect to discern, then certainly what it cannot discern seems identical to this intellect though the two alleged identical objects are not identical in themselves. Hegelian and Kantian logic have challenged the notion of the in itself and this is perhaps the reason why Leibniz's second principle seems controversial to us.

5 Ontological refers to all that is related to the nature of Being or existence. Ontology is known as the ancient

epistemological claim. It makes an ontological claim dependent on the structure of our knowledge-apparatus.

A related principle is the indiscernibility of identicals, discussed below. The indiscernibility of identicals is not the same as the identity of indiscernibles. Along with the principle of sufficient reason, this is one of Leibniz's great ontological principles though sufficient reason (or cause: the principle states that everything that occurs in reality and thus in experience has a cause or ground: in German it is known as the *Satz vom Grund*) and is sometimes taken to be an empirical but not an ontological principle since it depends on perception and experience.

> **THE IDENTITY OF INDISCERNIBLES**
>
> The **identity of indiscernibles**: there cannot be separate objects or entities that have all their properties in common.

The indiscernibility of identicals along with the identity of indiscernibles is given below and is formalized using quantifiers. Thus Leibniz (who did not grasp quantifiers in a clear way: they were developed by Peirce and Frege) could not formulate his principles in sentential order logic and needed first-order quantifier logic to express them. That identicals are indiscernible is a reasonable logical and ontological principle since we pick out objects according to their properties or according to the predicates they satisfy. If all of the above are the same then it is reasonable to claim that we have no means of distinguishing two objects. This is true of sense-objects though a nominalist about sensation would claim that there are no identical objects in nature (Nietzsche thought so) but even more so of objects of the mind such as complex numbers that possess the same real part. There is no good way of picking them out even logically or mathematically. There is no room here for a full discussion and we refer the curious reader to Brandom's *Tales of the Mighty Dead* (p.281, ff.). Brandom points out that there is no good way to distinguish and know with certainty if i or $-i$ is the algebraic square root of -1. For the mathematician it might not matter, but for the epistemologist (or knowledge theorist) it does. Brandom uses mathematical morphisms to get a handle on this knowledge issue. But the point is even a sophisticated logical system like the one of Frege (who made use of quantifiers) had problems establishing reference in a clear and unproblematic way. In order to discern we need both to be able to pick something out clearly and to refer to it in an unambiguous way which may not always be simple as the complex number examples shows

---

science of Being.

We state the two principles formally:

> **THE INDISCERNIBILITY OF IDENTICALS (PRINCIPLE I)**
>
> For any x and y, if x is identical to y, then x and y have all the same properties.
>
> $$\forall x \, \forall y \, [x = y \rightarrow \forall P \, (Px \leftrightarrow Py)]$$

> **THE IDENTITY OF INDISCERNIBLES (PRINCIPLE II)**
>
> For any x and y, if x and y have all the same properties, then x is identical to y.
>
> $$\forall x \, \forall y \, [\forall P \, (Px \leftrightarrow Py) \rightarrow x = y]$$

Principle 1 is not reflexive[6] or does not entail the logical property of the equality relation used in its statement. (If we substituted an arbitrary relation we would not be able to assume that it is reflexive either). However = and logical equivalence ($\leftrightarrow$) used together as in principle 1 entail or imply, both taken together, the symmetry and transitivity of P. For the reasons stated above principle 1 and the set of reflexive predicates P are used to define the relation of equality in a second order predicate calculus which possesses quantifiers. The *indiscernibility of identicals i*s taken to be a logical truth (despite the problem pointed out above with complex numbers) and has not been challenged seriously in the recent history of logic.

However, there is a problem with the formal statements of Principle 2 above. In the identity of indiscernibles, Principle 2, we must exclude the following predicates:

- *"is identical to x"*
- *"is identical to y"*
- *"is not identical to x"*
- *"is not identical to y"*

If these predicates are included in the list of predicates that may be said of x and y, for example "*if x is identical to y*", then there will always be a "bothersome" property that distinguishes them, namely "being identical to x."

However, in this way, the discernibility (which may not be achieved by picking out objects in terms of the predicates they satisfy, intuitively it is the other way around but

---

[6] Reflexivity is the principle that x = x in the context we are discussing. In general for a relation R, this relation is reflexive on set S if $\forall x \in S: xRx$ is true. In the case of real numbers equality is such a relation since all real numbers are self-identical and are equal to themselves.

modern logic is not intuitive but highly formalized and abstract: in this it was influenced by the modern physical theory of electro-magnetic fields which are not concrete but immaterial and intangible) is transferred to higher level concepts such as relations which may be discernible on their own from within their own logico-deductive structure and without being logically individuated from the terms, entities or substances that they serve to relate.

This insight is due to the great logician Charles Sanders Peirce whom we will study in the section on the Pragmatist worldview in this book. On the other hand, it is incorrect to exclude all predicates that are materially equivalent (i.e., contingently equivalent) to one or more of the four given above. If this is done, the principle says that in a universe consisting of two non-identical objects, the two non-identical objects are identical—which is a contradiction—because all distinguishing predicates are materially equivalent to at least one of the four given above.[7]

QUESTIONS

THE THREE LAWS OF THOUGHT

1. What is the difference between the principle of excluded middle and logical bivalence?

2. Give an example of a logic in which the principle of excluded middle does not hold but bivalence holds.

3. Are there logics in which the concept of bivalence does not hold but the principle of excluded middle does?

4. What is the difference between the indiscernability of identicals and the identity of indiscernibles?

5. Are these principles metaphysical and logical or empirical?

6. Give an example of a situation in science where you would apply the indiscernibility of identicals.

7. Give an example of a situation in science where you would apply the identity of indiscernibles.

8. Why are the three laws of thought (identity, non-contradiction, and excluded middle) at the same time logical, ontological and psychological notions?

9. Why is logic related to ontology in Fichte's, Schelling's, and Hegel's philosophical-idealist systems of scientific philosophy?

---

7 In fact, they are each materially equivalent to two of them.

KEY CONCEPTS & DEFINITIONS - CRITICAL THINKING

GENERAL FORM OF A STATISTICAL SYLLOGISM
A proportion Y of X, are Z
W is an X
_____
W is a Z

INDUCTION starts with known instances and arrives at generalizations.
DEDUCTION starts from the general principle and arrives at some individual fact.

FORMAL FALLACIES: Fallacies that do not respect the laws of logic and the forms of syllogism first analyzed by Aristotle. (E.g. *Affirming a disjunct; Affirming the consequent; Denying the antecedent*)

QUANTIFICATION FALLACIES: An error in logic where the quantifiers of the premises are in contradiction with the quantifier of the conclusion.

SYLLOGISTIC FALLACIES: Fallacies passed off as good syllogisms. (E.g.: *Illicit Negative; Fallacy of four terms (quaternio terminorum); Illicit process of the major term; Illicit process of the minor term; The illicit affirmative; The undistributed middle*)

INFORMAL FALLACIES

LINGUISTIC FALLACIES: Fallacies that err through a form of vagueness or equivocation in the meaning of terms. (E.g.: *Equivocation; Etymological fallacy; Fallacy of composition; Fallacy of division*)

FALLACIES OF OMISSION: Options or possibilities are left out of the premises so that the conclusion appears necessary (E.g.: *Straw man fallacy; Argument from ignorance (argumentum ad ignorantiam); Argument from silence (argumentum e silentio); False dilemma (false dichotomy, fallacy of bifurcation, black-or-white fallacy); Onus probandi or Burden of Proof*)

FALLACIES OF INTRUSION (relevance): *Argumentum ad hominem; Argumentum ad baculum; Argumentum ad verecundiam*)

FALLACIES WITH BUILT-IN ASSUMPTIONS: fallacies in which the conclusion is inferred from a premise that already contains part or all of the information that constitutes the conclusion in some implicit or tacit form. (E.g.: *Begging the question (petitio principii); Circular reasoning (circulus in demonstrando); Naturalistic fallacy*)

CAUSAL FALLACIES: fallacies in which a premise is mistaken for the cause of the conclusion. (E.g.: *Post hoc ergo propter hoc; Confirmation bias; Continuum fallacy or Sorites fallacy; Fallacy of the single cause; Gambler's fallacy; Historicist fallacy, paradox or aporia; Ignoratio elenchi; Referential fallacy*)

NECESSARY CAUSES: A is a necessary cause of B if, whenever B occurs this entails that A occurs concurrently and without fail.

SUFFICIENT CAUSES: A is a sufficient cause of B if, whenever A occurs this entails that B occurs concurrently and without fail.

CONTRIBUTORY CAUSES: A is called a contributory cause of B if the occurrence of A precedes the occurrence of B and if changing A implies a change in B.

MILL'S METHODS are a means of individuating causes and identifying them.

There are four: Mill's method of:
1. Agreement,
2. Difference,
3. Agreement and Difference,
4. Concomitant Variation and Residue.

CHAPTER 2
CRITICAL THINKING, INFORMAL LOGIC & INDUCTIVE REASONING

Logic has been traditionally looked at in at least two competing ways. One can be traced back to Aristotle, in which logic is compared to geometry and efforts are directed at developing a formal theory of argumentation. Other logicians such as Walton and Toulmin have returned to Aristotle in order to ground what Walton has called a "new dialectic". This new dialectic is, in fact, a hermeneutic or interpretative art of dialectic. It rejects the view of logic as a branch of pure mathematics. In fact in *The Uses of Argument*, Toulmin attempts to show that perhaps logic should be understood not on the model of computation or ratiocination that is familiar to us from mathematics whether it is of the analytical-geometrical or of the abstract algebraic school, but that logic should be understood rather on the model of jurisprudence. Argument is then seen to be something pragmatic, even though Walton still avers in informal logic that validity is a semantic concept insofar as a proposition can be taken to be true or false. It is not clear whether this still depends *somehow on the notion of analytic proposition or argument that has been forcefully* challenged by philosophers such as William Ormard Quine and Donald Davidson.

CRITICAL THINKING, WORLDVIEWS & LOGIC

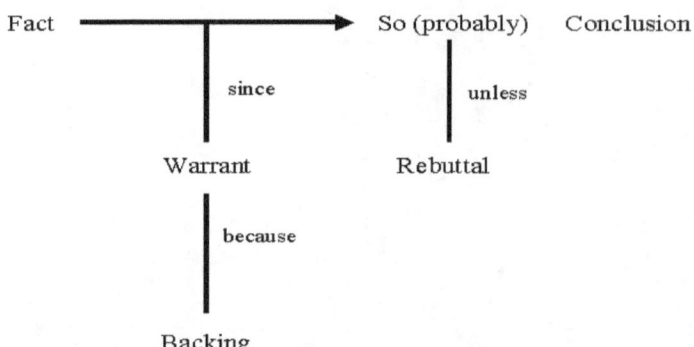

Courtesy of Ian Alexander, http://www.scenarioplus.org.uk/papers/argumentation/argumentation.htm

TOULMIN MODEL FOR ARGUMENTS
(From Uses of Arguments 1958)

In addition to proposing that arguments be understood according to the distinction between analytic and substantive types rather than the more common deductive-inductive distinction, Toulmin has provided us with a model for understanding and visualizing arguments. The basic components are facts or data and warrants that "back" or defend the facts and data that take the form of a thesis that may be challenged dynamically. Toulmin like Douglas Walton subscribes to the Aristotelian model of dialogical and dialectical argument, so the final claim comes or manifests through a debate or rebuttal process out of which the stronger thesis emerges as the victor. Of course, this is not a purely eristic model in which winning is sought at all costs. The process can mimick forms of deliberation but it is clear that this is a dynamic model in which the truth emerges through discussion, dialogue and debate in which alternative versions of the truth or the case are considered.

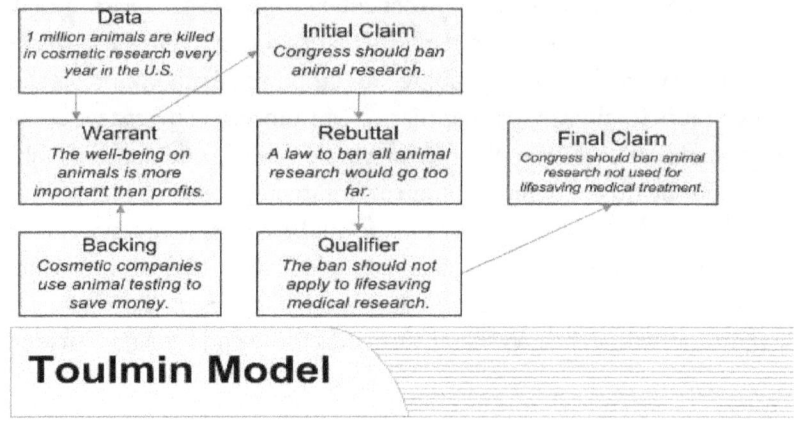

Courtesy Helena High Honours English, http://hhswritingguide.pbworks.com/.

2.1 WHAT IS INDUCTION?

Induction is a way of reasoning that leads from particular cases and evidence to statements about probable future events or general rules or laws.[1]

> **KEY NOTES**
>
> **Etymology of Induction**
>
> The word 'induction' comes to us from the late 14th century, where we have definitions such as "advancement toward the grace of God" and "formal installation of a clergyman," from the old French *induction* or directly from Latin *inductionem* (nom. *inductio*): "a leading in, introduction," noun of action from *inducere* "to lead".
>
> The term 'induction' was first used formally in logic by Cicero (early 1st century) when he gave '*inductio*' as the translation to the Greek *epagoge* (leading to) in Aristotle.

2.2 STATISTICAL SYLLOGISMS

Statistical syllogisms generally use qualifying terms like "most", "frequently", "almost never", "rarely", etc. These arguments may also possess a statistical generalization as one or both of their premises.

For example:

> *Almost all people are taller than 30 inches.*
> *Bob is a person.*
> ___
> *Therefore, Bob is taller than 30 inches*

The first or major premise is a generalization. From that generalization, the argument attempts to draw or derive a conclusion. This needs to be contrasted to a deductive syllogism in which the premises logically support or confirm the conclusion rather than strictly entail it. In the deductive syllogism it is possible for the premises to be true and the conclusion false, rare as it may seem. Furthermore, deductive arguments when valid and sound are characterized by the fact that the conclusion follows from the premises with necessity and certainty. In the case of statistical syllogisms as in the example above, the conclusion follows only with a certain probability or likelihood.

To make sense of the general example above, X is called the "reference class" and Z is the "attribute class". W is the individual object. In the first example we looked at, "(things that are) taller than 30 inches" is the attribute class and "people" is the reference class.

___
[1] Online Etymology Dictionary, http://www.etymonline.com/index.php?term=induction.

Even according to Aristotle's analysis of the form of arguments, most syllogisms are deductive. However, a statistical syllogism is inductive. In this case as with other inductive arguments, what we should be interested in when analyzing statistical syllogisms is whether the conclusion follows with high probability or whether there is a high likelihood for the conclusion to follow from the premises. We should also follow the rules associated with the analysis of inductive reasoning as opposed to deductive reasoning.

> **KEY NOTES**
>
> **GENERAL FORM OF A STATISTICAL SYLLOGISM**
>
> *A proportion Y of X, are Z*
> *W is an X*
> *W is a Z*

We study the general notion of fallacy (whether formal or informal) below. In particular, the so-called *dicto simpliciter*[2] fallacies can occur in statistical syllogisms. A *dicto simpliciter* fallacy is a fallacy in which a sweeping generalization occurs because one fails to specify something particular about a general instance that one can apply the argument to. A famous example is: *All kitchens must be examined by government officials. Therefore, your home kitchen must be examined by government officials.* The general stipulations apply to commercial and institutional restaurant kitchens, but because we have neglected this detail and simply said ('simply said' is the literal translation of *dicto simpliciter*) 'all kitchens', we have created a confusing situation in which one might believe that home kitchens need to be examined by government officials.

Faulty generalization fallacies can also affect any argument premise that uses a generalization. We will return to this issue when we study informal fallacies.

A problem with applying statistical syllogisms in real cases is the reference class problem: given that a particular case W is a member of very many reference classes X, in which the proportion of attribute Z may differ widely, how should one decide which reference class to use in applying the statistical syllogism?

---

[2] The example we give in the text is the "converse accident" *dicto simpliciter (a dicto secundum quid ad dictum simpliciter)* fallacy. But a fallacy of accident *(dicto simpliciter ad dictum secundum quid)* which also falls under the dicto simpliciter fallacies can also occur. All stealing is criminal. Paul stole the show. Therefore Paul is a criminal. Note that this fallacy is also based on equivocation though it also stems from applying a general principle to an accidental example to whom the principle clearly does not and should not apply. This is why it can be considered a fallacy of accident (*dicto simpliciter*).

> **KEY NOTES**
>
> **INDUCTION** starts with known instances and arrives at generalizations.
> **DEDUCTION** starts from a general principle and arrives at some individual fact.

Inductive Analogy as a Form of Inductive Reasoning

An argument from analogy is a kind or type of inductive argument. We will explain more clearly why it is inductive, below. For now we mention that like most inductive arguments, it does not depend on pure logical structure or form; but is also dependent on features or characteristics observed through sense-experience, which is a general characteristic of inductive reasoning and knowledge. In the case of analogical arguments, some perceived or allegedly similar properties or characteristics are used to infer some similar properties or characteristics that have yet to be observed. Analogical reasoning is really an attempt to look for patterns and similarities in the features of the world. It is an innate form of reasoning and so very common. Frequently this form of reasoning is employed in the discovery of new knowledge or to understand reality and novel situations or problems.

Reasoning from analogy is used in many walks of daily life. When someone has bought something from a given company and has had a bad experience, they will tend to believe that all the products made by that company have problems and will try to avoid the brand associated with that negative experience. In other cases, when scientists apply tests for certain forms of medication (contraceptives or Parkinson disease or Alzeihmer disease medication) with lab animals, they work from the premise that these animals are similar enough (in their nervous system in the case Parkinson disease and Alzeihmer disease or in their reproductive system in the case of contraceptives) to humans. Here again, they use a form of analogical reasoning to come to their conclusions. Even if they have shown (deductively) that these systems do not vary significantly in the areas of import; or have accounted for these variances where they do exist, the declaration or the finding of similarity is analogical for we 'know' these systems to be factually distinct: it is the bridging through similarity that operates the force of the conclusion.

The general form of an analogical argument is:

> *W and V are similar in respect to properties a, b, and c.*
> *Object W has been observed to have further property x.*
> ———
> *Therefore, V likely has property x also.*

It must be clear from the onset that an analogical argument does not affirm or assert that two natural or artificial objects are identical but merely that they share similar characteristics or properties. Thus an analogical argument is not a deductive argument. The analogy is never fool-proof and there can always exist a factor or property that has been neglected and that makes two objects dissimilar enough for the conclusion not to apply with a reasonable amount of likelihood or certainty. This is the reason why we consider analogical arguments to be inductive and that their conclusions do not follow with necessity from the premises, as is the case for deductive arguments.

Determining the strength of the argument requires that we take into consideration more than just logical form or structure: the content of the objects observed must also come under scrutiny.

In the history of philosophy at least two famous arguments from analogy have been presented and then refuted by various scholars. The first we consider is the teleological argument presented by Saint-Thomas and Paley. The world is compared to a watch and God is compared to a watchmaker who has built the perfect mechanism. David Hume gave a famous refutation of this analogy between the design of a watch and the design or purpose of the world. We omit its full discussion here but the curious student should read Hume in the original to consider whether the refutation is spurious or not.

The second example of argumentation in the form of analogy comes from Sartre's *Being and Nothingness*. Sartre considers the arguments presented for the existence of other minds to be false. His position is that, in their general form, these are arguments from analogy. Logically, they cannot provide an experiential ground for certainty. He presents a scenario: he considers a peeping Tom spying upon a couple of lovers through a keyhole. The peeper is unaware of himself, purely observing the couple and objectifying them. At the same time, they are pure images and forms to the peeper, not realities. Then suddenly he hears a noise behind him. He blushes. In an instant, he realizes that someone else had been witnessing him spying upon the couple and this is the most profound, emotionally-laden proof there can be of the existence of others and their consciousness or mind. The experience of shame is the best analogy to make us aware of the existence of others and of their similarity with ourselves. This example Sartre would argue, shows the impossibility of all arguments from analogy, which ultimately must be deemed spurious because of their abstract and formal inductive structure.

QUESTIONS
STATISTICAL SYLLOGISMS

Determine which of the following statistical syllogisms are weak and which are strong and justify your argument.

1. 92% of freshmen at McGill are Quebec residents. Jessica is a freshman at McGill University. Therefore, Jessica is a Quebec resident.

2. Very few employees at the Ottawa university are Ontario residents. Joyce is an employee of the Ottawa University. Therefore, Joyce is not an Ontario resident.

3. Professor Horst grew up in a small mining town. Most people who grow up in small mining towns have never read Plato. So Professor Horst has never read Plato.

4. I'm sure that if you adopt that abused Labrador, it will make a great pet for your kids. Labradors are generally very gentle, lovable dogs.

5. Most people in this town who voted-63 per cent of voters- voted for Mayor Coderre. You voted. So you supported Mayor Coderre.

KEY NOTES

Several facets or aspects affect the strength of an argument from analogy:

1. The number of properties or features that the things being compared share.
2. The relevance of the known similar properties or characteristics to the properties or characteristics inferred through the similarity in the conclusion.
3. The number and multiplicity of examples examined through the alleged or perceived analogy.

2.3 FORMAL & INFORMAL FALLACIES
2.3.1 Formal Fallacies

Formal fallacies have been analyzed since the time of Aristotle. They are errors or misapplications of deductive forms of reasoning. Because of this, the formal fallacies do not in fact depend on the contents of the statements made in their premises and their conclusions. They are fallacies simply because they do not respect the laws of logic and the forms of syllogism first analyzed by Aristotle. An important question in research on the nature of formal fallacies today is whether there are formal fallacies other than the ones already demonstrated in Aristotelian syllogistic logic. For example the following formal fallacies seem independent of classical Aristotelian syllogistic logic: (1) *Affirming a disjunct*; (2) *Affirming the consequent*; (3) *Denying the antecedent*. Rather, these formal fallacies depend on the development of the logic of propositions, relations and predicates stemming from the turn of the 20th century.

Though the denial of the antecedent seems to be a mere confusion or misunderstanding of the contrapositive which was already known in the 13th century by Jean Buridan (Buridan was opposed to the notion of the contrapositive, which he found misleading), most of these fallacies which we discuss below seem to be owed to the development of the understanding of truth tables and quantifiers due to Frege, Peirce and Wittgenstein. In fact, though we present the formal fallacies here for reasons of convenience, they could as well have been presented in the chapter on formal and mathematical logic since they are not in any way dependent on context of application or dialogue but merely on logical form and structure.

We briefly explain the formal fallacies mentioned above. It is ill-advised to give examples, though we will do so with a certain risk, because these are fallacies of form and giving them specific content might in fact mislead the student.

Affirming a disjunct

Affirming a disjunct is a fallacy that misunderstands the formal nature of a disjunction or inclusive or which is true as long as either one of its members is true. This type of fallacy would conclude from the truth of A or B and the truth of B, that A is false. This fallacy stems from misunderstanding the nature of the logical 'or'. The 'or' is inclusive and may have both members true when the logical union is true. "A or B" is a true statement if (1) A is true; (2) B is true; (3) both A and B are true. Here we see that we only need one of the statements to be true, but that this in no way 'implies' that if one is true the other is not (simply because it no longer needs to be).

EXAMPLE

Either you go to school or you will be poor
You will go to school

You will not be poor

Affirming the consequent

Affirming the consequent in this fallacy, one concludes that the truth of the second member of a logical implication (the de facto consequent) must imply the truth of the logical antecedent. But one misunderstands the nature of logical validity in doing so since we know that the conclusion of an implication or a consequent can sometimes be false if the antecedent is itself false. This is sometimes difficult to grasp for the beginner in logic but we have already dealt with this issue to a certain extent in Chapter 1. We also consider some examples here but first let us look at the fallacy in a purely formal manner: the antecedent in an indicative conditional is claimed to be true because the consequent is true. In formal terms if A, then B; B, therefore A.

EXAMPLE

If you eat a lot you will get fat.
You are fat.

You ate a lot.

This again is fallacious reasoning, though common-sense might seem to contradict it and most of us believe it to be sound. Some people get fat due to hormonal imbalances and illnesses and not necessarily through the increase of the quantity of calories or volume of food that they ingest.

Denying the antecedent

Here the consequent in an indicative conditional is claimed to be false because the antecedent is false; if A, then B; not A, therefore not B.

EXAMPLE

If you are born into a wealthy family, you will have a good and successful life.
You were not born into a wealthy family.

You will not have good and successful life.

Experience belies this example of formal fallacy as many a person has been born into modest means and has had a prosperous and productive life of achievement and happiness, while many wealthy people have not.

QUANTIFICATION FALLACIES

The quantification fallacies are also important formal fallacies which are independent of Aristotelian syllogistical logic. Again this is because quantifiers were only developed by Peirce and Frege in the 19th century. A quantification fallacy is an error in logic where the quantifiers of the premises are in contradiction with the quantifier of the conclusion.

Existential fallacy

This fallacy occurs when a statement is made that is general but that presupposes that there exists at least one person to which the general statement applies. However, from the general statement alone, one cannot determine that this single particular or individual to which the statement applies, does indeed exist.

> **EXAMPLE**
> *Everyone in this house is very rich.*

If it were the case that there are people in the house, then this statement might be true. However, until we know that the house is not empty, there is no guarantee that there is a single individual or person in the house to which the predicate (being rich) would apply and so the statement is not only nonsensical, but arguably false. This fallacy is sometimes called the fallacy of *existential import*.

KEY NOTES

FORMAL FALLACIES : fallacies that do not respect the laws of logic and the forms of syllogism first analyzed by Aristotle.

QUANTIFICATION FALLACIES: An error in logic where the quantifiers of the premises are in contradiction with the quantifier of the conclusion..

SYLLOGISTIC FALLACIES: Fallacies passed off as structurally sound syllogisms.

FORMAL SYLLOGISTIC FALLACIES

We studied syllogisms in Chapter 1. They are formal structures identified by Aristotle and which are comprised not only of major premises, minor premises and conclusions, but also middle terms, major terms and minor terms. The principal aspect of syllogisms is that they constitute a logic of classes and not a logic of propositions and predicates such as we studied in Chapter 1. Nonetheless, these classes are purely logical in form: the forms of the syllogism are limited and can be exhaustively studied and do not depend on particular contents of the statements or sentences, but on general form and structure.

Illicit Negative

The illicit negative fallacy concludes something positive (or an 'affirmative conclusion') from the combination of two negative premises in a syllogism. According to the logic of syllogisms, only a negative conclusion, not a positive one, can follow from two negative premises.

> **EXAMPLE**
>
> *All irrational numbers are not integer numbers*
> *All real numbers are not integer numbers*
> ―――――――――――――――――――――――
> *All real numbers are irrational numbers*

This argument is of the form: *All A are not B. All A are not C. Therefore, all C are A*, which is clearly false. From the premises we know that (1) All A is not B and so B implies not A; (2) All A are not C, so that C implies not A. We can picture the fallacy is as follows. Let A be the set of all irrational numbers, let B be the set of all integer numbers; and let C denote the set of all real numbers:

$$A \cap B = \emptyset \text{ and } B \cap C = \emptyset, \text{ then } A = C$$

while the following diagram illustrates that this is not necessarily so:

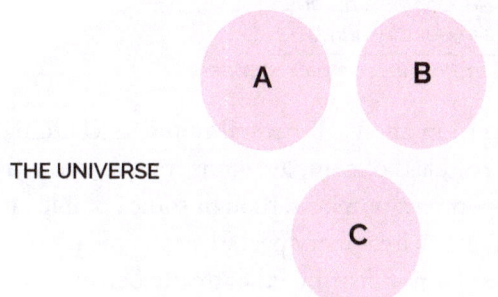

THE UNIVERSE

Fallacy of four terms (*quaternio terminorum*)

This fallacy occurs when a categorical syllogism has four terms. In traditional syllogisms only three terms are allowed and the major and minor premises must distribute the terms correctly for there to be a genuine and valid syllogistic conclusion that follows from the major and minor premises.

EXAMPLE

All attempts to end hostilities are efforts which should be approved by all nations.
All of Japan's present activities in China are attempts to end hostilities.

Therefore all of Japan's present activities in China are efforts which should be approved by all nations.

The problem is that there are four terms (in the major premise ending hostility excludes war as a means whereas in the minor premise, ending hostilities includes war as a means to end hostilities, this could also be a simple example of equivocation but there are effectively four terms and not three as are always required in a syllogism) because for reasons explained in the footnote below, war is not a way to try to end hostilities but is itself a form of hostility. This argument was used in the late thirties in order to justify Japan's war against China as way to "pacify China".[3]

Illicit process of the major term

A categorical syllogism that is invalid because its major term is not distributed in the major premise but distributed in the conclusion.

EXAMPLE

All imaginary numbers are complex numbers.
No natural numbers are imaginary numbers.

Therefore no natural numbers are complex numbers.

The conclusion makes an assertion about all natural numbers claiming that this class of numbers is excluded from the class of complex numbers. We know this to be absurd since all natural numbers are complex numbers, though some complex numbers are not naturals (those that possess a purely imaginary part). But the fallacy occurs because the major term 'imaginary numbers' is not distributed correctly between the major premise and the minor premise. Hence, a false conclusion is inferred.

Illicit process of the minor term

A categorical syllogism that is invalid because its minor term is not distributed in the minor premise, but distributed in the conclusion.

---

[3] This fallacy comes for Copi (Introduction to Logic, 1972). Japan was actually at war with China and its effort to end hostilities is interpreted differently in the Major premise and in the Minor premise. War is one way to try to end hostilities but more candidly and ingenuously it is correctly seen as a form of hostility.

> **EXAMPLE**
>
> *All fish are poisonous*
> *All fish are mammals*
> ___
> *Therefore all mammals are poisonous.*

The illicit affirmative

This occurs when a categorical syllogism has a negative conclusion derived from affirmative premises.

> **EXAMPLE**
>
> *All cats are dogs.*
> *All dogs are mammals.*
> ___
> *All cats are not mammals.*

The undistributed middle

Fallacy of the **undistributed middle.** This fallacy occurs when the middle term (M) in general form of syllogism is incorrectly distributed.

> **EXAMPLE**
>
> *All S are M*
> *All P are M*
> ___
> *All S are P*

A concrete example:

> *All scholars carry guns.*
> *My uncle carries a gun.*
> ___
> *Therefore, my uncle is a scholar.*

In this formal fallacy, in neither the major premise nor in the minor premise is the middle term distributed properly. For further information about distribution please consult the Appendix On Syllogistic Logic. A brief word about this concept can be given here. Distribution has to do with information possessed or fixed about one of the terms in syllogistic logic. When a term is not distributed we do not possess information about its determinacy or definition. In our example, formalizing, we get All P are M (in which M (guns) is not distributed) and Some S is M (in which again M (gun) is not distributed).

CRITICAL THINKING, WORLDVIEWS & LOGIC

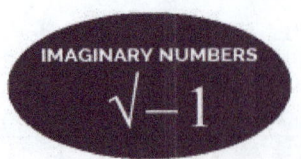

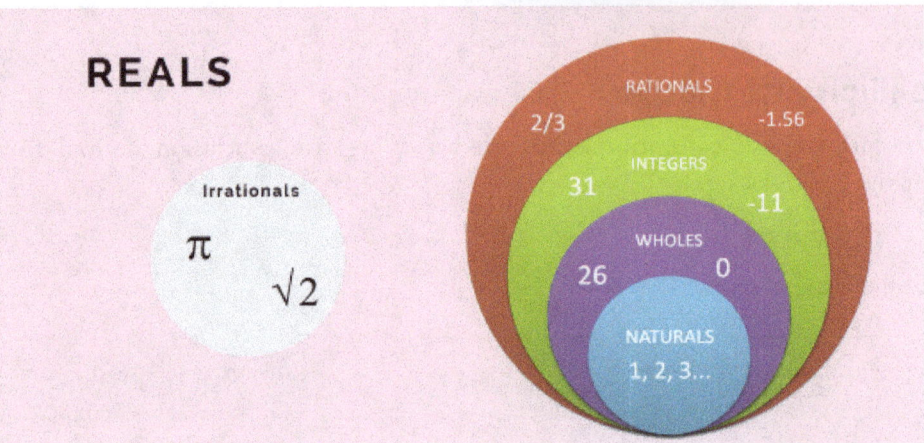

ⓘ FORMAL FALLACIES

Fallacies that do not respect the laws of logic and the forms of syllogism first analyzed by Aristotle.

Affirming a disjunct; Either you go to school or you will be poor. You will go to school. You will not be poor.
- ***Affirming the consequent;*** If you eat a lot you will get fat. You are fat. You ate a lot.
- ***Denying the antecedent:*** If you are born into a wealthy family, you will have a good and successful life. You were not born into a wealthy family. You will not have good and successful life.

QUANTIFICATION FALLACIES: An error in logic where the quantifiers of the premises are in contradiction with the quantifier of the conclusion.

SYLLOGISTIC FALLACIES: Fallacies passed off as structurally sound syllogisms.
- ***Illicit Negative;*** You can't conclude a positive from two negative premises.
- ***Fallacy of four terms (quaternio terminorum);*** The elementary form of a syllogism has only three terms.
- ***Illicit process of the major term;*** The major term is distributed in the conclusion and not the premises.
- ***Illicit process of the minor term;*** The minor term is distributed in the conclusion and not the premises.
- ***The illicit affirmative;*** You can't conclude something negative from positive premises.
- ***The undistributed middle:*** The middle term in the premises is improperly distributed.

QUESTIONS
FORMAL FALLACIES

Determine which formal fallacy is employed in the following false arguments:

1. If you vote Trudeau then Scheer will get elected. Scheer got elected. Therefore you voted Trudeau.
2. Either you study Nietzsche or you are a weak intellectual. You are a weak intellectual, therefore you did not study Nietzsche.
3. All students wear expensive brands, my uncle wears expensive brands. Therefore, my uncle is a student.
4. Either you smoke marijuana or you will not be cool. You smoke marijuana. Therefore you are cool.
5. No philosophers are cool people. No cool people are erudite. Therefore all philosophers are erudite.
6. All men are smart people. All women are clever people. Therefore all men are women.
7. All mammals are animals. Some pets are not mammals. Therefore, some pets are not animals.
8. All Quebecois love Justin because he legalized Marijuana. My cousin loves Justin. Therefore my cousin is a Quebecois.
9. All Quebecois are fans of Bill 21. No Anglo-Ontarians are Quebecois. Therefore no Anglo-Ontarians are fans of Bill 21.
10. If violets are blue then you are dancing in the rain. You are dancing in the rain. Therefore violets are blue.
11. All Americans love Trump. All Americans are democrats. Therefore all democrats love Trump.
12. All Bernie Sanders lovers are Americans. Some Florida voters are not Bernie Sanders lovers. Therefore, some Florida voters are Americans.
13. If Gandhi was a great man, then Mandela was a criminal. Gandhi was not a great man. Therefore Mandela was not a criminal.
14. Either you read Capital by Karl Marx or you are a bourgeois intellectual. You read Capital by Karl Marx. Therefore you are not a bourgeois intellectual.
15. Either you write a book or you will not be famous. You are not famous. Therefore, you did not write a book.
16. If Buddha is the Lord then Heidegger was a Nazi. Buddha is not the Lord. Therefore Heidegger was not a Nazi.
17. No students are talented people. No philosophers are students. Therefore all philosophers are talented people.
18. All whales are mammals. All mammals are animals. Therefore all animals are whales.
19. All students are smart. No artists are students. Therefore no artists are smart.
20. All Americans are erudite people. All erudite people are interesting people. Therefore all interesting people are Americans.

21. All Venn diagrams are beautiful. All students are beautiful. Therefore all Venn diagrams are students.
22. All globalist philosophers are frauds. All female artists are intelligent. Therefore all globalist philosophers are intelligent.
23. No men are good philosophers. No good philosophers are geniuses. Therefore all men are geniuses.
24. All Quebecois are separatists. Some separatists are immigrants. Therefore, some Quebecois are not immigrants.
25. Some people are not great artists. No great artists are women. Some people are women.
26. All Quebecois artists are total refusers. All Romanian writers are global assenters. Therefore all Quebecois artists are global assenters.
27. All tennis players are blue. All blues players are blue. Therefore all tennis players are blues players.
28. All Australians are rude people. All uneducated people are rude people. Therefore all uneducated people are Australians.
29. All Quebecois are natives. No Canadians are Quebecois. Therefore no Canadians are natives.
30. No fish are mammals. Some mammals are not animals. Therefore, some fish are not animals.
31. All philosophers are men. Some men are not good. Therefore, all philosophers are good.
32. No marijuana smoking is a good thing. Some learning is a not a good thing. Therefore all learning is not marijuana smoking.
33. All philosophers are wise humans. Some wise humans are fools. Therefore, some philosophers are not fools.
34. No women are wise. Some of the wise are not gifted people. Therefore, some gifted people are not women.
35. All mathematicians are not great human beings. Some great human beings are not poor. Therefore, all mathematicians are poor.
36. No graphic artists are talented people. All talented people are not humane. Therefore, some graphic artists are not humane.
37. All politicians are crooks. Some cooks are friendly. Therefore, some politicians are not friendly.
38. No graphic artists are talented people. All talented people are not humane. Therefore, some graphic artists are not humane.
39. All painters are not smart people. All smart people are not nice. Therefore all painters are nice.
40. No pettifoggers are cool people. Some cool people are not dullards. Therefore, some pettifoggers are not dullards.

2.3.2 Informal Fallacies

Informal fallacies have seen a recent resurgence in interest. They are almost more studied than formal fallacies which seem to be a closed subject-matter for research as almost all the forms and structures of fallacy are known and fairly well understood. Douglas Walton is a notable Canadian scholar who has studied informal fallacies and what he calls the new dialectic in order to distinguish it from the classic dialectic of Plato and Aristotle. Other important scholars in the field are Van Vleet, Van Eemeren, Grootendorst (there seems to be particular interest in argumentation theory in Holland as all these scholars are Dutch) and Hamblin. Stephen Toulmin also contributed to this field of research in the middle decades of the twentieth century. For these scholars, the turn taken from Aristotle towards the development of a formal, mathematical logic is actually a misunderstanding and takes away from the concrete uses of logic in spoken and argumentative contexts.

Except for a small resurgence during *German idealism* when logic was understood as the laws of thought, formalism has dominated the modern history of logic. To take Walton's important theses, logic has to be replaced within the field of everyday common discourse and understood as a study of forms of dialogue and argument schemes. Walton notes that dialectic was a lively form of debate that stemmed from the courts and public disputations of Ancient Greeks. In this he follows or is in agreement with Toulmin who, in *The Uses of Argument,* claims that logic should be conceived less as a mathematical pursuit but rather on the model of jurisprudence. It should be seen not as proceeding from general laws or principles but as arguing from particular examples, sounding out, reasoning and testing concrete premises given in language as to what would follow from its conclusion. Walton goes even further and claims that the idea that dialectic is tied to common or public opinion belongs to Aristotle. It is not clear whether Walton does justice to Plato's understanding of the dialectic which, though more technical and perhaps esoteric, was also seen as a form of dialogue which sought to establish understanding between two people who communicated with each other. It seems to us that Walton does not acknowledge the work of Hans-Georg Gadamer on the subject. Gadamer had already shown that the dialectic was rooted in dialogue and in the speech form of question and answer. Gadamer's rehabilitation of the tradition of philosophical rhetoric has made the work of Walton possible in great part, though he fails to acknowledge this influence or scholarly precedent anywhere in his works as far as we can tell.

Gadamer deepened the insight his master Heidegger had given us on dialogue in Aristotle. He does this by returning to Plato's notion of the dialectic and showing that it fundamentally determined Aristotle's own understanding of dialogue and dialectic.

If one were to classify informal fallacies as types of argument, one would probably have to classify them as inductive types of argument though other classifications have been proposed. Toulmin (in *The Uses of Argument*) proposes distinguishing between analytic and substantive arguments. This goes back to the analytic-synthetic distinction owed to Immanuel Kant but severely taken to task and challenged by the analytical philosopher William Ormard Quine. Fallacies are seen as bad inductive arguments because they do not depend on general logical form or structure, but instead on general schemes that pertain to the actual contents of the arguments. Though the schemes themselves are general, they can embody specific flaws that can only be identified by looking at the particular contents of each argument. An important point Walton does make, which Gadamer overlooks, is that informal fallacies are actually defendable arguments that may have a restricted validity in certain contexts. It is wrong to assume in general that fallacies are bad forms of arguments. By examining carefully the contexts of many fallacies, Walton manages to show that in certain contexts what seem like fallacies (the *ad hominem* for example) are legitimate critiques.

> **KEY DEFINITIONS**
>
> Van Vleet classifies **INFORMAL FALLACIES** into five broad categories:
>
> (1) Linguistic fallacies,
> (2) omission fallacies,
> (3) fallacies of intrusion or relevance,
> (4) fallacies with built-in assumptions and
> (5) causal fallacies.

Van Vleet classifies informal fallacies into five broad categories: (1) Linguistic fallacies, (2) omission fallacies, (3) fallacies of intrusion or relevance, (4) fallacies with built-in assumptions and (5) causal fallacies. We describe these fully.

LINGUISTIC FALLACIES

Linguistic fallacies are fallacies that err through a form of vagueness or equivocation in the meaning of terms. In general, we say a statement is a linguistic fallacy because its meaning is unclear and this lack of clarity vitiates the drawing of a strong conclusion from the premises. We consider briefly the main linguistic fallacies by also providing some key examples.

Equivocation

This fallacy occurs when a word is used with different meanings in at least two differing premises. Based on the different meanings of the term a spurious conclusion is inferred.

EXAMPLE

Murderers are inhumane kind of people. Since murders are inhuman they do not deserve to live and should be given the death penalty.

Here there is a conflation of the meaning of inhumane (which means lacks compassion) and inhuman which means lacking the quality of being human. This equivocation allows the conclusion to be inferred, though it invalidates the argument.

> **① KEY DEFINITIONS**
>
> **LINGUISTIC FALLACIES:** Fallacies that err through a form of vagueness or equivocation in the meaning of terms. In general, we say a statement is a linguistic fallacy because their meaning is unclear and this lack of clarity vitiates the drawing of a strong conclusion from the premises.
> (Equivocation; Etymological fallacy; Fallacy of composition; Fallacy of division)

Etymological fallacy

In this fallacy, one tries to deduce or infer the actual meaning of a word based on its original meaning. This fallacy obtains because sometimes, the conceptual understanding of a term has largely evolved due to refinements in the understanding of that term. Thus looking to the original meaning of the term might be misleading. But again, this type of fallacy also has to be relativized since looking at the original meaning of a term might give insight into something that ulterior conceptual developments might have covered over. Martin Heidegger the famous German philosopher and author of *Being and Time* was notorious for having complex and often controversial etymology to support his arguments. While we do not endorse some of his more spurious etymological research, we must note that some his etymologies are productive and insightful.

EXAMPLE

A deduction is not an inference. This is because inference comes from the latin 'in' and 'fero' which means to 'carry over'. Deduction on the other hand comes from the Greek 'apagoge', 'apa' and 'agein' in ancient Greek means 'removing things' or 'proving through contradiction'. Therefore only inductions and abductions are forms of inference.

The example is very technical but illustrates how looking at the etymologies of words may be misleading. A deduction in fact does draw conclusions from premises, but it is also truth-preserving given some specific conditions and so 'carries over' the truth and hence may be considered a form of inference. Some doubt remains, however: Is not deduction analytical in some way so that the truth of the conclusion is already implicit in the truth of the premise? In this case, the making explicit of the truth that was implicit in the premise through process of the argument is what 'carries over' the truth to the conclusion and so, it is still inferred. Therefore a conclusion is still inferred from the premises even in deduction.

Fallacy of composition

In this type of fallacy one assumes that what is true of some of the parts of a whole is true of the totality of the whole.

Here is a misleading example of the fallacy of composition advocated by some poor or weak economists:

> If everyone saves their money and spends less, then this will be good for the economy since less people will be in debt and there will be less personal bankruptcy.

Economists will claim that this is a fallacy of composition since if people spend less, the economy as a whole (which is the sum of the consumers treated as parts) will not grow, but possibly even start shrinking. While there might be some general truth that less consumer spending leads to a slowdown in retail sales and thus in some part of the economy, this is an example of a fallacy of composition since the spending has to be further dissected and understood to make a reasonable and informed economic claim.

We consider a second example of a fallacy of composition:

> **EXAMPLE**
>
> If I leave the show early, then I will beat traffic. If everyone leaves the show early then they will all beat traffic.

Obviously if everyone leaves early there will be traffic as opposed to the situation where only one or two people leave early.

Fallacy of division

In this kind of fallacy one assumes that what is true of a whole is also true of all its respective parts.

> **EXAMPLE**
>
> For Anaxagoras (as we have received his opinion in the historical record of Lucretius), the atoms of water were themselves wet, atoms of earth were themselves dirty, atoms of air were vaporous and atoms of fire were igneous.

This is obviously mistaken since the properties of water are understood in modern day science to be emergent (this a technical scientific term meaning that the properties somehow manifest to our sense-apparatus independently of the actual composition of the given substance, i.e. the properties emerge; hence the word 'emergent') and in no way dependent on the properties of its hydrogen and oxygen atoms.

FALLACIES OF OMISSION

Fallacies of omission occur when options or possibilities are left out of the premises so that people one attempts to persuade with the argument are only given a few options to choose from. Typical of this kind of fallacy is the false dilemma where we are only given two options and all other options on the spectrum of possibilities occurring between the two options presented are omitted. Another example of this type of fallacy is the argument from ignorance considered below with specific examples. Here the argument is that because something does not yet exist, one concludes that it can never exist. Sometimes this is expressed as 'proof of non-existence is non-existence of proof' or alternatively 'evidence of non-existence is lack of evidence for existence'. Considered in this abstract way there might be some validity to the arguments; but when we employ concrete examples the arguments quickly become spurious. For example, we cannot argue from the non-existence of a cure for cancer that no cure for cancer will ever be found. We have countless examples in the history of medicine that show the invention or development of cures hithero unknown. An answer to this critique is that the cure or its compound have always existed and that science only 'discovered' them.

Straw man fallacy

A straw man fallacy is a fallacy in which the position of an opponent is simplified and distorted so that it no longer represents his original point of view. Again and following Walton we might think that in some cases such a fallacy is a mere move in a conversational game in which we seek to win the argument. Following Plato and Aristotle, Walton classifies this type of dialogue or discourse as *eristic* and along with classic sources, sees it as a destructive type of dialogue where one seeks to win at all costs. However, one may imagine situations perhaps when simplifying an opponent's position and reducing it without distorting it would not be an inappropriate move in conversation, but would merely point out weaknesses in that opponent's position.

> **EXAMPLE**
>
> A: We should relax the laws on marijuana.

B: No, any society with unrestricted access to intoxicants loses its work ethic and goes only for immediate gratification.

This is an example of a straw man fallacy despite there being some power to the argument. The question very much in vogue these days, is whether marijuana should be decriminalized or legalized. Though this can be taken to be a fallacy, access to recreational drugs may in fact produce a greater increase in the desire for immediate gratification—an ill from which our society already suffers. There is however no direct link between work ethic and the desire for immediate gratification and so the argument overreaches somewhat. We have examples of high-functioning drug addicts in the history of philosophy (Jean-Paul Sartre, for instance). A further concern that is not addressed in the argument is the correlation between use of marijuana and mental illness. Though biologically there is no causation between these two issues, there is evidence of correlation and this should be taken into account when looking into the specifics of this argument.

> ⓘ **KEY DEFINITIONS**
>
> **FALLACIES OF OMISSION:** Options or possibilities are left out of the premises so that the conclusion appears necessary. (*Straw man fallacy; Argument from ignorance (argumentum ad ignorantiam); Argument from silence (argumentum e silentio) ; False dilemma (false dichotomy, fallacy of bifurcation, black-or-white fallacy); Onus probandi or Burden of Proof*)

Argument from ignorance (*argumentum ad ignorantiam*)

This fallacy consists in the belief that a claim or statement is true because it has not been or cannot be proven to be false. The equivalent fallacy is to state a claim is false because it has not been or cannot be proven true.

> **EXAMPLE**
>
> The typical example for this kind of fallacy is the one with yet to be developed cures for diseases. Here, one infers that no cure for cancer will ever be found from the fact that no cure exists presently. However, the fact that at some point in time there was no cure for tuberculosis could have been used in this same fallacious way. Granted, tuberculosis and cancer are very different diseases and perhaps the counterexample does not apply; but for the statement that 'no cure to cancer can be found' to be reasonable, it must be supported by a separate argument on the details and minutiae of what cancer consists in and not through a single overarching argument that proceeds in such a simplistic way.

Argument from silence (*argumentum e silentio*)

The argument from silence is an argument in which someone putting forth an argument uses the thesis that there is no evidence for a given fact or event and that this absence of evidence confirms the truth of their conclusion.

> **EXAMPLE**
> This argument is often used to disprove the historicity of Christ. While this view exists among some reputable historians it is a minority view just as the fact that Caesar or Socrates never existed is a minority view. In general, people who hold this view argue that the Gospels are a fabrication, that historians such as Josephus and Titus-Livius are biased and unreliable, and so shift the burden of proof to the historian. In this way the denial of the historicity of Christ could be a combination of the argument from silence and the burden of proof fallacy, seeing as the historical evidence for the existence of a Jesus from Nazareth is in general a well-accepted and non-controversial fact.

False dilemma (false dichotomy, fallacy of bifurcation, black-or-white fallacy)

In this fallacy, only two options are presented when in reality the two options are only two extremes on a wider spectrum of possibility purposely omitted in order to mislead.

> **EXAMPLE**
> Either you get a university diploma or you will be poor and miserable.

While there might be some truth to this and perhaps even more in the past. Present day examples of successful entrepreneurs such as Bill Gates and Mark Zueckerberg contradict this facile dichotomy. (Certainly Bill Gates and Zueckerberg are not poor though their degree of happiness might be questioned.) A false dilemma functions by setting up two poles on the spectrum of possible fact or opinion and forcing the person on the receiving end of the argument to choose between those two poles. In reality, there are many gradations to wealth and many more possibilities available to the college graduate or dropout such as trade schools, going into business or even municipal politics to name a few.

Onus probandi or Burden of Proof

In this type of fallacy an individual makes an assertion and then claims that the onus or burden to provide evidence against the claim he makes is on the person who contradicts the said claim.

> **EXAMPLE**
> Someone may claim that there is a car or a spoon in orbit around the moon. Because no one can immediately prove him wrong, he claims that his inference or belief is valid.
> The Apollo moon landing was a hoax.

The fallacy of burden of proof occurs when someone asserts something and claims that the onus or the responsibility lies with the people contradicting his belief or assertion to prove that he is wrong.

FALLACIES OF INTRUSION (relevance)

The *fallacies of relevance* are an important class of fallacies. Douglas Walton's work (which we both follow and critique) has shown that some of these fallacies (such as the ad hominem and the ad verecundiam) were given their names for the first time (as they would later appear in modern textbooks of logic) in John Locke's *Essay Concerning Human Understanding*. Walton also identifies a fourth kind of argument Locke provides called the *argument ad judicium*, though Locke does not consider it to be a fallacy at all but rather a form of argument that "disposes him to hear the truth in a position". It is from this classification that places fallacies within reasonable forms of arguments that led Walton to posit that fallacies are not always absolutely wrong, but that they need to be studied and understood in terms of context—and that in some contexts they may be reasonable forms or ways to criticizes an opponent's move within the conversation.

Argumentum ad hominem

In this fallacy it is the person making the argument or their character that is attacked, rather than the particulars of the argument the person is making. As Douglas Walton has shown, this fallacy may sometimes be a legitimate form of argument when there is an inconsistency in the person's affiliations and the actual position he is defending. In general, however, the *ad hominem* is an abusive form of argument that tends to insert irrelevant claims about an opponent when entering into a dialogue or conversation with him. Following Walton we may insert this type of fallacy mostly in the eristic form of debate in which each of the participants in conversation seeks to win the argument at all costs, as we often see in political campaigning debates.

> **EXAMPLE**
>
> Mr. Harper should not be elected prime minister again. This is because Harper is not a democrat. He is not a democrat since he has been found in contempt of parliament in 2011. Also it is believed that he has paid ex-Senator Mike Duffy's expenses in order to keep him quiet about the financial scandals in the Canadian senate.

The first claim that Harper is not a democrat is incorrect. Prime Minister Harper did not plot to undermine the authority of parliament in a way an anarchist or extremist leader might have. In this sense, Harper respects the principles of Canadian parliamentary democracy and this could be interpreted to be an *ad hominem* fallacy. *Ad hominem* fallacies are very common in politics and schoolyard arguments. It is not unlike Douglas Walton's example in which Bob argues for the privatization of the post, and an interlocutor attacks him for being a communist. It should be pointed out that, in this case, Walton would claim that to attack Bob with reference to his communist beliefs might be a valid argumentative move provided that there was a contradiction between Bob's general political position and his argument for the privatization of postal services.

Argumentum ad baculum

This fallacy is considered a fallacy of force of coercion or of imposition. It occurs when an opponent seeks to overpower his partner in conversation. The nature of this fallacy will become clearer when we consider an actual example, as we do below.

> **EXAMPLE**
> You should not read the work of Friedrich Nietzsche called *The Antichrist*. Doing so will compromise the eternal salvation of your soul. If you read Nietzsche's *Antichrist*, you will burn in Hell.

Sometimes known as the argument to the cudgel or to the stick, this argument proceeds through threat and menace. In this case, we are threatened of dire consequences to our personal salvation if we read certain controversial philosophical texts.

Argumentum ad verecundiam

This is an argument from authority. There might be interference in this type of argument with the use of expert argument or testimony. The line between when an authority or expert is used in an appropriate way and when the expert is actually cited or used as a source in an inappropriate way might be difficult to distinguish. For example, we might cite a specialist or credentialed expert in architecture to explain the demolition of the buildings in the 9/11 attacks in New York, when it would be better to seek the expertise of a physicist or of a materials engineer. Others examples may be more obvious, *"I am older, therefore I am right." "It is written in the Bible, therefore it is true." "Everyone agrees, therefore it must be so."*

> **EXAMPLE**
> Aristotle believed that objects fell to the ground because they possess a potential that is actualized by the fact that those objects reach their preferred state of rest. Because Aristotle said so it must be true.

This argument from authority is easily shown to be a fallacy since we now know that Newton's and Einstein's science provide a more accurate account of how and why objects fall to the ground. However, sometimes an argument from expertise is difficult to distinguish from a fallacy of authority. This happens, for example, when we need to resort to an expert opinion such as in a court-room where the prosecution or the defense will bring an expert doctor to testify. Sometimes the other party will bring the competency of the expert into question: It is sufficient to discredit the expert if one wants to cast doubt on the testimony.

FALLACIES WITH BUILT-IN ASSUMPTIONS

Fallacies with built-in assumptions are fallacies in which the conclusion is inferred from a premise that already contains part or all of the information that constitutes the conclusion in some (implicit or tacit form. Typical examples of this fallacy are fallacies like begging the question, circular reasoning, the 'is-ought' or naturalistic fallacy—a fallacy first fully identified in the work of G.E. Moore, though David Hume had already broached the issue).

Begging the question (*petitio principii*)

In this fallacy what already exists in the premises is repeated in the conclusion. In this way the argument (and the premises to be precise) has done no real work of defending the truth of the conclusion.

> **EXAMPLE**
>
> A contradiction to my theory of dream produced by another of my women patients (the cleverest of all my dreamers) was resolved more simply, but upon the same pattern: namely that the non-fulfillment of one wish meant the fulfillment of another. One day I had been explaining to her that dreams are fulfillment of wishes. Next day she brought me a dream in which she was traveling down with her mother-in-law to the place in the country where they were to spend their holidays together. Now I knew that she had violently rebelled against the idea of spending the summer near her mother-in-law and that a few days earlier she had successfully avoided the propinquity she dreaded by engaging rooms in a far distant resort. And now her dream had undone the solution she had wished for; was not this the sharpest contradiction of my theory that in dreams wishes are fulfilled? No doubt; and it was only necessary to follow the dream's logical consequence in order to arrive at its interpretation. The dream showed that I was wrong. *Thus it was her wish that I might be wrong, and her dream showed that wish fulfilled* (italics original)"[4]

This apparent circularity in Freud's theory is one of the reasons Popper considered psychoanalysis to be a non-scientific theory of the human psyche. It's a fact that through these circular aspects of interpretation, Freud could pretty much explain anything and its opposite. But for Popper you had to make a specific predictive claim that could not be contradicted. If never contradicted then the theory was potentially valid, but if no specific predictive claim could be made as he believed was the case with Freudian psycho-analysis, then one could not claim that that the theory was scientific.

---

4 Sigmund Freud, *The Interpretation of Dreams*, New York: Avon, 1966, 185.

> **ⓘ KEY DEFINITIONS**
>
> **FALLACIES WITH BUILT-IN ASSUMPTIONS:** fallacies in which the conclusion is inferred from a premise that already contains part or all of the information that constitutes the conclusion in some implicit or tacit form.
>
> *(Begging the question (petitio principii); Circular reasoning (circulus in demonstrando); Naturalistic fallacy)*

Circular reasoning (*circulus in demonstrando*)

In formal reasoning validly deductive arguments are in fact circular since they make explicit something that is implicit in the premises. So circular reasoning is not a fallacy in general, but only when we present a thesis, are challenged and attempt to provide independent grounds for our position while only re-stating our premise(s). By this means, although circular reasoning and begging the question are often taken to be somewhat interchangeable, in the context of informal fallacies they are not.

> **EXAMPLE**
>
> *God dictated the truth to Jesus, therefore the Bible is free of error.*
> *Because the Bible is free of error, it must have been dictated by God.*

Aside from being a show of misunderstanding of how the Bible has been transmitted, this is a circular fallacy because in attempting to defend the truth of the first statement, one employs the second in which, instead of introducing new information or independent sources of justification, one is in fact merely repackaging the first statement and not making any new claim or adding any new content in the second statement explicit that was not already so in the first statement or adding new content in the second statement that was not already implicitly there in the first statement.

Naturalistic fallacy

This fallacy does not respect the fact-value distinction and makes evaluative inferences from factual or informational premises. Hume had already pointed out some of these issues in the teleological argument and in the natural law principle in ethics. For him this was part of the 'is-ought' problem.

> **EXAMPLE**
>
> The naturalistic fallacy is usually applied to ethical theories like the theory of natural law. This theory claims that everything in nature has a purpose. But there are natural things that do not possess an obvious purpose. This is the case with sex for example. The theory of natural law made the claim that sex was uniquely devised for the purpose of reproduction. However, one

may also look at sex as a way for two adults to be together, to express a sense of mutual, inter-subjective and individual pleasure and at some deep level to exchange and communicate with each other. Thus one cannot infer from the nature of sex, from the fact that it exists and is in a certain way, what the 'ought' of sex or its teleology or purpose ought to be.

> ⓘ **KEY DEFINITIONS**
>
> **CAUSAL FALLACIES:** fallacies in which a premise is mistaken for the cause of the conclusion.
> (Post hoc ergo propter hoc; Confirmation bias; Continuum fallacy or Sorites fallacy; Fallacy of the single cause; Gambler's fallacy; Historicist fallacy, paradox or aporia; Ignoratio elenchi; Referential fallacy)

CAUSAL FALLACIES

Causal fallacies are fallacies in which a premise is mistaken for the cause of the conclusion. These fallacies are a misunderstanding of the phenomenon of cause and effect, not necessarily as it applies in nature, but as it relates to the structure of arguments. Though causality was thought to refer only to induction in the work of Hume, the work of later empiricists (who we explore in Chapters 4 and 7 of this book) such as Carl Hempel has shown that causality might be tied to deductive form and structure. Thus we may have ground to argue that causal fallacies are actually *formal* rather than *informal* fallacies. But this discussion is a bit abstract and deals with the method in which physical and natural phenomena are understood, which is a topic we deal with in Chapter 7 on the subject of scientific explanation and scientific method. We do not need to understand at this point whether Hume or Hempel are correct (in fact this discussion might be a bit beyond the scope of this introductory text) to understand causal fallacies. Rather we need to look at concrete cases of how cause and effect are understood in common day language. We follow Douglas Walton and Stephen Toulmin[5] in claiming that the dialectical and rhetorical use of causal fallacies is more important than determining with absolute formal rigor whether these fallacies pertain to deductive or inductive reasoning.

---

5 In fact Toulmin proposes in *The Uses of Argument* (1958) a scheme or distinction between analytical and substantive arguments. He then proceeds to dissect both these argument schemes or types in terms of the notions of data, warrants, backing and rebuttal. In some of the visuals that have appeared in the wake of his work, the word fact has been substituted for data. This is not a major straying but often students coming from high-school mistake or are not clear on the nature of facts. They assume that these are natural posits behind which one may not regress. Perhaps this is also what Toulmin means by data. But data may also come from the social sciences where information and data are treated and interpreted. However, the main point is that even data and facts may be interpreted to a certain extent are not purely given like numbers or geometrical shapes, especially if Toulmin wants to be consistent and apply his model of argumentation to everyday existence and base himself on the model of jurisprudence rather than geometry or pure mathematics such as algebra and analysis.

Post hoc ergo propter hoc

Latin for "after this, therefore because of this": Something happens after something else and one claims that the event that preceded the second event is the cause of the second event.

This is also a variation on Hume's critique of induction. Two examples can be considered, the example of a light turning green and someone's car begins to move so we naturally ascribe the movement of the car to the changing of the traffic signal. Another is Hume's famous example with the billiard balls. Just because a billiard ball hits another and that other ball begins to move does not mean that in fact there is a causal connection, between the collision and the movement: there is only a correlation between the two events and one cannot ascribe proper causal interaction between the two billiard balls.

> **EXAMPLE**
> *"I was just thinking of you when the phone rang. That must be why you called."*
> *"I prayed for rain and so it rained."*

Confirmation bias

This fallacy consists in processing or accepting only those facts and information that confirm or agree with one's predetermined beliefs or hypothesis. All other facts or information that contradict the preconceived opinion or thesis are ignored.

A confirmation bias can occur for instance when a doctor researching illness X assumes that a patient has illness X without carefully examining the symptoms. Since his mind is made up so to speak, every symptom he observes confirms his original prejudice or ready-made opinion. These types of biases can also occur in police work when racial profiling is used and certain individuals belonging to certain races might be suspected of having committed certain crimes in unfair ways.

> **EXAMPLE**
> *All lawyers are dishonest. I never met an honest lawyer.*
>
> *Society has never considered women equal to men nor allowed them the same political authority. Women like Thatcher, Merkel and Rousseff were anomalies and don't count.*

Continuum fallacy or Sorites fallacy

This paradox was known in Antiquity and is attributed to Eubulides of Miletus (part of the Megarian school philosophers). In Antiquity it was presented as a puzzle about a heap. If you remove pebbles from a heap or grains of sand from a heap of sand and replace the grains of sand with new ones at what point is the new heap no longer identical to the original heap? This puzzle has become a paradox in modern logic and it still causes problems for certain formal deduction systems that try to master it.

> **EXAMPLE**
>
> The continuum fallacy or the paradox of the Sorites is a complex fallacy that is known since Antiquity. It poses the question of when a heap becomes something other than it is by the constant removal or addition of small parts to it. An example of this is Theseus's ship: The ship never comes to shore to be refurbished or rebuilt, but while on the ocean, the sailors replace parts of it as needed until at some point—and this is the critical and difficult question posed by this fallacy—the ship is no longer logically identical with the original ship. The important question is: Can we determine or find a criterion for when the original ship is or becomes the new ship? There is no simple answer to this question.

Fallacy of the single cause

Often events are complex and require an explanation that appeals to more than one cause. However this fallacy tends to reduce an event to a single explanatory cause that supposedly captures its full meaning. The examples below should clarify the meaning of this fallacy.

> **EXAMPLE**
>
> *Mrs. Rivers gunned down three innocent people because she was on drugs.*
> *The terrorists attacked us because they hate us.*

These examples explain a complex event such as a terrorist attack or a tragedy in which three people get murdered by referring to a simplistic single cause. Complex events more often than not possess complex explanations. These might have deep causes and more superficial causes but in order to fully explain the event one needs to look at multiple sources of causation and at the broader context.

Gambler's fallacy

Also known as the Monte-Carlo fallacy, this is a fallacy which tends to infer a conclusion from the belief that events which possess independent random probability are somehow connected and have a bearing on the conclusion or the inference that is derived.

> **EXAMPLE**
>
> This fallacy occurs when one believes that because an unbiased coin has been observed to be tails for a great number of times in sequence (say, a hundred times) then the next result will be heads. This is a misunderstanding of the fact that the flipping of a coin in the case of an unbiased coin is an independent statistical event.

Historicist fallacy, paradox or aporia

This fallacy occurs when we tend to project the beliefs of the present into an interpretation of the past. Inevitably, we do not manage to fully put ourselves into the shoes of people from the past who had different values and different belief systems. But to assume that the present and the past are incommensurable realities is precisely to commit this fallacy. There is a way to bridge the horizons of the past and of the present, albeit imperfectly.

> **EXAMPLE**
>
> A typical example of this fallacy occurs in ethics and is actually a form of relativistic fallacy. There is no moral progress because the past cannot be criticized since it partakes of different ideals and values that are incommensurable with our own. Thus we cannot criticize the behavior of the Turks during the Armenian genocide because their values were different and the times were radically different from the ones we possess today. But this is plainly not true, genocide can be historically understood and studied along with other genocides. By studying the past there is the hope that we will not repeat its errors. As Santayana claimed, those who do not understand history are bound to repeat it.

Ignoratio elenchi
(irrelevant conclusion, missing the point)

These types of argument are fallacious because they do not relate to the issue at hand and bring in an idea that diverts the attention or changes the subject of the main theme under discussion. This fallacy is thought to be identical to the ***red herring*** fallacy.

> **EXAMPLE**
>
> An example of Red Herring fallacy often given in Eastern European countries before the fall of Communism in 1989 was the following: People would criticize socialist countries for the lack of freedom and democracy in those countries; the leaders of those countries would reply 'that in America, they kill black people'. Here we see that the actual issue is never taken into account. It is side-stepped by a statement that is not relevant to critiques about democracy and freedom in socialist countries. While this may be a logical fallacy, recent events in American history have proven there is a problem of racial injustice in America today. Despite this fact, racial injustice in America still has no relevance on whether or not democratic freedom exists in socialist countries. However, if what the socialist leaders were replying to was a relative comparison of social justice in society, then perhaps the answer would not be fallacious but a valid critique and debate point. Douglas Walton has put the thesis forth that fallacies are not always wrong, but can sometimes be interpreted as correct argumentative moves given the context of the dialogue or dialectical debate.

Referential fallacy

This fallacy assumes that because different words exist they must refer to different objects or meanings. But this is plainly not true, language can be accidental and contingent and sometimes two words refer to exactly the same object or meaning.

This is a common mistake made by more advanced thinkers and it lies in the belief that if different words exist then they must refer to different things. For example, some philosophers see no difference between metaphysics and ontology which they take to be essentially the same thing or to refer to the same discipline or objects of study. Others infer because of the difference in names that the two words ontology and metaphysics actually refer to different domains. This is a complex example though simpler ones can be found. For example, opium was thought to bring about sleep because it had a dormitive virtue. But this dormitive virtue turned out to be a simple effect of inhibition on the nervous system and does not exist as such. Just because the word "dormitive virtue" exists does not mean that it actually refers to something in reality.

> **EXAMPLE**
> To dispel or debunk this fallacy an example from the history of philosophy is required as well. Plato reified or hypostatized the Forms or Ideas. This means that Plato created a world of real existing entities called Ideas or Forms. But for Aristotle, the Forms or Ideas could only exist within actual objects in the world so that they were dynamic entities existing in the world and not static Ideas or Forms existing in another world broken off or dichotomous from the actual world. One can see that this is not always a fallacy because some Platonists still believe that the ideas and Forms actually exist in a different world.

Another more concrete example is provided with the concept of the human soul. For a long time people believed that thinking occurred in the soul. This belief blocked research into the functioning of the brain as the seat of consciousness and of actual thinking. The soul was hypostatized and became a metaphysical or ontological entity to which the attribution of thought was ascribed. Again, to some this is arguably no fallacy—there are still non-materialist philosophers who believe in the power and existence of a human soul.

ⓘ INFORMAL FALLACIES

LINGUISTIC FALLACIES: Fallacies that err through a form of vagueness or equivocation in the meaning of terms.
(Equivocation; Etymological fallacy; Fallacy of composition; Fallacy of division)

FALLACIES OF OMISSION: Options or possibilities are left out of the premises so that the conclusion appears necessary.
(Straw man fallacy; Argument from ignorance; Argument from silence; False dilemma (false dichotomy, fallacy of bifurcation, black-or-white fallacy); Onus probandi or Burden of Proof)

FALLACIES OF INTRUSION *(relevance):*
Argumentum ad hominem; Argumentum ad baculum; Argumentum ad verecundiam)

FALLACIES WITH BUILT-IN ASSUMPTIONS: fallacies in which the conclusion is inferred from a premise that already contains part or all of the information that constitutes the conclusion in some implicit or tacit form.
(Begging the question (petitio principii); Circular reasoning (circulus in demonstrando); Naturalistic fallacy)

CAUSAL FALLACIES: fallacies in which a premise is mistaken for the cause of the conclusion.
(Post hoc ergo propter hoc; Confirmation bias; Continuum fallacy or Sorites fallacy; Fallacy of the single cause; Gambler's fallacy; Historicist fallacy, paradox or aporia; Ignoratio elenchi; Referential fallacy)

EXERCISES

Identify the following fallacies and group them under the categories of 1) Linguistic Fallacies; 2) Fallacies of Intrusion; 3) Fallacies with Built-In Assumptions; 4) Causal Fallacies; and 5)Fallacies of Omission.

1) Criminal actions are illegal, and all murder trials are criminal actions, thus all murder trials are illegal. (Here the term "criminal actions" is used with two meanings. Example borrowed from Copi and Cohen: 113)

2) From the fact that logos is Greek for "word", Stuart Chase concluded in his book *The Tyranny of Words* that logic was mere manipulation of words.[6]

3) Atoms are colorless. Cats are made of atoms, so cats are colorless.[7]

4) A Boeing 747 can fly unaided across the ocean. A Boeing 747 has jet engines. Therefore, one of its jet engines can fly unaided across the ocean.[8]

5) Evidence of absence is absence of evidence.

6) There exists an extant document D in which no reference to an event E appears. It is known that the intention of the author of document D was to provide an exhaustive list of all the events in the class of events to which E belongs. Event E is assumed to be a type of event which the author of D would not have overlooked, had the event taken place. Therefore Event E did not take place.

7) Either you go to school and will get a good job or you will live in poverty for the rest of your life.

8) Kant: "I think that some people have psychic powers." Nietzsche: "What is your proof?" Kant: "No one has been able to prove that there is no condition of possibility that absolutely proves people do not have psychic powers."

9) Donald Trump says that whites are victims of police brutality just as often as black people… but honestly, would you believe a claim made by a racist?

10) Plato was a great philosopher and he had many lofty ideas but these notions are muddle-headed because he is known to have been a pederast.

11) If everyone goes shopping this will increase consumer spending and will help increase our country's GDP. Everyone needs to shop because the price of oil has dropped and the global economy will soon enter into a recession.

12) Euthanasia is a form of murder. We should resist any attempts to legalize it because the weakest and most vulnerable of our society will suffer if a law is enacted that legalizes this practice.

13) Socrates never existed. The only people who have ever written about him are Plato, Xenophon and Aristophanes. But they were all Sophists and wanted to deceive the people in order to create the myth of the philosopher-martyr.

14) There is a great meteorite heading towards the Earth. I have consulted my local astrologist

---

[6] Courtesy of Copi and Cohen, *Introduction to Logic, 10th edition.*

[7] Courtesy of Wilfred Sellars, *The Myth of the Given,* 1956.

[8] This exercise courtesy of *Public Speaking, Strategies for Success: Communication, Human communication,* 6th edition, by Dan Zarefsky.

and he has confirmed it. Of course if you do not think it is true you should prove it.

15) There will not be a referendum in Catalonia despite public opinion being in favor of it. The people have to obey the Constitution and the Constitution will only allow a national referendum on the autonomy of one of the regions of the country. Democracy is not the rule of the people by the people it is the submission of citizens to the rule of law and to the etat de droit.

16) God inspired the holy prophets. This inspiration made them write the holy Bible. The Bible is true because it is the word of God and its truth cannot be questioned.

17) Love is the natural law of all Creation. The purpose of all beings is to love each other and to live harmoniously. Even where natural beings apparently pursue their selfish goals and personal interests, the higher law of Love is the real explanation and source of their actions.

18) We can fully clone a human being by replacing and growing each one of her cells in a laboratory. However if we replace only half her cells she will still be the same person. As soon as we replace one extra cell she will become a different person.

19) I have been unlucky recently on the stock market. All the stocks I have bought have lost some of their value. However since the stock market as whole always increases its value in time, the next stock I buy will probably increase its net worth in the next month.

20) There is no progress in ethics. The Greeks used to have slaves and the Nazis used to kill Jews. This shows that what is right today was wrong yesterday and will be wrong tomorrow.

21) There are two different words to talk about Being and existence. Ontology discusses Being while metaphysics discusses existence. Therefore Being and existence are different topics. As soon as two different words exist this means that two different realities exist that are explained and talked about by these different words.

22) John A. Macdonald was a good administrator but his wife supported creationism. This means the whole family is opposed to natural science and to sources of evidence. This means Macdonald is not fit to govern and you should vote for Etienne Cartier for Prime Minister in the next federal election.

23) How do you know that people at CERN (note: This is an advanced particle physics laboratory located in Geneva, Switzerland and in France) will not create a black hole with their crazy experiments. They have to prove that their experiments will not destroy the earth or the United Nations should shut them down.

24) There was a big storm after that huge meteorite crashed in Russia in 2013. This means the meteorite must have caused the storm.

25) Obama does not really exist. You've only seen pictures of him on the Internet and on television. You have never met him in person. He is part of a government cover-up to install a world-dictatorship run by a puppet-figure.

26) Political parties should be able to use material aired on television in reports by journalists. After all the material in those reports does not belong to anyone, it is public so anyone should be able to use it. People who oppose this are anti-democratic and believe in censorship.

27) The Buddha was a great man but he should not be a role model for anyone because he had trouble controlling his appetite. In fact few people know this but he actually died of an indigestion.

2.4 NECESSARY & SUFFICIENT CONDITIONS & INDUCTIVE REASONING

We should not confuse sufficient conditions with sufficient causes when examining informal reasoning. Sufficient conditions are related to statements and thus to the logic of statements. Sufficient causes are related to reasoning about causality, which though related to inductive reasoning, is also independent of it and moves into the territory of the theory of knowledge or epistemology which we begin to study in the next chapter.

> **KEY NOTES**
>
> **SUFFICIENT CONDITIONS:** statements and the logic of statements.
> **SUFFICIENT CAUSES:** reasoning about causality and theories of knowledge

2.4.1 Necessary & Sufficient Causes

Causality is studied by the logic of induction which as previously stated is based on repetition of occurrence, enumeration to a certain extent but, more importantly, elimination followed by synthesis or rule and connection development. Causes are thus related to induction but conditions may be studied in a purely deductive fashion. Thus necessary and sufficient conditions may be studied as part of the deductive or analytical part of logic whereas necessary and sufficient causes presuppose some notion of sense-experience and some concept of necessary connection or synthesis. This is the heart of Hume's great critique of the habit of induction. For him there was no necessary connection lying within the heart of phenomena: it was a mere psychological introjection to suppose so. The human subject of knowledge was himself a spurious contraption. Hume was perhaps too strongly aware of the transitory aspect of knowledge. Nonetheless, synthesis and connection is possible. The fact that a self is writing these words is proof enough. We now proceed from possibility to necessity.

Necessary causes

We say A is a necessary cause of B if, whenever B occurs, this entails that A occurs concurrently and without fail. The fact that A occurs **does not** entail that B occurs.

Sufficient causes

We say A is a sufficient cause of B if, whenever A occurs, this entails that B occurs concurrently and without fail. The fact that *B* occurs **does not** entail that *A* occurs.

> **EXAMPLE**
> Lead in the blood stream is a necessary and sufficient cause for lead poisoning.
> Exposure to the rabies virus constitutes a necessary and sufficient cause for contracting rabies.
> Exposure to alcohol is a necessary but not sufficient cause for the development of alcoholism. Many people are exposed to alcohol and yet do not become alcoholics. There are other factors such as genetic and environmental markers that may explain the development of alcoholism.

Neccesary and sufficient conditions may be defined identically by replacing the word 'cause' with the word 'condition' in the above definitions for necessary and sufficient causes but they can be considered purely logical and mathematical notions. We consider some examples:

> "A number being divisible by 4 is a sufficient condition for its being even."
> "The fact that a figure A is a rectangle is a necessary but not sufficient condition for it to have four sides"

We see that these examples do not speak of causes in any way, but the logical structure is similar to that we used to define necessary and sufficient causes. To distinguish necessary *or* sufficient causes from necessary *and* sufficient causes, one must look at the nature of the specific examples that one is analyzing.

KEY NOTES

NECESSARY CAUSES: *A* is a necessary cause of *B* if, whenever *B* occurs this entails that *A* occurs concurrently and without fail.
SUFFICIENT CAUSES: *A* is a sufficient cause of B if, whenever *A* occurs this entails that *B* occurs concurrently and without fail.
CONTRIBUTORY CAUSES: *A* is called a contributory cause of *B* if the occurrence of *A* precedes the occurrence of *B* and if a change in *A* implies a change in *B*.

Contributory causes

A particular cause *A* is called a contributory cause of *B* if the occurrence of *A* precedes the occurrence of *B* and if changing *A* implies a change in *B*. All those objects or subjects upon which *A* acts will not experience *B* which may be considered the effect in this case.

> **EXAMPLE**
> An example of a contributory cause is that of smoking in the development of coronary heart disease. Smoking by itself is neither fully necessary nor sufficient to cause the development of coronary heart disease. Therefore smoking may be termed a contributory cause to the development of coronary heart disease.

Causality contrasted with conditionals

As explained above conditional statements are *not* the same as statements about causality. In the case of the examples with necessary and sufficient conditions there was no temporal sequence that needed to be respected (for example being divisible by 4 is not temporal in any way). In the case of causal statements the temporal sequence matter and the cause has to precede the effect temporally. However, the notion of material conditional does not possess this experiential structure to it and is in fact so general that the following statements may be trivially true even if apparently non-sensical:

> **EXAMPLE**
> If George Bush is president in 2014, then Toronto is is in Quebec.
> If Paul Catanu wrote War and Peace, then "any possible arbitrary statement".

Indicative Conditional

The ordinary *indicative* (as opposed to subjunctive conditional) has more experiential texture or logical structure (depending how one chooses to look at it) than the material conditional. It is closer to our common-sense intuitions of what we mean when we use an if-then statement.

However the sentence: *'If Homer did not write The Odyssey, then someone else did (or many people did)'* seems true even though there is no explicit causal relationship between the antecedent and the consequent in this presumed situation between Homer's not writing *The Odyssey* and someone else (or a group of people) writing it.

The ordinary *indicative* conditional has more structure than the *material* conditional. It is closer to a real statement in natural language than the material conditional. For instance, although the first example above is the closest, neither of the two examples seems true on an ordinary indicative reading. But the sentence: *'If Homer did not write The Odyssey, then someone else did (or many people did)'* intuitively seems to be true, even though there is no straightforward causal relation in this hypothetical situation between Homer's not writing *The Odyssey* and someone else's actually writing it.

2.4.2 Mill's Methods & Inductive Causal Arguments

Mill's methods are a way of individuating causes and identifying them. They presuppose that causality exists so that they do not face the problem of causal skepticism as expounded by Hume. Starting from the premise that causality is a fact, Mill searched for a way to organize and differentiate between different instances of cause. He did this at a symbolic level and then applied it to concrete examples. The topic is somewhat abstract but has many applications in industry. Mill's laws are at the bottom of what are called 'fishbone diagrams' in the world of engineering. The proper knowledge or epistemological issues related to Mill's laws are treated in Chapter 4 on empiricism. One may ask whether presupposing causality without proving its existence is warranted but these are not purely logical questions but require epistemological consideration.

Mill's Method of Direct Agreement

If two or more occurrences of the issue or phenomenon whose cause we are trying to discover or identify agree in only one common circumstance then this common circumstance is the cause or the effect of the phenomenon or issue under investigation. It is here that the notion of necessary cause intersects somewhat with the notion of necessary condition since we are interested in looking at the instance under investigation (which we treat as the effect or cause) and observing which properties or circumstances which we may take to be *necessary conditions* are present and which are absent, thus determining or identifying the cause of the effect under investigation. We may represent the **method of Agreement** symbolically as:

A B C D occur together with a b c d
A E F G occur together with a e f g
Therefore A is the cause, or the effect, of a.

EXAMPLE[9]
The endorsement of the Canadian Auto Worker's union is essential to getting elected in Oshawa. No one has ever been elected in Oshawa in Parliament without the support of the CAW.

The effect of which we are seeking the cause of is being elected into Parliament. The only property those who were elected in Oshawa have in common, is that they were supported by the CAW.

They may have other things in common, but we know that when they are not supported by the CAW they do not get elected. Thus we eliminate all other factors as being causally irrelevant as they are not necessary to the occurrence of the event. As such, we classify this under Mill's Method of Direct Agreement.

Mill's Method of Difference

If the issue or phenomenon whose cause we are trying to discover or identify, and if a circumstance in which the issue or phenomenon under investigation does not occur,

---
[9] The examples for Mill's Methods come from "The Power of Critical Thinking" (Lewis Vaughn, Oxford University Press, Second Canadian Edition).

have all things in common except for one, then the former circumstance (in which the phenomenon under investigation occurs) is either the *effect* or the *cause* or an indispensable part of the one thing (that both instance of the phenomenon and the circumstance in which the phenomenon was absent have in common).

We may represent the **method of Difference** symbolically as:

A B C D occur together with a b c d
B C D occur together with b c d
Therefore A is the cause, or the effect, or a part of the cause of a.

EXAMPLE
Forty-Five patients were admitted to Children's Hospital for pneumonia in December. They were all given standard treatment for pneumonia. After 5 days, 30 of them were well enough to go home. The other 15 however somehow acquired other infections and were not well enough to be released for two weeks. The only relevant factor common to these 15 is that they all stayed in the same ward (different from the ward that the other group stayed in). Therefore, something about staying in this ward is the cause of the prolonged illness.

This is a case of Mill's Method of Difference: Consider the group of 45 as an entity. The effect whose cause we are seeking is the fact that 15 of 45 did not get better (they in fact got over pneumonia so the treatment worked and we know this because the other 30 got better thanks to the treatment at least hypothetically). So why did the 15 not get better? We may look at this as a controlled experiment. We take 45 people and 30 stay in one ward and 15 stay in another ward but they are submitted to the same treatment.

Some people might argue that this is a case of agreement and difference or indirect agreement (as Mill called it), but it is not. People whose health improved differed in one circumstance only as compared with those whose health did not improve: they were in a different ward in the hospital.

In his *System of Logic (Ratiocinative and Inductive)*, Mill states that the Method of Agreement and Difference is applicable when substances (versus circumstances) are the variables, because these have a potentially infinite number of different properties—unlike circumstances which are external and may be counted).

2.4.3 Joint Method of Agreement & Difference

This method simply combines the methods of agreement and difference. Rather than enunciating in words we let the student study the symbolical relations which she will have to apply in the exercises. The example will also help the student develop intuition for this type of combination of the method

Symbolically, the **Joint Method of Agreement** and difference can be represented as:

> A B C occur together with a b c
> A D E occur together with a d e; and
> B C occur with b c
> ___
> Therefore A is the cause, or the effect, or a part of the cause of a.

EXAMPLE
Researchers report that an experimental vaccine persistently prevented women from becoming infected with a strain of the Human Papilloma Virus, HPV-16 that is associated with half of all cervical cancers. The study involved 2,392 women from 16 to 23 years of age. Participants were randomly assigned to receive three shots of either an HPV-16 vaccine or a placebo (a dummy substance). The study was double-blinded—that is, neither the investigators nor the patients knew who was getting the vaccine and who was being administered the placebo. Participants were followed for an average of 17 months after getting the third shot. Forty-one women developed HPV-16 infection. All forty-one women were in the placebo group. By comparison, no one who got all three vaccine shots developed HPV-16 infection. *(National Cancer Institute).*

This is a case of the Joint Method of Agreement and Difference. It is a controlled experiment and we can only have controlled experiments by employing the Method of Difference. So why isn't it a case by method of Difference alone? This is because we are testing a substance not a circumstance. The substance is the vaccine. So we are giving two substances: a placebo (a dummy substance) to a selected group and the real vaccine to the group.

This test could have been made even more refined by giving parts of the vaccine to different control groups. But then you would have to assume that the vaccine works and now you are attempting to improve upon it.

2.4.4 Method of Residue

This is typically the method of Sherlock Holmes. Eliminate all the possible effects of any given antecedents and whatever remains however improbable is the true cause of the effect you are seeking. All of Mill's methods except for concomitant variation base themselves on some form of elimination in order to achieve ampliative knowledge. However the method of residue is the most purely eliminative of Mill's methods.

Symbolically, the **Method of Residue** can be represented as:

> A B C occur together with a b c
> B is known to be the cause of b
> C is known to be the cause of c
> ___
> Therefore A is the cause or effect or a part of the cause of a.

> **EXAMPLE**
>
> Part of damage to the car was due to its impact with the truck. Another part is due to its impact with the tree. But some of the damage cannot be explained in this way. Investigators are examining the evidence closely to find out if there are no traces of explosives.

2.4.5 Method of Concomitance, Concomitant Variance or Correlation

This method is very intuitive for most students who have studied statistics. It is simply a statistical correlation. Once we have identified (through the method of necessary conditions) what aspect of the cause is connected to what aspect of the effect, we can seek a quantitative relation between the *cause* and the *effect*. This is the essence of the method of *concomitant variation*.

Symbolically, the **Method of Concomitant Variation** can be represented as: ('with' is taken as representing a shift):

> A B C occur together with a b c
> A and an increase/decrease in B C results in a and an increase/decrease in b c.
> Therefore A and a are causally connected

This method unlike the basic notion of *induction* is based on a *statistical correlation*. The more a certain quantity of cause occurs the more the quantity of the effect will be increased. Normally, induction is eliminative but in this case it is enumerative and quantitative.

> **EXAMPLE**
>
> *The more educated people are, the greater their income and health will be.*

This is also an example of correlation since income and health increase or decrease in direct proportion with the level of education.

> **KEY NOTES**
>
> **MILL'S METHODS** are a means of individuating causes and identifying them. There are four: Mill's method of:
> 1. Agreement,
> 2. Difference,
> 3. Agreement and Difference,
> 4. Concomitant Variation and Residue.

EXERCISES
INDUCTIVE REASONING AND INFORMAL LOGIC
I. ARGUMENTATION

For the arguments 1- 10 listed below:
- *Distinguish inductive from deductive arguments.*
- *Formalize or standardize each argument—that is, reduce them to their form or structure.*
- *For deductive arguments, ascertain whether the argument is valid and sound;*
- *For inductive arguments determine whether the argument is inductively strong or weak.*

1) And it must not be imagined that in this I commit the fallacy which logicians call arguing in a circle, for since experience renders the greater part of these effects very certain, the causes from which I deduce them do not so much serve to prove their existence as to explain them; on the other hand, the causes are explained by the effects. (Descartes, Discourse On Method, Part VI)

2) German criticism has, right up to its latest efforts, never quitted the realm of philosophy. Far from examining its general philosophic premises, the whole body of its inquiries has actually sprung from the soil of a definite philosophical system; that of Hegel. Not only in their answers but in their very questions there was a mystification. This dependence on Hegel is the reason why not one of these modern critics has even attempted a comprehensive criticism of the Hegelian system, however much each professes to have advanced beyond Hegel. (Karl Marx, The German Ideology, Part A).

3) More recent philosophy, as an epistemological scepticism, is, in a concealed or open manner, anti-Christian , although (and this is said for more refined ears) in no way anti-religious. Formerly, that is, people believed in "the soul," as they believed in grammar and the grammatical subject. They said "I" is the condition, "think" is the predicate and conditioned - thinking is an activity for which a subject must be thought of as cause. Now, people tried, with an admirable tenacity and trickery, to see whether they could get out of this net, whether perhaps the opposite might not be true: "think" as the condition, "I" the conditioned - thus "I" is only a synthesis which is itself created by thinking. (Friedrich Nietzsche, Beyond Good And Evil, Aphorism 54)

4) Self-indulgence is more like a voluntary state than cowardice. For the former is actuated by pleasure, the latter by pain, of which the one is to be chosen and the other to be avoided; and pain upsets and destroys the nature of the person who feels it, while pleasure does nothing of the sort. (Aristotle, The Nicomachean Ethics, III.12)

5) It is in the empiricist development, as we know, that the new psychology, which was required as a correlate to pure natural science when the latter was separated off, is brought to its first concrete execution. Thus it is concerned with investigations of introspective psychology in the field of the soul, which has now been separated from the body, as well as with physiological and psychophysical explanations. On the other hand, this psychology is of service to a theory of knowledge which, compared with the Cartesian one, is completely new and very differently worked out. In Locke's great work this is the actual intent from the start. It offers itself as a new attempt to accomplish precisely what Descartes's Meditations intended to accomplish: an epistemological grounding of the objectivity of the objective sciences. (Edmund Husserl, The Crisis of the European Sciences, 1937, Section 22)

6) This simple triad of desire-means-end is excluded by the increasing multiplicity and complexity of higher life. Now the complex of means is itself turned into a multiplicity in which the most important means are constituted by means and these by others. So in the practical life of our mature cultures, our pursuits take on the character of chains, the coils of which cannot be grasped in a single vision. (Georg Simmel, Schopenhauer and Nietzsche, Chapter 1).

7) The problem of perception presents itself to theoretical philosophy under a twofold aspect: it may be considered from a psychological and from an epistemological standpoint. Throughout the history of philosophy, the two have been in constant conflict; but the more sharply the oppositions develop, the more evident it seems that here precisely are the two poles around which the whole problem of perception must necessarily move. (Ernst Cassirer, The Philosophy of Symbolic Forms, Volume 3: The Phenomenology of Knowledge, Part I, Chapter 2).

II. Statistical Syllogism

Are the following statistical syllogisms inductively cogent (i.e. strong) or weak? Why?

(1) 93% of freshmen at Concordia are from Quebec.
Anna is a freshman at Concordia.
Anna is from Quebec.

(2) Very few employees at the Nortel Networks are from Ontario.
Paul is an employee of Nortel Networks.
Paul is not from Ontario.

(3) Approximately 91% of professional philosophers are men.
Bettina Sawyer, is a professional philosopher.
Therefore Bettina Sawyer is a man.

(4) Most of what R. Feynman has to say about the universe at the time of the Big Bang is correct.
R. Feynman says the universe was more highly disordered at the time of the Big Bang than it is today.
The universe was more highly disordered at the time of the Big Bang than it is today.

III. Analogical Induction

Analyze the following inductive analogies in terms of :

(a) The number of properties or features shared by the things being compared.
(b) The relevance of the known similar properties or characteristics to the properties or characteristics inferred through the similarity in the conclusion
(c) The number and multiplicity of examples examined through the alleged or perceived analogy.

A. The universe is a living organism. It comprises processes of exchange, transportation, regulation, and equilibrium. It actuates and changes just like a living organism. Its parts are coordinated so that the part does not destroy the whole and the whole fully encompasses the part. Furthermore, like an organism, the universe can birth smaller sub-worlds through the process of black holes and of mini Big Bangs. One is forced to conclude that the universe possesses all the properties of a living organism and thus is alive. (Argument adapted and paraphrased from Plato's Timaeus).

B. Democracy possesses many decision-making processes that are similar to that of a family. Parents often discuss with their children what they want to do and then decide what the proper course is for action. Similarly, in democracies, there are large consultation processes such as focus groups and town hall meetings where leaders listen to the people. Like in families, these leaders then discuss among each other, just like a mother and father do, and come to the right decision as to what course the country should be set upon.

C. The universe is extremely complex and harmoniously organized. Like a clock every wheel and cog has its proper role and place. There is a perfection in design and in symmetry so that this can only be explained through a preter-human intelligence. The clock must possess a clock-maker and the clock-maker of our universe is none other than our loving and benevolent God, our Lord. (Argument adapted and paraphrased from William Paley).

D. A beehive is like humanity on smaller scale. There is division of labor, there is hierarchy, there are historical cycles when the queen mates and creates offspring and a new generation of bees appears. Bees, like humans, are highly intelligent and organized. Thus it is no wonder that Tolstoy compared the totality of humanity to a gigantic beehive in his great historical novel War and Peace.

E. Human beings are a lot like apes. They are gregarious and can feel pain. They have alpha-males and strong females which dominate certain groups. Furthermore the study of apes has shown that they possess an elementary communication system and can identify certain basic concepts. There is no doubt that apes and humans are related in a biological evolutionary sense. Therefore we should treat apes with compassion just as we treat human beings compassionately whenever possible.

IV. Necessary and Sufficient Conditions.

Determine whether the following statements are true or false and explain why:

1. Being a circle is sufficient for having an infinite number of sides.
2. Being divisible by 8 is not sufficient for being an even number.
3. Hating someone is not sufficient for being hated. A person who hates someone might not be hated by anyone perhaps because there are only good people in the world.
4. Having no sides is sufficient for being a circle.
5. Being selfish is both necessary and sufficient for being a great genius.
6. Being stupid is necessary for being selfless.
7. Being talented is sufficient for being famous.
8. Being greater than 0 is sufficient for being a positive number.
9. Being a rational number is necessary for being a real number.
10. Doing your duty is sufficient for being a good person.
11. The consequences of one's actions are sufficient for having one convicted.
12. If you can plan things and engage in projects it is sufficient to be considered fit for trial.
13. Being a transcendental number is sufficient for being a complex number.
14. Being a complex number is necessary for being a transcendental number.
15. Being either e or π is sufficient for being a transcendental number.
16. Being a number that cannot be expressed as a solution to an algebraic equation is necessary and sufficient for being a complex number.

V. Discuss how these conditions are related & explain your answers:

    a) not being poor, being rich
    b) being an even number, being divisible by 2
    c) being an intelligent student, being the most intelligent student
    d) having ten dollars, having more than five dollars
    e) giving money to another person in exchange for a favour, corruption
    f) taking place on a weekday, not being held on Saturday

VI. Mill's Methods For Classifying Inductive Causal Arguments

Classify these arguments according to Mill's classification of inductive causal arguments.

A) An ounce of gold has hit $1000 Canadian on the world market only eight times in the last 30 years. Sometimes there were wars; sometimes there weren't. Sometimes the price of oil went up; sometimes it did not. But the price of gold always went up when the Global market went into a recession.

B) Simon was sad all week but then his mood improved remarkably. He started laughing a lot and went out to see his friends during the rest of the week. He was applying to law school and I think he got some good news this week with respect to his application.

C) We did a blind test with thirty customers. We gave them Coke and Pepsi in different cups. 80% of our customers preferred Pepsi without knowing what they were drinking. The only cause can be that Pepsi tastes better than Coke.

D) The reason there had been so many terrrorist attacks in the Austro-Hungarian empire is that the Slav minority and its rights had been unfairly oppressed. Every time a large number of Slavs had been killed, persecuted or unfairly jailed there had occurred a terrorist attack in the Austro-Hungarian Empire. The last attack started the First World War.

E) The risk of diabetes is related to the amount of blood sugar. The higher the blood sugar the higher the risk of diabetes. There is a direct connection between the level of blood sugar and the risk of diabetes.

F) We tested different ant exterminators over the years. They each had different methods of protecting the apartments that needed to get rid of ants; but over the years the best exterminators all used boric acid as part of their exterminating products.

LOGICAL CONNECTIVES & OPERATORS

OPERATOR	USAGE	SYMBOL
1. negation	not	¬
2. conjunction	and	∧
3. disjunction	or	∨
4. implication	if	→
5. bi-implication	if and only if	⇔ or ↔

TRUTH TABLES

TRUTH VALUES					
p	q	p∧q	p∨q	p→q	p⇔q
T	T	T	T	T	T
T	F	F	T	F	F
F	T	F	T	T	F
F	F	F	F	T	T

REPLACEMENT RULES

NAME	APPLICATION
1. De Morgan's Laws:	(1) ¬(p ∧ q) ⇔ ¬p ∨ ¬q ; (2) ¬(p ∨ q) ⇔ ¬p ∧ ¬q
2. Commutativity:	(1) (p ∨ q) ⇔ (q ∨ p); (2) (p ∧ q) ⇔ (q ∧ p)
3. Associativity:	(1) (p ∨ q) ∨ r ⇔ p ∨ (q ∨ r); (2) (p ∧ q) ∧ r ⇔ p ∧ (q ∧ r)
4. Material Implication:	(p → q) ⇔ (¬p ∧ q)
5. Double Negation:	¬¬p ⇔ p
6. Transposition:	(p → q) ⇔ (¬q → ¬p)
7. Distribution:	(1) [p ∧ (q ∨ r)] ⇔ [(p ∧ q) ∨ (p ∧ r)]; (2) [p ∨ (q ∧ r)] ⇔ [(p ∨ q) ∧ (p ∨ r)]
8.1 Idempotency of disjunction:	(p ∨ p) ⇔ p
8.2 Idempotency of conjunction:	(p ∧ p) ⇔ p
9. Material Equivalence:	p ⇔ q
10. Exportation:	(p ∧ q) → r ⇔ p → (q → r)

DIFFERENT THEORIES OF KNOWLEDGE & WORLDVIEWS

RATIONALISM TKO	EMPIRICISM TKO	IDEALISM WV	PRAGMATISM WV
Emphasis on Mathematics & Knowledge	More scientific or based on sense-data	More religious or based on ancient religious ideals	Emphasis on practical effects of knowledge and belief
Access to knowledge through reason and intuition (deduction) Belief in innate ideas and innate knowledge	Access to knowledge through sense experience – e.g. observation (induction)	Access to knowledge through the senses	Access to knowledge through Mind (Peirce) and through sense-data and varieties (William James)
All we know are concepts – senses can be faulty (e.g. math, definitions)	All we know are things that can be experienced through the senses (e.g. : (I see 20 students) Maxim: There is nothing in the intellect that was not previously in the senses	All we know are ideas (concepts, sensations…) Plato's & Plotinus's idealism • Kant's transcendental idealism • Hegel, Bradley's and Raddhakrishnan's absolute idealism	Knowledge as experience or as learnable only through experience; Forms of experience: Religious, Scientific, Artistic & Political-Social experience
These truths exist independently of me, though I do give them form through my reason and intellect • Kant's critical rationalism • Descartes' cogito • Spinoza's substance • Leibniz' monad	*The cause of these sense experiences exists independently of me and their existence may not be provable at all* (Hume's skepticism) *The representation theory of knowledge* (Locke: Primary and Secondary properties of objects)	*All that exists is ideas and Mind, dependent on thinker. The universe is one great Mind that processes forward through Firstness, Secondness and Thirdness* • Peirce's objective Idealism Berkeley: *God is the cause or source of my ideas*	*The truth exists in a community as much as in the individual* (Royce's beloved and loyal community) *The truth is not predominantly theoretical but grounded in practicity and praxis* Peirce called the movement pragmaticism from the Greek *pragmata* or practical things and objects.

✓ KEY CONCEPTS & DEFINITIONS - RATIONALISM

PEOPLE

PARMENIDES, SOCRATES, DESCARTES, SPINOZA, LEIBNIZ

RATIONALISM is "any view appealing to reason as a source of knowledge or justification".
RATIONALISM is "a theory of knowledge in which the criterion of truth is not sensory, but intellectual and deductive

PEOPLE	IDEAS
PARMENIDES	Being as the source of reason and non-contradiction
SOCRATES	Quest for Definition and Moral Rationalism
DESCARTES	The Importance of Method; Intuition-deduction thesis; cogito
SPINOZA	God or Nature; Substance, modes, attributes; Conatus; Amor Intellectualis Deus; Sub Specie Aeternitatis
LEIBNIZ	Theodicy and Optimism; The Algebra of Thought, Monadology, The Best of All Possible Worlds

CHAPTER 3
THEORIES OF KNOWLEDGE: *RATIONALISM*

The theory of knowledge is a branch of philosophy called epistemology. The word 'epistemology' comes to us via the Ancient Greek *episteme* (knowledge) and *logos* (rational discourse or speech, which also happens to be the root word for logic). If it were not circular[1] one could define epistemology as "knowledge about knowledge". Epistemology or the theory of knowledge studies notions and theories of truth. It attempts to show what a true statement is and how we can be certain of its truth. In this book, we study two theories of knowledge, rationalism and empiricism and two worldviews, idealism and pragmatism.

Rationalism is "any view appealing to reason as a source of knowledge or justification"[2]. Rationalism is "theory of knowledge in which the criterion of the truth is not sensory, but intellectual and deductive"[3]. Presently, rationalism covers a broad range of positions that apply this point with more or less flexibility. A moderate rationalist will claim "that reason has precedence over other ways of acquiring knowledge" while the radical rationalist claims that reason is "the unique path to knowledge".[4]

---

[1] We saw in the section on Formal and Informal Fallacies in Chapter 2, that a circular argument is a redundancy from the logical point of view. In hermeneutics or interpretation theory, circular reasoning is not always undesirable or avoidable. Heidegger famously speaks of the hermeneutical circle and of its role in human knowledge and understanding.

[2] Lacey, A Dictionary of Philosophy, 1st edition, Routledge and Kegan Paul, 1976. Routledge, London, UK, 1996, p. 286. Print.

[3] Bourke, "Rationalism", in Runes, *Dictionary of Philosophy*, Littlefield, Adams, and Company, Totowa, NJ, 1962, p. 263. Print.

[4] *Audi, Robert, The Cambridge Dictionary of Philosophy*, Cambridge University Press, Cambridge, UK, 1995. p.771. Print.

> **KEY NOTES**
>
> **RATIONALISM** is
> - any view appealing to reason as a source of knowledge or justification.
> - a theory of knowledge in which the criterion of the truth is not sensory, but intellectual and deductive

We associate Rationalism with a specific period in the history of philosophy[5] during which thinkers like Descartes, Spinoza and Leibniz dominated the field. However, rationalism also corresponds to a specific doctrine of thought that we may say occurred with the beginning of Greco-Roman philosophy.

3.1 PARMENIDES

Parmenides (500-540 BCE) was an ancient Greek philosopher born in Elea, a Greek city on the southern coast of *Magna Graecia*. Many Western historians believe that Parmenides knew the teachings of Heraclitus. There is a 200 line proem (poetic prelude) that has been handed down to us from Parmenides that hints at this. Parmenides, as opposed to Heraclitus, who observed the evolution of nature in order to develop his theory of Becoming and the strife of opposites, does not trust the senses. According to Parmenides' maxims, one must put all one's faith in reason.

Parmenides taught that the only convincing evidence was that of Being. He stated: "of what is, one can only say that it is, of what isn't, only that it isn't. Being is, it is one, unmoved, circular and infinite. It is the only thing that may be known."[6]

The world of the senses is unknowable because it is subject to perpetual change as Parmenides seems to grant to Heraclitus. But the contradictions of the sublunar world (the material world as opposed to the world of the heavens that the Greeks considered to be perfect) does not reproduce itself in the world of Being. Parmenides, with his disciple Zeno, establishes the basis of a logical, rational thought by affirming that *what is said and enunciated must be free of contradiction in order to be true and to be (or to exist) in an absolute sense of the word*. This was a critical step in the history of knowledge and logic in the

---

[5] The history of philosophy is different from the history of political events. It is made up of the different schools of philosophy or lone philosophers who defended different opinions. In the specific context of this history rationalism has a very specific meaning and it refers to philosophers from the European 17th century known as the Continental rationalists.

[6] Kirk, Raven and Schofield, *The Presocratic Philosophers*, Cambridge University Press: New York, 1957, fragments 293 and 294. Print.

Western world. Without insisting on the metaphysically immutable and unchangeable, one would not have the grounds for developing the logical concept of non-contradiction (which is important for the notions of logical consistency and coherence), which we saw in Chapter 1 of this book when we studied formal logic.

> **QUOTE**
>
> *"...what is said and enunciated must be free of contradiction in order to be true and to be (or to exist) in an absolute sense of the word."*
>
> — **Parmenides, via Zeno**

3.2 SOCRATES & RATIONALISM

Socrates is a real, historical figure; but because of the magnitude of his impact on the world, he has become greater than life. Many myths have been built around the figure of Socrates. These are the so-called Socratic legends. So much of myth and legend has been associated with the name and the figure of Socrates, that today, we cannot know with certainty how Socrates lived and if all the deeds and words attributed to him were truly his.

It is important to stress that Socrates never wrote an actual word himself. We know of Socrates from Plato and Xenophon, mainly. Socrates was not interested in disseminating his ideas and in acquiring the fame that might be associated with this dissemination.

The picture we have of Socrates is that of a man who wore no sandals and went about bare-foot in the Athenian market. This representation of Socrates shows us that Socrates was not interested in wealth and worldly matters: he was interested only in the pursuit of truth. In this way, Socrates looks like the classic sage of Antiquity: without responsibilities and attachments, he is free to wander about, challenging people by asking them whether they are leading a virtuous life.

Socrates places the moral question at the center of philosophical enquiry. What is the good life? What does it mean to live well? What does it mean to do the right thing in any circumstance? What does it mean to care for one's soul? What is virtue and can it be taught? Socrates brought about a moral revolution in philosophy. He believed that before one can understand the world, one must understand oneself, and that the only way to accomplish this was through rational thought. In order to understand what this means, one needs first to appreciate the Ancient Greek understanding of the world.

This Ancient Greek worldview is based on self-mastery and on the *logos* (in this context, signifies rational discourse, measured speech and even science). The *logos* of Socrates and Plato is opposed to the *muthos*[7] of the literary figures of Homer and Hesiod but also to the object of philosophy proposed by naturalist figures like Parmenides, Heraclitus, Anaximander and Empedocles who were interested in understanding and describing *phusis*[8] and not human nature.

Socrates is a crucial figure of the history of thought not just in ethics but in the history of Western knowledge because he shifted the interest from natural philosophy which the Presocratic philosophers like Anaxagoras, Anaximander, Heraclitus and Parmenides focused on (to name only the most important Pre-Socratics). Socrates brought about a moral revolution, but in so doing he challenged the authorities of his society and asked for rational grounds, reasons or causes (the Greeks were not necessarily clear on the difference between these two concepts) in philosophy.[9] In this way, Socrates' rational approach to philosophy and ethics greatly contributed to the development of knowledge.

3.3 DESCARTES & RATIONALISM

Descartes reacted not only to Scholasticism, but also to the Renaissance occultism and irrationalism of thinkers like Giordano Bruno and Pico of Mirandola. At the same time Descartes was beginning to philosophize, the sciences were developing at a very fast and dynamic pace. Physics, biology, agriculture were all challenging the traditional, religious way of looking at the world. Faced with this decline of the older medieval worldview, Descartes was pressed to come up with a new picture of the world that would account for the novelty and dynamism of science.

---

[7] Muthos is the Greek word for myth. This dichotomy between the muthos and the logos characterizes Greek culture and civilization to a great extent. In its beginnings Greece was under the sway of the muthos but as it progressed into the classical age which was dominated by Athens and its democratic system (the Attical age) the muthos gave way to the rational thought of logos begun by Socrates and perfected by Plato, Aristotle and the Stoics.

[8] Phusis means nature in ancient Greek. The philosophers who studied it: Anaximander, Anaxagoras, Parmenides, Zeno, Heraclitus, Xenophon, Empedocles and others (the list is not exhaustive) were called the Phusikoi by Aristotle.

[9] It is not entirely correct to see in Socrates an advocate for civil disobedience though this complex historical character can be read in this way as well. In order to understand the importance and even worship that Socrates practiced, one should study the Platonic dialogue of the Crito very attentively. There the Laws come alive in a wonderful Platonic allegory and Socrates debates them directly, though always with great respect and moderate restraint.

The Importance of Method

Descartes was obsessed by the problem of method. He writes in his *Discourse on Method*:

> "The first [principle, P.C.] was never to accept anything for true which I did not clearly know to be such; that is to say, carefully to avoid precipitancy and prejudice, and to comprise nothing more in my judgement than what was presented to my mind so clearly and distinctly as to exclude all ground of doubt.
>
> The second, to divide each of the difficulties under examination into as many parts as possible, and as might be necessary for its adequate solution.
>
> The third, to conduct my thoughts in such order that, by commencing with objects the simplest and easiest to know, I might ascend by little and little, and, as it were, step by step, to the knowledge of the more complex; assigning in thought a certain order even to those objects which in their own nature do not stand in a relation of antecedence and sequence.
>
> And the last, in every case to make enumerations so complete, and reviews so general, that I might be assured that nothing was omitted." (Discourse On Method, Part 2)

Descartes had had many teachers and had listened to many lecturers but wanted to know how one might possibly start philosophy on a firm basis. He was looking for what he called a *fundamentum inconcussum*, an unbreakable foundation for his philosophical system. Descartes wanted to break with Medieval philosophy whose main concern was the discourse on God, that is, theology.

He sought to establish philosophy on a firm principle. Before he could do so, he needed to find a method to set science on a firm ground. In 1637, he published the *Discourse on Method*, where he established certain principles for proceeding in the sciences. One of these principles is that of having clear and distinct ideas. From clear and distinct ideas, Descartes thought he could proceed methodically to certainty about statements of knowledge and of science.

Descartes is considered the founder of modern rationalism because he shifted emphasis from the scholastic obsession with the proofs of God's existence onto the human subject of knowledge. Additionally his treatise the *Discourse on Method* helped to systematize the scientific method and its way of attaining true and certain results.

Descartes' theory of knowledge is made up of some important theses. Descartes was very interested in geometry and developed mathematical and algebraic geometry, known as Cartesian geometry having been named in his honor. For Descartes, knowledge is certain because it possesses a deductive and intuitive structure.

The senses may deceive us but they cannot deceive us about mathematical knowledge and about introspection. Starting from what is called the position of methodological skepticism, Descartes developed a hyperbolic doubt through which he questioned the truth of each and every assertion which he receives. This is a sort of dark room experiment where everything is taken off the table of knowledge and knowledge is rebuilt starting from fresh foundations.

It is important to note the distinction between methodological doubt and existential doubt, in which we may question the meaning of life and fall into despair. Methodological doubt is a stance in the theory of knowledge and foundations of science where we assume nothing to be true; i.e., we doubt its truth until we can reconstruct from the base or foundation and prove its truth. This methodological doubt is tied to the thesis of foundationalism about knowledge which was challenged in the 20th century by philosophers like Heidegger, Quine and Sellars. These philosophers assumed that we cannot start from scratch and build science up from the bottom. Rather, there are pre-ontological or pre-epistemological truths that always already exist or are given and which we can only focus on or thematize partially but not reconstruct from nothing.

Tied into this method is the thesis also held by Descartes that we possess innate ideas or innate knowledge. Unlike the empiricists who believe we come into the world as blank slates, Descartes argued that we were born with certain innate categories of the understanding or of the intellect. These innate ideas or notions allow us to attain knowledge that is certain and infallible, unlike the knowledge that issues from the senses (which may deceive us).

> **KEY NOTES**
>
> **DESCARTES: KEY CONCEPTS AND DEFINITIONS**
> - Method as fundamental for knowledge.
> - Intuition/Deduction thesis: All knowledge is both deductive and intuitive.
> - The *Cogito*: The foundation for knowledge is the ego or the thinking thing (*res cogitans*).
> - Existence of innate ideas and innate knowledge.

Intuition-deduction thesis

In the *Regulae*,[10] Descartes develops further his method by introducing the method of deduction and intuition. He writes:

> "On pourroit peut-être se demander pourquoi à l'intuition nous ajoutons cette autre manière de connoitre par déduction, c'est-à-dire par l'opération, qui d'une chose dont nous avons la connoissance certaine, tire des conséquences qui s'en déduisent nécessairement. Mais

---
[10] This is the title of a work by Descartes published originally as *Regulae ad directionem ingenii* and usually translated as *Rules for the Direction of the Mind*. The book was not published during Descartes' lifetime.

> *nous avons dû admettre ce nouveau mode ; car il est un grand nombre de choses qui, sans être évidentes par elles-mêmes, portent cependant le caractère de la certitude, pourvu qu'elles soient déduites de principes vrais et incontestés par un mouvement continuel et non interrompu de la pensée, avec une intuition distincte de chaque chose ; tout de même que nous savons que le dernier anneau d'une longue chaîne tient au premier, encore que nous ne puissions embrasser d'un coup d'œil les anneaux intermédiaires, pourvu qu'après les avoir parcourus successivement nous nous rappelions que, depuis le premier jusqu'au dernier, tous se tiennent entre eux. Aussi distinguons-nous l'intuition de la déduction, en ce que dans l'une on conçoit une certaine marche ou succession, tandis qu'il n'en est pas ainsi dans l'autre, et en outre que la déduction n'a pas besoin d'une évidence présente comme l'intuition, mais qu'elle emprunte en quelque sorte toute sa certitude de la mémoire ; d'où il suit que l'on peut dire que les premières propositions, dérivées immédiatement des principes, peuvent être, suivant la manière de les considérer, connues tantôt par intuition, tantôt par déduction ; tandis que les principes eux-mêmes ne sont connus que par intuition, et les conséquences éloignées que par déduction."*
>
> (Rules For the Direction Of The Mind, Rule 3)

This passage from the Rules for the Direction of the Mind shows a certain Cartesian inconsistency in the fact that intuition and deduction are "put together" in a seamless way. Kant is guilty of this fault also, to a certain extent. Deduction possesses a transitional, process aspect. It is an internal connection from premises to a conclusion; but what is important is how one transitions from the premises to the conclusion in order to preserve the truth from the premises to the conclusion (especially in the notion of deductive validity). Intuition on the other side is a complete and self-enclosed whole, it is not a process (though one rightly speaks of intuiting something as a form of introspection or absorption within an intuitive whole) but rather is full and developed at any given moment. Another problem with Descartes' understanding of deduction (which will be later criticized by Charles Peirce and others) which comes out of this citation is that for the philosopher deduction is psychological (because related to memory). But deduction is not psychological (this is why deduction systems which are independent of memory may be built) but veridical and certain because it is formal.

Descartes' belief in this method is linked to the fact that he was a student of geometry. In geometry unlike in number theory and logic, intuition plays a paramount role.[11] Shapes and spaces are given to our intuition which we then attempt to express rigorously in statements, arguments and theorems which capture the truth of the geometric figures. But geometry is a science that presupposes some axioms. This was known to the great Greek geometer Euclid. Descartes was familiar with Euclid and the Greek philosophers, who favored the deductive form of argument. From intuition, Descartes thought he could build syllogisms

---
11 It is not true, in general, that intuition plays no role in logic. In fact, Kurt Gödel's metamathematical and logical theses allow for categorical or mathematical intuition to play a fundamental role in the development of logical proofs and theorems.

(studied in Chapter 1 of this book). But although syllogisms may capture the truth of geometry, it is less clear that they can capture the truth of the world of sense-perception and appearances whose reality cannot be formalized into theorems and arguments because it is radically particular and individual. We will see in Chapter 4 that Francis Bacon raises many objections to the deductive method because of this very inability to capture the essentially formless aspect of matter and its correlate nature.

The importance of the *cogito*

The central point for which Descartes is known is his argument of the *cogito* (I think). In the book called the *Meditations on First Philosophy*, Descartes attempts to find the foundation for science. As outlined above, he employs his method of hyperbolic doubt. Descartes engages in the specific thought experiment outlined in the next citation:

> "But as often as this preconceived opinion of the sovereign power of a God presents itself to my mind, I am constrained to admit that it is easy for him, if he wishes it, to cause me to err even in matters where I think I possess the highest evidence; and, on the other hand, as often as I direct my attention to things which I think I apprehend with great clearness, I am so persuaded of their truth that I naturally break out into expressions such as these: Deceive me who may, no one will yet ever be able to bring it about that I am not, so long as I shall be conscious that I am, or at any future time cause it to be true that I have never been, it being now true that I am, or make two and three more or less than five, in supposing which, and other like absurdities, I discover a manifest contradiction. And in truth, as I have no ground for believing that Deity is deceitful, and as, indeed, I have not even considered the reasons by which the existence of a Deity of any kind is established, the ground of doubt that rests only on this supposition is very slight, and, so to speak, metaphysical. But, that I may be able wholly to remove it, I must inquire whether there is a God, as soon as an opportunity of doing so shall present itself; and if I find that there is a God, I must examine likewise whether he can be a deceiver; for, without the knowledge of these two truths, I do not see that I can ever be certain of anything. And that I may be enabled to examine this without interrupting the order of meditation I have proposed to myself (which is, to pass by degrees from the notions that I shall find first in my mind to those I shall afterward discover in it), it is necessary at this stage to divide all my thoughts into certain classes, and to consider in which of these classes truth and error are, strictly speaking, to be found."

(Meditations On First Philosophy, Third Meditation)

At the end of his reflections, Descartes concludes that the only thing he cannot fundamentally doubt is the fact of his own thinking and its active existence. The fact that he is involved in an act of reflexion and thinking guarantees that something is thinking and that this something exists. He will baptize his ego a thinking thing (*res cogitans*) and will contrast it with extended substances which occupy real physical space.

It is through these reflections that Descartes sets the basis for what is known as the mind-body problem, for here he begins to think that his mind is of a radically different substance than the body. He believed for instance, that the mind (or soul as also referred to it) was situated in the pineal gland of the brain. Though science has disproved this theory, many still believe in the existence of a fundamental dualism between mind and body. However, Descartes has not established the necessary and certain existence of his ego. He has established the existence of himself and his own possible self-identity as a thinking process or synthesis.

3.4 SPINOZA : KNOWLEDGE OF THE NECESSITY OF GOD & THE WORLD

Descartes had a tremendous influence on his contempararies. One such contemporary who read Descartes and was impressed by his work was the Dutch philosopher Spinoza. Spinoza, who was also an avid truth-seeker, survived an attempt on his life by Jewish orthodox radicals (though he was a Jew himself) because of his views on Ancient Testament Scripture and how it should be correctly interpreted from a modern perspective.

Spinoza's two main works are the *Tractatus Theologico- Philosophicus* and *The Ethics*, which was published posthumously.[12] We will deal with the *Ethics* shortly. In that work Spinoza outlines his powerful metaphysical and philosophical vision. In the *Tractatus*, Spinoza argues that Scripture and miracles cannot be understood literally. He also argues that religion, theology and philosophy should be carefully distinguished and kept separate when interpreting Scripture. Furthermore and a bit more controversially, though history would vindicate this position to a certain extent, Spinoza argues that absolute sovereignty or almost absolute sovereignty should be granted to the civil government over religious clergy and institutions. Spinoza was willing to make allowances for a state religion that would cement civic sentiment but believed that government and its representatives should be fundamentally secular.

Because of his early difficult experiences with members of his own religious community and the general atmosphere of religious intolerance at the time in Europe—despite Holland being one of the most advanced and tolerant societies in Europe during the 17th century—Spinoza decided to publish his greatest work, *The Ethics*, posthumously.

---
12 Posthumously means after the death of the author.

God or Nature (*Deus sive Natura*)

God or Nature, is one of Spinoza's key distinctions or mottoes in *The Ethics*. For Spinoza, philosophers have distinguished God and Nature for too long. The *sive* in his expression is an identifying and inclusive 'or'. For Spinoza, there is no principled difference between God and nature.

The influences on Spinoza's philosophy are numerous. They range from Philo of Alexandria,[13] Maimonides,[14] Al-Ghazzali[15] and many others. But the philosopher that Spinoza seems to be the most critical of is Philo. Philo of Alexandria was the first philosopher to have established a connection between Holy Scripture and Greek philosophy. He did this by developing the notion of a difference between the concepts of essence and existence. Philo distinguished between the existence of God, which could be demonstrated, and the nature or essence of God which humans are not able to cognize. Philo also introduces the notion of the *Logos* (God's image). He claims that the sensible universe is the image of the *Logos*, that is "the archetypal model, the idea of ideas".[16] Because of this, because God can only be perceived negatively and not through our senses, we can intuit God's existence, though we cannot fathom his essence.

Philo thus makes a distinction between the existence and essence of God and the existence and essence of the world. This would influence all of later Christian philosophy from the Low Middle Ages (Augustine) to the High Middle Ages (Thomas). It is only with Spinoza that the essence and existence of God and the world of nature are identified. This marks in many ways the beginning of the challenge to God's exceptional and unknowable metaphysical status. For from Spinoza's thesis that God is the world or that God is immanent in the world and the world internal to God, it is only a step to the belief that God and the world are both contingent and unnecessary. This may have led Nietzsche to claim much later that "God is dead".

An important distinction in Spinoza's philosophical system is that between *natura naturata* and *natura naturans*. The former may be looked at as a form intuition whereas the latter may be looked at as a form of deductive process:

> "By *Natura naturans* we must understand what is in itself and is conceived through itself, or such attributes of substance as express an eternal and infinite essence,

---

13 Philo of Alexandria (20 BCE – c. 50 CE) a Hellenistic Jewish philosopher who lived in Alexandria, was also called Philo Judaeus. It is important to note, that Alexandria in Egypt, was under Roman dominion in Philo's time. Philo wrote in Ancient Greek.
14 Mosheh ben Maimon, known as Maimonides, was a Spanish Jewish philosopher, astronomer and physician in the Middle Ages.
15 Abū-āmid Muhammad ibn Muhammad al-Ghazālī (around 1058–1111) was a Muslim theologian, jurist, philosopher, and mystic of Iranian descent. His most famous work is *The Incoherence of the Philosophers*.
16 Philo, *On Creation*, (De Opificio Mundi), 25.

that is ... God, insofar as he is considered as a free cause. But by *Natura naturata* I understand whatever follows from the necessity of God's nature, or from God's attributes, that is, all the modes of God's attributes insofar as they are considered as things which are in God, and can neither be nor be conceived without God."[17]

There is a dualism here despite Spinoza's claim that both these natures are essentially one and identical. Nature is process and substance, but the dynamism of process cannot always be arrested and hypostatized[18] in the stasis[19] of unitary substance.

> **KEY NOTES**
>
> **SPINOZA: KEY CONCEPTS AND DEFINITIONS**
> - God or Nature: Both God and the world are necessary, not contingent.
> - Substance metaphysics: Everything in the world is either a mode or an attribute of divine Substance.
> - *Sub specie aeternitatis*: Rational mind (*mens*) is eternal, the human body is perishable.

Traditionally the metaphysics of Plato and of Aristotle has made God necessary and Nature or the world contingent. For Spinoza this is wrong. He reasons as follows: Any event B in nature follows from a preceeding event A. But if B follows from A in a contingent manner and all events in nature are the result of the will of God, then this implies that God may have willed two different things at any given moment in time. This then implies that God must have had two different wills at a given moment in time. Furthermore since God only possesses a single will this means that there would have been two Gods possessing two (different) wills at a given moment in time so that B could have followed from A as well as a different event B according to God's second will or according to the will of a second God. This shows that God and his will are not purely necessary. Spinoza believes he has derived a contradiction and hence he believes that he has proved that the thesis that the world is contingent is false. To Spinoza either both the world and God are necessary or they are both contingent.[20] This important point is

---

17 Spinoza Baruch, *Ethics* I P29, Scholium, Translation Edwin Curley. London: Penguin, 1996. Print.
18 Hypostatized means that something is frozen into a static configuration or ideal state.
19 Stasis means a state of suspension and lack of movement.
20 The discussion above is given in propositions XXIX and XXXIII in Part 1 of The Ethics (On God). This builds on Spinoza's argument that God is the only necessary substance in Nature. Spinoza proves that God is the only substance in the world in the following way. He first establishes that no two substances can share an attribute or essence (I proposition 5). Spinoza then proceeds to show that a substance with infinite attributes exists (by Ethics I proposition 11 this substance is identical with God). The existence of infinite substance precludes the existence of any other substance. It is here that Spinoza deploys the *reductio ad absurdum* strategy. Suppose a second substance other than infinite substance did exist. This substance would have to possess some attribute or essence according to Spinoza's system. But since God possesses all possible attributes, this second substance would have to possess one of the attributes of God. But I proposition 5 has already established that no two substances can possess an attribute in common. Spinoza has derived a contradiction and believes that this proves that no other substance than God exists.

made to ensure that God has free choice of will. For this can happen only if God's will is necessary. A contingent God or a God with a contingent will is not free since his will is now dependent on some other arbitrary source external to him.

Substance, modes, attributes

Spinoza's system proceeds through a proof method called *more geometrico* (the work is written syllogistically in the fashion of geometrical treatises). As they did for Descartes, mathematics and geometry play important roles for Spinoza as sources of absolute truth.

Spinoza's system is composed of three main concepts: *substance, modes* and *attributes*. God is the absolute substance according to Spinoza and God is identical to nature. But God also possesses modes and attributes. The modes are the parts of God and the attributes are the parts of the mode, so to speak. God and modes form wholes that are subdivided into parts; these parts are the attributes. But the whole is identical to the parts and the parts are all necessary for each respective whole (both for God and for the modes of God). This philosophical system results in a reality that is internal and immanent[21] to itself.

Conatus

The *conatus* is an appetitive mechanical and perhaps organic drive. It is what drives nature forward. The origin of the *conatus* comes from the Greek atomists and the Roman stoics and their concept of *nisus*. This same concept was also used by Thomas Hobbes who called it 'the impetus'; and Newton who termed it 'the endeavor'. These terms are not identical and they all possess different nuances, but for the purposes of this introductory text, they may be viewed almost as synonyms.

Amor Intellectualis Deus

Another important concept of Spinoza's is the *Amor Intellectualis Deus*. For Spinoza, once we understand that the system of nature is rational we can only accept it; and once we do so, we no longer feel sorrow in those moments of fortune which disadvantage and hurt us[22]. There is an internal and detached joy which we feel at the movements and

---

21 Immanence refers to the concept that all things are present within the first realm in the two world ontology (the two world ontology comes to us from Plato who distinguishes between a world of Being and a world of Becoming, Christianity then transformed this into the distinction between the worldly and the super-worldly realm of Paradise), in the realm of Becoming or of the here and now. If X is immanent to Y then it is somehow contained within it. Transcendence is the opposite of immanence and has to do with what is beyond the physical world. It is related to the second realm in the two-world ontology. God and Being transcend the world and Becoming. If X transcends Y, it cannot be contained within it and it somehow eludes it or goes beyond it.

22 This concept of Spinoza (the *Amor Intellectualis Deus*) has a clear influence on Nietzsche's notion of *amor fati* and eternal recurrence of the same. The will intuits the eternal recurrence of the same but reason allows us

wonderous works of nature. This nature is identical to God. We learn to perceive God and nature intellectually. We no longer look to His ways as mysterious, irrational and incomprehensible because everything in nature possesses a reason and it is only a matter of time before this reason becomes manifest to our intellect and understanding.

Spinoza is above all a debunker of superstition and irrationalism. He bemoans that the masses get manipulated by religious leaders and priests who use fear to inflame their imagination and make them act from emotional and irrational drives. This is why the notion of *Amor Intellectualis Deus* is introduced towards the end of the *Ethics*. The sad affects of religion, suffering and sorrow, are sublated into the great joy of the philosopher and his love of God. But the philosopher is joyful[23] because he understands God as a principle and not as an anthropomorphized idea. God is not a human-like figure according to Spinoza. He is the highest rational principle of nature and of the universe and identical with this nature. This is what Spinoza posits with his notion of *Deus sive Natura*.

In the context of the theories of knowledge which we are studying in this text, it is necessary to note that Spinoza also believed in intuition and this is grounded in his great respect for geometry. However, it is not clear whether Spinoza believed that humans possess an intuitive understanding also; not only a sensitive and rational understanding. Spinoza's God saw everything from an absolute point of view unlike humans, and though Spinoza resists any attempt to view God as a super-human and or to anthropomorphize him, he appears here to share still a bit in the view of God as an exceptional metaphysical entity. There are three types of knowledge according to Spinoza: intuitive knowledge, cognitive knowledge and discursive knowledge.[24]

Sub Specie Aeternitatis

Perhaps the most important concept of Spinoza is his notion of *Sub Specie Aeternitatis* which appears in the 5th book of his *Ethics*. Spinoza follows Plato in asserting the immortality of the soul. Even though the word he uses is not soul in Proposition 23

---

to will and materially affirm and actualize this eternal recurrence. Finally, we love God and the world because we become joyful in loving the logical necessity of God, the world and the eternal recurrence of the same which coexist together in nature. This is the highest thought of *amor fati* developed by Nietzsche.

23 Spinoza anticipates here the Nietzschean notion of the *Gaya Scienza*—Nietzsche will explicitly recognize in Spinoza one of his greatest predecessors and will link the *Amor Intellectualis Deus* with his own notion of *amor fati* and (perhaps unconsciously) with the eternal recurrence of the same.

24 Spinoza classifies them into knowledge of the first kind (*genus*), second kind and third kind. The first kind of knowledge is tied to opinion and imagination. It is the only type of knowledge that can be false. The second kind is discursive knowledge, which is based on syllogistic and inferential deduction. The third kind is intuitive knowledge, which leads to what Spinoza (he seems to follow St. Thomas here) the *scientia intuitiva*. The second and third kind of knowledge are essentially internal and occur in the mind of the subject whereas cognitive or knowledge of the first kind occurs externally and is based on sense-perception.

of the Fifth book of *The Ethics*, it is clear that Spinoza (despite his emphasis on the immanence of God and of Nature to the world) believes that something called the mind (*mens* in the original Latin in which the *Ethics* was published) survives the temporal dissolution of the body. The human *mens*, because it is somehow integrated and integral to the divine Mind or Godhead, lives perpetually and eternally under the species of eternity.

3.5 LEIBNIZ: LOGIC, MONADS & KNOWLEDGE OF THE BEST POSSIBLE WORLD

Leibniz, a German Philosopher and contemporary of Spinoza also possessed a rationalist theory of knowledge. In contradistinction to Descartes he held that metaphysical substance was not extended since that would imply that it was infinitely divisible.

Before we set out to outline Leibniz's metaphysical and logical system, it is perhaps appropriate to justify why Leibniz is considered to be a rationalist. He supports both the theory of innate ideas and the forms of deduction in his mathematical proofs. Whether he supports the geometrical thesis of intuition is perhaps less clear but he does claim that there exist *cognitio intuitiva* or intuitive cognitions. The following passage also shows why Leibniz can be taken to be a rationalist:

> The senses, although they are necessary for all our actual knowledge, are not sufficient to give us the whole of it, since the senses never give anything but instances, that is to say particular or individual truths. Now all the instances which confirm a general truth, however numerous they may be, are not sufficient to establish the universal necessity of this same truth, for it does not follow that what happened before will happen in the same way again... From which it appears that necessary truths, such as we find in pure mathematics, and particularly in arithmetic and geometry, must have principles whose proof does not depend on instances, nor consequently on the testimony of the senses, although without the senses it would never have occurred to us to think of them...[25]

It is clear that Leibniz shares the concern that reason should be a criterion for knowledge and that this reason is of a mathematical and perhaps non-sensible nature. The reason that Leibniz did not admit that substance was infinitely divisible is because that would have precluded the existence of his metaphysical monad. If substance is infinitely divisible, then there cannot be a basic unit of reality which Leibniz called the monad.

---

[25] Leibniz, G. W., *New Essays on Human Understanding, in Leinbiz: Philosophical Writings*, ed. G.H.R. Parkinson, transl. Mary Morris and G.H.R. Parkinson, London: J.M. Dent & Sons, 1973. Preface, pp. 150–151. Print.

Leibniz describes in his own words his evolution and how he came to believe in the existence of monads:

> But when I looked for the ultimate reasons for mechanism, and even for the laws of motion, I was greatly surprised to see that they could not be found in mathematics but that I should have to return to metaphysics. This led me back to entelechies[26], and from the material to the formal, and at last brought me to understand, after many corrections and forward steps in my thinking, that monads or simple substances are the only true substances and that material things are only phenomena, though well founded and well connected. Of this, Plato, and even the later Academics and the skeptics too, had caught some glimpses… I flatter myself to have penetrated into the harmony of these different realms and to have seen that both sides are right provided that they do not clash with each other; that everything in nature happens mechanically and at the same time metaphysically but that the source of mechanics is metaphysics.[27]

These monads are irreducibly simple, units of reality. Each monad has different levels of complexity, awareness and consciousness. All monads are programmed by a kind of divine reason, though some are inorganic, like stones.

Monads do not possess form or shape, for that would imply divisibility. Monads can neither be produced nor destroyed because that would alter their status as fundamental substances that make up the world. Monads are radically individual: there is no monad in the universe that is identical to another monad.

> **KEY NOTES**
>
> **LEIBNIZ: KEY CONCEPTS AND DEFINITIONS**
> - **Mathesis universalis:** A universal, absolute, deductive science is attainable.
> - **Monadology:** The universe is entirely composed of simple indivisible entities called monads.
> - **Theodicy:** We live in the best of all possible worlds and evil is an illusion that God uses to motivate us towards the Good.

Monads play a clearly defined role in nature and it is here that we see the influence of the Catholic doctrine of natural law in Leibniz's work. Some monads are perceptive beings like plants but they do not have memory. Other more sophisticated monads have sense (they can feel pain) and memory. Finally, at the top of the hierarchy are human-like monads that possess sense, memory, sentience, rationality, consciousness and self-consciousness.

Monads are self-enclosed. They are windowless and possess no entry points or doors. They are points of force and in this they anticipate some of Nietzsche's work and his concept

---

26 An entelechy is a purpose or final cause, it comes from the Ancient Greek *entelecheia*.
27 Leibniz, G. W., *Die philosophischen Schriften*. 7 vols. Edited by C. I. Gerhardt. Berlin, 1875–90. Reprint, Hildesheim: Georg Olms, 1965. III 606, L 654–55, Print.

called the will-to-power. For Leibniz substance is represented through its action. Monads can interact. They are programmed with information and they execute this information. The world is coordinated because there exists a pre-established harmony between the programs of all the monads. This pre-established harmony explains free will. Unlike Spinoza, Leibniz believes that he can explain the free will of both God and man. To Spinoza only God could be truly free, man as an attribute of substance was determined and all his actions were necessary and purely caused by the efficient cause called *conatus*.

This removal of man's free will was unacceptable for Leibniz. (Leibniz was a staunch Protestant and cared more for organized religion than Spinoza did). Through his system of monads, Leibniz sets to explain the concept of free will. The monads contain their own principle of action within themselves; like atoms, they possess a *conatus*, which allows them to freely swerve and determine their course. But through the principle of sufficient reason, God chooses and selects the right configuration for the world out of many possible worlds, that allow for the actions of the monads. Thus God's freedom is commuted to a universal free will that chooses between possible worlds: Each monad inside this actual world chosen by God possesses an internal principle of direction, which gives it its free will and which, Leibniz calls in a direct contradiction of Spinoza's concept, the *conatus*.

Leibniz's explanation is a good one, and predicts many of the dynamics inherent in biologic and ecologic systems. Since plants and animals—or perhaps, even their parts—may be taken to be monads, it seems that one has granted free will to these entities as well. We see that in the organism, even something so complex as the human being, the parts down to each cell act according to their own biological prerogatives for survival with a confused and partial awareness of the whole: but it is this perceptive, yet 'selfish' and self-directed behavior of the part, that constitutes the health of the whole body.

Leibniz delineated seven fundamental philosophical principles. We've already seen Leibniz's principles of the *identity of indiscernibles* and the *indiscernibility of identicals* in Chapter 1 of this book:

> *Although time and place (i.e., the relations to what lies outside) do distinguish for us things which we could not easily tell apart by reference to themselves alone, things are nevertheless distinguishable in themselves. Thus, although diversity in things is accompanied by diversity of time or place, time and place do not constitute the core of identity and diversity, because they (the different times and places) impress different states upon the thing. To which it can be added that it is by means of things that we must distinguish one time or place from another, rather than vice versa.*[28]

---

28 Leibniz G. W., *Sämtliche Schriften und Briefe*. Edited by the Deutsche Akademie der Wissenschaften zu Berlin. Darmstadt, 1923 ff., Leipzig, 1938 ff., Berlin, 1950 ff. Cited by Series (*Reihe*) and Volume (*Band*) (A

This passage is particularly problematic in light of Kant's philosophy. There is some confusion here as to whether space and time are objects in themselves and exist independently of our sense apparatus (at least from a Kantian and Hegelian perspective). Despite his sensitivity to the notion of monadic perspective, Leibniz seems sometimes to conflate the 'in itself' and the 'for itself' or things how they are and how they appear to be. In our context and related to the thesis of the identity of indiscernibles, things are not identical merely because our sensible faculty or intellect are too weak to distinguish amongst them. In general, indiscernibility is not identical to identity.

All of Leibniz's principles blend together seamlessly and build on each other. There is a force and an almost aesthetic beauty in the symmetries and organization of his philosophical system.

Another central concept in Leibniz's philosophy is his notion of complete individual concept. This notion helps to bridge the gap between the monads, God's free will, truth and the principle of sufficient reason. It is central to Leibniz's theory of knowledge. To Leibniz, a true concept possesses all of its predicates internally. It possesses the predicates of its past, its present and its future. Thus every monad that is an ontological construct becomes a complete individual concept (this is a knowledge or epistemological idea) and contains the entire history of the world within it. This history of the world may not be discernable by finite intellects, but God can read it off the nature of the monad, so to speak. Furthermore, though each monad is self-directed and has its degree of freedom of action, the action of every monad is controlled or subjected to the principle of sufficient reason. This principle has at least two distinct enunciations:

(1) "There must be a sufficient reason [often known only to God] for anything to exist, for any event to occur, for any truth to obtain."[29]; and
(2) "The principle of sufficient reason, namely, that nothing happens without a reason."[30]

Monads contain all of their concepts and predicates from the past, present and future. All of them also contain all of the history of the universe from a certain perspective (perhaps that of God). Monads cannot interact causally; they have their ground only in themselves and in God's choice of the actual world from a set of less perfect possible worlds.

VI vi 230)
29 Clarke, Samuel Clarke D.D, *Collection of Papers, which passed between the late Learned Mr. Leibniz, and Dr. Clarke, In the Years 1715 and 1716,* London: James Knapton, 1717, L 5, known as the Leibniz-Clarke Correspondence
30 Idem, L 2, AG 321

Theodicy and optimism

Leibniz is famous for having stated that we live in the 'best of all possible worlds'. In his opinion evil is always explainable through its instrumentalization for a greater or unseen good. This is a classical explanation of the problem of evil in moral philosophy and an answer to the argument of how the existence of evil can be consistent with the existence of (a benevolent) God.

In his famous novel *Candide*, Voltaire caricaturizes Leibniz in the character of Candide's tutor and mentor, Pangloss. No matter how bad things get for *Candide*, Pangloss insists that we live in the best of possible worlds and that *Candide* should take his suffering and sorrow in stride. While logical from Leibniz's point of view, Voltaire turns this into a satire of how the world is not as good as the optimists would have us believe. Voltaire's novel was written in the wake of the Lisbon earthquake—an event without precedent in European memory. It shocked many political leaders and philosophers and made them question their optimistic outlooks on life.

Symbolic thought

Leibniz prefigures modern formal logic as we saw and studied in Chapter 1 of this book. Leibniz treated sentences and propositions the way we treat numbers in algebra: by assigning variables to them. The goal then becomes to discover a universal formal or mathematical language through which disputes and conflicts may be avoided or resolved. Leibniz calls this universal language the *characteristica universalis*. Once armed with his universal formal language, Leibniz begins to develop a universal science of nature—science as seen from the point of view of God.

The project of *Logica Universalis* led by Béziau[31] attempts to retrieve this level of generality present in Leibniz and in the 20th century with the logician Tarski. After Tarski, logic was further formalized in order to deal with the emerging field of cybernetics and of artificial intelligence.

Thus many formal concrete logics were developed to cope with paraconsistent systems such as software repositories or logics to assist robots to parse and learn from partial and incomplete information. The project of *Logica Universalis* shows that even concrete formal logics can be axiomatized and re-formalized from the point of view of structures.

---

31 Jean-Yves Béziau (born January 15, 1965 in Orléans, France) is a professor and researcher of the Brazilian Research Council at the University of Brazil, Rio de Janeiro, Brazil. He has published on paraconsistent logic, on model theory and on the project he is spearheading called *Logica Universalis*. See Béziau (editor), *Logica Universalis*, second edition, Birkhäuser Verlag AG, Boston, 2007. Print.

Structure then becomes the fundamental logical notion. A number, a proposition, a set—all are considered to be structures. This projects competes to a certain extent but also harmonizes with model theory which was developed by Tarski and Gödel and treats a logic as composed of a set of symbols, a theory and logical consequence operator. The theory is the formal language within which well-formed formulae take on their meaning or their truth-valued interpretations. [32]

What we have perhaps neglected to consider in this section about Leibniz is that he managed in a way to mediate between Spinoza's necessitarianism and Descartes' mechanicism about free will, by proposing his theory of free will based on the inclination of the monad and its tendency to act in a certain way without being in fact necessitated by the laws of Nature. Even in Descartes, there is some left-over Augustinianism and Jensenism which may allow too much room for grace and not enough room for the notion of cooperation between the will of the human monad and that of the Divine one. Finally, Leibniz refurbished and analyzed all the main arguments for the existence of God, the ontological, the cosmological and the teleological arguments for God's existence were given new breath through his *Monadology* which is the real esoteric doctrine of Leibniz as opposed to the exoteric doctrine of the best of all possible worlds expounded in his book called the *Theodicy*.

---

[32] Godel's and Cohen's (there are marked differences between Godel's and Cohen's views but we avoid the details in this introductory text) alternate view of logic as based on strong axioms and mathematical intuition as opposed to the algebraic notion of structure defended by Béziau and Tarski.

CONCLUSION

We have studied the works and ideas of Descartes, Spinoza and Leibniz in this Chapter. We also looked at the genesis or prehistory of what has been officially called Continental rationalism. The main ideas that most rationalists agree on are the belief in innate ideas and innate knowledge, the deduction intuition thesis and the fact that knowledge is somehow related to the truths of mathematics and possesses an intellectual non-sensible element. Of course, beyond this agreement there is also disagreement and tension between Descartes, Spinoza and Leibniz. Descartes and Leibniz tend to agree that there is something like human freedom or what has traditionally been called free will. Spinoza is not a clear-out determinist though his critics seem to think so at times but a self-styled (this was his own self understanding) necessitarian. Beyond these disagreements, the rationalists are united in denying that knowledge is acquired merely through the senses. They also deny that knowledge is purely inductive as some empiricists may want to claim. A critical rationalist like Kant also believes (unlike Hume for example) that causality can be vindicated in the world, granted that it does not apply to things in themselves but only to appearances or phenomena. It is worth noting that rationalism was often in competition with the school of empiricism but that it may be a bit immature to always see these schools as at odds with each other. For example, a rationalist may grant that knowledge about physics and chemistry or biology is empirical and is based on sense-experience. Similarly an empiricist may grant that classes are mathematical and logical universals that possess some kind of deductive structure. However the empiricist may not want to go as far as the rationalist and claim that we need something some rationalists have called 'categorical intuition'[33] to relate to mathematical classes and deductive structures.

---

33 See Husserl's *Fifth Logical Investigation* for this notion of categorical intuition

QUESTIONS
THE RATIONALIST THEORY OF KNOWLEDGE

1. Why can Parmenides be considered a rationalist and what is the importance of his concept of Being in the history of Logic and Knowledge?
2. Why can Socrates be considered a moral rationalist? How is rationalism in ethics related to the rationalist theory of knowledge?
3. Why was method so important for Descartes and how is this related to the rationalist theory of knowledge?
4. What does methodological skepticism mean in the Cartesian theory of knowledge?
5. What is the difference between methodical doubt and existential doubt?
6. Explain the thesis of intuition-deduction and why it is so important for the rationalist theory of knowledge.
7. Explain the thesis of innate ideas and why it is central to the rationalist theory of knowledge.
8. Explain the thesis of innate knowledge and why it is central to rationalism.
9. Explain why Spinoza can be characterized as a philosopher of immanence. Clearly explain what immanence means in this context and contrast it to the concept of transcendence.
10. What does the concept of *Amor Intellectualis Deus* mean in Spinoza's philosophy?
11. Why has Spinoza sometime been interpreted as a determinist (or necessitarian) in the debate on free will in the 17th century?
12. What does the concept of *conatus* mean in Spinoza's philosophy?
13. What is a monad in Leibniz's ontological vision?
14. What are levels of monads and why do they exist according to Leibniz?
15. What is Leibniz's project of a *characteristica universalis* and how does it prefigure the modern logic we studied in Chapter 1 of this book?
16. What is the principle of sufficient reason and why is it important in Leibniz' theory of knowledge?
17. What is a theodicy and how does it explain Leibniz's optimism and how is it tied to the contemporary thesis of the fine-tuned universe?
18. How does Leibniz explain free will for humans?
19. Do Spinoza and Leibniz support the notions of innate ideas and the intuition-deduction thesis? Justify your answer.
20. Why could having distinct conscious monads as parts of a larger organism constitute a problem for the Leibnizian philosophy of monads?

KEY CONCEPTS & DEFINITIONS - EMPIRICISM

TIME: 400 BC - 1900 A.D.

EMPIRICISM: a "theory of knowledge in which the criterion of the truth is sensory and inductive, not intellectual and deductive as in rationalism".

Gassendi's **EMPIRICIST MAXIM**: *"there is nothing in the intellect that was not previously in the senses"*

PEOPLE	IDEAS
ARISTOTLE	Hylomorphism: Perception as the reception of a form within the matter of the senses.
ROGER BACON (1220-1292)	Emphasis on induction and natural sciences.
FRANCIS BACON (1561-1626)	Theory of matter, critique of deductive syllogism, the inductive method and the method of tables enumerative versus ampliative induction.
JOHN LOCKE (1632–1704)	The Tabula Rasa, The representation theory of knowledge, primary and secondary properties, induction and corpuscular ideas instead of innate ideas.
DAVID HUME (1711–1776)	Critique of induction and causality, Radical knowledge skepticism, the common or general point of view, enumerative versus ampliative induction.
JOHN STUART MILL (1806–1873)	Mill's presupposition of the existence and truth of enumerative induction and its implication for causality. Mill's classification of enumerative causal induction: Mill's methods: agreement, difference, difference and agreement, concomitatnt variation and residue.

CHAPTER 4
THEORIES OF KNOWLEDGE: *EMPIRICISM*

Aristotle's notion of *hylomorphism*[1] was influential in the development of empiricism because it first conceived of the senses as possessing a matter; and of sensory perception as being the transmission of a form that modifies this matter of the sensory apparatus in order to bring about knowledge of a given object in the intellect. Thus hylomorphism prefigures Gassendi's empiricist maxim which claims that "there is nothing in the intellect that was not previously in the senses."[2]

Before digging into Aristotle's influence on the history of the theory of knowledge of empiricism, we must note the distinction between the fact of acquiring a perception that is more of a psychological question than a physiological question (i.e. how is the human body and sense-apparatus constituted so that we may perceive objects in our surrounding world and the status of the truth of that perception). There is a deeper epistemological question, which is how do we know that what we think is knowledge of X (here X is something we perceive) is actually correct and not deceitful, wrong or an illusion. Recall that this was the question that obsessed Descartes and which we have seen in Chapter 3 of this book.

---

1 Aristotle has certainly been characterized under many denominations in terms of philosophical categories. Some have seen in him an idealist (Gadamer), others a realist (Duns Scotus), others still a nominalist or a proto-empiricist (as Locke implicitly does, via Ockham). The question we are asking is whether one can look at Aristotle as a predecessor or as pre-figuring the empiricist tradition that begins unofficially with Roger and Francis Bacon and officially with John Locke.

2 *Nihil est in intellectu quod non prius fuerit in sensu.*

Next we consider Aristotle's account of substance, matter and form. Aristotle's account is complex and often involves psychological, logical, epistemological[3] and metaphysical[4] claims. The central text that influenced the history of empiricism however, is *On The Soul (Peri Tes Psyches)*.

For Avicenna[5] (Ibn Sina), the tabula rasa consists in an empirical proximity with objects in this world from which universal concepts become abstracted. This tabula rasa is developed through a method of syllogism: observations lead to statements and propositions which when cumulated and synthesized lead to further universal concepts.

Ibn Sina is crucial to the history of empiricism.[6] His notion of *tabula rasa* was a foundation that Locke developed; but also because he appears to reverse the trend in medieval Christian scholasticism to think of sense perception as the reception of a form that modifies the matter of the senses. Ibn Sina begins instead with the material intellect (*al-'aql al-hayulani*), which is "a blank slate with the potentiality for grasping the intelligible forms or universals."[7] According to Ibn Sina the material intellect is "referred to as material not because it is actually material, but because it resembles matter in accepting the form".[8] Notwithstanding, the notion of a material intellect is important as it seems to be a shift away from considering the intellect and the soul as a substantial form and prefigures Francis Bacon's understanding of perception as a material process occurring in a material medium.

4.1 EMPIRICISM IN THE MIDDLE AGES

Roger Bacon (1214-1294)[9] was seeking to reform theological studies. He felt less importance should be given to minor philosophical distinctions than was done in the philosophy of the Scholastics.[10] Roger Bacon exhorted all theologians to study the totality of the sciences closely, and to add them to the normal university curriculum. In

---

3 Epistemology is the theory of knowledge.
4 Metaphysics is the study of ultimate matters or of what transcends the physical realm.
5 Avicenna (980-1037) was a Persian Muslim philosopher and doctor of medicine. He was a disciple of the Greek philosopher Aristotle. His most famous philosophical treatise is called *The Healing*.
6 Abubacer, an Andalucian Muslim philosopher from the 12th century wrote a novel about a feral child whose mind he compared to a blank slate or *tabula rasa* in Latin. A latin translation of this novel, entitled *Philosophus Autodidactus*, was known to Locke who later introduced this very notion of *tabula rasa* to the British empiricist theory of knowledge.
7 *Routledge Encyclopedia of Philosophy*, Entry on *The Soul in Islamic Philosophy* by Shams C Inati, New York: Routledge, 1998. Print.
8 Idem
9 Roger Bacon (1214–1294) was an English philosopher and Franciscan friar who placed importance on the empirical study of natural science.
10 See Chapter 3 on Rationalism for a definition of the term.

his understanding of the acquisition of knowledge Bacon was in favor of experimental study over reliance on authority, arguing that "thence cometh quiet to the mind" (from this comes quiet to the mind).

Lynn Thorndike writes the following of Roger Bacon, "[his experimental method…] is not like modern experimentation, the source but 'the goal of all speculation'. It is not so much an inductive method of discovering scientific truth, as it is applied science—putting the results of the speculative sciences to the test of practical utility."[11]

> **KEY NOTES**
>
> Gassendi's **EMPIRICIST MAXIM**:
> *"there is nothing in the intellect that was not previously in the senses"*

Aristotle's philosophy of knowledge and sense-perception was recovered in the Middle Ages through the influence of the Arab Aristotelians Ibn Sina (Avicenna) and Ibn Rushd (Averroes). Aristotle's treatise *Peri Tes Psyches* (*On The Soul*) which we've already mentioned, was the most influential work in the theories of perception and development of knowledge from sense-experience at the time. The Scholastic Christian Aristotelians believed in both natural substances and artificial substances.[12] The Scholastics gave mechanistic explanations of how natural substances interacted in nature by treating the natural substances in relation to the dominant element that was present in each natural substance (earth, fire, air, water).[13] By the same argument, the Scholastics believed that human beings possessed a substantial form called the soul. So the question became how perception and then knowledge of something entered into the soul. For the Scholastics, the human senses were composed of matter and the perceptions were shapes or forms. So perception and knowledge acquisition were modeled on the fact that the senses received a form when they perceived a colour or a sound or a smell. The senses' matters were modified by the forms given off by the external world.

Some more modern philosophers like Richard Rorty have claimed that even for a more mature empircist such as Locke, it is not clear how much is explanation of how the senses work and how much is justification of what knowledge gathered from the senses is.[14]

---

11 Thorndike Lynn, *A History of Magic And Experimental Science*, II, Columbia University Press, New York, 1929, p.650
12 For Aristotle the original distinction was between primary substances and secondary substances.
13 For example if an object contained more air it would move up and if it contained more earth it was considered a heavy element and forces were believed to pull the object down.
14 See Rorty *Philosophy And The Mirror of Nature*, Chapter 3, Section 2: *Locke's Confusion Of Explanation And Justification*. This is the problem of whether Locke fully espoused a representational theory of perception. There is disagreement about this in the literature. One could argue against Rorty's thesis that Locke reduces both primary qualities and secondary qualities (not to say tertiary qualities, which are sometimes referred to in Locke)

4.1.1 Francis Bacon: The Precursor to Empiricism and the Discovery of Induction

The deep origins of Empiricism probably lie in Aristotle's more practical approach to philosophy as opposed to that of Plato. However, historically we may trace the origins of empiricism to the works of some Islamic Aristotelian philosophers and in the West to the philosophy of the two Bacons: Roger Bacon (1220-1292) and Francis Bacon (1561-1626). We have dealt with the Islamic Aristotelians in the previous sections and we have also mentioned Roger Bacon briefly in the previous section. We now move to consider the voluminous and important work of Francis Bacon.

Francis Bacon was an advocate of the double-truth (following Averroes): the truth of reason and the truth of faith. By keeping them separated and presiding over distinct domains he hoped to avoid controversy and conflict whether political or theological.

Not unlike Descartes, Bacon starts by diagnosing the errors and illusions of his day before proceeding to give his own positive method of developing and acquiring certain and scientific knowledge. Bacon identifies four main errors, which he calls Idols from the latin *idola*. They are called idols because idolatry was a major Christian sin. To worship idols is to mistake God for the symbols and relics that represent him. In the same way, Bacon believes that men mistake knowledge for the idols that are passed off as true knowledge in society and in the world at large.

The first idol is the **Idola Tribus** of which he writes the following:

> "then it is that in struggling towards that which is further off it falls back upon that which is more nigh at hand; namely on final causes: which have relation clearly to the nature of man rather than to the nature of the universe: and from this source have strangely defiled philosophy"[15]

The main error that Bacon associates with the *Idola Tribus* is the fact that final causes are attributed to natural substances and confused with natural causes. This Aristotelian error comes from the human tendency to anthropomorphize[16] nature and attribute moral purpose to mechanical and natural occurrences. Furthermore it is an idol of the tribe

---

to representations and representations about ideas. But the secondary qualities clearly have some objective status in Locke despite being compared to powers in the perceived object of knowledge. Hence the object and its secondary qualities are not hidden in a pure veil of representation.

15 (WB IV, 57), WB stands for Bacon, Francis, *The Works of Francis Bacon*, Spedding, J. Ellis, R. and Heath, D. (eds), London, Longman and Co, 1858, Cited by volume and page number.

16 Anthromorphize means transform into something that has human shape, in this particular context it means projecting human categories upon nature, which is independent of humans according to the judgment of Francis Bacon.

that is of the whole human species. Since man is gregarious and possesses purpose in society, he derives or attributes this same type of cause to nature. This attribution is an error however, and blocks access to a correct understanding and knowledge of nature. Bacon was hostile to Aristotle but thought highly of Democritus.

Idola Fori

Of the *idola fori*, Francis Bacon writes "The idols of the marketplace are the most troublesome…"[17] and "Definitions cannot cure this evil…"[18] The idols of the marketplace are those due to our commerce with fellow humans. Inherent to language are many errors and biases. Language itself contains poorly defined predicates and words whose definitions are ambiguous.[19]

Idola Specus

The *idola specus* or idols of the cave are the mistakes that the individual man makes. Every unique human exemplar errs because of the limitations unique to his development and constitution. Individual diversity is most often considered a good thing, but for Bacon it is also a source of potential error. We are each, individually, the prisoners of a Platonic cave: "The idols of the cave are the idols of the individual man for anyone, besides the errors common to human nature in general (viz. The idols of the the tribe), has a cave or den of his own which refracts and discolours the light of nature; owing either to his own proper and peculiar nature; or to his education and conversation with others; or to the reading of books and the authority of those he esteems and admires or to the differences of impressions, accordingly as they take place in the mind."[20]

Idola Theatri

The *idola theatri* comes from studying the theories of the schools. Bacon argued that the schools put on a show of truth: they invert the true nature of things just like the theater does where we believe we see life but see only actors. In very much the same way, Scholastic hylomorphism believed that the soul was a substantial form and that perception was related to matter through the senses. But the inverse or opposite is true to a certain extent. Bacon does not fully reject the theory of form as some argue;[21] but

---

17 WB IV, 60ff
18 WB IV, 61
19 We suppose this thesis of Bacon's and his dissatisfaction with natural language would find agreement later in Leibniz. Bacon passed away twenty years before Leibniz was born. There is reason to believe that Leibniz was familiar with the work of John Locke in developing the **characteristica universalis** studied in Chapter 3 when we dealt with the theory of knowledge of rationalism.
20 WB IV, 54
21 See Carlin Laurence, *The Empiricists: A Guide For The Perplexed*, New York: Continuum Books, 2009. Print.

he does seek a theory of matter. Though not in full agreeement with classical atomism, Bacon does go through a phase where matter is central to his understanding of the world. However, his notion of matter was not a mechanism related to motion as it was for Galileo. Bacon is much more influenced by chemistry and the occult Renaissance tradition of magic[22] when he writes upon these questions. The separation of magical method and scientific method had not been clearly achieved in Bacon as we will see. As with Giordano Bruno, whom we will study in Chapter 8, the magical pre-figures and influences the scientific outlook. Magic, understood as the theory that nature can be operated on in order to undergo transformation, was linked to a theory of form. Nature's secrets were hidden in its matter, though this matter was not totally formless as it was for the Neo-Platonists.

Its shape and form could be affected by magical and scientific operations. The method for studying nature is the inductive nature and there is a rejection of syllogism and the four Aristotelian causes in attaining knowledge of nature.

Bacon's theory of matter is central to his empiricism. Even though matter is connected to motion, Bacon did not have a theory of material nor of mathematical mechanism as did Galileo. Rather he was more influenced by mathematical chemistry. In Bacon's view, method was required to rid oneself of illusions or *idola* as we have seen above. Two types of method were given as being possible:

> *There are and can be only two ways of searching into and discovering truth. The one flies from the senses and particulars to the most general axioms, and from these principles, the truth of which it takes for settled and immoveable, proceeds to judgment and to the discovery of middle axioms. And this way is now in fashion. The other derives axioms from the senses and particulars, rising by gradual and unbroken ascent, so that it arrives at the most general axioms last of all. This is the true way, but as yet untried.*[23]

Bacon who begins the great tradition of scientific method in England, argues that this method allows for objective knowledge. Bacon is known for having coined the famous word or motto "knowledge is power". Bacon is also a precursor of the Enlightenment worldview insofar as he claims that one should get rid of all one's prejudices in order to attain objective and scientific knowledge.[24]

For Bacon as for Descartes, method is primordial in order to achieve freedom from uncertainty and illusion. Their new method was primarily the inductive method with

---

[22] We will see more about this when we study the influence of humanities on knowledge in *Chapter 8: Knowledge and the Humanist Worldview.*
[23] WB IV, 50
[24] Bacon has started the trend that will be diagnosed much later by the German philosopher Gadamer who criticizes the Enlightenment theory of knowledge or worldview for having developed "a prejudice against all prejudices".

which we have already familiarized ourselves with in Chapter 2, where we studied inductive logic and reasoning. Bacon rejected the Aristotelian deductive method which would be later taken over by Descartes. (We know Descartes read Bacon while the contrary is probably not true).

Bacon opposes the syllogistic method and defines an alternative method "which by slow and faithful toil gathers information from things and brings it into understanding". In his *Novum Organum* (1620), he claims:

> *"[of] induction the logicians seem hardly to have taken any serious thought, but they pass it by with a slight notice, and hasten to the formulae of disputation. I on the contrary reject demonstration by syllogism....."* [25]

Induction is understood as an ascent to axioms, paired with a further descent to works, so that from axioms new knowledge in the form of particulars[26] is developed. The inductive method starts from sensible or sensory experience and moves through the study of natural history (sense-data are provided as warrants from the study of nature) to lower theories, formulae or propositions. These are derived from the tables of presentation organized by Bacon or by abstracting from percepts and perceptions.

Bacon claims that his method both corrects and develops sense-data into facts. This pairs well with his construct of tables for gathering information. The sequence of methodical steps does not, however, end here. Bacon assumes that from lower axioms more general ones can be derived (by induction); and so the process of induction is tantamount to a joining of parts into a systematic chain.

> **KEY NOTES**
>
> **FRANCIS BACON: THE IDOLS OF KNOWLEDGE**
> - *Idola Tribus:* Natural Causes are confused and taken to be final causes.
> - *Idola Fori:* We err because we share the prejudices of our fellow human beings.
> - *Idola Specus:* These are errors generated by our own limited understanding.
> - *Idola Theatri:* The schools (of philosophy and of Scholasticism) but also the modern schools (the novatores) mislead us by their false teachings.

The decisive instrument in the process described by Bacon is the discovery of a 'middle term' (this was true also of Ibn Sina for whom the finding of the middle term was crucial) to ascertain truthful knowledge. These middle terms are the middle or 'living axioms,' which mediate between particulars and general axioms.

---

25 WB IV, 24
26 Here particular means objects or sentences that refer to specific individual objects. In his logic, Aristotle originally distinguished between universal statements, particular statements and individual statements.

In Bacon's view, induction can only be efficient if it is eliminative through exclusion, which goes beyond the remit of induction by simple enumeration. There is an eliminative aspect to induction, which allows for it to develop new knowledge. If induction were purely enumerative and lacked what we have called elsewhere in this book an ampliative element[27], then it would be purely redundant and would lack an ability to construct and extend the body of knowledge. "Bacon's antipathy to simple enumeration as the universal method of science can be seen as derived primarily from his preference for theories that deal with interior physical causes (material but also occult and logical causes), which are not immediately observable."[28] This emphasis on internal, hidden forces is perhaps due to Bacon's interest in Renaissance magic. It also anticipates Newton's[29] challenge to the empiricist concept of mechanism developed by Galileo[30] and Gassendi[31] through the introduction of the notion of invisible attractive or gravitational force.

Bacon believed in the use of "tables of counter-instances, which may suggest experiments […] tables of presence and of absence and tables of comparison or of degrees, to move from the sensible to the real requires the correction of the senses, the tables of natural history, abstraction of propositions and induction of notions."[32]

Central to Bacon's development of the inductive method is his creative use of tables and permutation, and the correlation of information in those tables. There is an undeniable Lullian influence on Bacon. Lull developed in *Ars Magna* tables of the *Dignities of God* and other attributes. We will focus on Lull's influence on the development of the scientific method in Chapter 8 when we study the role of the humanities in the development of knowledge and of the humanist worldview.

Francis Bacon, building on the work of Roger Bacon and of the Islamic empiricists, is a precursor of the inductive method developed by Hobbes, Locke, Hume and Mill. As opposed to Hume who goes as far as rejecting induction completely as a valid source

---

27 In order to increase or amplify knowledge, some elements first have to be removed or eliminated: Bacon here anticipates Mill's law of elimination in his analysis of inductive causation. This will come nearly three centuries later.
28 Urbach, P. , *Francis Bacon's Philosophy of Science: An Account and a Reappraisal*, p. 30, La Salle, IL: Open Court., 1987. Print.
29 Newton is the famous 17th century physicist who discovered the law of universal gravity. One may read Newton as an empiricist or alternatively as a rationalist given his strong emphasis on mathematics and the calculus which bring him into greater proximity to Descartes than to someone like Locke.
30 Galileo is an early 17th century mechanical philosopher invented the telescope in 1613. He supported the heliocentric model of the solar system (he was put under house arrest by the Catholic Inquisition for this feat) and did a lot of work on dropping weights and establishing the independence of their acceleration to the ground from their weight. This would prove very important for Newton who would come to distinguish between the two notions of mass and weight.
31 Pierre Gassendi was an empiricist philosopher living in France in the 17th century who tried to reconcile Christianity with the philosophy of Epicurus and with Epicurean atomism.
32 Malherbe, M., 1996, "Bacon's Method of Science", in *The Cambridge Companion to Bacon,* Peltonen (ed.) 1996, p. 85. Print.

of knowledge and as opposed to John Stuart Mill who merely assumes the existence of enumerative induction and treats it as a form of causality, Bacon with a more subtle understanding which anticipates Charles Peirce, distinguishes between ampliative, eliminative and enumerative induction.

> **INTERESTING?**
>
> **Avicenna** (980-1037) was a Persian Muslim philospher, doctor of medicine and disciple of Aristotle. His most famous philosophical treatise is called "The Healing".
>
> **Abubacer**, an Andalucian Muslim philosopher of the 12th century wrote a novel about a feral child whose mind he compared to a blank slate or *tabular rasa* in Latin. A Latin translation of this novel, entitled *Philosophus Autodidactus*, was known to Locke who later introduced this very notion of *tabula rasa* to the British empiricist theory of knowledge.
>
> **Galileo** was an early 17th century mechanical philosopher and was said to have invented the telescope. He was put under house arrest by the Catholic Inquisition for supporting the heliocentric model of the solar system.

4.2 BRITISH EMPIRICISM
4.2.1 John Locke: The Founding of British Empiricism

John Locke (1632–1704) developed the view that knowledge acquired by human beings depended on experience. In this he was inspired by his forerunner Francis Bacon. Locke called this type of knowledge based on experience, *a posteriori* knowledge. Scholars often attribute the doctrine of the *tabula rasa* or blank slate to Locke, though Arab Aristotelians were already employing this expression, as we have seen.[33] Thomas Hobbes was another important philosopher who influenced Locke and served as an intermediary between Locke's thought and the work of Francis Bacon.[34]

Locke is famous for having criticized and rejected the notion of innate ideas that was developed by Rene Descartes whom we saw in the preceding Chapter. There are two accounts of innate ideas according to Locke: the naïve account and the dispositional account.[35] '*To come to the use of reason*' is a crucial concept for Locke as he uses it again to

---

33 See footnote 6 above.
34 Due to the limited space we have in this introductory text, we will not deal with Hobbes extensively but it is important to know that he was a materialist and believed in the existence of fundamental material particles called atoms that formed everything we perceive.
35 Locke distinguishes between the naïve and dispositional account of innate ideas. The first account is not a sophisticated one and Locke does not spend much time refuting it. The naïve account implies that we are born with certain internal impressions that give us knowledge. This is plainly not right for Locke. So instead he focuses on criticizing the dispositional account of innate ideas. On this account we have innate ideas that form

criticize the notion of innate idea. In this context, *'to come to the use of reason'* may have two meanings. It can mean:

1. to have innnate ideas which give us a criterion to distinguish between mathematical axioms and theorems. For Locke, innate ideas do not exist precisely because it is impossible to distinguish clearly between what is an axiom and what is a theorem in mathematics. The second meaning of 'to come to the use of reason' is that:

2. we use innate ideas when we reach maturity only. Before that we do not possess reason so to speak and hence have no access to innate ideas. But Locke also disagrees with the invoking of this unsderstanding of the relation between innate ideas and reason. Locke argued that children reason and ratiocinate before reaching the age of majority though this does not imply in any way, that they have access to the privileged information of innate ideas and innate knowledge.

This claim then, deals with the nature of the human mind and how it relates to the activity of engaging in mathematics and theorizing about mathematics. Presumably both axioms and theorems are discoverable by reason. However if that is the case, then how do we differentiate between them? Locke suggests that one way would be to immediately assent to the truth of an axiom whereas a theorem would require further argument and proof. But even if this is true, all we have here is a criterion for assent not for innateness. This represents Locke's anti-foundationalism in the philosophy of mathematics.

Locke makes a distinction between innate moral principles and innate theoretical/mathematical or scientific principles or ideas. He claims that for innate moral principles there is even less general assent than for, say, the principle of identity. There is a natural tendency to disagree when it comes to moral principles and so this weakens the possibility of holding on to the concept of innate ideas in morality or ethics. Locke famously analyzes the Golden Rule (*'Do unto others as you would have them do unto you'*) and claims that it may not be taken as a mathematical axiom to which the majority would automatically agree or assent.

Locke also distinguishes between simple and complex ideas. The former are unanalysable, and are broken down into primary and secondary qualities.[36] It is not clear that Locke

---

dispositions that are latent within our minds when we are born. These ideas are almost unconsciously there within us but we get to learn them by sorting ourselves out by becoming aware of the inner workings of our mind. This is also unacceptable to Locke and ultimately he believes that the source of knowledge does not stem from the mind but from sense-perception. He thus follows the empiricist maxim formulated by Gassendi: There is nothing in the intellect (or mind for Locke) that was not previously in the senses.

36 Properties and qualities are not identical. We do not distinguish them sharply in this introductory text but we may say a few things about their difference. Properties are somehow more essential to the constitution of an object whereas qualities, even primary qualities (shape, size, extension) which possess more objectivity than secondary qualities, are somehow detachable or distinguishable from the ontological or metaphysical substratum of an object.

held a representational theory of sensation/knowledge as some philosophers have argued.

To Locke, perception is a triadic relation between perceiver, idea, and object. Objects are not perceived or gotten at directly but are mediated by simple ideas or complex ideas or ideas of primary qualities and possibly, though this is less clear, ideas of secondary qualities. Locke often speaks of secondary qualities as powers of the ideas of primary qualities to generate a perception within our perceptual apparatus. This introduces what has alternatively been called a veil of ideas or a veil of perception between our sense apparatus and real world. In empiricist epistemology, the notion of primary and secondary qualities is very important; and this is especially true in Locke's theory of knowledge.

> **KEY NOTES**
>
> **JOHN LOCKE KEY CONCEPTS AND DEFINITIONS**
> - **Tabula Rasa:** Individuals are born as blank slates and all knowledge is learnable.
> - **Veil of representation:** We access and get to know objects, not first-hand, but through our representations.
> - **Importance of induction:** All real knowledge is obtained through contact with sense-experience.

Extension, form and size are primary qualities; density, viscosity and color are secondary qualities. However there are cases that make one wonder. For example, is mass a primary or a secondary quality? According to Newton, mass was a primary quality (and Locke agreed with him and was influenced by him on this particular point) whereas weight was a secondary quality since if the particular body was in gravitational vacuum it would still possess mass but would be weightless.

For Locke, there is an issue with the notion of substance in general. If we take Locke's theories to their ultimate end, then there appears a certain '*je ne sais quoi*' which holds primary qualities together in a metaphysical object. This weakness will lead to Hume's bundle theory of the object and of perception, which will point out that nothing, including any '*je ne sais quoi*', can hold the object of knowledge together. Hume will extend his radically skeptical critique to the Cartesian ego, the human subject of thought. If nothing holds the general substance together then nothing holds the self together either, and so it is a free-floating bundle of unattached perceptions and memories that has no center.[37]

---

[37] An important philosopher who may be taken to be an empiricist but has also been classified as a subjective idealist is George Berkeley. We deal with this writer and author in the chapter on the Idealist worldview in

4.3 PHILOSOPHICAL SKEPTICISM
4.3.1 Hume: The Radicalization of Empiricism into Philosophical Skepticism

In answering Berkeley's criticism of Locke, the Scottish philosopher David Hume (1711–1776) took empiricism to a new level of philosophic skepticism. Hume writes:

> "Mr. Locke, in his chapter of power, says that, finding from experience, that there are several new productions in nature, and concluding that there must somewhere be a power capable of producing them, we arrive at last by this reasoning at the idea of power. But no reasoning can ever give us a new, original, simple idea; as this philosopher himself confesses. This, therefore, can never be the origin of that idea."[38]

Here Hume is critiquing Locke's notions of complex and simple ideas. He wishes to replace this distinction with his own distinction between ideas and impressions. The two are distinguished by degrees of vividness in perception. An idea is less vivid; it is abstract; while an impression has a phenomenological quality—it feels like something to perceive an impression. In bouts of delirium we can mistake ideas for impressions, but this is not the normal, natural state of things and of human nature. In general, ideas and impressions can be distinguished through the criterion of vividness and phenomenological feel, or so Hume would argue.

> **KEY NOTES**
>
> **ASSOCIATIONISM** denies that there are any necessary connections in experience or reality. These exist only in the realm of deduction and mathematical ideas. Knowledge is reduced to the fact that things or events are contiguous in space or time.

Hume divided all of human knowledge into two categories: relations of ideas and matters of fact. Mathematical and logical propositions (e.g. "that the square of the hypotenuse is equal to the sum of the squares of the two sides") are examples of the first; propositions involving some contingent observation of the world (e.g. "the sun rises in the East") are

---

Chapter 6. It is sufficient here to note that he was very critical and downright hostile to Locke's understanding of the nature of knowledge and that he describes his understanding of matter as inconsistent and contradictory and sees his brand of empiricism as leading directly to atheism. In fact, Berkeley was right to a certain extent. The philosopher we study next, David Hume answered Berkeley's critiques of Locke, extended the empiricism of Locke into philosophical skepticism and staked an atheist position in *Dialogues Concerning Natural Religion* which he published after his death for fear of political persecution and repression due to the radicality of his theses on the existence of a supernatural Being (God).

38 Hume David, *An Enquiry Concerning Human Understanding*, Of The Idea Of Necessary Connection, Paragraph 8, footnote 12.

examples of the second. "Ideas" are derived from "impressions".

For Hume, an "impression" corresponds roughly to what we call a sensation. To remember or to imagine such impressions is to have an "idea". Ideas are therefore the faint copies of sensations.

Hume drops the concept of object of knowledge. As a consequence, the self or subject of knowledge also becomes intangible or ineffable. This is Hume's Berkeleyanism. Thus for Hume there is no longer a tripartite division of subject, representation and object of knowledge. One can thus say that Hume abandons Locke's representational theory of knowledge. However the most famous item in Hume's empiricism is his critical treatment of the problem of induction. Hume's criticism was as follows: the only way that reason can guarantee the certainty in the field of knowledge and therefore science is through thinking and deductive reasoning. But this kind of reasoning is never encountered and never applicable in ordinary life and experience. The favorite example of Hume concerned billiard balls in the *Enquiry Concerning Human Understanding*. We quote:

> The mind can never possibly find the effect in the supposed cause, by the most accurate scrutiny and examination. For the effect is totally different from the cause and can never be discovered in it. Motion in the second Billiard-ball is a quite distinct event from motion in the first..." [39]

Thus for Hume causality and the connected notion of induction were spurious. They were just based on habit and repeated association not on a fact of the matter or logical certainty and necessity that could be established a priori. These radically skeptical theses of Hume's would later rouse Kant out of his dogmatic slumber.

In chapter 8 we shall study the Renaissance philosopher Giordano Bruno. It is our thesis that this idea exists already in the literature, that Bruno's art of memory influenced Hume's theory of psychological associationism.[40] We postpone the discussion of the Brunist art of memory to Chapter 8.

Hume is part of the habit-tradition of philosophizing. According to this tradition which begins with Aristotle and knows perhaps its most recent important exponent in Charles Peirce (see chapter 6), knowledge is the result of accumulated practical experiences

---

[39] Hume, David, *Enquiry Concerning The Human Understanding And The Principles of Morals* Section IV, Part 1, 25.

[40] Associationism is a view of the theory of knowledge that denies that there are any necessary connections in experience or reality. These exist only in the realm of deduction and mathematical ideas. Hence knowledge is reduced according to this view to the fact that things are contiguous or that they appear together in experience by coincidence and that this appearance could always be contradicted by the non-necessary appearance or manifestation of another distinct contiguity. (Contiguous means two things appear next to each other when they are perceived).

that results in habits of thought and beliefs. These habits do not determine us and our behaviour—they are rational to a certain extent and we can rationally distance ourselves from them. We can examine them, though they resist full analysis and cannot be broken down into fully understandable parts as in Cartesian philosophy.

> **KEY NOTES**
>
> **DAVID HUME KEY CONCEPTS AND DEFINITIONS**
> - **Bundle theory of knowledge:** Objects and the self do not really exist they are merely cobbled together by our sense apparatus.
> - **Critique of causal induction:** Science and philosophical argument cannot prove the true existence of causes beyond a reasonable doubt.
> - **Knowledge skepticism:** We should carry on with life as usual even though we cannot find foundations for our scientific knowledge.

4.4 PHENOMENALISTIC EMPIRICISM

4.4.1 MILL: Phenomenalistic[41] Empiricism and the Methods for Understanding Causality

As John Stuart Mill put it in the mid-19th century, matter is the "permanent possibility of sensation".[42] Mill also claimed that "induction is necessary for all meaningful knowledge including mathematics." Mill believed that even mathematics was derived from experience. He argued that mathematics was a form of generalized induction. He eliminates the account left out in Hume's philosophy for relations of ideas. In general even in his logic, though he reawakens the quest for a deductive logic, he is not so clear on the notion of relations which we studied in Chapters 1 and 2. He makes use of the notions of denotation and connotation but cannot solve some basic problems associated with definite descriptions such as "'the actual king of France' or 'the actual king of Mexico' is bold".[43]

---

[41] Phenomenalism is the view that whatever is physical or phenomenal (can be perceived) is reducible to mental entities. For phenomenalists, in the end only mental objects really exist, which has made some claim that phenomenalism is reducible to subjective idealism. We study subjective idealism in Chapter 6 on the Idealist worldview.

[42] Mill John Stuart, *An Examination Of William Hamilton's Philosophy*, p.183.

[43] This problem of definite descriptions was solved by Bertrand Russell who built on Frege's work on logical quantifiers and the problem of reference. Some have argued though that Mill was not a psychologist (here pyschologist refers to the theory of knowledge of psychologism for which logic and mathematics could be reduced to the laws of empirical psychology) as some later German philosophers accused him of being. The most famous of these philosophers was the phenomenologist Edmund Husserl.

Mill's account of the relativity of knowledge and the fact that it is based not on direct experience but on inference from that experience creates a gap between knowledge and experience. The question then becomes, whether such a gap exists or if such a gap is even acceptable from a knowledge point of view. If we think it might be, then we must ask: What is it that fills the gap? For some philosophers like Berkeley, the indirect aspect of knowledge and the gap it generated, is what allows for the existence of God. Whatever it is that might exist in the gap created or observed by Mill when he pits indirect experience and possibilities of sensation against actualities or actualized sensations, there remain many unanswered questions and vague aspects about this so-called gap within sensation and the knowledge that proceeds from sensation.

> **KEY NOTES**
>
> **JOHN MILL KEY CONCEPTS AND DEFINITIONS**
> - **Mill's Laws:** We can organize and enumerate causes in nature according to a logical structure.
> - **"Mathematics is inductive":** Identity and number only exist because we derive them from experience.
> - **Phenomenalism:** Experience is a psychological construct and knowledge does not possess a real object (the psychologism denounced by German phenomenologists).

Some have argued that Mill's position falls back on a form of subjective idealism. We will investigate this argument in Chapter 5 when we consider the theory of knowledge of idealism. If the subject of knowledge is central to Mill's account, it is because the human beings that are the subject of this knowledge ultimately structure knowledge from possible sensation and indirect experience. This creates logical absurdities. For instance, from Mill's theories, it is not possible to explain how floor beams might continue to support a floor when there is no one there to 'sense' it. These and other phenomena and questions may be considered as unresolved from the point of view of a Millian account of knowledge.

We will return to the aspect of Mill's Laws of causality in the Chapter on Scientific Explanation and Method (Chapter 7 of this book). Mill was very influential on the understanding of causality and scientific method. What is not clear is whether his understanding of causality as a law of laws or as a generic law that is derived from experience is correct. Some great minds like Immanuel Kant have argued that it is impossible to understand causality without some *a priori* element that involves the categories of the understanding (and perhaps the faculty of imagination).

Who is closer to the truth? Mill or Kant? We postpone adjudication until Chapter 7 while admitting that both parties present strong arguments for their sides. While this issue may be controversial still, Mill introduced the principles of determinism and limited variety as methodological guides in conjunction with his laws of causality. These contributions to western thought are paramount, as we shall see.

The issues we discussed above surrounding Mill's application of empiricism and phenomenalism to mathematics, are in a class of their own.[44] Mill was also a philosopher of Utilitarianism in the realm of ethics and there his positions may be on better grounds.

What is perhaps even more problematic is Mill's methods of analyzing causality, which we studied in chapter 3. Though Mill may have identified something essential about the way causality and reality are organized and interact, there remain problems with his approach. These problems will come to the fore when we look at the Viennese and Berlin schools of logical empiricism. Briefly, the main issue here is that an imaginative step that is not inductive, but either deductive or abductive[45] is required in order to decide which of his four-five methods to use: Agreement, Difference, Agreement and Difference, Correlation and Residue. While it is not clear what the step is that governs the hypothetico-deductive model of scientific explanation and enquiry, the work of Hempel (whom we introduce briefly below, and discuss more broadly in Chapter 7) and others has made it clear that one must go beyond mere induction and experience to understand and organize causal explanation.

4.5 LOGICAL EMPIRICISM
4.5.1 The Vienna and The Berlin Schools

Induction was transformed by the logical positivist or logical empiricist school[46] through their application of probability to the notion of law and causality. Induction guarantees with a definable degree of confidence that something that occurs in a regular manner will recur in the future. If we take the example "All crows are black", the statement can never be made certain nor be guaranteed by deductive reasoning. However, Hume would

---

44 Mill's position on mathematics is that it rests on a form of induction or inference from experience. But most mathematicians and philosophers of mathematics clearly dismiss this stance claiming that mathematics possesses an internally consistent standard of evaluation for the truth of its statements that, in fact, is much more akin to a form of deduction system or deductive knowledge than to anything resembling experiential or inductive knowledge.
45 See footnote 47 in order to understand what abduction means.
46 The Logical Positivist school was situated in Vienna around figures like Gödel, Carnap, Schlick and Ayer, the Logical Empiricists were situated in Berlin around figures like David Hilbert (who is in fact more of a mathematician), Carl Hempel (whose deductive nomological model of scientific explanation we will study in Chapter 7) Richard Von Mises and Hans von Reichenbach. For the purposes of this introductory text we will not distinguish clearly between these two schools and will treat them as one general trend in the history of the empiricist theory of knowledge.

say that either a statement is certain or it does not provide knowledge. Since regularities are not certainties, Hume concluded that the statement "All crows are black" explained nothing of a scientific nature. However, the positivists or empiricists did not agree. Their answer to Hume's qualms about induction is that the statement "All crows are black" can never ultimately be proven, but it may still contribute to the body of knowledge by its positing, and it is the positing of such statements that make science possible.

> **KEY NOTES**
>
> **LOGICAL EMPIRICISM KEY CONCEPTS AND DEFINITIONS**
> - **Rejection of Naïve Inductivism:** Knowledge is also deductive and possesses empirical content.
> - **Carl Hempel's Understanding of Causality:** Causality possesses deductive and statistical aspects.
> - **Anti-metaphysical Thesis:** Metaphysics is contradictory, inconsistent and does not yield any serious knowledge.

This is because we can study any number of crows and arrive at a statistical and probabilistic law on the number of black crows versus crows of other colors. And this law of probability, which is based on a "rule of induction" is not nothing: It increases our knowledge and provides a scientific truth for the general case, though that truth can never be fully certain for any particular case. For the greater the number of crows we add randomly to our analysis, the surer we are of our conclusion. Induction is the link that allows us to arrive at generalized experience developed from particular cases.

The general statement must then be tested and qualified by performing additional checks. But if we did not have the concept of induction, we could not enunciate rules of general and universal law, even though these laws are sometimes statistical. (Many laws are not statistical in their expression. For example Force = mass x acceleration is an exact law; but its veracity or certainty is derived from experience by induction[47] and must be verified statistically by repeated experiment.)

Hempel, who is part of the Berlin circle of logical empiricism, argues that it is a 'naïve inductivism' that pretends we can observe nature without presuppositions[48] and

---

[47] Philosophers like Charles Peirce, whom we study in Chapter 6, have suggested that an additional component of scientific enquiry or method is an abduction or abductive step. This is essentially an imaginative, informed and educated guess that allows one to posit and derive a hypothesis. (We are not stating generally that the imagination and guessing are identical but there are elements of guessing which are related to the imagination. It is true that one can use the imagination in order to see something that was not there before or that was not seeable or conceivable before, and so the imagination can be a form of analogical seeing and not just a guess). The school of Logical Empiricism, however was more interested in induction than abduction and perhaps would have even denied the existence of an abductive step.

[48] See the *Introduction* Chapter (on p.4) for the notion of presupposition and its meaning.

preconceptions. Hempel argues that we need theory to determine what we classify and observe.[49] That is, classification and the object of our observations presupposes a theory or structure of knowledge already present.

Hempel's claim is that there are no neutral facts devoid of theory. Naïve inductivism consists in the following aspects:

> 1) the observation and recording of all accumulation of well-established facts;
> 2) analysis and classification of these facts;
> 3) the derivation of rules by induction or by general propositions derived from these facts, and
> 4) additional controls and checks on general propositions or statements.

Hempel's claim is that each of these four stages has methodological errors. A shortcoming of the generalized method of naïve inductivism is that one cannot make the assumption[50] that at stage 3 one can work through the hypothesis without an application of imaginative powers or faculties. Hempel argues that if you do not already have a hypothesis powered by imagination or guesswork you cannot even know what facts should be observed and recorded.[51]

ⓘ KEY DEFINITIONS

NAÏVE INDUCTIVISM consists in:
   1) the observation and recording of all accumulation of well-established facts;
   2) analysis and classification of these facts;
   3) the derivation of rules by induction or by general propositions derived from these facts, and
   4) additional controls and checks on general propositions or statements.

In criticizing naïve inductivism, the logical empiricists actually brought Hume back into fashion. Their critique or development was to introduce a deductive element into their notion of verificationism and falsificationism and into their understanding of the covering law[52] of causality. We go back to these themes in Chapter 7 of this book where

---

49 This can be seen as a subtle attack on Mill's method of inductive causality and it will be taken up and repeated by a philosopher of science, Karl Popper.
50 Which corresponds to step 1 in the scheme of the hypothetico-deductive method, stage 0 being the identification of the problem to solve or of the phenomenon in need of explanation or interpretation.
51 Again this is a subtle critique of Mill's methods but also an indictment of the whole empiricist tradition of Bacon, Hobbes, Locke and Hume who constantly undermine and limit the mental faculty of imagination (they sometimes call it a decayed form of sense) in favor of the concept of knowledge. In this sense, someone like Einstein should be seen as a rationalist, not an empiricist, when he claims famously that "Imagination is more important than knowledge".
52 The notion of covering law is related to the Deductive-Nomological model of Carl Hempel because, a covering law exhausts or covers all the possible instances of a given physical phenomenon and thus gives a full scientific explanation of it.

we examine the deductive-nomological model for scientific explanation developed by Karl Hempel. Falsificationism is the work of Karl Popper and it is also tied into the logic of scientific inquiry.

Popper argued that one needed to be able to devise an experiment that could contradict the scientific theory or law that one wanted to test. In the absence of this devisable experiment, the scientific theory could not be falsified and it should not even have been considered a candidate to become part of the body of scientific theories in the first place. In this way, Popper claimed to have shown that both psychoanalysis and Marxism were pseudo-sciences since no empirical experiments could be provided to test their hypotheses.

CONCLUSION

We conclude the chapter by comparing the empiricist theory of knowledge with the other theory of knowledge considered in this book, Rationalism and the Idealist and Pragmatist worldviews.

Empiricism rejects the innate ideas and the intuitions of Rationalism. While some empiricists accept that some domains of knowledge like mathematics are deductive, some like Mill rejected even this possibility.

In contrast to Pragmatism, Empiricism limits experience to sense-experience. In Pragmatism, experience is broader and can be extended to religious experience, educational and political experience, for instance. Most empiricists are strict representationalists (Hume is a notable exception) and sensationalists, and argue that knowledge can be derived only from sense-experience and representation.

As regards Idealism, Empiricism rejects the thesis that there is something like a cosmic mind or any form of dualism between the object of knowledge and the knower. For empiricists, the only minds in existence are finite human minds in which nothing enters that was not previously in the senses.

Logical positivists are opposed to all metaphysics. They argue that statements of metaphysics have no meaning. They concede that their criticism does not apply to art. The logical positivists are critical of metaphysics because it makes assertions and statements that cannot be verified nor confirmed by sense-experience. For the positivists, significance and meaning occur only in relation to a scientific hypothesis. Metaphysical assertions on the other hand, have no empirical content because they do not possess a referent in experience.

Metaphysicians discuss and debate questions and issues about God, the soul, free will, etc. that are not tangible. However, logical positivism, which was developed in Vienna, was contemporaneous with the Viennese Expressionists and with the founder of the Bauhaus architectural movement. Von Neurath, who was part of the Vienna circle of positivism, argued against rejecting propositions on art and artistic expressions since these propositions have aesthetic and artistic objects as referents. These objects are given to our senses much like the colors and shapes and sounds we hear. Neurath admitted however, that such statements were not as clear as scientific propositions made in modern physics, and needed to be worked on and refined in order to improve clarity.

We can see logical positivism as an essentially modernist movement that does not reject the statement of art, but does reject as archaic what it considers to be metaphysical statements. It employs Hume's critique of induction against the truth of any metaphysical statement and in this way the scepticism of Hume was put to work to clear the world's house of all and any of the metaphysical statements and propositions of its past. In a famous lecture, Carnap, a logical positivist, attacks Heidegger's use of the word nothingness in a text for being completely meaningless.[53]

In conclusion, we have studied the empiricist movement with its beginnings in Aristotle and up to the 20th century in Vienna and Berlin. This movement is extremely influential and crucial in the development of the scientific method and the understanding of scientific explanation that we will study in Chapter 7. It is this movement that has made possible in great part, modern atheism (though there is a case to be made for continental atheism in the works of the Hegelian, Ludwig Feuerbach). Empiricism has influenced education, pedagogy and all other areas of modern life. It becomes critical, then, to have a solid grasp of the theory of knowledge it expounds in order to understand modern culture and society.

Up to now we have considered the rationalist and empiricist theories of knowledge. Another important aspect of the curriculum of the humanities for which this book serves as an introductory text are worldviews. Worldviews have three main aspects: ontological aspects, knowledge or epistemological aspects, and axiological or practical-ethical and moral aspects. In the next chapter, we begin with the Idealist worldview. In all, we shall consider four worldviews and compare them to each other: the Western Idealist worldview, the Pragmatist worldview, the Scientific worldview and its accompanying method and the Humanist worldview, which is at the core of what we understand by the Humanities.

---

53 20th century phenomenology and logical positivism were often in a relation of rivalry and competition even though Husserl did his PhD in mathematics in Berlin and frequented Weierstrass, who was the teacher of some of the later members of the logical empiricist school of thought in Berlin.

QUESTIONS
Empiricist Theory of Knowledge

1. What is the empiricist maxim (attributed to Pierre Gassendi) and how is it related to knowledge?
2. Why could the rationalist and the empiricist theories of knowledge be seen as being in opposition or competition?
3. Is there a way to be both an empiricist and a rationalist in various domains of knowledge? Give and example of how this would work.
4. What is the role of Aristotle and his theory of hylomorphism in the history of empiricism?
5. What role does Avicenna's material intellect play in the history of empiricism?
6. Why might Francis Bacon be seen as the modern originator of empiricism?
7. Why is Francis Bacon's theory of matter so important for his philosophy of science and for his understanding of the empiricist theory of knowledge?
8. What is the influence of Bacon's understanding of magic (with its associated concept of operations upon nature) on his development of the scientific method?
9. Describe Locke's theory of knowledge and why he is considered to be the true founder of British empiricism.
10. What is the representational theory of perception and does Locke hold that theory or not?
11. What role do simple and complex ideas play in Locke's corpuscular theory of knowledge?
12. What is Hume's dinstinction between impressions and ideas and how does it place limits upon the imagination?
13. How does Hume relate matters of fact to relations of ideas?
14. What is the problem of logical connection and how does it relate to the problem of induction in Hume?
15. Why does Hume critique the notion of theodicy and of divine perfection in his *Dialogues Concerning Natural Religion*?
16. What is the phenomenalist theory of knowledge held by John Stuart Mill and how is it related to his methods of classification of causal arguments?
17. How does the empiricist theory of knowledge experience a revival in the twentieth century through the work of the logical empiricists?
18. Why is the notion of verificationism and falsificationism so central to logical empiricism?
19. Why does logical empiricism reject any form of metaphysical statement?
20. How is logical empiricism different from classical empiricism?
21. How does logical empiricism refine the scientific method?
22. Why is naïve inductivism in line with Hume's critique of induction and why is it rejected by the proponents of logical empiricism in favor of a more deductive approach to hypothesis-creation or discovery in the natural or empirical sciences?

✓ KEY CONCEPTS & DEFINITIONS - IDEALISM

2400 BC to Present

PEOPLE

PLATO, PLOTINUS, AUGUSTINE, KANT, HEGEL, PEIRCE (WHO IS ALSO A PRAGMATIST) BRADLEY, RADHAKRISHNAN,

IDEALISM is a theory of knowledge that defines reality as a mental phenomenon or something mentally-formed; and emphasizes the thesis that reality is fundamentally immaterial.

IDEAL: What is most perfect or most desirable. E.g. 'the ideal husband', 'in an ideal world'. The word **ideal** shares a root with the word '**idea**'.

SUBJECTIVE IDEALISM places the human subject and the subjective experience at the center and source of knowledge.

OBJECTIVE IDEALISM claims that there is an objective ideal apart that, while it may inform, is independent of the human subject. This is the position of Charles Peirce and perhaps of Plato.

TRANSCENDENTAL IDEALISM claims that perfect knowledge can never cross the bounds, limits and boundaries of sense and experience. One must 'transcend' these limitations in order to perceive the perfect knowledge.

ABSOLUTE IDEALISM: "ALL IS MIND." The human mind and the Cosmic, Universal Mind can reach communion in absolute knowledge through the combination of both discursive and intuitive knowledge and data.

PEOPLE	IDEAS
PLATO	the existence of certain universals called **ideas** or forms (eidos)
PLOTINUS (204-270)	the One (*Hen*), the Intellect (*Nous*) and the Soul (*Psyche*)
AUGUSTINE (358-430)	Christian cleric who developed notion of Trinity, criticized Manichaeism and integrated the works of Plato, Philo and Plotinus with the truth of Biblical Scripture and the New Testament Gospels. He may be viewed as a Christian idealist.
KANT (1724-1804)	German (Prussian) philosopher who lived towards the end of the Age of Enlightenment and who wrote the famous work, *Critique of Pure Reason*. By developing and describing the antinomies of reason he criticized the proofs of the existence of God and developed transcendental idealism.
HEGEL (1770–1831)	German (Swabian) philosopher who was a student or disciple of Kant. Hegel developed the philosophical position of Absolute Idealism. His main works are *The Phenomenology of Spirit* and *The Science of Logic*. Hegel criticizes Kant's refutation of the ontological argument claims there exists a deep identity between the subject and object of knowledge

CHAPTER 5
WORLDVIEWS: IDEALISM

Idealism is a worldview[1] that defines reality as a mental phenomenon or something mentally formed. This worldview strongly upholds the thesis that reality is fundamentally immaterial. It is mental (cognitive) or mentally-formed; and can be perceived only by human beings, who influence and contribute to the shaping of the nature of the reality they perceive, as a mental phenomenon. This is modern Cartesian (perhaps Hegelian, but not quite Hegelian) idealism; Plato did not think that reality (relative or absolute) was mental.

---

1 Worldviews have three main aspects, ontological aspects, knowledge or epistemological aspects and axiological or practical-ethical and moral aspects. In the next chapter we begin with the Idealist worldview. We define ontology on p. 224, footnote 2 of this book. The ontological aspects of a worldview deal with what it posits as reality claims about the world. The knowledge aspects of the worldview encompass truth claims about what is valid and sound about the world. Finally, the axiological aspects of the worldview make value claims about what is right and wrong or good and evil in the world. The three aspects are embedded and often distinguishable only analytically. What characterizes a worldview is that we seek to enter into dialogue with it rather than judge it and evaluate or criticize it as a whole. Theories of knowledge are criticizable in contrast since they are not a broad totality, like worldviews. Epistemologies or theories of knowledge make more limited claims and can therefore be criticized clearly as opposed to worldviews. Ideologies are also important concepts that need to be contrasted to worldviews. Ideologies are criticizable in themselves and the discipline of critique of ideologies is a subset of the humanities and social science. Typically, ideologies are both conscious and unconscious and this brings them into comparison with worldviews which may also be unconscious, but the notion of ideology comports the idea that there are false beliefs or erroneous concepts and actions that are associated with ideologies. As an example there is the Capitalist and the Communist ideology but, as the example of China shows, this is distinct from the Chinese worldview which is more intricate and much deeper. Finally, a country like China may possess an ideology, a worldview and economic system that are distinct. China has a communist ideology, it possesses an Ancient worldview and it operates in a capitalistic way in the global economy despite its communist ideology.

In the philosophical branch of epistemology or the theory of knowledge, idealism generally manifests as skepticism about the possibility of knowing any mind-independent object. Its philosophical opposite—epistemological realism—asserts that there is an object independent of the mind and of which we may attain knowledge.

As an ontological[2] doctrine, idealism goes further, asserting that all entities are composed of mind or spirit. Idealism thus generally rejects physicalist and dualist theories that fail to ascribe priority to the mind. This claim must be qualified. For Plato for example, there were two ontological levels (i.e., two metaphysical realms or two levels of reality). Seen in this way, classic idealism is not incompatible with ontological dualism.

> **ⓘ KEY DEFINITIONS**
>
> **IDEALISM** is worldview that defines reality as a mental phenomenon or something mentally-formed; and emphasizes the thesis that reality is fundamentally immaterial.

Religious and philosophical thought which privileges the immaterial or the supernatural over the material and natural is ubiquitous and ancient. However, the earliest extant argument that the world of experience is grounded in the mental or the supermental, derives from Greece and India. This occurs in the *Nous (Intellect-Mind)* for the Greeks, in the *Atman* (the Self) and its identity with the *Brahman* (the Absolute, or Cosmic-World-Ground), for the Hindu interpreters of the *Vedas* and the *Upanishads*.

The Hindu Idealists in India and the Greek Neo-Platonists gave pantheistic arguments for an all-pervading World-consciousness as the ground or true nature of reality. However, modernity has individualized and atomized the Plotinian World-Soul and World-Psyche. This development occurs throughout the works of Augustine and Descartes.

Some philosophers, the most famous one in the Western philosophical tradition being Kant, have argued that objects do not exist entirely apart from the human mind because the human mind shapes them. It is not the world that shapes the mind, but the mind that gives reason to the world by bringing it under the categories of its understanding, so that the mind alone is the source of all reason. In Descartes, who precedes Kant, this is further connected to the possessing of an inner light, an innate moral goodness and an understanding of what is good.

---

2 Ontology is the study of Being. *To on* means entity in Ancient Greek. Rational debate since Plato about what Being means, what the Being or existence of objects is i.e., What does it mean for a plant to exist or be and how is that different from it just being green. The difference between the statement "God is" and "God is omnipotent" is an ontological question pertaining to the existence and reality of God. Similar statements are made about the existence and reality of any given object. Thus we can first analyze the difference between the statements: "The table is (in the sense of exists)" and "The table is red" to get a better handle before tackling a difficult concept such as 'God'.

This claim needs to be qualified as it is perhaps one of the first characteristics of modern man that manifests in history. Insofar as this modern man believes that he can shape his reality, gods and the divine are written out of the equation of knowledge our out of man's worldview. Let us now trace the history of idealism and of the idealist worldview.

5.1 ANCIENT & MEDIEVAL IDEALISM
5.1.1 Ancient Idealism

The most important ancient idealist is Plato who is most famous for his theory of 'Ideas'. Plato continued the work of Socrates who had wanted to know whether it was possible to find something like a definition of virtue. He was interested in knowing whether we could find an explanation for all of the occurrences of virtue.

For Socrates, it is easy to say that it is good to treat your parents with respect and to pay back your debts, but is this all there is to virtue?

Consider the example of someone coming to you in the middle of the night asking for a weapon in a state of distress. Would you really, if you had a weapon, give it to him or would you deceive, even lie to that person in order to protect them from themselves? Could we say that you acted virtuously?

In chapter three we saw that Socrates asked for definitions in ethics. Starting from this Socratic search for a general and abstract definition of virtue, Plato went further. He posited the existence of certain universals which he called ideas or forms after the Greek word *eidos*. *Eidos* is the perfect tense of the verb *orao* meaning 'to see' in ancient Greek.

In the dialogue called the *Republic* Plato stated that the ideas were associated with the intelligible, invisible world. All that was sensuous, all that could be seen was not an idea but a manifestation of the idea. Let us take the example of the table or of the chair we have in front of us. It is Plato's claim that it is a chair by virtue of participating (*methexein*) in the idea or form of chair. The chair possesses "chairness" because it participates in the idea of chair. The chairness of the chair is something that is shared with all the physical chairs that exist in the world that is given to our sense-perception. But only the idea of the chair has reality according to Plato, only the *idea* of the chair can be true in the real and full sense of the word. Chairness functions here as both a defining or definitory property that allows knowers to pick out the invidualsor particulars in the world that refer to chair-like objects. But Plato goes even further and for him the theory of ideas (that "noble lore" as he refers to it in his fifth Letter) posits chairness as an independently existing form or metaphysical reality. The ideas of Chair, Justice, Goodness… exist in an independent realm called the ontological realm of ideas, which is radically independent from the world where real chairs exist, where just acts occur and where good actions manifest.

> ### ⓘ KEY DEFINITIONS
>
> **IDEAL:** What is most perfect or most desirable. E.g. 'the ideal husband', 'in an ideal world'
> The word **ideal** shares a root with the word '**idea**'.
> **PLATO** posited the existence of certain universals he called **ideas** or forms (eidos).

In a dialogue called *The Meno*, Plato states the problem of rational enquiry, which is of particular interest to us in our study of his theory of knowledge. Plato (or Socrates, to be precise, since we never know exactly what Plato means to say[3]) claims that we need to obtain knowledge of X, but he presents the following dilemma or paradox. In order to know X we must already possess some knowledge of X; but if this is the case, then it seems that rational enquiy is useless since we know ahead of time what we are looking for. Otherwise Socrates further claims, we have no knowledge of X. But in this case, we cannot get started in our enquiry for the truth of X since we have absolutely no clue of how to begin to enquire into the truth conditions or criteria of knowledge of X.

Plato solves this problem. However, in another dialogue, called *The Phaedo*, he claims that, in order to solve the dilemma of how to obtain knowledge of X, we must have known X previously. Plato claims that we have access to innate ideas which our rational soul knows and forgets as it enters the body. This myth of anamnesis is what explains our knowledge of the ideas according to Plato. Since we forget our knowledge of X or of the idea of X at birth, the task of the life of learning is to recollect, to enquire in a rational way and to remember what the idea and truth of X was that we knew before we were born and the soul entered into the body. The platonic forms (beauty in itself, good in itself, justice in itself, truth in itself are distinguished from the simple ideas, idea of a chair, idea of a table) as objects of knowledge.

Plato's theory of forms or "ideas" describes ideal forms (for example, the platonic solids in geometry or abstract objects and universals such as Goodness and Justice), as abstract objects existing independently of any particular instance. One should try to determine whether this doctrine is an example of a metaphysical idealism as transcendental idealism or whether Plato is the earliest representative of metaphysical objective idealism.

No matter where the final judgment lies, Plato holds that matter is real, though transitory

---

[3] This is part of the authorship problem in Plato, caused in part by the fact that he always expresses his opinions through interposed characters in his dialogues.

and imperfect, and is perceived by our body and its senses, while it is given existence by the eternal ideas that are perceived directly by our rational intellect (*Nous*). Plato was therefore a metaphysical and epistemological dualist, an outlook that modern idealism has striven to avoid: Plato's thought is thus significantly different from idealism in its modern sense.

Plotinus[4] reworks the Platonic dialectic and dualism by integrating Aristotle's critique of Plato. Aristotle had claimed that Plato had 'split the Forms'. The Forms or Ideas had to be given in a substantial, subsistent substratum. This is what Aristotle called *ousia*.[5] The specificity of the Form or Platonic idea was embodied in substance, which could be distinguished from accident. Aristotle distinguishes matter from privation of Form (or shape). Contrariwise, Plotinus holds that matter is what makes for the lesser reality of the sensible world since, according to him, all natural things are distinguished by the fact that their essence consists in being forms embodied and circumscribed by matter. According to Plotinus, matter lacks all intelligibility, but is somehow still dependent on the One.

> ### ⓘ KEY DEFINITIONS
>
> **ANCIENT IDEALISM KEY CONCEPTS AND DEFINITIONS**
> - **Plato's theory of ideas:** the idea of table gives an independent perceivable object the quality of tablehood or tableness in virtue of which it becomes a table. This idea exists in an independent metaphysical realm.
> - **Socrates' quest for Moral Definitions:** What is the ideal characteristic or nature of X?
> - **Plotinus and the One:** The One as Ideal, otherworldly entity, that structures our reality here "below".

What is of central importance in Plotinus' philosophy is the relationship between the One (*Hen*), the Intellect (*Nous*) and the Soul (*Psyche*). The One is *epekeina tes ousias*, beyond everything including the essences and Being. Out of the One, the (World-) Intellect and the (World-) Soul are precipitated. This thesis of Plotinus is of paramount importance in trying to counter the arguments of someone like Heidegger for whom on the contrary, the pragmatic (*zuhandene*) precipitates the theoretical (*vorhandene*).

As Idealism manifests itself closer to the modern era, a definite move towards the subjective is made. Some have claimed that modernity should be understood according to the principle of subjectivity.[6] In this case, its great inaugurator and founder is doubtlessly René Descartes.

---

[4] Plotinus was a neo-Platonist philosopher of the Hellenistic era and lived between 204 and 270 ACE.
[5] *Ousia* is Aristotle's Greek word for substance.
[6] This has been argued by the German philosopher Habermas in his book *The Philosophical Discourse of Modernity*.

5.1.2 Medieval (Christian) Idealism

The most important medieval idealist we consider is Augustine. John Duns Scotus may also perhaps be understood as an idealist despite his realist and empiricist leanings;[7] but we will focus on Augustine in this section.

The idea of World-soul is recast and reshaped by Augustine into the notion of a finite human soul-intellect (*mens*) as opposed to the infinite Mind-Intellect (*intellectus*) of God. This reshaping prepares the work of Pico della Mirandola whom we discuss in the last chapter of this book; Giordano Bruno (Bruno is the anti-Christian element in this triad) and Descartes. All three prepare the finitization of the human subject with respect to Ancient Idealism to some degree.

According to Augustine, there is a certain amount of perfection that is beyond human thinking yet which allows this thinking to occur. This means that something infinite and immaterial exists which precedes human thought. It is this something essential and infinite that makes my finite thought possible. We can get in touch with this infinity within our finite, situated first-person self by going within ourselves. Within man, *in interiore homine*, there exists this infinite source of Goodness and perfection which is called God. Later when Descartes develops his ontological argument by referring to God's perfections, the influence is clearly Augustinian.

But while an infinity is discovered within man, this infinity is somehow outside the world and not immanent within it. Augustine also accepts, it seems, the platonic dichotomy between the two ontological realms of Being and Becoming. It is true that this dichotomy is mediated by the emanationist[8] ontological model of Plotinus. But whereas in Plotinus, the world-soul inhabits even the rational man, the philosopher, in a directly immanent way, for Augustine, there is a clear delimitation between man's powers and God's.

---

7 This is due primarily to work on the notion of universals, which may be taken to be coterminous with ideals to a certain extent.

8 *Emanationism* is a cosmological and ontological concept which occurs in some philosophical and religious systems. The most famous use of the concept of emanation is in the ontology of Plotinus and the Neo-Platonists. Emanation is the way or mode in which all things are derived from the One in Plotinus's ontological and metaphysical system. All things are derived from the One, which is a first reality or perfect God, by steps of degradation to lesser degrees of the first reality or God, and at every step the emanating beings are less pure, less perfect, less divine. The last level or grade of reality is matter which is a form of privation from the perfect forms of the One. It must be stressed though that in emanationism some degree of the perfection of the One or first principle is preserved even in the less perfect entities which derive from it such as matter. Emanationism is a transcendent principle (See Chapter 3 for meaning of transcendence) from which everything is derived, and is opposed to both Creationism (which is a system in which the Creator is a sentient God who independent of the universe it creates) and materialism or empiricism, for which there is no underlying ontological reality behind the immanently given phenomena.

Only God is omnipotent and in being omnipotent, he necessarily limits man's free will. This was the upshot of the controversy with Pelagius. Divine justice and grace entail that man can come towards God, but God has to first choose him, to move towards him. Unless the movement is initiated by God towards man, man cannot move towards God. The movement of God towards man described here is both theological, ontological and logical in Augustine's philosophy.

With Plotinus, mystical union[9] destroys the self. Even though man cannot choose to enter into union with the One, he must detach himself and wait for union to manifest, so to speak. What is crucial is that once the union with the One is attained, there is no longer a self, finite or infinite.

In Augustine, the picture is different. God is an infinity which lies, at least potentially, within the human soul. This soul is a part of the indivisible, divine totality. The human self does not vanish in the mystical union with God. God is found within, in the vast apartments of inner memory. Since God is discovered and somehow recollected from within the inner workings and caverns of the human self, what happens when the union with God occurs is not loss of self, but self-clarity through the discovery of God within. Of course, at the same time, a delimitation occurs.

> ### ⓘ KEY DEFINITIONS
>
> **MEDIEVAL IDEALISM KEY CONCEPTS AND DEFINITIONS**
> - **Augustine and the Two Cities:** An ideal city of God that is virtuous as opposed to the sinful, corrupt city of man (Jerusalem the Holy versus Babylon the Harlot).
> - **Augustine on Free Will:** Anti-pelagianism; God first allows man to turn his head towards Him through the gift of grace.
> - **St-Thomas:** The Church as an ideal otherworldly entity or institution that understands and defends the natural law.

One realizes that God is infinite and that the human self is finite, but memory gives to the human self the security and power to realize the divine proto-adamic origin of the human soul. Man becomes dependent: though he is made free, it is God who gives him his freedom and this only (if we heed Nietzsche) to make him accountable and responsible for his will.

According to Augustine, Pelagius misconstrues 2 Peter 1:4 (*we are sharers in the divine nature*) which claims that man is sinless because the human soul is somehow like God without sin (*sine peccatum quemadmodem Deus*). In this way, according to Augustine, human nature can never attain the perfection of the divine substance. Augustine's

---
9 Plotinus calls this mystical union *henosis* in the Ancient Greek.

idealism is particularly visible when he reworks Plato's two-world or two-realm ontology into the Christian theological narrative of the City of God and the City of Man. The providential city is virtuous and pure: it is the celestial Jerusalem, while the City of Man is full of sin and pride; it is the earthly, material and venial city of Babylon.

5.2 MODERN IDEALISM
5.2.1 Subjective Idealism

Subjective Idealism (immaterialism or phenomenalism) describes a relationship between the experience of the human mind and the world in which objects can be construed as collections or "bundles" of sense data in the perceiver. Traditionally, this kind of idealism is associated with Berkeley and is heavily influenced by the empiricism of the British tradition. Later, Hume will develop his account of knowledge in terms of a bundle theory of sense-data. It is perhaps anachronistic to project such a model back onto Berkeley's idealism. Berkeley himself never really accepted this name for his philosophy and preferred the title of immaterialism or phenomenalism. Berkeley's famous motto is '*esse est percipi*' or 'to be is to be perceived'. This form of idealism is usually associated with René Descartes, with Berkeley or with the German philosopher Fichte. Subjective idealism is different from Objective, Transcendental or Absolute Idealism. Subjective idealism is based on the human subject and subjective experience as the center of knowledge, whereas the last three discount the purely human or subjective as incomplete. On the other hand, though the human mind is central as the source of innate ideas as we saw in the theory of knowledge of Rationalism, Subjective Idealism is accused of subjectivism or solipsism in that it cannot attain the truth of the object of knowledge as independent of the human mind.

> ### ⓘ KEY DEFINITIONS
>
> **SUBJECTIVE IDEALISM** places the human subject and the subjective experience at the center and source of knowledge.
>
> **OBJECTIVE IDEALISM** claims that there is an objective ideal independent of the human subject, but which may inform it.
>
> **TRANSCENDENTAL IDEALISM** claims that knowledge can never cross the bounds, limits and boundaries of sense and experience.

Though Subjective idealism may be a complex notion, it can be narrowed down by concretely examining Bishop Berkeley's and J. G. Fichte's philosophies. These are the main and most articulate representatives of Subjective idealism we have. Paradoxically or anecdotally, neither of these philosophers accepted this term for their philosophies. Berkeley saw himself as an "immaterialist" and Fichte saw himself simply as a critical or Transcendental idealist clarifying what Kant had left unclear and incomplete in his critical project.

5.2.2 Objective Idealism

While it may be conceded that idealism is mostly a modern phenomenon, this claim may also be questioned. The criterion for a philosophy being called Idealistic is not necessarily its self-awareness of itself as idealistic. This is a modern anachronism and fallacy. Self-awareness was first introduced by Descartes as one of the fundamental criteria of knowledge. Historical self-awareness came later, in the Enlightenment period. To project the criterion of historical self-awareness back onto Plato and Plotinus and to claim that their philosophies cannot be called idealistic is to take an errant view of history. In fact, it is the truth of the theory of historicism[10] that we are developing in this text that both Plato and Plotinus are idealists.

> ⓘ **KEY DEFINITIONS**
>
> **MODERN IDEALISM KEY CONCEPTS AND DEFINITIONS**
> - **Subjective Idealism:** The mind is that of an individual; ideas are located in the mind; existence of innate knowledge and innate ideas.
> - **Objective Idealism:** Reality is ideal; there exists a great cosmic Mind and the World is identical to it.
> - **Transcendental Idealism:** Reason and Idealism are limited; the bounds of reality cannot be transcended and if they are reason becomes nonsensical and antinomic.
> - **Absolute Idealism:** The Absolute and God are the highest concepts: They constitute both ultimate Being and ultimate knowledge. God, the Absolute and the World are one unity and one identity.

Objective idealism is sometimes taken to be the position defended by Charles Peirce although we study him in this text as a defender of the pragmatist worldview. The thesis of objective idealism writ large is that the whole world is a world-soul or Mind. Every aspect of the world has a structure that is similar to a divine mind. While Plato and Plotinus seem to endorse this view, theirs is an idealism which precedes the modern subject-object distinction, so it may be improper to call them objective idealists. Some German idealists like Novalis have been also called objective idealists but their idealism is tainted with Romanticism and magical, almost alchemical, properties. In the end, it might be difficult

---

10 Historicism is the thesis every conceivable object, be it science, religion, Being, God or intellect can be explained historically or with respect to its historical origins and development. Radical historicism claims that we can never understand the values of an epoch different from ours, and that there is no unitary science or religion because history introduces a radical flux within values, science and religion.

to tell knowledge-realism apart from objective idealism. One possible distinction is that most forms of realism assume that there is an object independent either of the knowledge that engages in the knowing of the object or of the mind or intellect that engages in the knowing of the object. So there is this subject-object break that is still presupposed in the realist theory of knowledge. Objective idealism, on the other hand, does not believe in the subject-object dichotomy but rather claims that all that exists is a seamless universal mind and that what appear to be different objects are in fact illusory differences that hide the true mental identity at the bottom of all things.

5.2.3 Transcendental Idealism

Transcendental idealism was coined by Immanuel Kant toward the end of the eighteenth century. Kant claims that the mind plays an active role in shaping the contents of experience through intuitive perception. This is the case according to Kant because reality is made up of the matter of intuition, but the human understanding possesses certain categories which organize and contribute to shaping the material furnished by the senses via the matter of intuition. In order to ground the truth of synthetic *a priori* propositions, Kant examines how knowledge is established through the application of categories of the understanding to the contents of experience. These experiences or their contents are perceived by the sensitive part of our mind, and then recast through intuition into the final synthetic unity of apperception. The first half of his famous work, *Critique of Pure Reason*, is devoted to examining the process of knowledge itself through which the understanding shapes what it receives and is given to it in sense-experience. In this sense, the role of the thinking subject, inherited from Descartes, is central. Kant writes:

> ...if I remove the thinking subject, the whole material world must at once vanish because it is nothing but a phenomenal appearance in the sensibility of ourselves as a subject, and a manner or species of representation.[11]

Thus Kant's epistemological model is essentially dependent on that of the Cartesian subject despite Kant's claim that in the second edition of the *Critique* that his idealism—the transcendental kind—differs from that of Descartes'. This is the case, according to Kant, because it addresses Hume's notion of experience, which in some way must be external to thought and mind. Transcendental Idealism then, is defined by the fact that knowledge can never cross the bounds, limits and boundaries of sense and experience.

Kant's claim is that the transcendental is both included in all categories of reality and still is somehow above or beyond these categories and that, finally, the understanding of the transcendental is something that cannot cross a certain limit or a bound. Transcendental ideas and regulative ideas are thus ideas under whose rule reason is allowed to govern

---

11 Kant Immanuel, *Critique of Pure Reason*, A383.

itself, but which somehow lack the reality of the phenomena. To see how Kant delimits transcendental idealism from both Descartes' (skeptical) idealism and Berkley's dogmatic idealism, the following citation is important:

> The dictum of all genuine idealists, from the Eleatic school to Bishop Berkeley, is contained in this formula: "All knowledge through the senses and experience is nothing but sheer illusion, and only in the ideas of the pure understanding and reason is there truth." The principle that throughout dominates and determines my [transcendental] idealism is, on the contrary: "All knowledge of things merely from pure understanding or pure reason is nothing but sheer illusion, and only in experience is there truth." [12]

In the second half of the two editions of the *Critique of Pure Reason* Kant famously deals with the antinomies of reason. These antinomies and a large part of the second half of the first *Critique* are devoted to claiming that the arguments for the existence of God, which Kant numbers to five (following the classification of Thomas Aquinas), and which have been handed down from the Scholastic tradition. These traditional arguments for the existence of God are the teleological argument, the ontological argument and the cosmological argument. Aquinas gives five forms of the teleological argument[13] which he calls (i) the argument of the first cause, (ii) the argument of the first mover, (iii) the argument from contingency, (iv) the argument of from degree and finally (v) the teleological argument. The particular thesis of Kant which interests us in this context is the one claiming that the cosmological proof of God's existence presupposes the ontological proof. This thesis was later attacked by Hegel and we will deal with Hegel's criticism later in this chapter in the section on Absolute Idealism.

It seems that Kant was intent on proving that cosmological arguments for the existence of God are connected to ontological ones.[14] This is because Kant conceives logical and ontological necessity as the opposite of an impossibility, while possibility is that which does not contradict itself. Thus, in Kant both necessity and actuality are always

---

12 Kant Immanuel, *Prolegomena to Any Future Metaphysics That Will Be Able to Present Itself as a Science*, 374.
13 There could be debate as to whether or not the sub-arguments are all versions of the teleological argument. For example the argument of contingency though Aristotelian in form might be judged to be different from a purely teleological argument.
14 The cosmological argument is an argument for the existence of God which argues from first causes. It involves the notion of the impossibility of an infinite regress. Causality regresses back onto first causes and then discovers that there must exist a First Cause or Original Principle if not the regress onto first causes would be infinite. Since such a regress is irrational or illogical, the cosmological argument concludes that a First Cause or First Motor (as Aristotle called the First Cause) must exist. There are some variants of the argument, each with subtle yet important distinctions: the arguments from in *causa* (causality), in *esse* (essentially) and in *fieri* (becoming). An ontological argument is any one of a category of philosophical arguments for the existence of God using ontology. The ontological argument is typically based on some affinity or identity between the ontology or Being of Mind and the Being of reality. From a certain perfection of the Mind, the argument claims that this perfection can only be made greater if it actually exists. Thus since God exists in the human Mind and is a kind of supreme Mind, it can reach its optimum (nothing greater than which can be thought as St-Anselm argued) or maximum only by really existing or by attaining the Being of Reality.

subordinated to possibility and non-contradiction. There is, however, an inconsistency in Kant's work here. In the first part of the *Critique* where he lists the contents of the category of modality, Kant opposes necessity to contingency, not to impossibility.

Kant's approach is in direct contrast with Hegel for whom it is more important to ascertain and preserve God's freedom by identifying him and his necessity within the Absolute. Hegel argues that both necessity and freedom, both essence and existence are unified and identified within the Being of the Absolute. The Absolute as concept is the highest determination both of Being and of God. Both Being and God are sublated within the Being of the Absolute through the developmental movement and process of greater determination which is given in the *Logic* and the *Phenomenology of Spirit*.

In this way, Hegel shifts the problem of freedom and necessity of the third antinomy from the freedom and necessity of the finite thinking subject to the freedom and necessity of God. God must be free insofar as he is not bound by any determinations within the world for it is God's being as the highest Idea and the highest Concept that first makes freedom possible. Yet at the same time God as Concept, Idea and Mind is identical with the world understood under the guise of reason.

Through this move, Hegel makes God immanent to the world while preserving God's transcendence from the world. However, it is an important thesis of the author that Hegel's move to immanentize God while preserving his transcendence is unstable because it rests on the identification of God's essence with his existence. All the same, Hegel's attempt to equate God's essence with God's existence is an important development in Western views on God's nature.

5.2.4 Absolute Idealism

Absolute Idealism finds its greatest and most formidable hero in the philosopher Hegel. Some later figures such as the English Bradley and the Indian Radhakrishnan—two other philosophers—have also come to adopt this position. Radhakrishnan's philosophy has connections to Hindu Idealism and non-dualistic Advaintaism that distinguish it from Hegel's absolute Idealism, grounded as it was in Lutheran Christianity. Though the Young Hegelians and the Left-Hegelians have questioned the possible grounding of Hegel's philosophy in Christianity, there is little doubt that (the *Wirkungsgeschichte*[15] of) Christianity played a defining role in shaping Hegel's philosophy. Similarly, Bradley's idealism is much closer to the subjective idealism of Berkeley and was influenced by the

---

15 *Wirkungsgeschichte* is a concept developed by the German philosopher Hans-Georg Gadamer. It means the work of history or the history of the influence of a given concept which is sometimes in the background but which works nonetheless to influence the way an idea is treated and received at a later historical time. It is almost like a historical unconscious in Freud's understanding of the term unconscious.

empiricist and quasi-nominalist aspect of English philosophy.

How then does Absolute idealism distinguish itself from Transcendental, Objective and Subjective idealism?

We must appeal to its greatest champion, Georg Wilhelm Friedrich Hegel (1770 – 1831). God and Being are two absolutes as Paul Tillich has clearly argued. God is the Absolute of theology and Being is the Absolute of ontology, but even though Heidegger is right that we do not have to accept the onto-theological construction and embedding of these two concepts given by the Hegelian synthesis, it is clear that the relation and understanding of *God and Being* has not been exhausted in our Western tradition.

There are linguistic and terminological issues that need to be clarified before considering further what this relation consists in. Being is written as *einai* in Ancient Greek. It becomes *esse* in Medieval Latin. The distinction between essence and existence is perhaps a formal one if we follow Duns Scotus, but both essence and existence are related to Being as some aspect of it. Furthermore, the philosophers of the Middle Ages analyzed God in terms of the relation and distinction between his essence and his existence. By relating these terms back to the Aristotelian notion of Being, they connect and return it to one of the first onto-theological syntheses of the notions of Being and God.

There are problems with the very language and terminology that we must wrestle with here. First, the distinction between *esse* and *id quod est* appears in Boethius' *De Hebdomadibus*. *Esse* is being and *id quod est* is that which is. We may take Being to be independent from that which is. Being is the general concept and that which is said of any individual or particular entity that is or that exists. But there is also a conceptual difficulty in the very language. Graham[16] claims that Aristotle was clear on the existential and predicative uses of to be. But not everyone in Ancient Greece was clear on this distinction—Parmenides for example, is famous for not having known the distinction between the existential and predicative uses of 'to be'.

Aristotelian thought influenced the Arabic and Islamic metaphysicians and scholars, Al-Farabi, Al-Ghazali, Avicenna and Averroes. According to Graham, since Arabic is a semitic language, it needed to distinguish between the existential and predicative uses[17] of the verb 'to be'. So it developed a new vocabulary: It used *wujud* for existence and *mahiyyah* for quiddity/essence. It remains unclear how *wujud* and *mahiyyah* are translated into Western Latin Medieval philosophical discourse.

---

16 A.C. Graham, *Disputers of the Tao: Philosophical Argument in Ancient China*, Open Court, Chicago 1999. Print.
17 The predicative use of the verb 'to be' is employed to express that an object has a certain attribute, such as 'X is red' or 'X is square'. The existential use of the verb is used to express that an object X exists; in this case: "X is" and may be replaced semantically by "X exists".

However, the couple *essentia-existentia* and their distinction is fundamental to understanding how the Being of God is dealt with in Western thought. The various explanations for this distinction, its role in the understanding of God and his Being are what differentiate the main schools of the High Scholastic, whether they are Ghentian, Thomistic, Scotist or Ockhamistic.[18] In accepting the identification of essence and existence within the Being of God, Hegel was doing precisely what Thomas Aquinas and other philosophers from the Middle-Ages had done. In this context, Hegel reconstructs his analysis of the relationship between freedom and necessity in Kant's third Antinomy of the *Critique of Pure Reason* and recasts this discussion in terms of the freedom and necessity of the Absolute subjectivity of God—not on the basis of man's finite subjectivity.

Where Hegel and Kant find room to agree is in their claim that God must be immanent to Creation and to the world of phenomena. For if God's essence were not given within the phenomenal world, the concept of God could not even be conceived without contradiction. For Kant, possibility consists solely in the absence of contradiction. Clearly God's concept is not self-contradictory for Kant, but that does not mean that an intuition is ever given for this concept. The concept of God does exist within the realm of our ideas, but it is a mere regulative idea—one which we heuristically use to orient our action, which we can never perceive, but which we can perhaps barely intuit.

Hegel, on the contrary, makes the claim that God's freedom and necessity form an identity. This allows him to unify and identify the ontological and cosmological proofs and the arguments Kant had dichotomized. (Kant is aware, however, that the two arguments, the ontological and cosmological are only analytically separable but are in fact inherently connected.) Hegel identifies these two approaches, the ontological and cosmological under the one principle of subjectivity. God is a principle, the highest principle of Mind and Cosmos and in Him, essence and existence, Self and Absolute, Subject and Object, Ego and World, Being and Becoming are united and identified.

However, this is where Hegel errs since the essence and existence of God are forever distinct and non-identifiable—God's essence, his concept, as our analysis makes clear, is unknowable and can only be intuited as such.

---

18 Ghentian, Thomistic, Scotist and Okchamistic refer respectively to Henry Ghent, Thomas Aquinas, Duns Scotus and William of Ockham. Henry of Ghent was a medieval, Scholastic philosopher who lived from 1217 to 1293 and who lectured on topics such as Being, essence, intentionality and illumination. He influence Duns Scotus on the notion of formal distinction; Thomas Aquinas is the most famous Catholic philosopher. He lived from 1225 to 1274 and is famous for his book the *Summa Theologica*; John Duns Scotus is a famous Irish philosopher known as the subtle doctor due to his talent in making subtle logical and ontological distinctions. He lived from 1266 to 1308. William of Ockham is a famous medieval philosopher who took the nominalist side in the debate on universals that occurred in the middle ages. He is known for having developed the principle of parsimony and he lived from 1287 to 1347.

QUESTIONS

WORLDVIEWS: The Idealist Worldview, its Ontology, Epistemology and Axiology

1. How many types of idealism are covered in this chapter? Describe two or three.
2. How is ancient Idealism different from medieval idealism and modern idealism?
3. How is subjective idealism different from objective idealism?
4. Describe the relation between knowledge and transcendental idealism.
5. Describe the relation between knowledge and absolute idealism.
6. How is idealism different from rationalism, pragmatism and empiricism?
7. What is the role of knowledge in idealism?
8. Why can Plato be considered an idealist though some consider Idealism to be a *modern* theory of knowledge?
9. Why does religion and ontology seem more prevalent in the theory of knowledge of idealism than in the other theories of knowledge we have studied?
10. Describe briefly Kant's theory of knowledge.
11. Describe briefly Hegel's theory of knowledge.
12. Can one possess an idealist ontology and a realist theory of knowledge or is that a contradiction?
13. Why could Descartes be considered both a rationalist and an idealist?
14. Explain what the cosmological argument is and how it relates to the idealist theory of knowledge.
15. What are other types of arguments for the existence of God?
16. What is the difference of the predicative versus the existential use of the verb to be?
17. Why does Kant think that the human subject shapes the object of knowledge? Who might have influenced him in this line of thought?
18. What does *emanationism* mean and what role does it play in the idealist theory of knowledge?
19. Aside from Plato, who were the first proponents of idealism?
20. What role does the distinction between essence and existence play in the theory of knowledge of idealism?
21. What are the main aspects of a worldview?
22. Describe the ontological aspects, knowledge aspects and moral-practical aspects of the idealist worldview.

🎁 INTERESTING?

William of **OCKHAM** was an English Franciscan friar, scholastic philosopher and theologian who took the nominalist side in the debate on universals that occurred in the Middle Ages.

He is known for having developed the principle of parsimony or *lex parsimoniae*. Today we speak of **OCKHAM'S RAZOR**, and colloquially we say,

"the simplest explanation is the best."

KEY CONCEPTS & DEFINITIONS - PRAGMATISM

TIME: 19th century to Present

PEOPLE

Emerson, Charles Peirce, William James, John Dewey, Richard Rorty, Robert Brandom

THE PRAGMATIST MAXIM: Consider what effects, which might conceivably have practical bearings, we conceive the object of our conception to have. Then, our conception of these effects is the whole of our conception of the object. (Peirce, 1902)

PEOPLE	IDEAS
EMERSON	"Truth comes in knocks"; it must have practical effect. Importance of practical experience and life.
CHARLES PEIRCE (1839-1914) Founder of Pragmatism.	Firstness, Secondness and Thirdness, pragmatic enquiry in science, fixation of belief, how to attain clear beliefs and find a middle way between religion and science, the importance of habit, the habit tradition of philosophizing (synthesis of Emersonian transcendentalism and Humean-Aristotelian skepticism); induction, deduction and abduction as part of the scientific method; (development of algebraic logic and point-set topology, the Listing theorem); the logic and phenomenology of continuity.
WILLIAM JAMES (1842-1910)	The will to believe, religion, science and the problem of praxis; the varieties of religious experience and of human experience, pragmatist psychology; simplification of pragmatism as a theory of knowledge; continuity and growth as psychological experiences, the philosopher's psychologist.
JOHN DEWEY (1858-1952)	The importance of democracy and pragmatism; simplification of Peirce's theories of knowledge and integration and application of Hegel and Peirce at the level of a theory of education; education as growth and continuity.
RICHARD RORTY (1931-2007)	Pragmatic relativism: the subordination of knowledge and science to democratic imperatives; the loss of the Peircean spirit of pragmatism.
ROBERT BRANDOM (1950–)	Neo-pragmatism. The logic of social norms and inferential role semantics. Recovery of the spirit of pragmatism but reduction of the Peircean project to logic. Loss of the religious, transcendentalist moment of pragmatism (Emerson, Peirce and James). Theory of democracy based on social engineering as opposed to educational growth and continuity (Dewey).

CHAPTER 6
WORLDVIEWS: PRAGMATISM

Some scholars trace a connection between the educational aims of Dewey and the vocations of self-reliance[1] and citizenship in Emerson.[2] They use this connection to support their thesis that New England Transcendentalism was a form of proto-pragmatism and a precursor to the Pragmatist worldview. This thesis is not without its critics, however, as some see a fundamental cleft between the moral and spiritual-religious perfectionism in Emerson and Dewey's democratic political objectives. One could see the pietistic and metaphysical roots of Emersonian and New England Transcendentalism being essentially in tension and perhaps even opposition with the pragmatism of James and Dewey for whom the only real metaphysical distinctions are the ones which have efficacy and instrumentality in practice and in action.

This assessment caricaturizes James's and Dewey's positions to some extent; nonetheless, there remains a sense of tension between the political philosophies of Emerson and those of a Jefferson or of a Madison.

---

1 Self-reliance is a famous concept of Emerson's and the name of a text published in his *Essays* (1841). It describes the value of being independent and autonomous (to be able to give oneself values, principles and modes of conduct) from external coercion, but also support; and to be able to be one's own person and to be ruggedly independent.

2 The most famous scholar to defend this view is Cornel West. See his *The American Evasion of Philosophy: A Genealogy of Pragamatism*. University of Wisconsin Press, 1989.

Since we wish to capture the spirit and origins of American Pragmatism it is necessary to examine the Transcendentalism and philosophy of Emerson. One thing is clear: If Peirce[3] offers the possibility of accounting for metaphysical distinctions which may or may not have a consequence in practice or action, James[4] and Dewey[5] lack the philosophical and theoretical sophistication and nuance which gave way to what some have called instrumentalism (as exhibited by Sydney Hook[6]) and Americanism.

However, it still seems in Peirce's philosophy that the only type of distinction that ultimately has bearing once the evidence of experience is overcome and left behind, is a type of formal-logical distinction.[7] It seems that for Peirce, it is logic that gives metaphysics its direction in the ultimate sense. This is why Peirce characterizes his idealism as an 'objective' or 'logical' idealism.

The question is whether the distinction between thought or logic and existence is a logical-metaphysical distinction or an existential distinction. Do we have evidence for it in experience and sensation and phenomena, or from thought alone? From where is the distinction between thought and existence conceived? From within existence or from within thought and logic?

The two terms *metaphysical* and *ontological* are not coterminous nor interchangeable. We want to make a short digression to elucidate the difference between these two terms and the differentiated way in which we use the two words:

Metaphysics means an account, a *logos* or a discourse that explains the fundamental nature of reality. This can be done by appealing to a transcendental ground or by explaining reality immanently, strictly from principles that occur within it.

---

[3] Charles Sanders Peirce (1839–1914) is one of the most important of all the American philosophers. He founded the movement of Pragmatism and was a brilliant logician and mathematician who developed symbolic logic and topology and developed the logic of relations.

[4] William James (1842–1910) was a personal friend of Peirce and the first one to use the term Pragmatism publicly in his lectures on Pragmatism in 1907.

[5] John Dewey (1859–1952) is also a famous pragmatist and the last classical American pragmatist. He took Peirce and James' insights and applied them to education and knowledge. He developed a naturalist theory of experience and had a famous debate with Santayana about the nature of experience and its metaphysics. Dewey's theory of education sees education as a form of continuous growth and development and it draws some of its inspiration from the Hegelian notion of education as *Bildung*.

[6] Sidney Hook was a student of Dewey but he somewhat reduced Pragmatism to Americanism and Instrumentalism thus diminishing its potentially universal scope. He was also active in the defense of American ideology against Soviet ideology during the Cold War (1945-1989).

[7] The Middle Ages loved the notion of philosophical distinctions. There were four major forms of distinction identified by Duns Scotus: the real distinction, the conceptual or formal distinction, the rational distinction and the modal distinction. The formal distinction was the one favored by John Duns Scotus. Thomas Aquinas favored the real distinction. The rational distinction influenced Descartes in the development of his version of the ontological argument. The formal distinction is a distinction that occurs between the logical space of the merely conceptual, and what is fully real or independent from the mind.

Ontology, on the other hand, is the attempt to specifically explain or describe both the Being of reality and the Reality of being—from the 'Beingness' of things to the fundamental nature of Being. One assumption that our definition of metaphysics and ontology makes is that Being and reality are not coeval or identical.

There is indeed common ground that is touched upon in the discussion of Being and reality, but philosophy and the theory of knowledge (and implicitly worldviews) can distinguish between these two notions and phenomena. God, for instance, has traditionally been part of the Being of reality and this is why ontology intersects with theology and becomes onto-theology. Finally, ontology must also explain the relationship between Being and Becoming.

> ⓘ **KEY DEFINITIONS**
>
> **METAPHYSICS**: an account that attempts to explain the fundamental nature of reality.
>
> **ONTOLOGY**: an attempt to explain or describe the Being of reality and the Reality of being.

Pragmatism was strongly influenced by the Empiricist movement we studied in Chapter 4. Pragmatism arose from the Scottish philosophy of common sense which. in turn, influenced the radical empiricist David Hume, whose contributions would later influence William James when he introduced the notion of pragmatism to the literary public.

Pragmatism is more closely related to empiricism than rationalism on one end, and closer to idealism than to realism on the other. What pragmatism does not share with empiricism is its sceptical thread. This is the case at least with respect to Peirce and Dewey and perhaps not so much so with James who characterized his philosophy alternatively as radical empiricism or pluralism and allowed for some form of skepticism in his analyses.

6.1 AMERICAN IDEALISM & PRAGMATISM
6.1.2 Ralph Waldo Emerson

Emerson's worldview may be characterized as a combination of Romanticism, idiosyncratic neo-Platonism and Pietism. This worldview is particularly suited to the soil of America: It is perhaps determined to a certain extent by the American myth of the rugged and boundless Western frontier. What is so fascinating in Emerson, for our purposes at least, is that he encompasses both a form of proto-pragmatism, albeit without the fascination for science and enquiry (as in Peirce), and an American form of Idealism.

> **💬 KEY QUOTE**
>
> Ralph Waldo Emerson: *"The Eye is the first circle."*
>
> *-from his essay "Circles". The eye or the observer, is the first delimiting factor: all knowledge is in this way subjective and subjectively limited.*

The first aspect of Emerson's philosophy that brings him into proximity with pragmatism is his emphasis on the notion of process and Becoming.[8] Natural history laid a strong influence on the idea of constant evolution and upon Emerson who was perhaps familiar with Darwin's theories. Being,[9] for Emerson, is not represented or portrayed as a fixed "wall" but as a sequence of "interminable oceans". For Emerson "permanence is but a word of degrees".[10]

Process is especially perceivable in Emerson's philosophy of moods which he relates to his concept of experience. Experience is a series of moods and one has to position oneself correctly to come into the right mood at the right time. While the moods are controllable to a certain extent in this way, there is no notion of Platonic self-mastery (*enkrateia*) in Emerson (also present in the Stoics and perhaps the Cynics and Cyraneics). True to his Pietistic heritage Emerson avers that our moods do shape us and make our self-activity relative.

But while moods have power over us, we also have power over them through our thought and will. There is a tension in Emerson between a certain contemplative side and a thought that sees thinking and reflection as a deed and activity. This idea of thinking and reflection as activity clearly anticipates Peirce's pragmatism.

Emerson's notion of power is complex. He often invests children and other improbable actors with power. As with moods, power is elusive in Emerson though there does seem to be a great man/hero aesthetic and ethic that manifests throughout his works that may have been obtained caused through a cross-influence by Thomas Carlyle whom he met.

---

8 *Becoming:* Becoming (and non-Being) are the counter-concepts to Being in the philosophic tradition since Plato. The notion was mostly developed by the philosopher Aristotle in his book *The Metaphysics*. It means something that is always evolving, changing, transforming itself. It sometimes means life-process but it can also be a historical process or physical process (i.e. The histories of given atomic particles i.e., The path that they have taken measured against a time-line). Aristotle divided Becoming into three phases or states. Becoming's potentiality (the ability of an entity A to move from state x to state y in time); Becoming's actuality (the ideal state of a given entity A, that what it strives to attain but never quite does in the realm of Becoming) and Becoming's entelechy (what an entity A strives towards; the purpose it seeks to fulfil); as we can see entelechy and actuality are more closely related than potentiality.
9 *Being:* Being is a concept first developed by Parmenides and Plato, two Ancient Greek philosophers. It refers to something that is always the same, that never changes and cannot contradict itself or be the subject of a logical paradox.
10 Emerson, *Essays,* Essay 10, Circles. (1847)

The great man/hero ethic will also be inherited by Nietzsche to a certain extent, though it is further refined into the difference between Zarathustra, the superman and the free-thinkers who may all be taken to a certain extent as forms of heroic typologies.

> **ⓘ KEY DEFINITIONS**
>
> **EMERSON: KEY CONCEPTS AND DEFINITIONS**
> - **Everything is process, there is no permanence.**
> - **The hero or great man ethic:** the "bruisers" of history.
> - **Ethical and moral perfectionism:** Favored the good of the elites as opposed to the American democratic ethos of Jefferson and the Federalists.

For Emerson these men who have the power to shape the arc of history are sometimes named. They are the Platos, Moses, Jesuses, Luthers, Copernicuses, Caesars and Napoleons of this world. Emerson claims somewhat poetically that these great men are "ploughed into the history of the world".[11]

Hence, the two aspects in Emerson's philosophy which stand out as possible anticipations of the philosophy of American pragmatism are:

- his emphasis on the notion of Being as Becoming as an ocean immersed in waves of change and transformation and
- his notion that activity is a form of thinking and is perhaps to be valued over and above thinking alone (or thought without activity).
- The American philosopher Stanley Cavell, for instance, provides cogent arguments for how the perfectionism and transcendentalism of Emerson stand contrasted to the liberal democratic ethos of the Federalists and their influence on the spirit of Pragmatism. However the basis of the idea that Being is at bottom Becoming and process, and that acting is a form of thinking certainly finds an early echo in Emerson. This echo will be heard and developed in the wonderful melody of Peirce's original foundation and historical launch of the notion of American Pragmatism. What is prefigured in Emerson's work is the idea of pragmatism as a broad theory of knowledge, worldview and perhaps methphysics that emphasizes process and experience.

In Emerson as in the ulterior pragmatist movement, experience takes a much broader understanding than it had in Empiricism. In Empiricism which may be characterized as a form of sensationalism, experience is reduced to the perceptions that came from the senses. In this way, experience is reduced to sense-experience. In Emerson and in Pragmatism, experience is broadened to understand communal experience, religious experience, aesthetic experience, educational experience and even political experience.

---
11 Emerson, *Selected Essays and Addresses*, ed. L.Ziffe, New York, Penguin 1982, Print. pg. 112

6.2 ORIGINS OF AMERICAN PRAGMATISM
6.2.1 Charles Peirce

The initiator of Pragmatism is Charles Sanders Peirce. In what have become seminal texts, he defined and outlined as clearly as possible what Pragmatism was. As an interesting note, Peirce thought of calling his new method of philosophizing Pragmaticism, but came to the conclusion that most people would be put off by this name and settled on Pragmatism instead.[12]

Menand[13] asserts that Pragmatism had appeared on the American scene of ideas during discussions held at a "metaphysical club" in Harvard around 1870. This club brought together teachers and intellectuals (some of its members were pragmatically inclined lawyers) who were interested in debating and understanding the nature of metaphysical ideas and the import such ideas had for their own conceptions of knowledge, science, ethics, aesthetics, psychology, religion and community.

> ⓘ **KEY DEFINITIONS**
>
> **Emerson's** anticipations of **American Pragmatism**, are :
> - the notion of Being and Becoming as change and transformation.
> - the proposition that activity is a form of thinking and is perhaps to be valued above thinking alone (that is, thought without activity).

Belief and Truth

For Peirce, the notions of truth and belief are tied to action. Peirce is categorical about the fact that thinking is a deed or a form of action. It is with this somewhat Faustian thesis[14] that Peirce sets off to explain his theory of belief as a form of behavioral, social and communal tendency and habit-formation that induces people to cohere around a common perception of objects of knowledge and scientific enquiry.

Whereas belief is tied to the pragmatist maxim in Peirce's work, there is more to it than this. Belief is also tied to Peirce's understanding of probability and its effects on

---

12 These texts (*The Fixation of Belief, How To Make Our Ideas Clear* and others) are from the end of the 1870's. James lectured on pragmatism in 1907. Peirce's philosophical system had moved away from the idea of pragmatism in his own researches but he was in dire financial need so he updated and actualized his old lectures and revisited the original notion of pragmatism which, according to Peirce's own judgment, had been somewhat distorted and simplified by James.
13 Menand L, *Pragmatism*, New York: Random House. 1998.Print.
14 In the beginning was the Deed as Goethe claims in his famous German poem, not the Word as is claimed in the Gospel of John. But the Word could be taken as the most fundamental form of action or deed if language is what essentially characterizes man and God.

knowledge. Furthermore, belief functions as Peirce's critique of both Cartesianism's punctual and adequationist notion of doubt and his rejection of Empiricism's grounding in singular sense-perception (Empiricism's reduction of experience to sensationalism) and the bundle theory of sense-data. For Peirce, belief is tied to the philosophy of common-sense (drawn largely from Scotland). Common-sense is based on belief and habit insofar as it does not attempt to reconstruct reality from scratch, as Descartes and some proponents of empiricism attempt to do. Thus belief is the touchstone for Peirce's critique of both Descartes' foundationalist theory of knowledge and the reduction by certain empiricists of sense to sense-perception.

Peirce's Understanding of Logic

In the 1865 lectures *On The Logic of Science*, Peirce sketches the difference between two fictional schools in the history of logic. The first treats logic as an extension or as somehow related to the discipline of psychology. The other focuses on the connections between the actual objects that are manipulated by our thoughts. This is already the thesis of his later objective idealism or of scholastic realism *in nuce*. What Peirce is concerned with, is how objects interact in reality and as a self-contained system of signs and symbols, without reckoning with the subjective, intuitive perceptions of our senses, which may influence the operations of logic. One could speak in this sense of an internal, objective logic.

Subjective logic (or the attempts to ground logic in subjectivity) are errors according to Peirce. One must understand the context of Peirce's work in the history of logic to appreciate this statement. For a long time, and even during Aristotle's time, logic had concerned itself with metaphysical substance. Later, in Descartes and Leibniz, this substance began to be subjectified. This process continued in Kant and Hegel until Hegel finally asserted that his goal was to transform substance into subject through his *Logic and Scientific Philosophical System*. For a long time, logic was considered to be concerned with and designed to describe the laws of thought and of judgment.

Our own definition of logic in Chapter 1 of this book is indebted to a certain extent to this tradition. We defend this tradition because it seems that logic must possess some component that relates it to the consciousness and thought of human beings. If this were not the case how could causality be understood? There can be no causality completely independent from the human mind; and the fact that the mind contributes to a certain extent to shape reality through its categories of the understanding would have to be dismissed. Thus, we agree with Kant and Hegel to a certain extent and oppose Peirce's purely objective logic.[15]

---

[15] Peirce's logic is connected to the truth of the object of experience and is thus more inductive. But there is a paradoxical tension in his logical project. One the one hand, he develops a purely formal treatment of deduction

The thread of thinking in the history of logic defended by Peirce led to the purely formal logics of the twentieth century, which concerns the first chapter of this book. This is why it is necessary to follow his argument to a certain extent here. As Peirce arrives on the scene, logicians like Boole and De Morgan begin to question the foundations of Hegelian and Kantian logic. They begin to detach logic from the study of the faculty of thinking (which is the object of psychology) and study the objects of logic as an independent subject-matter.

In relation to this, Peirce along with Frege and Boole, are credited with having developed a logic of relations,[16] the first step in overcoming the dominion of substance and subject in the history of logic. Peirce understands induction, deduction and abduction as forms of reasoning and inference, and as steps in the scientific method.

This represents a subtle but important difference. Theoretically, systems of inference (deductive ones already exist developed by Tarski and Quine in the 20th centuries) might exist independently of experience. In fact, in Peirce there is a tripartite treatment of induction, deduction and abduction:

1. as part of a theory of signs,
2. as part of a critique of argumentation; and finally
3. as part of a method of inquiry or scientific method.

The moment induction, deduction and abduction become steps understood to be part of the scientific method, they henceforth can apply to experience alone—for science is a theory of nature, of the experience of nature and not of the transcendental and the supernatural.

One thing we must be clear about is Peirce's understanding of induction, which is central to his notion of scientific inquiry. Peirce is thoroughly opposed to conceiving of induction as a form of counting or as enumeration. For him, induction is both evaluative and ampliative in the sense that it adds information through a form of synthesis; it does not single out particulars but parses them under universals. In this, he is influenced by the legacy of Francis Bacon, as we have shown in Chapter 4.

Peirce possesses a sophisticated "scientific" metaphysics. The putting together of the two

---

through the invention of logical quantifiers (the existential and universal quantifiers we studied in Chapter 1). This logic is purely mathematical and objective and has nothing to do with the Cartesian subject of knowledge that influenced Kant and Hegel. On the other hand, Peirce also studies inductive logic through his concept of abduction and here there may be psychological traces of the subject of knowledge's arrangement of the object of knowledge through his sense faculty. Here, Hume and Mill may have to be given their due against Peirce.

16 As mentioned in footnote 35 in Chapter 1, relations are the most general forms of logical connection that can be established between objects. This was discovered independently by Peirce and Frege around the same time.

terms might surprise most scholars of a positivistic bent, since science and metaphysics are usually considered to be opposed or dichotomous, at least according to a post-Enlightenment understanding of things. So why is metaphysics scientific for Peirce? There are two separate, but related points to this question.

First, metaphysics is not completely independent of mathematics and physics and hence is related to what Peirce considers as fundamental for it: logic. Second, metaphysics is related to Darwin's theory of evolution. The essence of metaphysics for Peirce is its process or evolutionary aspect. The following passage from his *Collected Papers* provides evidence for our thesis:

> The evolutionary process is, therefore, not a mere evolution of the existing universe, but rather a process by which the very Platonic forms themselves have become or are becoming developed. [17]

One question we might want to ask is whether these two points or issues (that of logic which is connected to physics and mathematics, and that of evolution, which is connected to living systems and organisms) do not possess an internal tension and hence undermine to a certain extent Peirce's claim that metaphysics is scientific.

The architectonic of Peirce's metaphysical system revolves around the terms *Firstness, Secondness, Thirdness*. Peirce has an elaborate theory of the relationship between Firstness, Secondness and Thirdness. This relationship is also related to his understanding of signs, semeiotics, and reality as somehow shaped by semeiotic or sign-relations. We will list the most important triads for our interpretation and then analyze and draw out how Peirce sees them fitting together into his system. In our description of Peirce's theory we will focus on the obviously metaphysical aspects of Firstness, Secondness and Thirdness.

TRIADS

Firstness	*Secondness*	*Thirdness*
Possibility	Actuality	Necessity
Fact	Habit	Rule or Law
Entity	Relation	Representation

In Section 20 in Volume 6 of *Collected Papers,* Peirce writes: "Mind is First, Matter is Second and Evolution is Third". An important other triad is the traditional Aristotelian-

---

17 Peirce Charles S., *Collected Papers*, Harvard University Press, Cambridge, 1935. Volume 6 paragragraph 194, will be quoted as CP from now on and using paragraph numbers, not page numbers.

metaphysical one: possibility is (a) first, actuality is (a) second and necessity is (a) third. Yet another, quality is (a) first, fact is (a) second, habit (or rule or law) is (a) third. Yet another triad is: entity is (a) first, relation is (a) second, representation is (a) third. We limit our discussion to these three in this section devoted to Peirce's metaphysics. It must be said that there are a great number of triads that we are neglecting; after all Peirce notes that everything, including reality, was triadic. Thus, the category of triad in Peirce is not exhausted in this section of this introductory book. Another important thesis of Peirce's is that metaphysics and logic are indivisibly connected—they form a grounded and grounding circular totality.

> ### ⓘ KEY DEFINITIONS
>
> **CHARLES SANDERS PEIRCE: KEY CONCEPTS AND DEFINITIONS**
> - **Logic dominates and clears up metaphysics.**
> - **Tychism:** Chance and contingency;non-determinism are more important than the doctrine of necessity (anti-Spinozism).
> - **Synechism:** Continuity and order are more important and fundamental than chaos and discreteness as basic structures of the world and cosmos.

The inseparability of logic and metaphysics can perhaps most clearly be expressed by the fact that in some sense, Peirce saw the world as evolving, moving, processing away and changing through the lens of his logical categories. He thought the entire cosmos, the *phaneron* as he idiosyncratically calls it, is a self-moved totality that abduces, deduces and induces itself forward and perhaps backward. There is a sense in which the move is rather forward from chaotic, pure un-refined matter to a totally connected, perfectly symmetrical, self-aware, ordered Mind which manifests eschatologically at the end of History or of the Cosmos/Universe.

This perfect state of full, self-aware, balanced, and fulfilled mind is reached and coincides with the end of inquiry when Mind possesses and masters a perfect science and possesses a fully developed understanding of knowledge and itself. This state may correspond to the state of Absolute Knowledge in the *Phenomenology of Spirit* or of the Concept which knows itself as the identity of subject and substance at the end of the Hegelian *Logic*. It also has echoes of the Aristotelian *noesis noeseos*,[18] the circularity of the Divine Intellect which thinks itself thinking itself in full actual self-possession and eternal happiness.

Peirce's Aristotelian-Scotistic-Hegelian roots are undeniable, but he does innovate with respect to them insofar as he integrates the notion of evolution, both biological and conceptual, and radicalizes and draws the consequences of Darwin's great naturalistic

---
[18] This is the Greek that Aristotle uses to describe the Divine Mind or Intellect.

discoveries. There are also Platonic elements in his philosophy as in the philosophies of all the great thinkers who wrote after Plato and Aristotle. Some of these Platonic elements are apparent in his emphasis on Mind.

Peirce possesses a concept of time that is unreal or ideal. He claims that time itself "is an organized something". He describes in what have become his *Collected Papers*, the fact that originally in the universe there was "a state of just nothing at all"[19] which is not identical or equivalent to emptiness. Using a medical or psychological qualifier he claims that "the only sane answer is that where freedom was boundless nothing in particular necessarily resulted".[20]

Peirce emphasizes that the logic of evolution is not the logic of events. This implies that contrary to what Hegel believed, the order of necessity is not identical or equivalent to the evolutionary order.

Peirce explains that "the zero of bare possibility leapt into the unity of some quality".[21] In his view, this leads to a hypothetic inference of the form "Something is possible, red is something, therefore red is possible".[22] This is why Peirce believes that quality is first, fact second, and relation third.

> **KEY QUOTE**
>
> Charles Sanders Peirce:' *Matter is effete Mind'*

Peirce's universe is a universe that evolves from chaos to order. The perfect, fully integrated state of the World and Cosmos at the end of history (both human and cosmic), is a perfectly symmetrical, mathematical, fully self-aware Mind. Peirce famously asserts that 'Matter is effete Mind'. Peirce's objective idealism is shot through with Empiricist and Materialist influences. He admits himself that he makes atoms swerve to a certain extent. But this swerving is minimal since a radical swerving might undermine the ability of Mind to order the Cosmos. However the swerving of the atoms is also necessary to explain man's freedom or free will which Peirce is committed to in his philosophy.

Peirce ratifies the connection between metaphysics and logic. Traditionally, metaphysics grounded logic and was its foundational epistemic guide. Peirce reverses this relationship and claims that Metaphysics must be grounded in a thorough understanding of logic so that one does not lose his way in this difficult discipline.

---

19 Peirce, CP 6.218
20 Peirce, CP 6.215
21 Peirce, CP 6.218
22 Peirce, CP 6.220

In many ways, Peirce attempted to regress to a form of Metaphysical, logical and epistemological scholasticism. What was different from his historical vantage point was the fact that Natural Science (including the science of Natural History and thus Evolution) and mathematics had taken on a dominant role in the life of the mind. One can perhaps propose as an explanatory hypothesis, that Peirce understood this new situation as bringing about a reversal in the traditional priority of metaphysics over logic.

Logic functions in Peirce as a methodological guide to organize the material of knowledge provided by scientific enquiry. This allows for the possibility of metaphysics; but whenever this metaphysics comes in conflict with scientific enquiry (even if this enquiry is not interpreted in the narrow terms of the pragmatist maxim and its many formulations given by Peirce), logic adjudicates what the facts are and where the truth lies, and metaphysics takes the back seat, so to speak.

Peirce is in line here with the thought of Aristotelian philosophers, though like all great philosophers there are platonic and neo-platonic influences in his thought. The major influence aside from Aristotle on Peirce is without doubt John Dons Scotus and his thesis of the ultimately infinite and complex nature of God's essence.

In his time, Scotus had to absorb Christianity and reformulate the Aristotelian heritage given the new development of Christianity. He accomplished this by distancing himself from Augustine's more Platonic or neo-Platonic interpretation. Peirce on the other hand, who is still working mainly within an Aristotelian framework, must absorb the discovery of biological evolution and accommodate this new fact within the Aristotelian system.

Peirce intuited and anticipated the appearance of the wave-continuity notions of quantum-physics even if the did not know or possess the mathematical formalism underlying these notions. Tychism[23] and indeterminacy are, from a physical, cosmological and metaphysical perspective compatible, perhaps even equivalent to the uncertainty principle.

What Peirce saw less clearly perhaps is that the continuity of synechism[24] and the indeterminacy of tychism are in tension and perhaps opposition. For how can we have continuity without any form of determinacy and determination? Continuity requires perhaps not full determination and determinacy but at least determinability. It is this

---

23 *Tychism* is a central part of Peirce's philosophy which can be defined as the belief that the world, reality and knowledge are indeterminate. World, reality and knowledge contain a component of freedom and non-determinism within their essence and nature, according to Peirce. Peirce was especially opposed to the necessitarianism which he thought followed out of the positions of people like Laplace and perhaps Auguste Comte.

24 *Synechism* is an important aspect of Peirce's philosophy. It deals with the thesis of the continuity of reality. For Peirce continuity is a central concept that ties into the fact that reality has an order and organized aspect to it. The centrality of continuity is also very important to modern physics. In a dialogue with the great Indian poet Rabindranath Tagore, Einstein used the idea of the logic of continuity to defend his theory of relativity against the claims of the Absolute put forth by Tagore.

determinability of the concept (*Begriff*) that a disciple of Hegel (and Spinoza) might later inveigh against Peirce's tychism.

What is striking about the discovery of genes and which was also missing from Peirce's theory of knowledge and his ontological system, is that genes possess both the capacity to bind—to enter into a point of fulfilling contact with nucleotides—as well as the ability to fold upon themselves. Life may be understood as a principle of organization of a higher order than the merely inorganic, since at each step a choice occurs: to bind or to fold. Furthermore, this organization itself would not occur were it not for the physical nature of space which needs to allow for both the binding and the folding of carbon molecules and proteins within its locus.

This is the thesis of the **fine-tuned universe** which has become a central concern for scientists, philosophers and even creationist-intelligent-design theologians. This thesis of the *fine-tuned universe* is related to another idea for which there might be some evidence—namely the notion that organisms consume (negative) entropy and so have the capacity to reverse the entropic forces to a certain extent. The argument is that organisms should be considered open systems which transact or exchange matter and energy. This is in contrast with the Universe as a whole, which may be taken to be a closed system from the point of view of the total sum quantity of entropy present within it.

> ⓘ **KEY DEFINITIONS**
>
> **THE THEORY OF THE 'FINE-TUNED UNIVERSE'**: A principle of organization is inherent and manifest in all life, energy and matter. This architecting force or principle then, informs and directs all facts, knowledge and processes, including the subject, the observer, and the event and act of observation or thinking, and even the structure of this very sentence and language.

These considerations though interesting in themselves, do not directly concern Peirce or the origins of American pragmatism. Peirce is a central figure in the development of American philosophy and perhaps the greatest thinker that the North American continent has known. To place Peirce alongside Hegel and Kant and perhaps more imprudently in the same company as Plato and Aristotle is to err only slightly. Peirce stands head and shoulders above all the other American Pragmatists and though some other pragmatists like James and Royce possess undoubted genius, they lack the breadth of Peirce.

One can speak of a certain form of decadence of American thought after Peirce. With Dewey and Rorty[25], there appears a lack of sophistication and dialecticity in American

---

25 Richard Rorty (October 4, 1931 – June 8, 2007) was a neo-pragmatist American philosopher who was

philosophy. While these thinkers made important contributions, they tended to politicize Peirce's legacy. They set up a dichotomy among metaphysics, logic and democracy. An attempt at such a dichotomy is not only misleading, but also dangerous. Democracy, despite its grounding in a form of pluralist relativism, must also be defended from a high-minded idealist and pragmatic metaphysical ethos.

To dichotomize democracy, reason and metaphysics as some philosophers have done is detrimental for democracy, reason and metaphysics. It produces a weak democracy and a weak philosophy and is the sign of a form of cultural decay.

6.3 SUBJECTIVE PRAGMATISM

6.3.1 William James: Psychological & Subjective Pragmatism

Charles Peirce was a personal friend of William James. Being the older figure and the inceptor of the idea of pragmatism/pragmaticism, Peirce dominated for some time the younger James. James did come into his own with time. He departed from the shadow of his great mentor to create his own original position within the history of Classical American Pragmatism. James was much more interested in psychology than Peirce, whose main interests were mathematics, logic and the exact sciences.

One of the first books written by James was a textbook of psychology that he was asked to write by an American publisher. However, the book sometimes delves into purely epistemological and phenomenological analyses so one may not easily classify this text as a work of clinical psychology. Nonetheless, the work that made James famous or that is best known to most of his readers is *The Varieties of Religious Experience*.

Essentially, James may be classified as a psychological or subjective pragmatist. Others have called him a radical empiricist. In his constant preoccupation with religion one may also term James a proto-existentialist pragmatist or a proto-phenomenologist. This is because the questioning of the meaning of life or of existence, the study of the problems of religious and moral pessimism and optimism, are constants within James' writings.

Although there are elements of metaphysics and moral reflections on faith in Peirce,[26] one may safely claim that with James there is a deepening of the understanding of the

---

influenced by James and Dewey as well as other philosophers such as Heidegger and Wittgenstein, to name only a few.

26 One can provide as an example, Peirce's reflections on the history of the Church and his theory of *agapastic* evolution, notably in the volume of his works called *Scientific Metaphysics*, Volume Six.

recesses of human subjectivity and of religious experience. With James, experience is no longer an object of scientific and perhaps metaphysical analysis; in his work as a whole, experience is not a purely scientific and methodological starting point.

Rather, experience is understood both naturalistically as in Peirce, but also phenomenologically (and psychologically) as in Nietzsche and Husserl. James is often engaged in pure description, barren of construction and explanation. Perhaps description is insufficient to guarantee knowledge, but it is a natural starting point along with the observation expected of any scientific endeavor. Description often (though not always) carries deep understanding and truth within itself.

James rejects the standpoint of absolute idealism. He criticizes Systematic, Dogmatic and Natural theology for not making any "pragmatic" difference—difference in the *praxis* or comportment of the life of religious faith. In order to understand James's rejection of absolute idealism (which we take to be a reaction to Hegel's philosophy published at the beginning of the 19th century) it is useful to compare his philosophy to that of Josiah Royce who has been categorized alternatively as an "absolute idealist" or "absolute pragmatist".

ⓘ KEY DEFINITIONS

WILLIAM JAMES KEY: CONCEPTS AND DEFINITIONS
- The will to believe: belief as a voluntary and practical act.
- No absolute knowledge or standpoint: truth is a matter of temperament.
- The mathematical infinite as standing or growing.

James had a public debate with Royce about the nature of truth and of pragmatism. Initially it was Royce who launched an attack on James's position which he felt did not answer correctly the challenge of epistemological and metaphysical skepticism. Before reconstructing the debate, it is useful to note that James might seem to give a psychological answer to Royce's essentially epistemological and metaphysical question.

This fares well in terms of James's own positions with respect to technical philosophy and his favoring of common-sense answers. (Psychology's virtue in James' appraisal was that it was more accurate than pure philosophizing as it was closer to the common sense of the common man). Nonetheless, it is hard not to see that the Jamesian reply somehow evades Royce's challenge.

It appears that James' adoption of a certain form of realist pluralism or relativism is based on his suspicion of any absolutist standpoint in philosophy. His reply to the absolute standpoint is a form of descriptive *ad hominem* combined with a *non sequitur*. James might say that certain temperaments require the absolute standpoint given their innate psychological constitution, but that this absolute standpoint is not required in general by all human individuals who might be inclined or pre-disposed to a more subjective temperament.

Those who require the absolute standpoint are the tender-minded souls of the idealists and the classical rationalists.

Again, one cannot escape the feeling that James is not really taking the argument of absolute standpoint seriously. He is pre-empting any discussion of it because he reduces its meaning to the temperament of the one who defends such an argument. James seems to be begging the question to a certain extent.

It is unclear that this lack or failure is either due to James' unwillingness to engage in abstract argument or if one wants to push further and perhaps a bit unfairly, due to a certain lack of intellectual rigor or integrity on his part. His retreat into a form of subjective psychologism might be warranted but he never makes the argument clearly on why objects of discourse can be intended and referred to independently of the mood, temperament or disposition within which we find ourselves at any point.

Certainly some states of powerful mood might find us deluded and confused about the objects of our consideration and deliberation, but surely these states are extremes of mood and temperament and not the norm. What is the justification then for focusing on these states alone to make one's argument? Is it because religious emotion is more akin to these extremes of mood and temperament? But surely religious temperament and mood, though never finding us to be satisfied and replete, for that might be the definition of impiety, also allows for lucidity, clarity, contentment and quiet detachment.

James has been called and this is perhaps not unwarranted, a "philosopher's psychologist". There seems to be a natural flow and grace to James' spiritual and intellectual composure. He compensates for what seems like a lack of intellectual and technical precision, with a penetrating intuition.

Despite our qualms that the precision of philosophical and spiritual science may not be sacrificed in favor of the point of view of common sense, we understand the venerable tradition (which includes Hume and Scottish common-sense empiricism) within which James works. Peirce also works within this tradition to a certain extent, though he creatively reshapes and re-casts it into historical significance by adapting it to the American situation and predicament.

When analyzing James' purely philosophical positions it is not clear whether these can be detached from the positions of a writer in the tradition of the New England Preacher and of a great psychologist of the human Mind in the tradition of Nietzsche (and not only coincidentally, almost contemporary with him). Some of his more technical and precise analyses are available in his volume, *Works*.

However, a lot of the essays published (e.g.: *The Will to Believe, Does Life Have Any Meaning* and many others) were given at the time in the form of lectures which significantly simplified his positions and attempted to popularize them. These lectures were given to an audience of not only intellectuals (philosophers or theologians) but also to the lay public. As a consequence some hermeneutic caution is necessary in distinguishing where James attempts to state his position rigorously and precisely in terms of the philosophical technical language and where he attempts to edify, convince, persuade, motivate and quicken men to faith as New England preachers did.

There is no doubt that James wanted to write "serious" philosophy and to be taken seriously by "serious" philosophers like Peirce, Royce, Russell and Dewey. James was interested at first in Psychology in the 1880's, then ethics and religion in the 1890's and finally there seems to be an interest in fundamental philosophical i.e. Metaphysical problems from the 1900's on. This is a rough sketch and James was no doubt interested in ethics and religion much earlier as his essay on Spencer of 1878 shows. Nonetheless, his interest in pure philosophy and metaphysics comes at a later stage.

James' fundamental metaphysical reflection is presented through a collection of his works as under the title, *Some Problems of Philosophy*. There is some contradiction or murkiness regarding the goals the text pursues. It is simultaneously intended to be an introductory text into the thorny issues of metaphysics and a serious treatise in metaphysics.

Thus James seems to be confused to a certain extent about the audience he is aiming for and the writing style he wishes to employ. He both wants the style to be simple and accessible, not unlike the one adopted in his public lectures and yet does not shy away from taking on very complex and difficult problems in traditional metaphysics for which traditionally philosophers have developed terms of art which seem to be required or necessitated by the inner intricacy of the issues themselves.

Ultimately, we cannot claim that *Some Problems in Philosophy* is a thoroughgoing success. All the same, James raises an interesting point about fundamental metaphysical reflection: Must this reflexion always be technical as it appears to be in Aristotle, Spinoza, Kant and Hegel or is it the case that fundamental truths can have a literary, stylistically satisfactory enunciation without being complex and technical? Is it the case that the wiser the philosopher is, the simpler his expression and his sayings?

These questions raise an important issue and constitute the means by which James attacks the rationalists and the idealists since in his assessment, the ultimate radical empiricism will express itself through terms that come directly from practical experience. Thus, radical empiricist, in James's view is in some way closer to the truth as it bears a simpler less technical expression than the expressions of the rationalists and the absolute idealists.

This leaves us with the question of what 'less technical' and 'simpler' when it comes to philosophy. Surely a philosopher may be the friend of beautiful and simple expression, but his duty is to be a greater friend to truth. *Amicus pulchritudine et simplicitas sed magis amicum veritas* or "A friend of beauty and simplicity, but a greater friend of truth". If truth is complex (the attack about technicality is more difficult to refute, but may perhaps be answered along the same lines) then surely to refuse to express it in its complexity is not to do justice to it. But then the Absolute is at once simple and complex; at once, finite and infinite; one and many; at once, rich and poor. It encompasses all the attributes of the Universe and of God so to argue that simplicity of expression should be the norm does not do justice to the reality of the Absolute and to the manifold of reality.

As for technicality, James's attack might strike home. It is more difficult to claim that we need to be technical when we do metaphysics. Metaphysics is supposed to be the most general discipline. If specific disciplines like psychology, physics and mathematics require technical terms and a discipline-bound vocabulary, then one must ask whether the most general discipline and science, the science of Being, (here we are equating metaphysics with ontology though they are by no means co-terminous and co-eval) requires technical terms.

> **INTERESTING?**
>
> The real numbers are said to be 'dense' compared to other numbers (e.g. integers or irrationals) because between any two Real numbers we can find another Real number and so on indefinitely. Georg Cantor proved that the size or cardinality of the Real numbers was much greater than that of the Natural numbers. Cantor proposed the continuum hypothesis and established the existence of levels or orders of infinity.

Should metaphysics be expressible in common language and be perfectly accessible to common-sense? Here, one cannot help but recall a thesis of Hegel's about the relationship of science (philosophical science and thus metaphysics) to common-sense. Hegel is anti-empirical and anti-common-sense insofar as he claims that even if the beginning of absolute knowledge is identical with the beginning of knowledge in the *sensus communis*, there is a dialectical reversal and absolute knowledge can never be perfectly adequate to common-sense. The metaphysician, just like the moralist, is always both inside the worldview of common-sense and simultaneously outside it, so that he may gain a critical distance and exert the labor of the concept on the false identifications and misconceptions of common-sense. In this sense the metaphysician must practice a negative dialectic.

Common-sense is sublated and sublimated in absolute knowledge, but never identical with it. This relationship between common-sense and metaphysics can also be observed in the contemporary world in the relationship between common-sense and advanced physics. Advanced physics is non-common-sensical (or one may want to shorten *with some loss of specificity* to non-sensical!). This means that the ontology of advanced quantum mechanics contradicts or is at odds most of the time with the ontology of common-sense and ordinary sense-perception.

But let us tackle the text of *Some Problems of Philosophy*, directly. One of the seminal texts in this collection is *The Problem of the Continuum and the Infinite*. This essay is deeply flawed, as was acknowledged by Peirce in Vol. 6 *Scientific Metaphysics*. It is flawed insofar as James never attains to the essence of what is at stake in the problem of the continuum[27] and which is both: a mathematical-logical debate on the nature of the continuum of Real numbers; and a metaphysical-ontological debate about the reality of the actual infinite versus the potential or possible infinite.

The fact that James does not make this twofold distinction and instead chooses to characterize the infinite as 1) growing or 2) standing (we would re-translate this within more sophisticated vocabulary as dynamic and static, as again we find James' terminology unsatisfactory even at a basic level) vitiates almost the totality of his discussion. His understanding and discussion needs to be compared with the much deeper and precise analysis of Peirce on the subject.

It must be emphasized that James characterizes his latest or later philosophical position as that of pluralist or radical empiricist. He is both opposed to the position of rationalism and absolute idealism and to conceiving of the world as one Substance or Mind. Here, James comes into conflict with his philosophical mentor Peirce, for whom ultimately Matter was 'effete mind', and who ultimately believed that at the end of inquiry and at the end of the universe, everything would turn out to have been manifest Mind all along.

---

27 The continuum is the fact that the real numbers are dense. Between any two real numbers we can find another real number and so on indefinitely. In the beginning of the twentieth century mathematicians like Georg Cantor proved that the size or cardinality of the Real numbers was much greater than that of the Natural numbers. Cantor proposed the continuum hypothesis according to which the cardinality of the Reals was 2 to the power of the cardinality of the Naturals. Cantor could never prove this but there are now indications that the size of the continuum might be a lot larger than Cantor anticipated. Cantor's merit lies in the fact that he managed to establish the existence of levels of infinity and to relate cardinalities to ordinal numbers which allow us to count past natural infinities of numbers.

6.4 END OF CLASSICAL AMERICAN PRAGMATISM

6.4.1 Dewey

John Dewey's theory of Knowledge claims knowledge is participatory and active. It is grounded in the pragmatist concept of experience which is a very rich and complex notion. Knowledge is valuable if it is effective: this is an application of Peirce's pragmatist maxim according to which an object or action should be judged in terms of its practical effects and results. This was a direct reaction against the traditional dualisms metaphysical, epistemological, political and social, which result in a spectator theory of knowledge.

In *Democracy and Education*, Dewey considers the theories of knowledge which underlie the classical views of education that have existed in the Western world starting with Plato. We will consider Dewey's critique of Plato's spectator theory of knowledge and the attendant Platonic epistemological dualisms. Dewey was not a dualist, though he was opposed in some ways to metaphysical and epistemological monism. We will attempt a characterization of his metaphysical and epistemological position and see what consequences this has. Finally, we will consider a critique that may be leveled against Dewey: that there exists a certain dualism between experience and principles, standards or concepts, which must transcend this experience.

> **KEY QUOTE**
>
> John Dewey: *"knowledge is participatory and active."*

Our thesis is that a commitment to a pluralistic, dynamic democratic understanding of knowledge and philosophy cannot be undertaken without differentiating between experience, principles, standards and concepts, which go beyond experience itself and so are in some way transcendental or transcendent. However, Dewey's view of experience is replete with principles which he derives from experience and then tests in the light of this experience. One of the challenges of this section will be to show how Dewey derives these principles and concepts from experience. We will also be asking the question whether Dewey needs to resort to a realm different from that of experience when deriving these principles.

Dewey's concept of experience is central to his critique of the spectator theory of knowledge and its attendant dualisms. Starting from Emerson's deepening of the concept of experience in the *Essays* (see especially the second chapter in the *Essays* entitled *Experience*), Dewey develops a concept of experience that goes beyond the empiricist's sensationalist understanding of sense-experience. Building on James's notion of religious experience, Dewey extends the concept of experience to the notion of a social and political *fundamentum* in which all dualisms can and must be sublated.

This is particularly apparent in his seminal *Experience and Nature*, in which he develops what may be termed a metaphysics or an ontology of experience. There is almost a consensus in the literature that Dewey has something which may be termed 'a metaphysics'. (See Santayana, *Dewey's Naturalistic Metaphysics*, Rorty, *Dewey's Metaphysics* and Bernstein, *Dewey's Metaphysics of Experience*). Of what this metaphysics of experience consists, is less clear. Dewey is best understood by contrast to four major tendencies in his time. On the one hand, he was reacting to the sociological positivism of someone like Comte and to the British idealist appropriations of Hegel. On the other hand, he also situated himself in contradistinction to the logical positivism of the school of Vienna (which we briefly looked at in the Chapter on The Empiricist Theory of Knowledge) and the emerging phenomenological existentialism of someone like Heidegger.[28]

Dewey may be contrasted to three major tendencies in his time:

(1) the sociological positivism (Comte and Hegel).
(2) the logical positivism of the school of Vienna (See Chapter 4) and
(3) the emerging phenomenological existentialism (e.g.: Heidegger.)

Dewey tried to find a middle road which avoided all of these extremes and did justice to the truths of the natural sciences. In *Experience and Nature* he characterizes his position alternatively as natural empiricism or an empiricist naturalism, but claims that his philosophical position could also be called naturalistic humanism.

> **ⓘ KEY DEFINITIONS**
>
> **JOHN DEWEY: KEY CONCEPTS AND DEFINITIONS**
> - Democracy as participatory and fundamental to a healthy society.
> - Education as a form of growth or continuity based on practical experience.
> - **Knowledge instrumentalism:** Theories as tools of the trade; what matters is the consequences of usage of the given instruments not the theories in themselves.

If it is truly the case that Dewey has a metaphysics of experience as is my thesis, the next question of importance is how this metaphysics of experience is related to epistemology. In Dewey's view, experience functions as a *fundamentum* that is somehow naturalistic.

---

28 Heidegger (1889-1976) was a famous German philosopher of the beginning of the twentieth century who wrote the famous book called *Being and Time*. For more information about this philosopher see Catanu, Paul; *Heidegger's Nietzsche: Being and Becoming*, 8th House Publishing, Montreal, 2010. Print.

Dewey argues that experience is part of nature—an inherent constituent of it and not something which is apart and distinct from it, as this latter view is required as a starting point for the dualisms he is intent on avoiding. Nature and Experience are two sides of the same coin; they are fundamentally indistinct in terms of their ontological status.

But experience has at least two aspects for Dewey: it can be primary or secondary and reflective. Primary experience, to use Dewey's term, is "had" and "undergone". It is, in this respect, pre-reflective (and hence also pre-analytic). Reflective experience or second-order experience is what allows for the development of an epistemology of learning that can have consequences in political practice and in the theory of knowledge.

However, even reflective experience is naturalistic. Dewey is clear about the fact that he does not believe in the mind-body dualism proffered by Plato and reinforced by Descartes' epistemology. But is there not a weakness here? Namely, how can the second-order reflective experience still be sublated into the first-order experience which Dewey refers to?

It seems that Dewey claims that the quality of experience can be a criterion allowing one to differentiate inanimate life from animate life. His argument against mind-body dualism is an intricate and difficult one to follow. It is layed out in *Experience and Nature* in one of its central chapters: *Nature, Life and Bodymind*. Two critical threads in this chapter do not cohere harmoniously, as Richard Rorty has pointed out: a physiological (naturalistic) aspect and a historicistic aspect. If the body and the mind are identical and continuous and if the history of one can be explained in terms of the other, there still remains a tension between nature and history writ large. What needs to be clarified in the context of Dewey's metaphysics and his epistemology is how they relate to his social and political ideas. Dewey clearly believes that knowledge and education "are a mode of participation". Though we may grant that knowledge and education "are a mode of participation" and need to be understood in terms of action and dynamism, we still may want to invoke the fundamentally contemplative aspects of knowledge and education, which Dewey does neglect. Knowledge is theory: it is the abstract contemplation of the idea, which provides standards and principles for action. This depends on the nature of the knowledge under discussion. In order to understand this universalistic commitment to the abstract and contemplative aspects of politics and knowledge, it should be made clear that certain concepts transcend experience and that in order to provide justifications for these concepts, principles and standards, one needs to go beyond experience to a quasi-transcendental form of argumentation.

An example of this is Hegel's reading of the historical Socrates. Hegel claims that, in order to respond to the challenge of decadent Athenian democracy, Socrates evaporated its reality through his thought and went into himself in order to find the source of right and wrong and so discover the right moral action. But by going within himself and creating the internal as a moral source for action, Socrates also prepared the way for Augustinian and Cartesian inwardness, which discovered the divine or the purely transcendent and transcendental within memory and within the life of the soul.

The need to withdraw within oneself, in order to create a self that is not purely naturalistic but that rather transcends and goes beyond the social and the natural, occurs from time to time in human history and it is only through this withdrawal from society and nature that a transcendent and transcendental consciousness is created.

> **ⓘ KEY DEFINITIONS**
>
> **JOHN DEWEY: CONTRASTED TO TENDENCIES OF HIS TIME** Democracy as participatory and fundamental to a healthy society
> (1) the sociological positivism (Comte and Hegel);
> (2) the logical positivism of the school of Vienna (See Chapter 4) and
> (3) the emerging phenomenological existentialism (e.g.: Heidegger.)

Dewey was perhaps correct in his statement that Plato creates a spectator theory of knowledge. But Plato has also given us the immortal and divine *Sokratesbild*.[29] Socrates proves through his actions and through his persistence to his ideals that principles and ideals are transcendental and that they do transcend experience. Socrates finds the code for his action nowhere in the society and nature of his time. He creates these codes because, like the Laws of Athens at the end of the *Crito*, Socrates becomes the embodiment of a new historical law for moral action. He revolutionizes both philosophy and world-history by creating the moral revolution in both philosophy and the world.

Dewey's and the later pragmatists' suspicion of principles and standards is understandable given the conflictual history that principles and standards led to on the Old Continent and on the New. We can mention the Salem witch hunts[30] and the civil war to name only two historical events that radically shaped America's self-understanding and self-consciousness.[31] In Dewey's view, a theory of democracy and education that is not grounded in experience ultimately leads to very damaging absolutisms and becomes the recipe for tyranny. One can turn this argument on its head

---

29 German for portrait or figure of Socrates.
30 The witch hunts are important and shaped American history and experience because they sparked debates about tolerance and intolerance that were couched in religious principles or standards.
31 These events are important for Dewey's hostility to principle and standard based argumentation in politics, ethics and education because he was influenced by the Hegelian WT Harris' critique of the radical abolitionists who advocated violence to achieve their ends during the American Civil war.

however, and notice that the historicization of philosophy that Dewey brings about has negative consequences for political and educational practice. It has been documented[32] that pragmatism was appropriated by certain ideologues of Nazi Germany who were interested in pragmatism's relation to naturalism and 'vitalism'.

If one had heeded the Kantian notion of the transcendental and its applications to developing a moral and political theory of democracy and education, many of the excesses of the Second World War in Germany might have been avoided. Hitler did believe that his anti-semitic views and Nazi ideology had a philosophical underpinning in Schopenhauer and Nietzsche,[33] which added strength to his convictions.

As Habermas[34] has pointed out, quasi-transcendentalism as a ground for legal, political (and educational) theory is necessary to combat the excessive historicization that was brought about in philosophy by the experience of the Holocaust. Without contemplation and the establishment of a dialectic between action and contemplation, theory and practice, there can be no knowledge and no education in the true sense of the word. It seems clear then that certain logical principles cannot be derived from experience or at least from primary experience. A reason for this is that experience and primary experience are the subject of constant change and becoming, while certain principles such as the logical principle of identity ($A = A$) are not subject to change. The question then is: If we did not arrive at the principle of identity through experience, where did we get it from? Dewey would answer this question by asserting that even if the principle of identity is not derived from experience, we need experience in order to determine what thing is identical to what other thing. If it is true that we can manipulate things symbolically in terms of identity, the issue becomes: How does our logical and mental apparatus access experiential data? This way of framing the problem leads to the famous Humean problem of skepticism on knowledge and induction. But Kant's answer to this issue and his attempt to offer a solution grounded in the transcendental usage of the categories of the understanding is an important rebuttal of Hume's skeptical attack.

---

[32] Hans Joas, *Pragmatism and Social Theory*, University of Chicago Press, London, 1993
[33] In his book, *The Destruction of Reason (Die Zerstoerung der Vernunft)*, Gyorgy Lukács has attempted without much success to show how this might be true.
[34] Juergen Habermas is a present-day Germany philosopher. His most famous work is "The Theory of Communicative Action".

QUESTIONS

WORLDVIEWS: The Pragmatist Worldview, its Ontology, Epistemology and Axiology

1. How is pragmatism pre-figured in the work of Emerson?
2. Why can Peirce be considered the official founder of American Pragmatism?
3. Describe Peirce's understanding of the relationship between belief and knowledge.
4. What is the relationship, according to Peirce, between logic, knowledge and ontology or metaphysics?
5. What is the problem of the mathematical-physical continuum?
6. How is the Pragmatist worldview different from the rationalist and empiricist theory of knowledge?
7. What is the pragmatist maxim and how is it related to knowledge?
8. How is the pragmatism of Peirce different from the pragmatism of James and of Dewey?
9. Why is religious experience and its variety so central to William James' pragmatism?
10. What role does the philsophy of common-sense play in William James' brand of pragmatism?
11. How does Dewey define education and its purpose or goal?
12. Why is educational experience so central to Dewey's pragmatism?
13. What does experiential learning mean for Dewey and how is it central to the classroom?
14. What is the relationship between knowledge, democracy and metaphysics in pragmatism?
15. Is pragmatism closer to the empiricist or to the rationalist theories of knowledge we have studied in Chapters 3 and 4?
16. Why does Dewey oppose the use of abstract principles and standards in ethics and politics?
17. Does Dewey possess a metaphysics? Why or why not?
18. What is the influence of the theory of evolution on the pragmatist worldview?
19. Why can William James be considered a subjective or psychological pragmatist?
20. What is the logic of relations developed by Peirce and what is the scientific context that influenced the development of this type of logic?
21. Describe the ontological, knowledge and moral-practical aspects of the pragmatist worldview.

KEY CONCEPTS & DEFINITIONS - THE SCIENTIFIC WORLDVIEW

TIME: Early 20th Century to Present

SCIENTIFIC WORLDVIEW: The scientific worldview subscribes to a naturalist, materialist or physicalist theory of knowledge and ontology. In general it believes that it can reduce truth-statements about the world to truth-statements about particular states of affairs that hold about fundamental particles. In general, the scientific worldview is value-free or value-neutral, but great advocates of science like Husserl and Peirce have supported the concept of a normative science.

PEOPLE
Karl Hempel, Otto Neurath, Carnap, Von Schlick, Wesley Salmon, Thomas Kuhn, Hilary Putnam

SCIENTIFIC THEORY: a logical model or representation of a process in reality that is confirmable by data available to our senses.

THE POSITIVISTIC MODEL OF THE SCIENCES
1) Emitting a hypothesis.
2) Conceiving of an experiment to test the hypothesis.
3) Gathering of data from experiment.
4) Comparing the data of experiment to the hypothesis.
5) Refining the hypothesis or dismissing and replacing it with another hypothesis.

DEDUCTIVE-NOMOLOGICAL MODEL
A 'scientific explanation' is comprised of:
(1) the *explanandum:* a statement "describing the phenomenon to be explained";
(2) the *explanans:* the class of statements adduced to account for the phenomenon.

HEMPEL'S CONDITIONS OF ADEQUACY:

R1: The *explanandum* must logically follow or must be a logical consequence of the *explanans*.
R2: The *explanandum* must contain general laws of nature and the statement of these laws in the *explanandum* must be used to derive the truth of the *explanans*.
R3: The *explanans* must have empirical content.

THE THESIS OF THE UNITY OF SCIENCE: All of science can be explained by a single, simpler and more fundamental science.

HISTORICIST CRITIQUE OF SCIENTIFIC WORLDVIEW: Science is not fully deductive and law-like. It is dependent on historical context, circumstance and contingencies.

CHAPTER 7
SCIENCE, CRITICAL THINKING & THE SCIENTIFIC WORLDVIEW

What is a scientific theory and what distinguishes it from knowledge which we may deem unscientific? A scientific theory is a model or a structure that exists either in our minds or in reality. This model or representation must be confirmable by data available to our senses. It is here that scientific theories meet the philosophical discipline of the theory of knowledge or epistemology. The question is: If we want to acquire scientific or certain knowledge about our surrounding world, can our senses be trusted?

When we devise a scientific theory, a model or a logical, mathematical and empirical structure, we use quantitative means such as mathematics: calculus, statistics and probabilities. But these quantitative or formal methods are given content by the acquisition of data. This acquisition of data happens by referring to experience, i.e., what is given to us by our five senses. Thus, as we can see, scientific knowledge requires both deductive and inductive knowledge. Deductive knowledge and deductive reasoning are not the same; just as inductive knowledge and inductive reasoning are not the same. They are related but knowledge is a type of content, an achieved and complete type of information, whereas reasoning is a form of argument and thus much more of a process, a way to preserve truth from the premises to the conclusion than an entailment/if-then type of relation.[1] Apart from being a form of content, knowledge is also a form of practical understanding, a know-how. This takes us back to Aristotle and his notion of prudential, practical knowledge. (Heidegger reactivated this ready-to-handness aspect of knowledge by studying Aristotle from a phenomenological perspective which eventually led to the publication of his monumental book (perhaps the most important philosophical text of the 20th century) *Sein und Zeit* (*Being and Time*, 1927).

> **ⓘ KEY DEFINITIONS**
>
> **SCIENTIFIC THEORY:** a logical model or representation of a process in reality that is confirmable by data available to our senses.

7.1 NATURAL SCIENCE, THE HUMAN SCIENCES & THE SOCIAL SCIENCES

One of the important questions we tackle in this chapter and in the conclusion to this book is the question of the relation of the Humanities to the Social Sciences and to the Natural Sciences. Also, how and under which aspect are the Humanities different from the Social Sciences?

This may be largely a matter of tradition of the disciplines. Humanities translates the German *Kulturwissenschaften* that Ernst Cassirer and other German Neo-Kantians conceptualized around the turn of the twentieth century. The reason that the Humanities play such a distinctive role in the curricula of the English CEGEPS around Quebec is proximity to the United States. The Humanities (or the study of the human being and human nature) in North America is seen as a broader subject than philosophy, history, literature or religious studies alone; and in fact the Humanities include all of these more specific disciplines within their scope of study. This is associated with the traditional belief in the United States of America that an education in the Liberal Arts prepares one well for all sorts of professions whether they be law, medicine or even business, economics and engineering. The 1980's *Rockefeller Commission "On the Humanities"* described the vocation of the humanities in its report, *The Humanities in American Life*:

> Through the humanities we reflect on the fundamental question: What does it mean to be human? The humanities offer clues but never a complete answer. They reveal how people have tried to make moral, spiritual, and intellectual sense of a world in which irrationality, despair, loneliness, and death are as

---
1 See Intro chapter for difference between argument and entailment.

conspicuous as birth, friendship, hope, and reason.[2]

The social sciences, on the other hand (they are usually taken to translate the German *Geisteswissenchaften* consecrated by the great German scholar Dilthey who analyzed their methodology and their relation to the problem of historicism[3] thoroughly), comprise sociology, geography and many other disciplines in which *quantitative* methods are usually applied to data. This is not to say that quantitative and empirical methods may not be fruitfully applied in the Humanities. Regardless of the enterprise, the subject could only benefit from submitting it to different methodologies, whether speculative, critical, logical or analytical, especially in the development and defense of its theories—for such argument and proof could only be made more robust by confirmation along all these planes of examination. However, in general the method of the Humanities is of a more speculative and critical nature—and this is what finally distinguishes it from the qualitative Natural sciences if not from Social Sciences.

In his famous essay *Interpretation and the Sciences of Man*,[4] Charles Taylor claimed that the essential difference between Natural Science and the sciences of man or the Humanities was that Natural Science relied on verification of data and the facts of the matter, whereas the Humanities relied on experience as a form of text, as the basic data for its theses, theories and interpretations. According to Taylor, engaging in the Humanities is equivalent to jumping into the middle of reading a text. Taking Heidegger[5] and Gadamer[6] as an inspiration, Taylor claimed that there was something fundamentally hermeneutic about the Humanities.

Knowledge in the sciences of man presupposed a form of pre-ontological understanding. It is only because we had this fore-knowledge that we could always already engage in acts of the understanding and of self-definition. Thus understanding a work of literature or of history meant engaging in a dialogue with the reality of the author and with the text that exemplified this intended mind of the author or *mens auctoris*. It is only starting from personal self-definition and insight that we could actively and productively engage with the text and intentions of an author from long ago.

Thus the Humanities were not engaged in a 'verificationist and falsificationist' form of project.[7] The goal of the study of Humanities was not seen to be—as it was in the

---

2 *The Humanities in American Life*, Berkeley, University of California Press, 1990, Chapter 1.
3 Historicism is the thesis that all phenomena (human or even divine and religious) possess a historical nature.
4 Charles Taylor, *The Review of Metaphysics*, Vol. 25, No. 1 (Sep., 1971), pp. 3-51.
5 See Chapter 2, p.136 for discussion of who Martin Heidegger was.
6 See Chapter 2, p.134 for who Gadamer was and his main achievement.
7 Verificationism and falsificationism are not necessarily continuous and seamless protocols in the scientific method. See discussion below.

Natural Sciences:

1. the idea of finding a meta-language in which no paradox or contradiction would occur;
2. to employ this meta-language to clarify how this language related to the object-language of a given natural science; and finally
3. to explain how the object-language related to the phenomena of nature in need of explanation.

On this reading, the Humanities have a radically different methodology from that of the deductive-nomological model developed by the positivists Carnap, Hempel and Popper who thought of scientific explanation as a form of deductive argument. In Taylor's view, the human sciences were sciences that relied not so much on *Erklaerung* (explanation) as on *Verstehen* (understanding). Here Taylor follows in the great tradition of understanding in the *Geisteswissenschaften* first developed by Wilhelm Dilthey[8] who was himself following Giambattista Vico in great part.

Thomas Kuhn and others who saw cultural elements in the Natural Sciences challenged Taylor's view. To Kuhn and (later) the philosopher Richard Rorty, the lines between the Humanities, culture and natural science were not so clear.[9]

Because the science of the Greeks was determined by their astronomical taxonomies which were essentially different from ours, Kuhn argues that they inhabited a different world-picture or worldview. Furthermore, the worldview of the Greeks and that of the modern world is incommensurable—there are large enough gaps between them he argues, so that we cannot guarantee sufficient agreement to ensure the objectivity of Natural Science.

We will not seek to adjudicate this debate in any final manner. While we do admit that keeping a clear demarcation line between the Humanities or the human sciences and the natural sciences seems a bit fruitless, it does seem to us that the knowledge-relativisitic picture that is entailed by the views of Rorty is in many ways self-defeating.[10]

---

8 Here it is appropriate to understand the Humanities as *Geisteswissenschaften* even though we claim that in general Humanities translates the German *Kulturwissenschaften* of Ernst Cassirer. In fact the reason the *Geisteswissenschaften* have been translated as social sciences might be a bit arbitrary and contingent. It probably rests in a certain materialistic, naturalistic and unspiritual understanding of the notion of social science. But this is not necessarily correct; one could think that the Humanities are the sciences of the (human) spirit and then Humanities would become the appropriate translation of the *Geisteswissenschaften*.
9 Rorty's and Kuhn's positions on science should not be taken to be equivalent, however. Rorty is in the end something of a relativist and suspicious of the rationality of science, whereas Kuhn believes that science is the best example we have of a rational enterprise and endeavor.
10 There is some truth to the historicism of Kuhn about the philosophy of science. There is, however, a danger when this historicism is pushed into and becomes relativism, of losing the basic insight that science is historical and claiming that scientific statements from previous eras are incommensurable. The thesis of the historicity of

It does seem like some descriptions of natural objects are more privileged than others. For example, if there is a blackboard in my classroom, there are very good scientific and objective reasons for claiming that the board is black, not green. There is evidence that can be gathered statistically about how many people see a black board and how many see a green board.

> ⓘ **KEY DEFINITIONS**
>
> **NATURAL SCIENCE VS HUMAN SCIENCES VS SOCIAL SCIENCES: KEY CONCEPTS AND DEFINITIONS**
> - **Natural Sciences:** Constituted by instrumental knowledge, manipulation of natural causes of live and dead nature.
> - **Humanities or Human Sciences:** Understanding and critiquing human nature within its social and historical context.
> - **Social Science:** Emancipation and critique of social institutions, social practices and policies.

This evidence can then be further correlated or corroborated with a spectroscopic analysis which may tell us more about the color of the board. We can do a sociological analysis that can perhaps give us information about the populations, which see the board in different colors. In the end there is something like a fact of the matter or an agreement about the color of the board devoid of argument but based empirically or on agreed evidence. Modern science then eliminates the possibility for more radical forms of knowledge-relativism, whether they are correct and fruitful or not.

It is true that a black-board may be considered a social-cultural object and not merely a natural object. This is the case because in order to know that in a given classroom, in a given learning institution the blackboard is something that is written on and used to explain the concepts and ideas that are being taught by the teacher and learned by the students, as opposed to being an object of worship for which these students have gathered in a religious ceremony, one does need to be acculturated into a specific type of socio-cultural horizon and understanding. So the demarcation problem between natural objects, which are the object of natural or pure science, and socio-cultural objects, which are studied by Social Science and the Humanities, is not easy to solve. But we believe that the demarcation problem does not completely collapse our distinction between knowledge-relativism and socio-cultural or values-relativism which may be accepted and perhaps promoted in inter-cultural and multi-cultural societies such as the Quebecois and Canadian societies.

---

science, while generally correct, does not entail the incommensurability of the science of different epochs and of different worldviews.

Other forms of relativism, such as pluralist relativism in ethics and politics, may certainly be arguable and debatable, though the relativism Rorty envisions following his understanding of the nominalism[11] of science and knowledge is philosophically weak in our opinion because it reduces knowledge and metaphysics to a form of questionable culturalist politics for which knowlege has to subject itself to the broader imperatives of democracy. But this way of dichotomizing knowledge, metaphysics and democracy shows a shallow and superficial philosophy: one which the fathers of pragmatism—Peirce, James and Dewey—would probably reject.

It must be stated that from our perspective (and this crosses the Natural/Social Science/Humanities divide), the human mind is closer to the notions and concepts of sets and relations than to the ideas or realities of fundamental particles, quarks, bosons or even the alleged and controversial strings and branes of recent physics because sets, numbers and relations are both real and ideal (we follow Charles Peirce and Kurt Gödel here) whereas particles are only real, if they are not in fact the fictions that Helmholz and Mach asserted them to be.

> **ⓘ KEY DEFINITIONS**
>
> **NOMINALISM:** a theory of knowledge dating back to the Middle Ages which asserts that all concepts and notions are merely names and words that are parts of language whose relations are internal to our minds.
>
> *"There are no universal essences..."*

7.2 THE POSITIVISTIC MODEL
7.2.1 THE POSITIVISTIC MODEL OF THE SCIENCES & ITS CRITICS

In introducing this chapter, we discussed how a model of scientific theory or scientific explanation would have to be deductive in some way. The model must resort to mathematical, formal methods upon which it is founded—hence we say it is deductive. But because we can have no scientific theory without referring to the world of sense-experience and because this predetermines our conception of the object, the experiment, the question and the truth, it is also inductive. This inductive aspect is a challenge to the nominalist/mentalist view of scientist-philosophers like Stephen Hawking, since the <u>model or structure</u> we apply to nature in conceptualizing it, not only predetermines what

---

11 Nominalism is a theory of knowledge that dates back to the Middle Ages according to which all concepts and notions are merely names and words that are parts of our language or that relate internally to our minds.

we seek the truth about, but requires that we step out of this model or conceptualization to obtain evidence from our senses which are perhaps more directly in contact with nature.

Other theorists of science, like Karl Popper, have rejected the fact that induction plays any role in the acquisition of scientific knowledge. They believe that observation is theory-laden or already fully deductive in some way.[12]

We will discuss the problem of free will and determinism in the context of theology and the debate between Erasmus and Luther in Chapter 8. There is also a problem of determinism in science. Human beings have a biological and chemical make-up. This biology and chemistry can be studied and brought under broadly mechanistic or physical laws. If this is the case, then how is it that human beings make free choices? How can they choose between what is right and wrong, good and evil? How can they decide whether to go to work or come to school every morning? There is a tension and perhaps even a contradiction between the fact that we are material-biological beings who are subject to the laws of matter and biology and the notion that we are free and unique and that we are responsible for our choices.

Some thinkers, like Stephen Hawking, have articulated this issue within the context of the search for a grand unified theory of physics. They claim that this theory would have to explain even the level of freedom which we have in searching for such a grand theory. Stephen Hawking seems to propose a solution in his book *A Briefer History of Time* that is akin to the evolutionary epistemology research programme.[13]

We find this a little shortsighted and take a more 'Kantian position' in which there are really two levels of explanation: (1) A moral level at which humans function according to a causality of freedom; and a (2) scientific-mechanistic-biologistic level at which we can study humans like automata in terms of systems subject to laws that circumscribe and predetermine their will. But the two levels, the noumenal and the phenomenal are necessary for justifiable freedom and morality to exist. Natural selection is not sufficient to explain this freedom, nor is the language of ethics and morality reducible to an evolutionistic vocabulary, as Nietzsche argues in the *Genealogy of Morals*.

---

12 Theory-ladenness means that something that is thought in general to have no relation to a theory or thesis is in fact determined or full of theoretical assumptions.
13 Evolutionary epistemology is the thesis that theories somehow compete in the realm of knowledge and that the best theory is somehow selected over weaker and less relevant theories. Sometimes evolutionary epistemology is tied to a secondary thesis which claims that those individuals who hold onto or defend the strongest theories benefit from some sort of evolutionary advantage and that they will be naturally selected over those individuals who defend the weaker theories. Evolutionary epistemology is a research program and no strong evidence has been provided for its truth. As such it is not supported by the author of this book.

7.2.2 THE POSITIVISTIC MODEL, SCIENTIFIC METHOD & THE ROLE OF EXPLANATION

In general, the scientific method may be sketched along the following stages or steps:

1) Generating a hypothesis
2) Conceiving of an experiment to test the hypothesis
3) Gathering of data from experiment
4) Comparing the data of experiment to the hypothesis
5) Refining the hypothesis or dismissing and replacing it with another hypothesis

Carl Hempel whose deductive-nomological model of scientific explanation we will look at shortly, provides us with an example of how the scientific method works. Hempel tells us the story of Dr. Semmelweis who was attempting to find the cause for the high death rate of pregnant women. His first hypothesis was psychological and was related to the role of the priest in the mortality of pregnant women. He varied the behavior of a priest with regards to the pregnant women to verify his hypothesis. He found that the changes in the priests' behaviors had no effect on the mortality of the women.

He then observed Dr. Kolletschka during an operation and inferred that there was cadaverous matter in the blood of the dead women (bacteria which transmitted puerperal fever[14]) and that this matter was transmitted to pregnant women. His assumption came to him all at once and guided his empirical testing. He proceeded to test his hypothesis—he told the students to wash their hands and statistically tested the mortality rate of women to conclude that this hypothesis was correct.

> ⓘ **KEY DEFINITIONS**
>
> **THE SCIENTIFIC METHOD** involves the following iteration
>
> *1) Emitting a hypothesis.*
> *2) Conceiving of an experiment to test the hypothesis.*
> *3) Gathering of data from experiment.*
> *4) Comparing the data of experiment to the hypothesis.*
> *5) Refining the hypothesis or dismissing and replacing it with another hypothesis.*

In understanding and critiquing the scientific method, it is important to keep in mind that we can never observe nor record *all* the facts. Each hypothesis is hypothetico-deductive in method and presupposes a result or a conception, so that one selects evidence and focuses only on some facts and ignores others.[15]

---

14 Puerperal fever is a type of fever contracted by women after childbirth and due to an infection of the uterus.
15 On this point there was disagreement between Popper and Hempel on the one hand and Carnap who

Can we describe all of the grains of sand that appear in the desert to reach a conclusion about the molecular composition of the sand? The analysis and classification of facts also has some issues. What matters in the hypothetico-deductive method is not only how the facts are analyzed and classified but *how* the facts are connected and linked together (synthesis of facts in a theory).

The derivation of general rules from facts or evidence by induction faces the same critique Hume levied against induction. How can simple regularities become rules or scientific laws? It is in the collection of data and the basic construction of an experiment that the problem arises here, because any rule or law includes a general and theoretical component that cannot be derived in a mechanical way through induction.

If we make a hypothesis it is because we use 'imagination' and a form of theoretical divination—a kind of leap in knowledge—that then organizes the facts to form an experiment and a means of collecting data, all with the aim of proving some preconceived notion. Hempel gives the example of gas and its temperature. He compares the variability of the length of a bar of metal in terms of its temperature. One can make a curve that shows the proportional variation between the temperature and the length of the metal bar but this illustration is a description, not a law like that which governs gas and temperature. If we redo the same exercise with gas and temperature, the law will not be discovered because temperature also depends on pressure.

> **ⓘ KEY DEFINITIONS**
>
> **POSITIVISTIC MODEL OF SCIENTIFIC METHOD AND THEORY: KEY CONCEPTS AND DEFINITIONS**
> - **Scientific theory is an argument with thesis and premises.**
> - **Deductive nomological aspect:** Every scientific theory must contain a deductive rule or law.
> - **Inductive Statistical aspect:** Whatever is not deductive in the scientific theory must be quantified statistically.
> - **Unity of Science Thesis:** All science can be reduced to one unique aspect: particle physics.

Therefore a theoretical assumption, one which is reached by an act of the imagination or by an act of divination[16] is the cornerstone of the hypothetico-deductive method.

thought that one arrived at the hypothesis from the ground up by noting all of the facts and observations and then mechanically deriving a hypothesis. Hempel and Popper thought that the hypothesis was an imaginative and deductive guess (others like Peirce might call it more correctly an abduction, to distinguish the guessing, divinatory, imaginative element from the logical-deductive element in the method) that would allow to organize the results of experiments under a hypothesis or general thesis which in the end could become a scientific law or a law of nature.

16 The American philosopher whom we studied in Chapter 6, Charles Peirce, calls this divination of the hypothesis 'abduction'.

The hypothesis is conceived as an act of divination or theoretical imagination, but if the hypothesis is not verifiable through repeated experience, it must either be abandoned or refined. The idea that the verification of the hypothesis of a scientific theory is the cornerstone of its method is due to the work of the logical empiricists Rudolf Carnap and to Karl Hempel. It was further developed by the Austrian philosopher of science Karl Popper in his 'procedure of falsification',[17] now a necessary step in the verification procedure or protocol of scientific theory.[18]

7.3 DEDUCTIVE-NOMOLOGICAL MODEL
7.3.1 Explanation as a Kind of Argument

According to the Deductive-Nomological Model, a 'scientific explanation' is made up of two "constituents":

(1) the *explanandum,* which is a sentence "describing the phenomenon to be explained"; and

(2) the *explanans,* which is "the class of those sentences that are adduced to account for the phenomenon."[19]

One of the major challenges to this view is the fact that, logically an explanation is not coeval[20] or coterminous with an argument (nor a deductive argument in the case of the deductive-nomological model). Karl Hempel and the logical positivists or empiricists we studied at the end of Chapter 3, would have us believe that a scientific explanation is very much like or identical to a deductive argument. Let us consider and entertain this possibility.

If the purpose of the *explanans* is to consistently and efficiently explain the *explanandum,* a few conditions need to be fulfilled. For one thing, "the *explanandum* must be a logical consequence of the *explanans*" and "the sentences constituting the *explanans* must be true".[21] Thus as mentioned above the explanation should take the logical form of a sound deductive argument. In this sound deductive argument (we refer back to Chapter 1 in which we studied validity and soundness in the context of deductive arguments) the

---

17 Popper's procedure of falsification is discussed on earlier in this book on p.218.
18 Verification was already developed by Rudolf Carnap.
19 Hempel and Oppenheim, 1948, reprinted in Hempel, 1965, p. 247
20 Coeval and coterminous are synonyms for the word 'identical'.
21 Hempel, 1965, *Aspects of Scientific Explanation and Other Essays in the Philosophy of Science,* New York: Free Press. p. 248.

explanandum must follow logically from the premises of the *explanans*.

This is what makes the deductive-nomological model "deductive". Second, there must be nomological or law-like aspects to a scientific explanation for it to fulfill the deductive-nomological model. This means that the scientific explanation (and specifically the *explanans* within this explanation) being scrutinized must possess an element of generality that likens it to a "law of nature". To be even more precise, the *explanans* must contain at least one premise within it that is like a "law of nature" and this premise must be so essential to the scientific explanation under analysis that if one were to remove this law-like premise from the *explanans,* the deductive link *itself* between the *explanans* and the *explanandum* would no longer be valid.

Hempel claims that any form of scientific explanation must possess logical conditions of adequacy and empirical conditions of adequacy. The logical conditions of adequacy are:

> R1: The *explanandum* must logically follow or must be a logical consequence of the *explanans*. One must be able to logically deduce the *explanandum* from the sentence expressing the *explanans*. Otherwise, the *explanandum* would not be a logical or adequate ground for the *explanans*.
>
> R2: The *explanandum* must contain general laws of nature and the statement of these laws in the *explanandum* must be used to derive the truth of the *explanans*. The general law of nature in the *explanandum* must do the logical work of a premise to defend the truth of the *explanans* and not just be an empty or redundant premise.
>
> R3: The *explanans* must have empirical content i.e. one must be able to devise a test or experiment through which to verify the factual truth of the *explanans* (this is Hempel's famous verificationist criterion complemented later by Popper's falsificationist procedure).[22]

Hempel goes on to list one final empirical condition of adequacy: That all of the sentences in the *explanans* actually be true. This is a necessary injunction in his view, because claiming that there is ample evidence for the truth of the sentences of the *explanans* is not logically strong enough to rule out statements, which were thought to be true in the past and for which evidence was provided, but which ultimately turned out to be untrue. For example, the world was flat and there was no sensory or evidential data to discount this until the globe was actually traversed.

As we studied in Chapter 1 when we looked at deductive arguments, we know that a sound argument must possess actually true sentences not just potentially true sentences

---

[22] Hempel, Carl and Paul Oppenheim, *Studies in Logic of Explanation, Philosophy of Science* 15 (2):135-175 (1948)

(which is good enough to guarantee an entailment relation or validity). This seems to be the requirement that Hempel is making at this stage of his deductive-nomological model.

> ### ⓘ KEY DEFINITIONS
>
> **DEDUCTIVE-NOMOLOGICAL MODEL**: a 'scientific explanation' comprises:
> (1) the ***explanandum:*** a statement "describing the phenomenon to be explained"; and
> (2) the ***explanans:*** the class of statements adduced to account for the phenomenon.

Hempel complemented his Deductive Nomological model of scientific explanation with an Inductive Statistical model of scientific law and explanation. He noticed that many of the phenomena in science were subject not to logical deductive necessity, but to inductive probability and regularity. This is an important evolution in Hempel's work who started out with Carnap and Von Reichenbach by objecting to Hume's account of induction and its role in scientific explanation. We refer the reader to Chapter 4 in the section on Logical Empiricism for a more detailed account of this critique. Let us briefly consider the inductive statistical model of scientific explanation.

The first thing that Hempel noticed is that laws of nature are not all deterministic. The development of quantum physics, which in most of its interpretations is non-deterministic[23], must have led Hempel to consider that his model did not explain almost half of reality (the microscopic part). So he revised some of his theses developed under the dominion of Einstein's mostly rationalistic and deterministic theory of relativity and inserted some inductive non-determinism into his model of explanation.

However, one of the classical examples considered by Hempel does not concern sub-atomic particles (though he looks at those examples as well) but someone recovering from a streptococcus infection. This John Johnes is said to recover more quickly because it is a general fact (and perhaps a law) that penicillin cures the streptococcus infection more quickly by helping the body create anti-bodies and accelerating the rate of the diseased body's recovery. However, claiming that a particular John Johnes recovers from the strep infection more quickly is a particular statement, not a general law of nature. In fact, it is like the statistical syllogisms we studied in chapter 2. Hempel claims then, that if a statement which is general enough like "penicillin helps cure all streptococcus

---

23 The Schroedinger unitary evolution formalism which describes the behavior of the electron as a wave does comport a deterministic element so it is wrong to claim in general that quantum physics or quantum mechanics is non-deterministic. The Heisenberg formalism describes the movement of an electron on the orbitals of an atom in a statistical, indeterminate way. That there is a tension between these two ways of looking at electrons as waves or particles is nothing more than the wonderful adventure of science which exhibits both dualism and continuity even at its most microscopic and undeterminable levels.

infections more quickly" confers truth upon a particular statement of the kind "John Johnes recovered more quickly from a streptococcus infection" (because he took penicillin), then we are in the presence of a statistical law.

But things are not as clear here as they were in the Deductive-Nomological model. Wesley Salmon adduces the following critique to the Inductive Statistical model developed by Hempel.[24] Consider the statistical argument:

> **P1**: Almost no cases of antibiotic-resistant streptococcus illnesses recover through the intake of penicillin.
> **P2**: John Johnes took penicillin.
> **P3**: John Jones had an antibiotic-resistant streptococcus.
> **Conclusion**: John Johnes did not recover quickly from a streptococcus infection.

These two versions of the argument have truth-compatible premises but contradictory conclusions. The problem is that we did not specify what type of streptococcus John Johnes was infected with. Hempel tried to tweak and respond to these types of critique, but in the end the Inductive Statistical model does not seem to have stood the test of time like the Deductive Nomological model has.

One of the basic intuitions behind the Deductive Nomological model is that at the basis of any type of scientific law there is something like a regularity. To achieve the generality of law one subsumes regularities under broader regularities until one arrives at a general enough statement which one may consider to be a scientific law or a law of nature.

> ### KEY NOTES
> **HEMPEL'S CONDITIONS OF ADEQUACY:**
> **R1**: The *explanandum* must logically follow or must be a logical consequence of the *explanans*.
> **R2**: The *explanandum* must contain general laws of nature and the statement of these laws in the *explanandum* must be used to derive the truth of the *explanans*.
> **R3**: The *explanans* must have empirical content.

Other strategies have been attempted to develop statistical models of scientific laws and scientific explanation but they often encounter similar issues or they try to describe a model of explanation that could work both for the natural sciences and the social sciences and humanities in a similar way. The issue with this is that the perception and interpretation of Heisenbergian non-determinism of quantum mechanics cannot be the

---
[24] See Wesley Salmon, *Scientific Explanation And The Causal Nature Of The Universe*, Princeton University Press, 1988.

same as explaining why juvenile delinquents seem to come from broken or impoverished homes. In fact the assumption seems to be in the previous case (as opposed to quantum mechanical indeterminism) that the statistical datum is first taken to be true, or taken to be determinately (as opposed to non-determinately) normative and true in order for the social workers and intervening agents to be able to have an efficient praxis in society.

What seems to clearly differentiate social science from natural science is the relation to practice or a form of the pragmatist primacy of practice thesis. The praxis aspects of social science are not mirrored in any similar or significant way in the natural sciences. So to try to explain statistical regularities in quantum physics in the same way as regularities are explained or questioned and challenged in the social sciences and the humanities seems to be misled.

Besides the existence of examples of problems with the *explanans* being a necessary condition for the *explanandum*, there are also examples that show there might be problems of logical sufficiency associated with Hempel's model of scientific explanation.[25]

7.4 OTHER POSITIVISTIC MODELS OF SCIENCE
7.4.1 The Causal Mechanical Model

The causal mechanical model is based on the idea of a mark moving continuously and being accounted for at any given moment in space-time. Thus any spatio-temporal object which could possess a mark and moves across space time could be explained by this causal mechanical model. A spatio-temporal object like the shadow of an object cannot be marked and so it would not qualify as the cause of an event in space-time. The shadow example is called a pseudo-process as opposed to the causal process generated by an object moving and that can support a mark. For this model, causation is descriptive, not prescriptive: it does not take the form of an argument. This model views scientific explanation, unlike Hempel's Deductive-Nomological Model as incompatible with the argumentative form.

Instead, scientific explanation seems much more descriptive. It considers conditions and what follows from these existing conditions in the world. There is an idealized or

---

25 One of the problems that the DN model has difficulty explaining is that of Explanatory Asymmetry. An example of this type of asymmetry is when we derive the length of a pole from the length of its shadow. While this derivation is possible given the angle of the pole and height of the sun on the sky, it seems like the right causal explanation is to claim that the pole causes the length of the shadow and not the other way around. The DN model cannot clearly distinguish one derivation from the other.

consequential component in this model insofar as it considers what would follow from a given object under certain conditions; however, the causality explained does not possess the same structure as an argument as in Hempel's model. The conditions studied are real situations or idealized ones. Furthermore, following Hume's critique of causation, this model is also somewhat suspicious of all attempts at determining causation. Instead, the model depends on the notion of counter-factual statements, which is problematic from a logical perspective. A counter-factual is a statement of the form "if x were the case, y would follow". But the counterfactual depends on a notion of hypothetical causality (causality given a hypothetical, but not necessarily true premise or proposition). This notion of hypothetical causality cannot be taken to be necessary or to obtain in all cases, which causes problems for the causal mechanical model.

There are some issues with this model, however. The causal-mechanical model does not have a way of distinguishing between certain basic entities like angular momentum and the mark that would be set upon billiard balls that would be engaged in a theoretical elastic collision.

The mark and the causal-mechanical model is descriptive of the process of collision that occurs and keeps track of this process, so to speak, but it cannot really explain what happens since this explanation would have to take into account the notion of the mass of the billiard balls and the notion of angular momentum, which are fundamental and specific to any particular collision that can occur. In similar ways, the causal-mechanical model has difficulty explaining the example developed by its author Wesley Salmon[26] to contradict or to show the weakness of the deductive-nomological model of scientific explanation we saw above. Consider the example of John Johnes taking contraceptive pills and not getting pregnant. This could be stated in the following argument-like form:

John Johnes takes contraceptive pills.
John Johnes is male
___
John Johnes does not get pregnant

Obviously, in this case the real cause for John Johnes not getting pregnant was his being male and not his taking contraceptive pills. But the fact that the end-result or outcome was the same as that of any female taking contraceptive pills did not allow the deductive-nomological model to track the causal process properly. In a similar way, one could think of a way of marking the pills that go through the metabolism of John Johnes and one could build a theoretical correlation between the metabolization of the

---

[26] See Wesley Salmon, *Scientific Explanation And The Causal Nature Of The Universe*, Princeton University Press, 1988.

pills and its markability in a forward and pseudo-causal process. However, one would miss the main definite specificity of this phenomenon which is that John Johnes does not avoid getting pregnant because he has ingested contraceptive pills, but because he does not possess a reproductive system allowing him to carry a child. Both deductive-nomological and causal-mechanical aspects of scientific explanation function at too great a level of generality and cannot effectively and efficiently track the required specificity of the phenomenon that they have set out to explain.

7.4.2 The Unity of Science Thesis

Hilary Putnam[27] and Paul Oppenheim[28] argue in a famous paper from 1958 that the thesis of the unity of science is a workable hypothesis. Fundamentally this is a thesis about reductionism. One of the questions that scientific philosophers and methodologists have always wondered about is whether all of science could not be explained by a single simpler and more fundamental science such as particle physics.

This thesis is complex and it presupposes first that one could reduce sociological, economic and anthropological laws (to take only some important disciplines) to psychological laws or the laws that govern single individuals and particular human beings.

> **KEY NOTES**
>
> **THE THESIS OF THE UNITY OF SCIENCE:** All of science can be explained by a single, simpler and more fundamental science.
> E.g.: Particle Physics can explain electromagnetism, gravity, materials, chemistry, nuclear fission, the solar system, etc.

Furthermore, this is only one of the steps in the overall reduction sought. What one truly seeks is to then reduce psychology and its laws to the laws of molecular biology, then to go further down so to speak and reduce biology to chemical processes and atomic forces in order to finally reach the sub-atomic level of quarks, bosons and possibly of strings and branes.[29]

There is also something more to this thesis of the unity of science. It hearkens back to the ideal of the speculative university and the speculative faculties of man tied to the development of the German higher schools and universities. In these institutions, there

---

27 Hillary Putnam (1926-) is an American philosopher of science teaching at Harvard University.
28 Paul Oppenheim (1885-1977) was an Austrian American scientists, industrialist and philosopher of science.
29 String-theory and Brane-theory is a research program in fundamental physics which claims that there are fundamental extremely small entities called strings (in fact these entities are so small they cannot be detected even indirectly. This is why string theory is a research program that has not been accepted by scientific establishment as a full-blown scientific theory. What is missing is the empirical evidence to confirm the theory or to falsify and verify it (Popper). String and Brane theory have not been verified by any independent empirical experiment.

was an ideal often voiced and effectively acted upon that all the disciplines could work together to harmonize their knowledge. Teachers and professors of various disciplines would attend the courses of teachers and professors of other disciplines in order to recognize that science and knowledge are not distributed among various faculties of the institutions or various faculties of man, but that there is a fundamental unity of knowledge that pervades and transcends the disciplinarization[30] of knowledge and of the education system.

This ideal has in many ways been lost because of specialization and the increase in the accumulation of the amount of knowledge in the different disciplines. There is also a tendency of different domains to use radically different methods to establish the truth of propositions. Thus beyond any factual divergences, what seems to be at stake is a problem of divergence in method and methodology between the social and human sciences and the natural sciences.

A more modern ideal which seems to have replaced the ideal of the speculative university is the ideal of inter or trans-disciplinarity. This ideal claims that each discipline has something to teach the other and that an exchange between the disciplines can only be fruitful. Philosophers like Gilles Deleuze[31] have defended this ideal forcefully and we subscribe to his position on this issue, at least partially.

7.5 THE HISTORICIST CRITICS OF THE POSITIVIST MODELS OF SCIENCE

As mentioned at the beginning of this chapter, some philosophers of science do not accept that the methods of the Human Sciences should be different from the methods of Natural Science. The major philosopher of science representative of this view is the philosopher Thomas Kuhn. His view is outlined in his now famous classic, *Structure of Scientific Revolutions*[32] (which we abbreviate to SSR from now on). Kuhn takes issue

---

30 Disciplinarization is also a consequence of workforce or labor organization and division. The disciplines are separated from each other according to the needs of society, which is itself subject to compartementalization, departmentalization, and division of labor. This is perhaps unavoidable to a certain extent but is also detrimental in many ways.

31 Gilles Deleuze (1925-1975) was a French philosopher who wrote extensively on the history of philosophy and on philosophers like Nietzsche, Spinoza, Leibniz and Kant. Deleuze was also influential outside of philosophy by proposing often daring theses on the nature of capitalism, labor and the scientific enterprise.

32 Kuhn, Thomas S. *The Structure of Scientific Revolutions*. 3rd ed. Chicago, IL: University of Chicago Press, 1996.

with some of the most famous theses defended by the positivist school of thought and its understanding of scientific explanations and theories.

Kuhn's major thesis is that science is not cumulative in a general way. It proceeds through upheavals or paradigm shifts. Often new discoveries precipitate novel ways of looking at problems and sometimes even new methodologies—in such cases the new paradigm or way of looking at things replaces an older paradigm. The period before the new paradigm replaces the older paradigm is typically a period of crisis within the scientific community that practices the particular science referred to. This period is characterized by rabid disagreement. Kuhn compares scientific revolutions to political and social revolutions. There is some reason to question this analogy. More will be said about this later.

Another important dichotomy or distinction rejected by Kuhn is the difference made between the context of discovery and the context of justification. For philosophers of science like Carnap, Hempel and Popper, there is something clearly distinct between the way a theory is discovered and the way a theory is justified. One has to do with the history of science and the other with the philosophy of science. Carnap, Hempel, Popper and Reichenbach (in whose work this distinction first appears in a formal way) are interested in maintaining a fairly rigid demarcation between the origin of a discovery and its subsequent justification.

Kuhn on the other hand, probably under the influence of Nietzsche and other philosophers, operates a genealogy on the origin of scientific theories. Genealogies are methods of analysis of a theory which look at the origin of the theory in order to understand the deeper mechanism of how the theory works and is justified—and also, whose or what interests the theory serves. The genealogist is not unlike the psychoanalyst who looks for the source of a psychological conflict in the patient's history to understand how the conflict works in the present. Similarly, Kuhn looks in the past to uncover the hidden roots of scientific theories and show that what seem like purely logical and deductive issues in the context of justification of a theory are in fact connected deeply and intrinsically to the context of discovery and the origin of a given scientific theory.

> ### ⓘ KEY DEFINITIONS
>
> **HISTORICISM AND SCIENTIFIC EXPLANATION: KEY CONCEPTS AND DEFINITIONS**
> - All science is historical: its methods are not universal and necessary but particular and contingent.
> - Scientists "convert" themselves to a new scientific belief or theory.
> - Science is the best example of a rational endeavor or enterprise (Thomas Kuhn).

Another point of disagreement between Kuhn and the positivists like Hempel is that Kuhn does not believe there are general rules for determining what is a better scientific theory or to adjudicate between two theories. In Kuhn's view, it is a haphazard process in which for whatever reason, at some point in the scientific community the majority of its active members convert to the new theory. Because this seems to reject the objectivity of scientific theories in a way, Kuhn has been accused of relativism and irrationalism. However, Kuhn has also said that science is the best example that we possess of rationality. Towards the end of his career Carl Hempel recognized some of the truth of Kuhn's objections to the positivistic model of science and entered into dialogue and debate with this thinker.[33]

One of the major points of contention between someone like Kuhn and Hempel is the nature of the objects that scientific theories and language refer to. Hempel argues that when a change occurs in the theories used to describe the universe, this is just a change within the language of science, not a change in the objective features of the world that this language attempts to describe.[34] Kuhn on the other hand seems to argue that a change in scientific vocabulary changes our world-picture[35] and the nature of the objects that exist in this world-picture. In other words, the so-called objective world and objects within it, are relative to the world-picture that is shaped by the language of our scientific explanations and scientific theories.[36]

There are some important ideas that distinguish Kuhn from the school of logical empiricism and its theses and theories about scientific methodology. As we have mentioned, in Kuhn's view, science is not cumulative as it is for the empiricists and positivists. Kuhn argues that a science evolving at a fast pace does not possess a tight deductive structure. Living scientific concepts, he argues, are not precise. Furthermore, the thesis of the unity of science is false—disconnected tools are used for different types of scientific inquiry in various scientific disciplines. Kuhn's underlying thesis, which suits our modernist opinion better, is that science exists in time and is essentially historical. Science is not trans- or extra-temporal in some way. In fact, the thesis of historicism—that all human (and even divine or godly) phenomena possess a historical aspect, while nature is very old—took root during the age of Enlightenment. However, during the Enlightenment, historicism was applied to the traditional power structures of the Church and the divine right of kings. The claim that Jesus Christ was somehow extra

---

33 See for example Carl Hempel, "Valuation and Objectivity in Science." In R. S. Cohen & L. Laudan (Eds.), *Physics, Philosophy and Psychoanalysis*. Dordrecht, Holland: D. Reidel Pub. Co.1983.
34 Carl Hempel, "Valuation and Objectivity in Science", 1983.
35 This brings us back to a certain extent to the distinction that Tarski and the neo-positivists or nominalists like Carnap (and Hempel belongs in this category as well at least he acts under their influence) wanted to maintain between a meta-language and object-language. But even work in set-theory and the foundations of mathematics has shown that this rigid distinction may lead to something called Skolem's paradox.
36 Kuhn, T.S. *The Copernican Revolution: Planetary Astronomy in the Development of Western Thought*. Cambridge: Harvard University Press, 1957.

or trans-temporal was severely criticized during the Enlightenment when protestant theologians set out to search for the historical Jesus. For a long time however, it was thought that science was different from religion and it could escape the issues and problems of historicism. This thesis has come under attack with the work of thinkers like Kuhn, Lakatos and Feyerabend to name only the most important recent philosophers of science.

We now examine the influence social and radical constructivism had on the understanding of science, scientific explanation and scientific method.

Social constructivism (and post-modernism under which it is sometimes subsumed or which subsumes it) describes science as not being about an independent reality, but as about the methods and practices of science. Thus 'science creates reality' for social constructivism or post-modernism. Reality here is viewed as a social construct and there is no independent reality (not even science) which science is able to explain or even describe. Essentially, social-constructivism is an anti-realistic thesis about the nature of scientific objects. However, as an epistemological theory it faces a number of problems: Social-constructivism does not want to commit itself to an anti-realist epistemological position; instead, it claims that epistemology is a form of conservative and domineering philosophical discipline that hides power relations in the academy.

Instead, social-constructivism is committed to the truth of rhetoric and the defusing of any claims about the objectivity of science or of the world. In respect to this, the Sokal hoax[37] is very instructive and shows the inability or reluctance of many social-constructivists to engage with science, logic, mathematics meaningfully. The politicization of science by social-constructivists and epistemological radicals like Feyerabend is entertaining, but contains so little truth for the amount of words one is required to read that one wonders whether such poorly argued positions and such simplistic understandings of the reality of science and of the world even require a refutation. We refer the curious reader to the excellent work of Paul Boghossian for a more thorough treatment of these issues and a generally correct refutation of post-modernistic and social-constructivist approaches within the philosophy of science.[38]

---

[37] In the Sokal hoax, a known and reputable physicist called Sokal submitted a paper to *Social Text* a leading journal of cultural studies. In the paper he argued, using examples from physics and mathematics, that physics and mathematics supported progressive social constructivist theses. But Sokal later revealed to the Journal *Lingua Franca* that his text was in fact an intellectual fraud because it deliberately used the language of physics and mathematics in a pseudo-logical way without evincing material understanding or efficacy of those concepts. In short his paper submitted to *Social Text* was a hoax to test whether the editors behind that journal (all leading proponents of social constructivism or post-modernism) would evaluate the text on scientific grounds or on purely rhetorical or political ones. The reader is left to decide what this shows about the validity and credibility of politicized social-constructivism and post-modernism.

[38] Bhogossian, Paul, "What the Sokal Hoax Ought to Teach Us," The Times Literary Supplement, December

QUESTIONS
Science, Critical Thinking and the Scientific Worldview

1. What is the scientific method and how is it related to the theories of knowledge that we have covered on rationalism and empiricism?
2. What roles do deduction, induction and abduction play in the Scientific method and scientific explanation?
3. What role do induction and deduction play in Hempel's Deductive-Nomological model of scientific explanation?
4. What is deductive and what is nomological about Hempel's model of scientific explanation?
5. How is the Causal Mechanical Model of Scientific Explanation different from the Deductive-Nomological model?
6. What is the thesis of the unity of science or of unified science?
7. What is the thesis of reductionism when it comes to human knowledge and its relation to scientific knowledge?
8. What are some typical weaknesses for Hempel's deductive-nomological model of scientific explanation?
9. What are some typical weaknesses for the causal Mechanical Model?
10. What are some typical weaknesses for the unity of science model of scientific theory and explanation?
11. What is the connection between scientific explanation and the Humanities?
12. What is the connection between explanation and understanding in the Humanities?
13. According to Charles Taylor, what differentiates the Human Sciences from the Natural Sciences?
14. What is a critique of Taylor from the point of view of Thomas Kuhn?
15. Why does claiming that science is shaped entirely by cultures and worldviews potentially lead to relativism?
16. Why is knowledge-theoretic relativism untenable and how is it different from ethical and political relativism?
17. What is the difference between the Humanities and the Social Sciences?
18. What is the difference between the Humanities and the Natural Sciences?
19. How is scientific description different from scientific explanation?
20. How is an explanation different from an argument? How does this cause problems for views of scientific explanation which try to understand scientific explanation as a form of argument?
21. How is the historicistic view of science different from the positivistic view of it?
22. Describe the ontological, knowledge and ethical aspects of the scientific worldview.

13, 1996, pp.14-15.

✓ KEY CONCEPTS & DEFINITIONS—KNOWLEDGE & HUMANIST WORLDVIEW

SUBJECT MATTER: The Problem of Human Freedom and Determinism and its Application in Western and Global History

TIME FRAME: Inception of Humanism and the Humaniora in the Renaissance and Development Up To The Present

PEOPLE	IDEAS
RAMON LULL	Divine Permutations and Combinations and the Origin of Computer and Information Science: Development of an art of calculation that will lead to Leibniz's *mathesis universalis*.
BOCCACCIO	Naturalization of Christian Eros of the Middle-Ages: Critique of Christian Sexual Ethics and Reorientation of Philosophy towards the Worldly.
PICO DE LA MIRANDOLA & MARSILIO FICINO	The Dignity of Man and Renaissance Syncretism: The Rediscovery of Plato in Florence and the Renewal of the Syncretic Roots of Christianity through Cabbalah and Hermeticism.
ERASMUS	Polemic with Luther on free will: The will of God and the will of Man: Negative Theological Freedom.
THOMAS MORE	*Theodicy and optimism; The Algebra of thought, Monadology, The Best of All Possible Worlds, Utopia, Conscientious objection, Authority vs Justification and Autonomy, Divine Power vs Temporal Power, Priority of Theological Virtues over Moral Virtues.*
GIORDANO BRUNO	Art of Memory & Its Role in Shaping the Scientific Method: From Bruno to Bacon to Hume, the career of psychological and esoteric associationism.

CHAPTER 8
KNOWLEDGE & THE HUMANIST WORLDVIEW

This textbook has covered logic, the scientific method, theories of knowledge and worldviews. But what is the connection of these topics to the humanities?[1] What is the relationship between logic, science and the Humanities? In French, Humanities is "sciences humaines". In German, it is "*Geisteswissenschaften*". Both French and German conserve in their appelation for the Humanities the connection to a concept of a science of man or of the human.

Traditionally, in the history of philosophy and thought, humanism is a period that hearkens back to Renaissance[2] thinkers such as Ramon Llull (1232-1315) Boccacio (1313–1375), Pico of Mirandola (1463–1493), Marsilio Ficino (1433 –1499), Erasmus (1466 –1536), Luther (1483 – 1546), Thomas More (1478 – 1535) and Giordano Bruno

---

[1] Humanities is sometimes translated into *Kulturwissenschaften,* whereas *Geisteswissenschaften* is translated by the term 'social sciences'. This is a questionable translation, however, since social sciences could also have the German equivalent of *Sozialwissenschaften*.

[2] The case for a historical period called the Renaissance was made by Jakob Burkhardt and Jules Michelet in the 19th century.

(1548–1600).

There is some debate over whether Luther should be included in the history of the Reformation or the history of the Renaissance. The Reformation and the Renaissance can be seen as concurrent and perhaps competitive streams of thought in the history of ideas but there was also a lot of cross-influence and spiritual commonality between the two movements. The Renaissance possessed at its core, at least in its Florentine representatives, Pico and Ficino, a drive toward religious reformation even though this drive, its objectives and yearning, were very different from those of Luther and Calvin—the traditional figures associated with the Reformation.

It will be the thesis of this chapter that humanist interest in esoteric philosophy (magic was the central type of esotericism[3] but other types such as *prisca theologia*[4] and Cabbalah[5] also played a central role) and knowledge led to Francis Bacon and his interest in the inductive method which we have seen to be a foundation upon which the scientific method rests. The deductive methods at play in the humanities (and in mathematical logic) are older than Bacon and they hearken back to Euclid's geometrical methods and to Parmenides', Plato's and Aristotle's theses about the deductive nature of nous, logos and Being.

We will also claim that the debate between free will and determinism with respect to human nature or within human nature constitutes the priviledged object or subject-matter of what has commonly been called the Humanities.

---

3 Esotericism is a form of knowledge (in this context it is tied to the notion of occultism) that is supposed to be accessible only to an initiate few. It is a "secret" or "rejected" form of knowledge as opposed to a general or public form of knowledge.

4 *Prisca theologia* is a tradition of talking about God that was thought to be pre-Christian by Mirandola and Ficino. It comprised the work of Zoraster, Hermes Trismegistus, Orpheus, Aglaophemus, Pythagoras, Philolaus and lastly Plato. Most of these figures are pre-Christian with the exception of Hermes. For Hermes who is sometimes conflated into Hermes Trismegistus (but this conflation is not always accepted by sources as reputable as Cicero) there are scholars who claim that he pre-dates Christ (Copenhaver) while others like Fowden believe that he appeared after the birth of Christ.

5 Kabbalah is an art of transformative interpretation. The Cabbalah is the Christian appropriation of the Jewish art of esotericism and number interpretation called Kabbalah. Kabbalah is a complex domain of expertise, almost a science, and we cannot hope to do justice to it in this short footnote. Important for it are the concepts of a key that could possibly allow to interpret and influence the nature of the universe (in this sense there seems to be some overlap between Kabbalah and magic). An art of transformative interpretation of a graph called the Tree of Life (and which in some ways anticipates mathematical Graph theory) who possesses Sephira or Sephiroths which allows to link the interpretative Kabbalistic key to states and modes of Being. The Cabbalah though inspired from the Jewish Kabbalah becomes a different tradition in the hands of Pico and Reuchlin and is appropriated to develop the Christian notion of a pentagrammaton that allegedly or perhaps supersedes the Judaic tetragrammaton.

8.1 RAMON LLULL
8.1.1 Ars Magna & the Influence on Calculus & Induction

Ramon Llull (1232-1315) was a Christian Catalan philosopher and mystic. He is a philosophical giant but is also known as the father and precursor of information science. Llull developed a system of 'correspondences' whereby he associated elements, concepts and colors with given letters in the alphabet. From this he attempted to find rules and correspondences that were rational and that led to arguments about the true nature of reality. Llull thus paved the way for someone like Leibniz who sought a universal logical language through which he could express all scientific truth: this was called Leibniz's *characteristica universalis* and it was part of an ideal science of universal learning called the *mathesis universalis*.[6] But Llull also influenced Giordano Bruno and his 'art of memory', which in turn influenced Francis Bacon and his 'tables of induction'.

Plates from Llull's *Ars Magna*

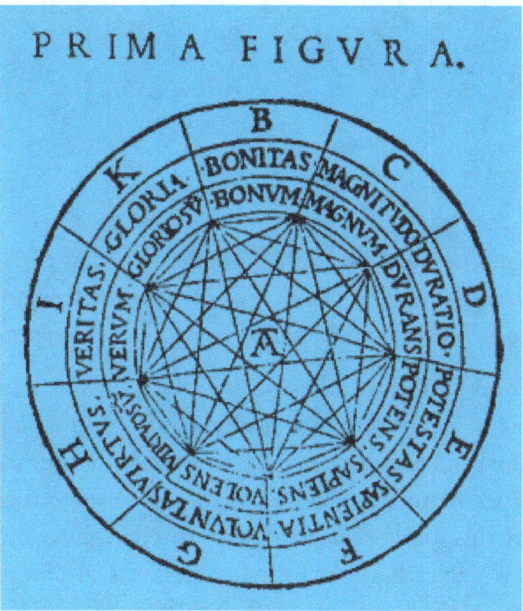

Figure 1 is directly influenced by Aristotle's triangle of oppositions we have studied in Chapter 2 of this book. On the diagonal, Llull uses the same oppositional logic as Aristotle by claiming that elements or contents opposed on the diagonal of the squares are ***combinatio impossibilis*** or impossible combinations.

---

[6] We have already discussed the *characteristica universalis* in Chapter 3 of this book.

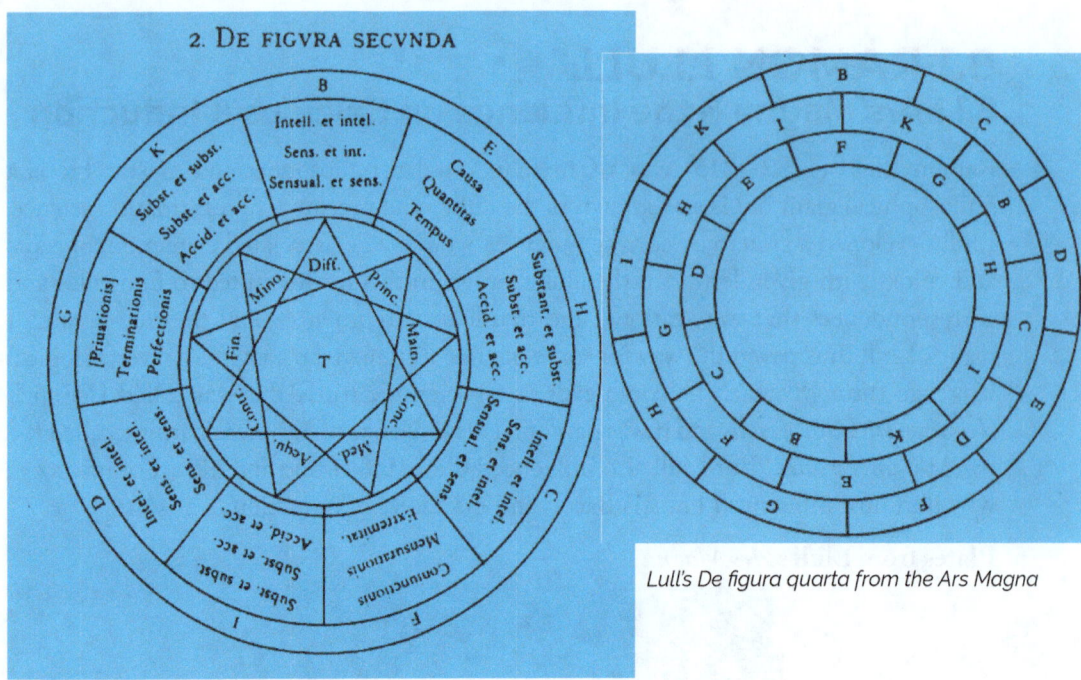

Lull's De Figura Secunda from the Ars Magna

Lull's De figura quarta from the Ars Magna

In this way Llull bridges the great logic of Aristotle with that of Leibniz. He seems to fill a void in logic (with the possible exception of Ockham whose nominalist logicistic is important but concrete) which occurs between Aristotle, Chrisyppus and Leibniz.

The idea that information is stored and associated with various letters is a precursor to the idea of storing specific information in specific tables from which inductive rules are derived to generalize the facts of experience. In modern computer software, variables are often associated with specific memory cells and the contents of those memory cells are abstracted from the way this memory is physically stored in the computer hardware. This process of abstraction which is familiar to many students of computer science was, in fact, pre-figured in Ramon Lull's *ars magna* of circular tables and associations.

A very important aspect of these plates in the *Ars Magna*[7] is that they use a system of numeration that is pseudo binary: 8 (2 to the power of three) and 16 (2 to the power of 4). The combinations might be arbitrary but the fact that he thought to arrange information in this way—the terms used are sometimes natural elements, sometimes

[7] This is the title of the work published by Llull in 1305 and which outlined his combinatorial method for developing arguments about the nature of reality.

moral qualities or what he calls the *Dignities of God*—paves the way for a logic that is formal and abstracts from contents as does Leibniz's and the formal logic of Boole, De Morgan, Frege and Peirce. This abstract formal logic is found later in the twentieth century deduction systems of Tarski. To connect back to the main thesis of this book about the Humanities one may say that through the infinite play of permutation and divination, Lull has anticipated the modern dilemma of free will and determinism. The fact that information can be abstracted from its immediate historical context and be projected onto a wider, cosmological and perhaps supernal scheme allows Lull to use esoteric and cabbalistic methods to anticipate and make possible the work of both De la Mirandola, Bruno, Heinrich Cornelius of Agrippa and John Dee. These, in turn are a major influence on the Francis Bacon who then becomes the mouth-piece of nascent empiricism.

> ⓘ **KEY DEFINITIONS**
>
> **RAMON LULL: KEY CONCEPTS AND DEFINITIONS**
> - Combinations and permutations of God's attributes and dignities
> - Bridges between Aristotle and Leibniz
> - Permutations and combinations of divine attributes both make possible and determine human freedom

8.2 BOCCACCIO
8.2.1 Naturalization of the Middle-Ages Christian Eros

Another important development of the Renaissance and of humanism that affected the nature of knowledge was the work of the writer Giovanni Boccaccio. In his *Decameron*, Boccaccio tells the story of a group of seven young women and three young men who flee from plague-ridden Florence to a deserted villa in the countryside of Fiesole for two weeks at the time the *black death* was plaguing Italy—the end of the Middle-Ages and the beginning of the Renaissance.

The ten youths recount stories to pass the evenings. There are ten days and ten evenings so in the end one hundred stories (taking the form of novellas) are told. Some have argued that the mercantilist economic philosophy is at play in the *Decameron*. But while there is definitely a greater emphasis on the reality of this world with its concreteness and its economic and financial issues, the true center of the *Decameron* is a form of Platonic *eros*. In the proemium it is clear, that in the fashion of the troubadours, the stories are meant to heal problems of the heart by allowing one to contemplate and revisit the passions and conflicts that were common around many medieval and beginning of Renaissance courts. The *Decameron* thus stands in the tradition of *amour courtois* literature that was common in the period of the Middle Ages and at the beginning of the Renaissance.

> **ⓘ KEY DEFINITIONS**
>
> **BOCACCIO'S NATURALISTIC EROS: KEY CONCEPTS AND DEFINTIONS**
> - Love is both worldly and other-worldly
> - Look away from Heaven and bring humanist gaze back to human nature
> - Religious toleration is key to living together (tale of Melchizedek)

Dioneo is the philosopher of all the recluses and some have believed that he represents the point of view of Boccaccio himself. Boccaccio transforms the medieval outlook: he writes prose in the vulgar—that is in Italian and not Latin like Petrarchus, the most accomplished Latin poet of that period. Boccaccio's prose is rhythmic and naturalistic. Boccaccio inaugurates the use of the novella in Europe even though he has Arabic predecessors. He makes use of a cornice[8] as a literary device to provide continuity to the whole work. The novella is one of the most modern literary forms, championed by Maupassant in French and Conrad, Hemingway and Steinbeck in English to name only a few. The English novella seems to have developed seriously as a genre only in the twentieth century. An important tale told in the *Decameron* and later picked up by Gottfried Lessing in his famous 18th century novel, *Nathan The Wise* and in the *Gesta Romanorum*[9] published around the end of the 13th century and the beginning of the 14th century, is the one of Melchizedek. The tale tells us of Saladdin, a famous sultan in dire need of money and an affluent Jew called Melchizedek who had plenty of money sitting idly, but who would not readily volunteer a share of his riches. The Sultan was not prepared to take the money by force. So he called Melchizedek to his court and asked him the following question: Which of the three great revealed religions (Judaism, Christianity and Islam) is the true religion?

Melchizedek sensed that this was a trap and responded with a parable: There was once a man who had three sons. He had received a precious ring from his own father. Afraid that the sons would quarrel over the ring and his estate, this man made two identical copies of the original ring. Each son got a part of his estate and one of the rings. Saladdin

---
8 A cornice in this sense is not an architectural structure but rather the narrative structure of how the stories are welded together by the narrator who bridges the stories that are told by the three men and seven women in Fiesole.
9 *The Deeds of The Romans* was essentially a preacher's manual containing a hodge-podge of excerpts from literary works.

understood that each of the rings symbolized one of Judaism, Christianity or Islam. He thanked Melchizedek for his allegorical tale and asked him directly for a loan which was granted by the Jew and was repaid in full by the Sultan in due time.

This tale of religious tolerance and its embroilment in a financial, worldly issue captures the spirit of the *Decameron* well. Religion, passion and cultural division are at its center; but the world is never far from this center, always pressing, naturalistically on the mystical and allegorical issues discussed and narrated.

Boccaccio focused on the naturalness of sex by combining and interlacing sexual experiences with nature. In this way he criticized the prudish Christian ethics of the Middle Ages. His is a humanist worldview which takes the human and his psychology as the main center of observation for the writer. Thus, Boccaccio participates in shifting the gaze of the Middle-Age writers and philosophers away from the city of God and back to the city of man.[10] As with Pico and his example of Adam,[11] man is placed at the center of creation and is lauded as its most beautiful creation. The humanism and the Humanities which will develop out of this humanism, take the human subject as the object of their study by applying psychology and a form of natural analysis to human relations, among which the most central of human relations of all: sexuality. Thus Boccaccio participates in the dialectic of the Humanities by discussing and challenging traditional, determinate modes of sexual and social conduct. He inaugurates a search for freedom beyond conventional and conservative Middle-Age sexual ethics and raises the modern humanistic question of freedom and determinism.

The reason Boccaccio is so central to the Humanities and to their development in the Renaissance is his modernism. In this aspect, he antedates Freud's insight that sexuality shapes individuals and civilizations. After a certain regression in the work of Luther and Calvin, this latent modernism of Boccaccio makes apparent the central role that sex and sexuality play in the psychological constitution of man and his shaping of the world. This insight shows Boccaccio to be perhaps more modern than Nietzsche insofar as he understands that life and sexuality form a totality that is grounded not in the will to power[12] but in a primeval and eternal eros. Boccaccio's bringing of the Middle-Ages to earth and to human concreteness and society anticipates to a certain extent later Protestant and more earthly based systems of religious thought (his mercantilism will be important in the France of the 16th and 17th century). In reaction, the writers and

---

10 See Augustine's book of the *City of God*.
11 See footnote for quote 15 from the *Oration On The Dignity Of Man*.
12 In fact Nietzsche's will to power is not opposed to the Greek notion of *eros*. Rather Nietzsche opposes the will to power to the selfless Christian notion of *agape*. *Eros* is good because it increases life and power but *agape* is bad because it humiliates and shames the self into servility and self-hatred according to Nietzsche's interpretation of the psychology of Christianity.

humanists we study next returned to a more theological and Christian approach to humanism and knowledge of human nature.

For Pico and Ficino, whom we study next, *eros* does not return or frame the argument in the world as in Boccaccio, but instead points to the invisible and to the primeval—to an original religious tradition in which all of the great religions of Judaism, Christianity and Islam are united. This religion or original theology is called the *prisca theologia* and it is to its influence on the development of knowledge that we turn next.

8.3 Pico de la Mirandola & Marsilio Ficino
8.3.1 The Dignity of Man & Renaissance Syncretism

In a letter to Pico of Mirandola, the other great Renaissance humanist Marsilio Ficino writes: *"Knowledge and learning are a form of remembering"* (the Platonic anamnesis-P.C)[13]

Pico then replies to Ficino in a letter that has also become famous: "For if I were to believe that what Pythagoras claims is true, I would say that Plato had been born again in Ficino."[14] It is obvious that these philosophers were influenced by the Platonic school of thought. But their interest in Platonic philosophy (we owe to Ficino the first translation of the complete works of Plato in a modern language—into the Italian of his native Florence) was mediated through their abiding Christianity and through what has been called the Hermetic[15] tradition in the case of Ficino and the Jewish Kabbalah in the case of Pico. Both of these traditions converged in the concept of what both Pico and Ficino referred to as the *prisca theologia*.

Pico proposed a reconciliation of all schools of thought through the *prisca theologia*. In his famous book *De Ente et Uno* (*Of Being and the One*), Pico claimed that he could prove that there was a hidden harmony between the philosophical systems of Plato and Aristotle.

Pico of Mirandola (1463–1494) was a 15th century Christian humanist best known for writing the manifesto of the Renaissance: *The Oration on the Dignity of Man*. In this book he celebrates man as the center of creation and for whom anything is possible: even the surpassing of angels and becoming equal to God. This could be accomplished if man uses

---

13 Ficino Marsilio. The Letters of Marsilio Ficino, Volume 7, p.44. Letter 35, Shepheard-Walwyn, 1975-2003. Print.
14 Idem, Volume 7, pp. 89-90
15 The Hermetic tradition can be taken to be co-extensive in this introductory text with the movement of the prisca theologia defined and discussed in footnote 3.

reason and free will. Heeding only his senses, man degenerates into animal brutality.[16] Interested in many aspects of learning, Pico mixed Greek knowledge, Christian teaching and the Jewish practice of the Kabbalah to arrive at what has been described as a form of philosophical syncretism.[17] Pico who was personally acquainted with Marsilio Ficino may also be termed a neo-Platonic philosopher.

> **QUOTE**
>
> *"Knowledge and learning are a form of remembering."*
>
> Pico of Mirandola

Pico sought to harmonize Christian beliefs with Kabbalah, which he considered a primal form of Jewish doctrine or gnosis originating in Moses and thus long presaging the teachings of Jesus. Pico tried to prove, through the teaching of the Kabbalah, that Jesus Christ was the savior of humanity and its redeemer. In his attempts to do so, he claimed to discover a means of linguistically and numerologically equating the name Jesus Christ with the God of the Ancient Testament, *Yahweh*. Of prime importance to Pico and his successor Reuchlin who was also familiar with Pico's Cabbalistic ventures, was to find a way to interpolate the name of the God of the Old Testament with the God of the New Testament.

Pico and Ficino's main contribution was to develop a science of man and to prepare the way for a more radical questioning of Christianity in the work of Giordano Bruno. This challenge to Christianity and its view of science and the universe was what allowed for the development of modern science and its revision of the understanding and knowledge of the universe that was prevalent in the Middle-Ages.

---

16 Adam, we give you no fixed place to live, no form that is peculiar to you, nor any function that is yours alone. According to your desires and judgment, you will have and possess whatever place to live, whatever form, and whatever functions you yourself choose. All other things have a limited and fixed nature prescribed and bounded by our laws. You, with no limit or no bound, may choose for yourself the limits and bounds of your nature. We have placed you at the world's center so that you may survey everything else in the world. We have made you neither of heavenly nor of earthly stuff, neither mortal nor immortal, so that with free choice and dignity, you may fashion yourself into whatever form you choose. To you is granted the power of degrading yourself into the lower forms of life, the beasts, and to you is granted the power, contained in your intellect and judgment, to be reborn into the higher forms, the divine." *"Nec certam sedem, nec propriam faciem, nec munus ullum peculiar tibi dedimus, o Adam, ut quam sedem, quam faciem, quae munera tute optaveris, ea, pro voto, pro tua sententia, habeas et possideas. Definita caeteris natura intra praescriptas a nobis leges cohercetur. Tu, nullis angustiis cohercitus, pro tuo arbitrio, in cuius manu te posui, tibi illam prefinies. Medium te mundi posui, ut circumspiceres inde commodious quicquid est in mundo. Nec te caelestem neque terrenum, neque mortalem neque immortalem fecimus, ut tui ipsius quasi arbitrarius honorariusque plastes et fictor, in quam malueris tute formam effingas. Poteris in inferior quae sunt bruta degenerare; poteris in superiora quae sunt divina ex tui animi sententia regenerari."* Giovanni, Pico of Mirandola, *Oration on the Dignity of Man*. Pp 7-8, Regnery Publishing, Washington DC, 1956. Print.

17 See p.308 in this section for the meaning of the term 'syncretism'.

It is no coincidence that the Renaissance emerged around the same time though perhaps a bit earlier than the Reformation. The movements are roughly contemporary and there is a lot of cross-influence and cross-polination between the two. Some disciples of Erasmus studied the Renaissance theater of Giulio Camillo[18] who was a Venetian Renaissance occultist very much influenced by Ficino and Pico. However, the Reformers would later be more interested in recovering the purity of the ancient Christian tradition and of scripture than in the syncretism of the Renaissance humanists.

Nietzsche claimed that Luther and the Reformation had ruined the legacy of the Renaissance; but the Renaissance movement spearheaded by Ficino and Pico of Mirandola, already had its own spirit of reform—of wanting to heal theological and sectarian conflicts that had arisen among the religions of Judaism, Christianity, and Islam and even the conflicts and competitions that had arisen in the Middle Ages within the Catholic Church between the Dominican, Franciscan and Augustinian orders.

Syncretism consists in the bringing together and melding of apparently contradictory beliefs originating from different and distinct traditions. Syncretism can be religious or philosophical or even political. It mixes elements of a religion, a doctrine, a worldview or an ideology in order to develop a new one. The origin of the word syncretism comes from the pan-cretan league or federation which was made of distinct disparate members who would often feud and disagree internally but who would all rally against an external enemy and unite in their fight against this enemy. The essence and method of the Humanities is effectively syncretistic and inter-disciplinary. Because there is a definitional problem as to what disciplines belong or not to the Humanities, the idea and method of syncretism is what fits best to describe its character.

> **KEY DEFINITIONS**
>
> **FLORENTINIAN PLATONISM (MIRANDOLA & FICINO): KEY CONCEPTS & DEFINITIONS**
> - There is no absolute contradiction between Plato and Aristotle
> - Truth is both rational and mystical
> - Freedom can be attained through historical and Platonic recollection

Logically and perhaps ontologically, syncretism is objectionable but from a social, political and religious point of view this movement marks the beginning of modernity in its openness to other traditions. It assumes, perhaps erroneously, that all religions are rooted in one primeval religious tradition, but at the same time, by claiming that

---

[18] Giulio *Delminio* Camillo 1480–1544 is an Italian philosopher and occultist of the Italian Renaissance. He is remembered for his *Theatre of Memory*. This Theater was a physical construction that was built to help practice the art of memory of which Camillo was a practitioner. Camillo described his theater in the work *L'Idea del Theatro,* published posthumously.

all the great religions encompass and comprise a kernel of truth, syncretism paves the way for secularism and religious tolerance. Syncretism may be viewed as a pre-condition to the Enlightenment notion of freedom of religion and freedom of conscience. Even Christianity has had to absorb some parcel of syncretism in order to open itself up and transform itself into a perennial religion. In fact the roots of Christianity itself are syncretic when one looks at the fact that it was melded together, so to speak, out of the Platonic and Aristotelian philosophical system, Gnostic dualism and contempt for the world and the Judaic concept of a monotheistic God of life, inspiration and movement. The tensions within the Christian worldview and ontology are no doubt due to this syncretistic origin.

So in reanimating and renewing Christian syncretism Ficino and Pico were in fact going back to the roots of Christianity in some way. They perhaps erred and found in the *prisca theologia* things that were different and entirely absent from the things that the Christian Fathers had in mind when they elaborated Christian doctrine. For one thing, Pico's thesis that the Qabalah/Kabbalah could be the source of original Christian teaching does not match the historical fact that the historical development of the Kabbalah occurred more fully into what it is known as today as the early second millenium after Christ.

But Neo-platonic emanationism developed around the same time as the Kabballah and it proved to be an answer to some of the challenges that the process aspects of the Kabbalistic Tree of Life launched against Christianity. At the same time Neo-Platonic emanationism helped Augustine understand some of the challenges put forth by the Hermetic and the Kabbalistic tradition to Christianity. Furthermore, we possess, in the Renaissance movement of Ficino and Mirandola a precursor of the pantheism that was to inspire Spinoza in his thesis of *Deus sive Natura* that we have studied in Chapter 3.

8.4 ERASMUS'S POLEMIC WITH LUTHER ON FREE WILL

Erasmus wrote an important text called *De Libero Arbitrio Diatribe Sive Collatio* in 1524. In response, Luther wrote his *De Servo Arbitrio* (On the Bondage of the Will) (1525). Erasmus began his argument in favor of free will by arguing from the ambiguity of Scripture. He was influenced by the neo-Platonism we studied in the previous section of this text and specifically by the appropriation that Ficino and Mirandola made of the platonic doctrine of ecstasy in the *Phaedrus*. While not being a Catholic in the strict sense, Erasmus developed the hermeneutic tradition of St. Paul and St. Augustine in claiming that parts of Scripture were not clear but rather ambiguous.[19] If this is the case, then an office of interpretation is required according to Erasmus. This office had to be the office of the Roman pope since he was the first among all bishops in Catholic or Western Christianity.[20] But since Scripture is ambiguous, Erasmus allows that within the will and the self there must be a capacity to freely appropriate the interpretation of Scripture. Thus what Erasmus seems to be arguing for, is not an unfettered free will, but a disciplined and organized will, which can select passages from Scripture to argue for its position, but which must also submit to a central interpretative authority of scripture: that of the Roman pope.

Erasmus considers the case of Adam and Eve who must have been free to some extent in order to receive the commandments of God. For Erasmus, if God commands something, this presupposes that those who are commanded must have the freedom of choice necessary to obey the command. Thus command presupposes freedom.

Luther's theology of the cross claims that God does not find humans and their choices already in the world but creates them through his will. Grace begins with God, not with an appropriative human choice. Luther argued that "freedom of the will after the fall, exists in name only".

For Erasmus[21] the essential point is that humans have the freedom of choice. Erasmus claimed that all humans possessed free will, and that the doctrine of predestination was wrong. He argued against the belief that God's foreknowledge of events was the cause of events. In other words for Erasmus, God's perfections, foreknowledge and omnipotence were distinct but non-contradictory powers of God. Erasmus also thought that the sacraments and practices of repentance, baptism and conversion depended on the existence of free will.[22] For Erasmus grace brought man to a knowledge of God

---

19 Erasmus adopted a position of neutrality in the conflict between Luther and the Pope, though at times he was perceived by both parties as engaging in a form of double-dealing.

20 Erasmus criticized the Pope's usage of St-Jerome's vulgate (translation of the original Biblical text) and provided his own somewhat controversial translation (translating logos by sermo instead of verbum for example). Behind this translation controversy laid a deeper attack upon Aristotle and scholasticism which Erasmus and Luther saw as a common foe.

21 Erasmus also looked at the work of the 'via moderna' school of Lorenzo Valla on the problem of free choice of will. But Erasmus later rejected the ideas of this school.

22 This debate of free will and determinism is central to most of the history of philosophy. A few centuries earlier Aquinas and the Molinists debated the nature of free will but this was centered not so much on sinfulness and grace as on the possibility of freedom given that God had to know in advance (he possesses foreknowledge) how all things will unfold until the end of time. The Molinists spoke of a middle knowledge that would solve this problem, while Thomas is typically thought to have prioritized the intellect of God to solve this problem. The semi-pelagianism (based on a half way position between that of Pelagius and that of Augustine) of Erasmus and his notion of cooperative grace had at some time in the history of the Christian Church been judged

and sustained humans as they used their free will to choose between good and evil. The choices of humans would eventually lead to salvation through the atonement and expiation of Jesus Christ. Christ had expiated the ancestral sin of Adam and Eve and this would redeem and save humans. Thus Erasmus developed a notion of collaborative or cooperating grace. His position was not unlike what has been called Semi-Pelagianism.[23]

For Luther there is no free will for humanity because any will humans might have is overwhelmed by the influence of sin. Luther believed in the power and complete sovereignty of God and it is from this position that he launched his critique of Erasmus' position.

Luther believed that unredeemed human beings are under the influence of Satan. Satan, the prince of the mortal world according to Luther, pursues all in his dominion and would be victorious were he not overpowered by a stronger power, that of God. Luther believed that when God redeems a human being, he redeems the entire being, including his will. This will then becomes liberated for the service of God.

According to Luther, no one can achieve salvation or redemption through their own choices. People do not choose between good or evil, because they are naturally dominated by evil. For Luther salvation is simply the product of God unilaterally changing a person's being and turning him or her towards good ends. If this were not so, Luther argues, then God would not be omnipotent and would lack total sovereignty over creation; and to argue differently became an insult to the glory of God according to Luther's righteous but austere soul.

Luther developed what he called a theology of the cross. In it he emphasized that even God died on the cross during Christ's crucifixion. His thesis was that God placed himself in the position of man and suffered in a way similar enough to human beings to be able to redeem them. His theology of the cross was thus opposed to a theology of glory in which God was seen as a triumphant king or emperor. This emphasis on sorrow and suffering in Luther's theology goes hand in hand with the emphasis on the weakness of the will and on sinfulness. We suffer because we sin, and we sin because we are weak and in need of God's redemption.

It seems at least from our point of view that despite Luther's theology of the cross and

---

heretical. It is interesting to note that Greek Christians and Orthodox Christians espouse a form of theological semi-pelagianism whereby man chooses to first turn towards God and then God meets him and comes towards him with his all-powerful grace.

23 Cooperative or collaborative grace was not discovered or coined by Erasmus, it is an older notion that goes back to the Egyptian Church Father and monk, John Cassian. He is also the teacher of the mystical orthodox doctrine of *theosis*, in which man may become divine on Earth during his lifetime.

Christ-God's suffering on this cross of redemption, that Erasmus is somewhat closer to logical and theological integrity on this issue. An omnipotent God must grant man the power to turn away from him. It is only if man has the free choice of will that we can call man a rational creature endowed with knowledge. Man's freedom is in some ways a negative freedom, a freedom to stay away from God. However, paradoxically even this freedom must ultimately be granted to him by God.

The issue of free will and determinism is connected to knowledge and the Humanities as it is central to the debate between science and the Humanities. Many scientists who look for ultimate and unifying theories claim that these theories must account for some freedom within their laws. Most of these scientists explain freedom naturalistically through the concept of biological evolution and natural selection. But these answers are in the end unsatisfactory. Freedom of the will is necessary so that we may act morally. This was Erasmus' great point. Morality does not follow from evolutionism. This does not mean that evolutionism is wrong, but that it functions at a level of explanation distinct from that at which we explain value, norms and ethical behavior.[24]

8.5 THOMAS MORE'S UPHOLDING OF CATHOLIC DOGMA AGAINST HENRI VIIITH

The controversy surrounding Thomas More's execution exemplifies the question of knowledge and the challenge knowledge, especially new knowledge poses to the establishment which embodies the structures and laws of old knowledge. It also contributed to the development of the modern notion of conscientious objection and objector, which was already touched upon by both Luther and More in separate but related ways.

Luther developed his notion of freedom of conscience in a publication of ninety-five theses. More, on the other hand, applied his ideas politically.[25] When More became Lord High Chancellor in 1529, he 'objected' to the King asking for a divorce from Catherine of Aragon so he could marry Anne Boleyn. Although Luther preceded his action by a few years, More developed the notion of freedom of conscience and conscientious

---

[24] This does not mean that we adhere to a position in which stasis has more value than process and Becoming. But one cannot reduce value and norm-attainment processes to biological and evolutionist-naturalist and selectionist processes. There exists process and evolution at the level of norms and values but this evolution is historical not naturalistic-evolutionistic.

[25] Luther also applied his conscience politically at the diet of Worms, in 1521.

objection from within the system of Catholicism.[26]

More argued that no temporal power could be the representative of God on earth. The doctrine of the Catholic Church, which claims that spiritual power and authority have precedence over temporal power and authority, supported his position. This debate, rooted in the doctrines of the pope Boniface VIII (in his papal bull *Unam Sanctam*[27]) and his struggle with Phillip IV, eventually led to the weakening of the papacy and the move of the pope to Avignon in what was termed by historians, the Babylonian captivity of the papacy.

The point to retain is that More was willing to accept the supreme sacrifice for this belief and lose his life. He never denied that the supreme power of God was represented by the Pope in England, even after people like Thomas Cromwell attempted his rescue by attesting that More had told him that he believed King Henry was the supreme power in England.

Beyond the specifics of this controversy, is a common pattern: Human beings slowly begin challenging the supremacy of authorities and developing the notion of an autonomous human subject[28] able to ground his beliefs in both conscience and rational argument. The arguments deriving from institutional authority[29] and tradition gradually lose their power as we enter the Renaissance and continue through to the Reformation of the Catholic Church.

More was a part of the Renaissance Humanism group of intellectuals. But while Erasmus' Catholicism is a subject of debate, More remained a staunch and devoted Catholic. Erasmus wrote a work called the *Praise of Folly* which in Latin is *Encomium Moriae* (literally the praise of Morus, or More). More's famous work *Utopia* is partly a criticism of Plato, an attempt to correct and develop the notions present in Plato's *Republic*.

As Lord Chancellor, Thomas More presided over executions of Protestants in England. While it is not clear that he actively persecuted Protestants and wanted to exterminate

---

26 This is not entirely correct: challenges to absolute papal authority had already been launched by people like Dante in his *De Monarchia* and other historical scholars but there is a definite novelty in a Catholic willing to die for his conscientious beliefs, as is the case with More. More may be fruitfully compared to Socrates who is earlier and to Giordano Bruno, who is a later figure. In all three cases political and religious authorities sinned against the free conscience of the philosophers and this has left an indelibile, tragic but also heroic mark on the history of philosophy.
27 *Unam Sanctam* means "one holy" in Latin and it refers to the unity of the Church, its holiness and the unity of the Pope's authority over the temporal world or order.
28 A notion that will become fully clarified only in Kant's ethical theory at the end of the 18th century.
29 They are considered fallacies of authority, a topic we have studied in Chapter 2 under the heading of informal fallacies.

them, his position towards them was certainly hostile. Some have argued that he betrayed his earlier humanism and the position of religious tolerance advocated in his famous book *Utopia*.

> **KEY DEFINITIONS**
>
> **THOMAS MORE CONTROVERSY: KEY CONCEPTS AND DEFINITIONS**
> - More refused to recognize Henry the VIIIth's divorce based on his conscience
> - One of the first conscientious objectors with Martin Luther
> - Author of *Utopia*: Model of Ideal society based on Plato's *Republic*

While More admired Plato and his work of the *Republic*, he saw his work of *Utopia* as a corrective to Plato's *Republic* in many ways. The ideal of religious tolerance is developed in *Utopia* but is now limited in scope. It does not extend to atheists, for instance, whom Utopians do not trust (according to More) because they do not believe in an after-life, are free to act unethically and perhaps criminally in this world.

While More admired Plato's theology with its other-worldly asceticism and its monotheism, he felt that there was something essential missing from Plato's account. He did not favor *sophia* and *eros* as the main virtues in his *Utopia*. Rather faith, charity and hope were more central to his account. In this context, one may question More's thesis that the moral virtues are preparatory to the theological virtues. What would one make of all the morally corrupt theologians of the ages (there have been many) and especially of the time of the Reformation who, rightly, incensed Luther?

In the end, More believed that Plato did not go far enough in his account because he was lacking the living Christ: the God who has walked with men and spoken to them of His creation. More wrote Christ with capital letter in his *Utopia* and Christianity was a central model for developing his ideal community. He saw no clash between the communism (lack of private property) of his *Utopia* and the Christian Gospel. In the end, More died like a true philosopher, when faced with death he was 'unafraid like Socrates'. Philosophy had taught him to die, to prepare for death. Serene, he positioned his head and his beard on the other side of the axe that was to separate his head from his body. He joked that at least his beard had to be safe and preserved after his death.

8.6 GIORDANO BRUNO'S ART OF MEMORY & ITS ROLE IN SHAPING THE SCIENTIFIC METHOD

Giordano Bruno is a dominant figure of the Renaissance. In 1600 he was burned at the stake by the Catholic Church. One can say that, not unlike Ancient Athens with Socrates, the Church sinned against philosophy and one of its brightest representatives in Giordano Bruno.

It is not clear whether Giordano Bruno got burned at the stake for his complex esotericism,[30] his belief in (the truth of) the Copernican system, his belief that the Earth moved or that an infinity of worlds existed. What will interest us here is the influence of what is called his system or *Art of Memory* on the development of the scientific method.

The art of memory proceeds by assigning loci or places for objects or things which one tries to memorize. By associating concepts or names with a specific physical place one builds and develops an artificial memory that is added to our natural capacity to remember things. The art of memory is a form of magic. It is developed by Bruno in two of his major works, the *Shadows*[31] and the *Seals*.[32] What Bruno sought in his art of memory might be difficult for the modern mind to comprehend. Bruno believed there were three levels of existence: the earthly images, the celestial images and the supercelestial ideas.

He believed that by somehow developing a system of organization of the celestial images one could work on the supercelestial ideas or realities and influence reality here below.

There was a double aspect to his art of memory and its connection to his magic. One was to master the external world, which would prove influential on Descartes and Bacon, who would later claim that the goal of science was to develop mastery over nature. But there was also a goal of self-mastery in Bruno's art of memory. He believes, not unlike the modern psychologist Jung, that we possess these universal symbols through a collective unconscious imprinted in our internal memory. These symbols of the zodiac exist in us internally though in a state of chaos. By organizing our internal nature and the symbols that exist within it, we can obtain mastery over ourselves a bit like in a system of yoga where concentrated and directed consciousness plays a salvific role by destroying the conditioning of the mind and other naturally and instinctively inherited

---

30 Esotericism is a form of knowledge that is supposed to be accessible only to an initiated few. It is a "secret" or "rejected" form of knowledge as opposed to a general or public form of knowledge.
31 *De umbris idearum* (Paris, 1582), *On The Shadows of Ideas* Print.
32 *Sigillus sigillorum* (1583), *The Seal of Seals* Print.

tendencies. The influence of Llull on Bruno who we studied at the beginning of this chapter is paramount. Bruno argued he could organize his hundred and fifty images or symbols on wheels and that through their combinations and permutations could achieve a total system of memory and knowledge. He employs Llull's idea of *mathesis* or of a combination of symbols, though his symbols were primarily pagan and had very little in common with Llull's trinitarian and Christian understanding of the *Dignities of God*.

Bruno reintroduced imagination into the discussion, which later influenced rationalists and even empiricists. Though the Brunist imagination was not a rational imagination, but a creative, emotional and religious generator of images, the re-examination of this faculty prepared the way for others like Kant and Einstein, who famously quipped (contrary to the theses of the empiricists) that imagination was more important than knowledge.

Bruno's art of memory and the magic associated with it were also influential on Francis Bacon whom we studied in Chapter 4. It led Bacon to develop his system of tables upon which induction is based. The idea that we make associations, connections and links in tables to develop rules that we remember and can formulate rigorously in mathematical, quantitative language as opposed to the occult use of number, which was qualitative and symbolic is novel and contributed to developing the scientific method. We see a definite Brunist influence on Bacon's table associationism and organization of inductive knowledge. A Brunist influence appears again in the psychological associationism of David Hume, who appears much later in history.

This chapter has been remarkably different from the other chapters in this book which dealt with epistemology, logic, science and the scientific method. Often the Humanities are relegated to a sort of back-seat in our education system. Recently a Canadian newspaper of serious repute wrote that unless students are super-rich or super-smart they should study something like mathematics, science, engineering or commerce, but not consider registering in a Humanities program. It is clear that such a thesis needs to be debunked and this is partly the motivation of the subject-matter covered in this chapter. The humanities have shaped science and the scientific method through the work of humanists and philosophers who despite the lack of quantitative methods or formulae, anticipated these practices in our modern society.

The spirit behind Renaissance magic is the same as the one that animates the 17th century's search for method. The humanists of the Renaissance want to have and to operate an effect on the world. They anticipate Bacon and Descartes' desire to rule over nature. An enlightened didactic and pedagogy would not separate the Humanities and the sciences in the curriculum. This is largely a political and disciplinarian distinction.

The *Geisteswissenchaften* and the *sciences humaines* possess within themselves the noble spirit of *Wissenschaft* and of science. It is only the limited and narrow mind of the 21st century which sees a dichotomy between the knowledge that stems from the Humanities and knowledge that stems from science. It is our hope to have demonstrated this thesis throughout this largely historical chapter.

> ⓘ **KEY DEFINITIONS**
>
> **GIORDANO BRUNO-MAGIC & SCIENTIFIC METHOD: KEY CONCEPTS & DEFINITIONS**
> - Influence on Francis Bacon through tables of association
> - One can effect changes on nature through individual concentration and application of magical methods
> - There exists a collective unconscious of symbols that can be accessed and controlled through magic (influenced Carl Jung)

QUESTIONS

Knowledge and the Humanist Worldview

1. How did the system of combinatorics developed by Ramon Llull pave the way for Leibniz' calculus and for Francis Bacon's tables of induction?
2. Why is the *Decameron* so important for the development of a naturalist understanding of sexuality and for a shift away from God and towards human relations and interactions?
3. How does Boccaccio anticipate the work of Freud and his thesis of the role of the unconscious in human knowledge?
4. How is the worldly aspect of money tied into the mystical aspect of religion in the *Decameron*?
5. How does the tale of Melchisedek represent religious tolerance?
6. How is humanism related to the humanities and to knowledge?
7. Why is Pico's *Oration on the Dignity of Man* so important for the Renaissance and

the development of knowledge about man or humans?

8. What was the role of Marsilio Ficino in reawakening interest in Plato in Renaissance Italy?
9. What is the role played by Hermeticism in the development of a syncretic understanding of knowledge in the humanist systems of Ficino and Pico of Mirandola?
10. Why is the idea that man does not possess a fixed nature so central in the Oration on the Dignity of Man? How does it anticipate modernist and existentialist views of human nature and its role in the acquisition of knowledge?
11. What is the role of religious syncretism in anticipating the secularism and tolerance of the Enlightenment age?
12. Why was the controversy of Luther and Erasmus surrounding free will so central to humanism in the Renaissance?
13. How does Erasmus defend the notion of free will through the notion of cooperative grace against Luther's critique of free will as bound by sin and the weakness of man?
14. Why is the notion of free will necessary for the understanding of the relationship between science and ethics or morality?
15. Why does Erasmus reject biblical predestination when he argues for the doctrine of free will?
16. How does Thomas More contribute to the modern notion of conscientious objection and objector which was already developed by Luther to a certain extent in his opposition to the Pope?
17. What could be a problem in agreeing with Thomas More that morality is a mere preparation for religion?
18. What is Giordano Bruno's *Art of Memory* and how does it prepare Francis Bacon's work on induction?
19. What is the influence of Bruno's *Art of Memory* on the scientific method?
20. Is humanism and the humanities the same thing? Why or why not? What is the difference between the humanities and natural science?
21. Is there a dichotomy or gulf between humanism and science? Does one have to choose between humanism and science or between religion and science?
22. Describe the ontological, knowledge and ethical aspects of the humanist worldview.

CONCLUSION

In this book, we have introduced formal and informal logic and its relation to argumentation theory and critical thinking. We have also covered the two theories of knowledge of rationalism and empiricism and the worldviews of idealism and pragmatism. In chapter 7 we looked at the relation between the humanities, the social sciences and the natural sciences, as well as their various methodologies and forms of explanation. In chapter 8, we set knowledge within the broader context of the humanities. We studied how the humanities developed in the post-Middle-Ages and how they were shaped by the humanistic syncretism of Florentine neo-Platonism (Ficino and de la Mirandola) and the origins of the humanities and of modern formal logic. We also studied Ramon Lull and how he mediated between Aristotle and the work of logicians like Leibniz, Pascal and Hobbes.

We have traced the development of the 17th century Scientific Revolution and the establishment of the scientific method. Our general view, shared by scholars like Frances Yates[1] is to propose a connection between the systematic desire to operate changes in reality, the world and nature through the manipulation of symbols and images—as seen in the works of Renaissance magic—and in the work of the scientist who methodically notes information and data in his tables in order to generalize and abstract laws and then proceeds to laboratory manipulations of his own, collects data and checks the original hypothesis. In this way, Giordano Bruno anticipates and influences the work of Francis Bacon on induction and inductive tables (Bacon and Bruno were contemporaries though Bruno died 26 years prior to Bacon, when he was burnt at the stake by the Catholic Inquisition) and Bacon's belief, shared with Descartes, that science should accomplish mastery over nature.

---

1 Yates, Frances, *The Art of Memory*, London, Routledge, 1966. Print. Also see *Giordano Bruno and the Hermetic Tradition* by the same author.

Other scholars such as Ion Culianu have worked on Giordano Bruno and his art of memory and his magic,[2] but perhaps the connection between magic, logic and science is not so clear in their work as it is in Yates'. Culianu likens Bruno's work to that of a public relations specialist who directs and shapes the image of his customers or clients who may be musicians, politicians or bank executives. He creates perceptions in the larger public by manipulating the image of the product that he is attempting to sell. In this way the work of Bruno would anticipate the work of marketing specialists and public relationists like Bernays.[3]

We have attempted in this book to trace and document the crucial historical steps in the evolution of the connected development of Logic, the Sciences of Man and of the Natural Sciences.

The formal chapters (Chapter 1 and sections of Chapter 2) are in many ways open-ended. The history of logic is not finished and is undergoing fascinating transformations. But this aspect of logic is only the deductive or formal side of it. It is coeval with mathematics insofar as it attempts to treat everything as reducible to a fundamental formal structure. People like Hilary Putnam[4] have argued (correctly I think) that one can look at mathematics and logic as entities in which something is reducible to some kind of basic structure such as a set (every mathematical object is at some level transformable into a set). Another way of appreciating this is to view mathematics as structurally equivalent to an entity in which everything is expressible in terms of modal logic. Putnam argues this point because ultimately he would like to affirm that mathematical structure is real and not ideal. While it is not our goal here to debate Putnam, it seems that the constituted Platonism of Kurt Gödel (which is pursued by contemporary mathematical logic scholars like Hugh Woodin[5]) is at least following a better direction in attempting to understand

---

[2] Culianu, Ion Petru, *Eros et magie à la Renaissance. 1484*, Paris, Flammarion, 1984.

[3] Edward Louis Bernays (1891 – 1995) was an Austrian-American developer of the notion of public relations and propaganda. Bernays is referred to as "the father of public relations". Bernays used the ideas of Gustave LeBon and Wilfred Trotter in social and crowd psychology and integrated them with the ideas of his uncle, Sigmund Freud, on the unconscious mind.

[4] For references about Hilary Putnam see Chapter 7 footnote.

[5] Hugh Woodin's approach is only one pursued in mathematical logic at the moment. Saharah Shelah's open gap research program, which asserts that the cardinality of the continuum is Aleph 2 rather than Aleph 1 presents an argument for discontinuity within our ability to complete the counting and quantification of the continuum of real numbers. It is our thesis that V is not equal L because not all sets are constructible: The real line is not constructible for two reasons: constructibility contradicts real as opposed to apparent continuity and the Real numbers may be constructible starting from the rationals, but transcendental numbers are not geometrically constructible, are not algebraic, hence cannot be added to the real interval if they are not supposed to be there in the first place and attributable to analytical and real continuity. The set of all transcendentals between 0 and 1 may have Lebesgue measure 0, but a measure of 0 is not equivalent to saying that the transcendental numbers could be arbitrarily injected or projected onto the real line. They have to pre-exist inside the real numbers and inside

mathematics.[6] There seems to be a dualism between mathematics and logic; attempts either to logicize mathematics (Frege) or to mathematize logic (Leibniz) have never been fully successful or convincing.

Logic not only deals with the mathematical. It also deals with rationality and reason and hence, the importance of studying inductive logic. With our definition of logic as 'the study of relations between reasoning, intelligence and truth and reality', we preserve this inductive, non-structural aspect of logic. Logic is learnable and relational and involves the structuring of a possible experience, as Kant[7] would say. This connection to reality, to the world, to experience must be preserved in order to have a viable and concrete philosophical logic, but also in the application of logic. However, the logic of induction is a logic of scientific explanation and is used extensively in the Deductive Nomological model of Hempel studied in chapter 7, it is not the same as the hermeneutical[8] logic of

---

reality so to speak for us to be able to discover them through our inferences and and mathematical constructions. Furthermore we follow Woodin in claiming that V is not equal L implies real and ideal continuity but that it does not support the generic multiverse thesis. Other worlds may exist mystically (the Judaic doctrine of Olam) or from a physical cosmological perspective (the parallel universes of modern physics) or may be derived from the semantics of language (the possible and impossible world semantics of Robert Brandom and others) but from a set-theoretic perspective. We need to fix the domain of discourse syntactically so to speak in order to differentiate the non-generic universal reality of models and sets from the genericity of mysticism, physical cosmology and linguistic semantics. All other domains of knowledge may shift including ontology, but logic has to be set still and work somehow foundationally as Charles Peirce clearly saw at the turn of the last century. (note of the author: V is the so-called cumulative hierarchy or the set of all sets obtained through successive recursive power-setting on the cardinality of sets. It is the set in which all of mathematics is possible but is likely not consistent since it falls prey among others to Russell's paradox. L is the constructible hierarchy or the set obtained by doing only countable unions of the elements at a preceding step within the recursive process. As such and intuitively, L should have a lower cardinality than V, but no one has been able to prove decisively that V is not equal to L. There are various arguments such as the one given in this footnote. For another argument given by Hilary Putnam see Evolution of Logic by W.D. Hart, 2010, Cambridge University Press, pp.173-174). To summarize my argument in this footnote; the real numbers are a lot more like V since one cannot generate a measure greater than 0 for the uncountable number of trancendentals present within the 0 and 1 interval. But then this means intuitively that cannot construct the reals through countable unions unless one is already at V. The density and continuity of the reals precludes us from identifying them with the constructible hierarchy.

6 In fact, Putnam and Béziau's approaches are not as necessarily dichotomous as may appear from my discussion. Béziau works with the assumption that all is needed for a logic is a consequence operator (Tarski), a set of logical symbols and strings of sentences that are well-formed and part of a formal language. His approach is thus more general in a way than Putnam's, whose approach may be taken to be a special case in which modal logic (which is equivalent to first-order logic with the modal connectives built into the language) plays a central role. There are, however, tensions between Putnam's approach and that of Béziau. The thesis that mathematics is about real existing objects is in some way opposed to Béziau's approach that mathematics is about ideal formal structures. It seems to us that the more general approach is better though we do not subscribe to the thesis that all of logic can be subsumed under the notion of abstract formal structures.

7 Immanuel Kant is a famous German philosopher from the 18th century who wrote, among other things, *The Critique of Pure Reason* and *The Critique of Practical Reason*.

8 For the notion of hermeneutics and how it is used in the context of the Humanities see the beginning of Chapter 7.

the human and social sciences. The Humanities and the social sciences are shaped by an often circular self-understanding and self-definition. This self-understanding grows and is deepened through the method of concentric circles or broadening spirals. Circularity can never and should never be fully removed from the logic of the Humanities.

This circularity is what gives the Humanities their speculative and imaginative power. The imagination negates the logical and deductive identity principle and helps develop productively the quantity of knowledge in the Humanities. The absence of circularity in the logic and knowledge of the Humanities should not be even sought after as a regulative ideal. This does not mean that there aren't clear demarcation lines between the Humanities and Natural Science.

Though Rorty[9] and Kuhn[10] should be granted their due, I believe that the logic of the Humanities is qualitatively distinct from that of the Natural Sciences. This is not an advocacy for the separation of the disciplines—we subscribe to the ideal of the speculative faculty and university[11] and to some form of the ideal unity of science and to the ideal of inter-disciplinarity[12]—but this ideal unity should not blind us the fact that the methods of the Humanities and of the sciences are qualitatively distinct. Science is in many ways plural and historical. This is one of its great strengths and sources of fertility. The positivistic ideal of confirmation, verification and falsification is in many ways dated and though still of historical and pedagogical interest, it is doubtful whether the nature of scientific discovery and scientific activity really conforms itself to its stringent idealized methods.

As we move into the 21st century, science is characterized by its multiplicity rather than its unity and universality. This is not to say that the key to this multiplicity is not some form of universal logic. Science still has to be seen as the embodiment of an ideal universal quest: as a quest for the universal. However, what we have learned by contrasting science and the Humanities is that the Humanities can enrich science's aspirations and openness to the universal by acknowledging the historical, situated origins of science and its roots in the more particular and plural Humanities. Science and the Humanities are not two different objects of study, they participate in the universal method of seeking to raise oneself from the individual and the particular to the universal. Their core is an ethical one

---
9 See Chapter 7 for background on who Richard Rorty is.
10 See Chapter 7 for background and the ideas of the philosopher of science Thomas Kuhn.
11 See the section on the Unity of Science in Chapter 7.
12 Inter-disciplinarity is the belief that knowledge is not clearly separated off into academic disciplines and that these are largely academic and political differences derived and determined by the organizational structure of educational institutions.

and a science or a humanity which does not acknowledge the existence of the (universal) Golden Rule, for example, is not a science or a humanity worthy of calling itself by those names.

We began this book with considerations on logic. This logic is understood to be both formal and concrete, both inductive and deductive (and perhaps abductive[13] as well). It must function as a critical method to discern science (and authentic, genuine true discourse about Humanities and human sciences) from pseudo-science, rational and reasonable thinking from non-sense, quackery and muddle-headedness; and fair, honest research from intellectual fraud.

---

[13] See Chapter 5 for the concept of abduction as understood by the great American philosopher, Charles Sanders Peirce.

SELECT BIBLIOGRAPHY

Aristotle, *The Works of Aristotle*, translated into English under the editorship of W. D. Ross. Oxford : Clarendon Press, 1952. Print

Carlin, Laurence, *Empiricism: A Guide for the Perplexed*, Continuum: London, 2009. Print

Descartes, Rene, *A Discourse on the Method of Correctly Conducting One's Reason and Seeking Truth in the Sciences*, translated with an introduction and notes by Ian Maclean, Oxford : Oxford University Press, 2006.

Descartes, Rene. *Meditations on First Philosophy.* Cambridge: Cambridge University Press, 1996. Print.

Dewey, *Logic-A Theory of Inquiry.* New York: Henry Holt and Company, 1938. Print.

Feynman, Richard, *The Character of Physical Law.* New York: Random House, 1994. Print.

Greene, Brian, *The Elegant Universe: Superstrings, Hidden Dimensions, and the Quest for the Ultimate Theory*, New York: Random House , 2000. Print.

Gribbin, John, *In Search of Schrödinger's Cat: Quantum Physics and Reality*, New York: Bantam Books, 1984. Print.

Hume, David, *An Enquiry Concerning Human Understanding*, New York: Barnes and Noble, 2004 (1772). Print.

Hume, David, *A Treatise of Human Nature : A Critical Edition*, Oxford: Clarendon Press, 2011. Print.

Hume, David, *Dialogues Concerning Natural Religion and Other Writings*, Cambridge: Cambridge University Press, 2007. Print.

Kant, *The Critique of Pure Reason*, New York: St-Martin's Press, 1965 (1781, 1787). Print.

Leibniz, Gottfried Wilhelm, *Theodicy : Essays on the Goodness of God, The Freedom of Man and the Origin of Evil*, London : Routledge & Kegan Paul, 1952. Print

Leibniz, Gottfried Wilhelm, *Monadology and Other Philosophical Essays*, Indianapolis: Bobbs-Merrill, 1965 (1714). Print.

Locke, John, *An Essay Concerning Human Understanding*, Oxford: Oxford University Press, 2008 (1690). Print.

Peirce, Charles Saunders, *The Essential Peirce : Selected Philosophical Writings*, Bloomington: University of Indiana Press, 1992. Print.

Penrose Roger, *The Road to Reality*, New York: Random House, 2004. Print.

Plato, *Complete Works*, Indianapolis: Hackett Publishers, 1997. Print.

Rorty, Richard, *Philosophy and the Mirror of Nature*, Princeton University Press: Princeton, 1979, Print.

Spinoza, Baruch, *Theological-Political Treatise*, translated by Michael Silverthorne and Jonathan Israel, Cambridge : Cambridge University Press, 2007. Print.

Spinoza de, Baruch /Benedict, *The Ethics*, Preceded by *On the Improvement of the Understanding*. New York: Hafner, 1955 (1677).

IDEAS & NOTIONS

Abductive 4, 10, 12
Absolute Idealism 198, 201, 202
Associationism 181, 254, 272
Atman 192

bound variable 79-80

Categorical logic 48-49
Causal fallacies 116, 126
Classical Rules of Inference 63
Conjunction 27, 63
Connotation 37-39, 58, 60, 182
Consistency 61, 68, 72, 80
Contraposition 53, 54, 61

Deductive 10, 40-42, 186, 233, 242, 244-246, 253, 277
Deductive Nomological model 244-245, 277
Deductive reasoning 12, 16-17, 23, 40-41, 48, 102, 181, 184, 233
De Morgan's Laws 22, 31, 66, 144, 297, 327
Denotation 37, 58, 60, 182
Disjunction 22, 28

Empiricism 136, 169-172, 174, 177, 180-182, 184-189, 198, 205, 209, 211, 213, 222, 224, 227, 244, 251, 253, 275
episteme 147
Epistemology 4, 8, 147, 170, 205, 231
Esse 203
explanandum 232, 242-246
explanans 232, 242-246

Fallacies of omission 119
Fallacies of relevance 122
Falsificationism 187
Free Variable 79, 82, 85

Hermenutics 11
Hylomorphism 169, 173, 189

Idealism 115, 182-183, 190-195, 198-203, 205, 208-209, 213, 217, 221, 225, 275
Identity of indiscernibles 94-97, 162-163
Inductive v, 10, 103, 133, 135, 137, 143, 244, 245
Inference 9-11, 14, 22, 39, 40, 41, 44, 57, 58, 60-62, 64-69, 75, 82-85, 87, 88, 117, 118, 121, 128, 183, 184, 214, 217
Instantiation 80, 82, 84-87

Joint Method of Agreement and Difference 137-138

Linguistic fallacies 116
Logic iv, v, 22-24, 38, 43, 70, 74, 82, 137, 146, 167-168, 190, 192, 194, 202, 206, 213, 216, 218, 232, 234, 237-238, 240-241, 243-245, 248, 250, 259, 276-277
Logos 147, 208

Material conditionals 28
Metaphysics 170, 201, 208, 210, 220, 224-225, 227, 235
Method of Concomitant Variation 139
Mill's Method of Difference 137
modus ponens 58, 60, 62
modus tollens 61, 66
Monads 161, 162, 163

Natural Science 218, 233, 235, 236, 249
Necessary and sufficient 133-134, 142-143
Necessary cause 98, 133-134
Negation 27, 66
Nous 190, 192, 195

Objective idealism 199-200
Ontology/ Ontological 39, 94

Phenomenology 11, 188
Postivistic Model 238-240
Pragmatism 205, 207, 209, 210-212, 219-221, 230-231
Predicate logic 25, 45, 48-49, 57, 61, 70, 73, 75, 82-85, 87
Principle of Bivalence 93
Principle of Excluded Middle 97
Principle of Non-Contradiction 93
Propositional Logic 24

Quantifiers 25, 48, 61, 73, 75-79, 80, 82-85, 106, 108, 182

Rationalism 146-148, 151, 167, 170,173, 187, 189, 205, 209, 225, 253,
Replacement rules 66
Rules of inference 22, 39-40, 57, 61-62, 65-69, 82-85, 87-88,

Soundness 22, 40-43
Specification 80, 82
Straw man fallacy 119-120
Subjective idealism 198, 203
Sufficient cause 98, 133, 134
Syllogism / Syllogistic logic 41, 48-53, 57, 76, 101-102, 106, 108-111, 170, 174-175

Transformation rule 58

Validity 40, 42-43

PEOPLE & WORKS

Aquinas 201, 204, 208, 266
Aristotle 18, 23, 25, 41, 45, 48-51, 60, 93, 99, 101-102, 106, 108, 115-116, 119, 123, 130, 140, 157, 169-172, 175, 177, 181, 188-189, 195, 201, 203, 210, 213, 216-219, 223, 257, 258, 262
Ars Magna 49, 176, 257-258
Augustine 156, 192, 196-197, 218, 261, 265, 266

Being and Nothingness 104
Being and Time 39, 117, 227
Berkeley 179, 180, 183, 198, 201, 235
Boccaccio 259-262, 273
Brandom 60, 95

Charles Peirce 10, 37, 181, 185, 199, 212, 220, 241
Charles Taylor 235, 253
Critique of Pure Reason 19, 200, 201, 204, 277, 280

David Hume 104, 124-127, 135, 179-182, 184-189, 198, 200, 209, 222, 230, 241, 244, 247, 272
Descartes 17, 19, 140, 148, 150-155, 158, 160, 167, 169, 172, 174-177, 192, 195-201, 205, 208, 213, 228, 271-272
Dewey 207-209, 219-220, 223, 226-231
Dignities of God 176, 259, 272
Donald Davidson 99
Douglas Walton 35, 100, 115, 122, 126
Duns Scotus 37, 169, 196, 203, 204, 208

Emerson 207-212, 226, 231
Erasmus 239, 255, 264-269, 274
Ethics 4, 8, 13, 18, 69, 140, 155-157, 159-160
Experience and Nature 227, 228

Francis Bacon 154, 169-173, 176-177, 189, 214, 256-257, 272-275
Frege 25, 37, 48, 73, 95, 106, 108, 182, 214, 259, 277

Genealogy of Morals 239
Giambattista Vico 236
Giordano Bruno 150, 174, 181, 196, 255-257, 263, 271, 274-275

Hans-Georg Gadamer 115, 202
Hegel 17, 140, 201-205, 213, 217, 219, 221-224, 227-229
Heidegger 11, 20, 38, 39, 116, 117, 147, 152, 188, 195, 203, 220, 227, 229, 235
Heraclitus 148, 150
Hilary Putnam 248, 276

Ibn Sina 170, 171, 175
Interpretation and the Sciences of Man 235

John Duns Scotus 196, 204, 208
John Locke 122, 169, 177
John Stuart Mill 182, 189

Kant 18, 19, 116, 163, 181, 183, 192, 199-205, 213, 219, 223, 230, 249, 269, 272, 277
Karl Hempel 187, 242
Karl Popper 186, 187, 239, 242

Leibniz 23, 49, 60, 148, 160, 161, 162, 163, 164, 167, 173, 213, 249, 257, 258, 259, 273, 275, 277, 280
Llull 255, 257, 258, 272, 273
Locke 19, 122, 140, 169-172, 176-180, 186, 189,

Nietzsche 17, 18, 20, 21, 95, 123, 140, 141, 156, 161, 197, 211, 221-222, 227, 230, 239, 249-250, 261, 264

Oppenheim 242, 243, 248

Parmenides 23, 148, 150, 167, 203, 210
Pico of Mirandola 150, 255, 262-264, 274
Plato 14, 36-37, 115-116, 119, 130, 142, 149, 157, 161, 172, 191-195, 199, 205, 210, 217, 219, 226-229, 256, 262, 269-270, 274
Republic 14, 193, 269, 270
Roger Bacon 170-172

Sartre 104, 120
Schelling 91
Socrates 3, 5, 36, 41, 45, 49-51, 121, 149, 150, 167, 193-194, 228, 229, 270, 271
Spinoza 148, 155-160, 162, 167, 223, 249, 265

The Phaedo 194
Thomas Hobbes 158
Toulmin 99, 100, 115-116, 126

Upanishads 192

Van Eemeren 115
Van Vleet 115, 116
Voltaire 164

Walton 35, 99, 115, 116, 119, 122, 126, 129
Wilhelm Dilthey 236
William James 163, 207-209, 212, 219-225, 227, 231
William Ormard Quine 99, 116

Zeno 148

APPENDICES

Appendix on Syllogistic Logic

An important notion in Syllogistic Logic is the notion of class or term distribution. Briefly, this notion has to do with the amount of information we possess about a class. In the Venn Diagram method, shading indicates that there are no logical individuals in the logical space that is shaded. An x means that there is a guarantee that there is at least one logical individual that is present in the sub-class or sub-region of the diagram that contains the x. White space expresses the possibility that there are individuals but it is only a possibility or a possible condition, not a certainty or an actual reality.

An A statement (All S are P) contains only a distributed predicate class or term. An E statement (No S are P) contains both a distributed predicate term and a distributed subject term. An O statement Some S are not P contains a distributed predicate term only. This may be hard to grasp for the beginner in logic. The fact that we have information about what is not in P is a determination that gives us information about P, not about the individual that is not in P. This may remind the student of Philosophy of Hegel's paraphrase of Spinoza: *Omnis negatio est determinatio* (All negation is a determination).

The notion of distribution is very useful when considering the more difficult and abstract notion of conditional validity or existential import. In this case because and often because of distribution issues or ambiguities about the distribution of a class we are required to use a third premise claiming that there is at least one logical individual that exists in S, P or M classes. We offer an example of conditional validity and the related notion of existential import below:

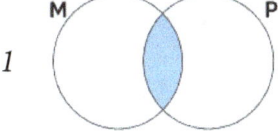

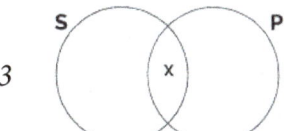

This syllogism is conditionally valid and it needs the assumption that the S class actually exists or that there is at least one logical individual in the S class in order to guarantee the validity of the syllogism. This is the case because the S class is not distributed (See above for the notion of class distribution), so we do not know what happens in the SM sub-class unless we make the assumption that S possesses at least one logical individual within its scope.

Existential Import is related to the notion of whether any given statement A, E, I, and O guarantees that there is something existing that the logical claim is made about. There is divergence between Ancient Logicians and Modern Logicians on this issue. For Aristotle only A and I possessed something like existential import even though the notion was not explicit in his philosophy. Negation is particularly tricky for existential import: as an example *Some man is not white* could be false for two separate reasons: 1) because there is no man who is white; or 2) because there is no man whatsoever. Thus, there are two ways or two causes for a negative statement to be true. This is simply different for affirmative (or positive statements) in logic.

Modern Logicians such as George Boole have suggested that the particular statements I and O should be taken to have existential import whereas the A and E statements should be taken to lack it. This is a shift in perspective in modern logic towards both nominalism or particularity and generality. The universal is no longer the category that interests modern logicians. This category has been replaced by a stronger emphasis on the particular and the notion of generality. This was forced into consideration by Axioms such as the axiom of choice in modern set theory. Here we know, for example, that elements and sets exist and that there is a way to individuate subsets and elements from these sets but we have no constructive evidence, proof or explicit rule to do the mapping. Thus the existence of logical individuals within classes or sets can no longer be taken for granted but must be assumed axiomatically and through a positing of existence.

This notion or issue also manifests in the square of opposition. For example, if we affirm the truth of *No man is white* then its sub-altern is *Some man is not white* but we cannot affirm with certainty that *Some man is not white* is false. *No man is white* could be true because: 1) there is no man who exists; or 2) there is not whiteness that exists in our logical universe of discourse.

APPENDIX ON INFORMAL ARGUMENT DIAGRAMS
Formalizing (Standardizing) & Diagramming Structured Arguments

In the Theory of Argumentation there is more than one convention in formalizing and diagramming arguments. The one adopted here is:

For Formalization (or Standardization):

- Premises are noted with P and followed by number Conclusions are noted by C followed by number
- We write the argument starting with premises and finishing with conclusion

    P1
    P2
    therefore
    C

In Diagramming

- Premises and Conclusions are indicated with numbers in the sentence following their natural text sequence.
- The diagram starts with the premises and goes towards the conclusion using arrows to indicate the direction of the support. Two conventions are used: writing the premises at bottom and going upwards to the supported conclusion or, as in more common "flow" diagrams going from top to the conclusion at the bottom. The arrows direction and the context will be the final indication of the premises -conclusion truth transfer.

TYPES OF DIAGRAMMED ARGUMENTS
SERIAL ARGUMENTS

A *serial* argument is a string of reasons and conclusions in which every conclusion is supported by one reason. Consider the following argument:

(1) The will to power is a metaphysical concept (2) all metaphysical concepts lack empirical content. So (3) the will to power cannot be empirically validated

In this argument, (1) is offered as a reason for (2) and (2) is offered as a reason for (3). Both the final conclusion (3) and the intermediate conclusion (2) are supported by one

CRITICAL THINKING, WORLDVIEWS & LOGIC

See how this works for the claim *All men are white* and its subaltern *Some man is white*. If *All men are white* is true then *Some man is white* is also true.

(1) The will to power is a metaphysical concept

(2) all metaphysical concepts lack empirical content

(3) the will to power cannot be empirically validated.

We can also give the diagram just in terms of the numbers of the statements. In this case the diagram looks like this:

CONVERGENT ARGUMENTS

Sooner or later most financial frauds get discovered. Even if you were to get away with a financial fraud you would eventually come to despise yourself for it. You should avoid perpetrating a financial fraud.

This reasoning has a single conclusion: avoid perpetrating financial frauds. It also has two separate and independent reasons for this conclusion. We diagram this argument as follows:

(2) Sooner or later most financial frauds get discovered.

(3) Even if you were to get away with a financial fraud you would eventually come to despise yourself for it.

(1) You should avoid perpetrating financial frauds.

Convergent arguments compare with *linked* arguments. *Linked* arguments also offer two or more reasons for the one conclusion but in this case the reasons are dependent on each other. For example:

(1) The concept of Being has become forgotten in Western philosophy (2) Being is the most fundamental concept that defines the identity of the Western philosophical tradition (3) The Western philosophical tradition suffers from an identity crisis.

This argument has one conclusion: The Western philosophical tradition suffers from an identity crisis.. It also has two reasons but these reasons do not work independently of each other. Since the reasons work together to justify the conclusion we diagram the argument like this:

(1) The concept of Being has become forgotten in Western philosophy

(2) Being is the most fundamental concept that defines the identity of the Western philosophical tradition

(3) The Western philosophical tradition suffers from an identity crisis.

It is important to distinguish *linked* and *convergent* arguments accurately. There is no standard method of indicating the distinction in English so we have to determine whether an argument is *linked* or *convergent* by examining the meaning of the argument.

In a *convergent* argument the reasons work independently of each other. This means that if one of the reasons is a bad reason, the other will not be affected. Look at the argument below:

Heidegger was a Nazi.

THEREFORE

Students should not
be compelled to study
Heidegger's philosophy.

Both reasons are different and independent from the other. If it turned out Heidegger had not been involved with the Nazi party of Germany in 1934 and after, then Heidegger's philosophy not being scientifically verifiable would still be a valid reason for not compelling students to study Heidegger's philosophy. On the other hand, if Heidegger's philosophy had been scientifically verifiable, then the fact that he was a Nazi philosopher would still remain a reason for not compelling students to study his philosophy at the university. Consequently, the argument should be diagrammed like this:

Heidegger was a
Nazi

Heidegger's
philosophy cannot be
verified scientifically

Students should not be compelled to study
Heidegger's philosophy.

In general, an argument offering more than one reason for a conclusion is *convergent* if the effectiveness of each reason remains unaffected even if all the other reasons turn out to fail. Otherwise it is *linked*.

To test whether an argument is *linked* or *convergent*, examine each reason in turn. Would the link between reason and conclusion remain just as strong even if everything else in the argument failed? If it does, then the reason is part of a *convergent* argument. If not, it is part of a *linked* argument. The ideal comparison term for a linked argument is the formal rule of inference modus ponens.

In other words:

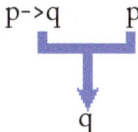

is the ideal linked argument. Furthermore, critical thinking and informal logic experts such as Douglas Walton have identified what they call an erasability test for linked arguments. If one of the premises can be erased and the argument seems to remain as strong, we are in the presence of a convergent argument. If the argument is thoroughly weakened, we are probably in the presence of a linked argument since the premises in a linked argument are semantically (or according to meaning) connected.

Look at the following example:

> The red car's board is heavily dented at the back.
>
> The white car has red paint at the front
>
> **THEREFORE**
>
> The white car has hit the red car.

This argument fails our test for convergence. If one reason turned out to be false, then the other reason would be affected. If the red car's board were not heavily dented at the back, then the white care having red paint at the front is no longer such a good reason to conclude that the white car has hit the red car. If the red car is not heavily dented at the back, then the fact that the white car has red paint at the front becomes a less compelling reason to conclude that the white car has just hit the red car. The argument is therefore *linked*, not *convergent*, so it should be diagrammed like this:

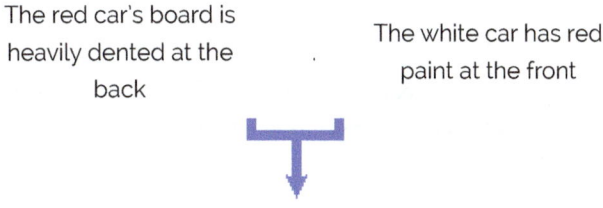

Examples of solved exercises

Exercise 1

1) It is pointless getting a university degree, since (2) everybody has one (3) other people will get better degrees than you have (4) Bill Gates and Mark Zuckerberg never graduated from university.

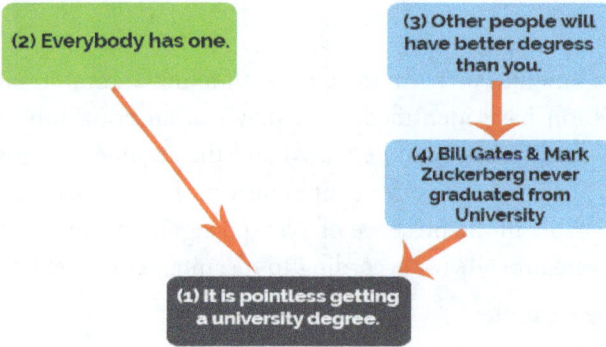

Exercise 2

(1) Until an artist has created a work of art, he does not yet know what art is. (2) The act of expressing his talent in a work is therefore an exploration of his craft.

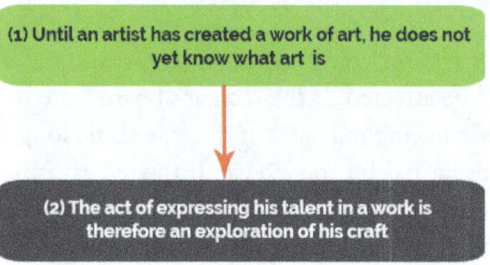

Exercise 3

1) What sort of life one chooses depends on what sort of person one is; for (2) life is not a dead piece of furniture that we can accept or reject as we wish; (3) it is rather a totality animated by the spirit of the person who lives it.

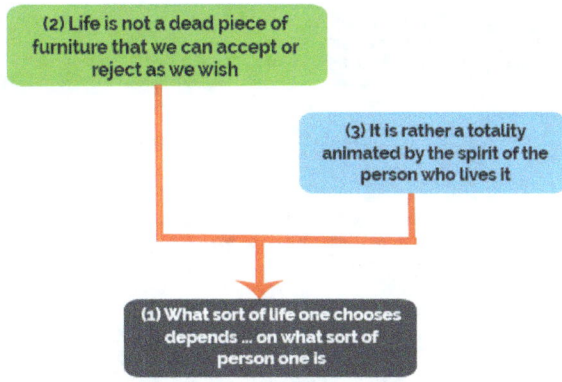

Exercise 4

(1) We should oppose the dumping of recycling products in third world countries because, firstly, (2) any such proposal would be rejected by local governments, since (3) people will react with resentment vis a vis rich countries that are unaccountable, and secondly, (4) because the long-term environmental effects are as bad globally as if we were not doing any recycling at all.

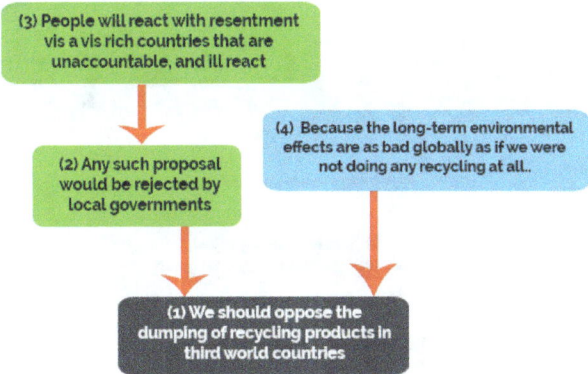

Exercise 5

(1) The most barbarous and the most fantastic behaviors translate some human trait, some aspect of life, either individual or social. (2) In reality, there are no comportments which are inappropriate. (3) All are true in their own way; (4) all express though in different ways, given aspects of human existence.

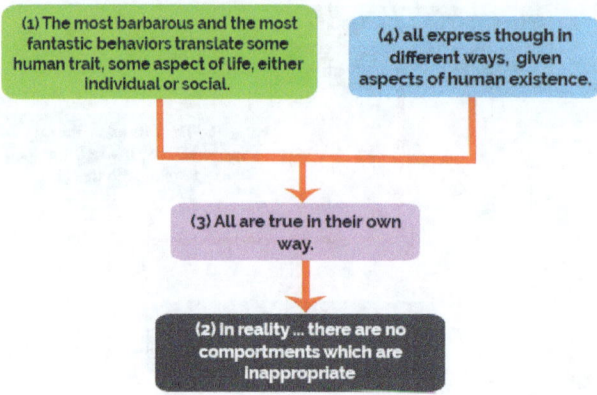

Exercise 6

That (1) this planet had received some visit from aliens, was evinced by (2) the knowledge that earthlings had of laser beams; (3) they imitated the act of shooting those lasers when we first came to the planet, and (4) when a laser beam was fired at the of the request of the earthlings, were not much alarmed.

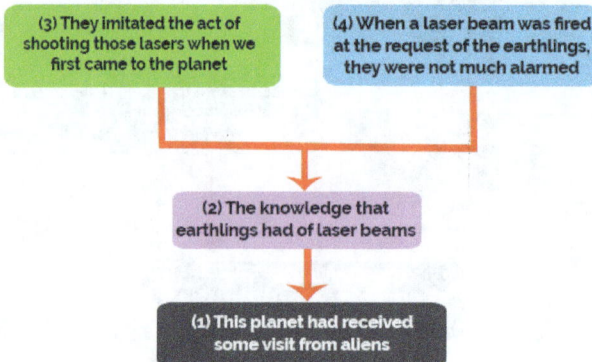

Exercise 7

(1) We say that pain is the starting point and the end of living well. For (2) we recognise pain as an evil which is primary and innate. (3) We begin every act of choice and avoidance from pain and (4) it is to pain that we return using our experience as the criterion of every bad thing.

APPENDICES

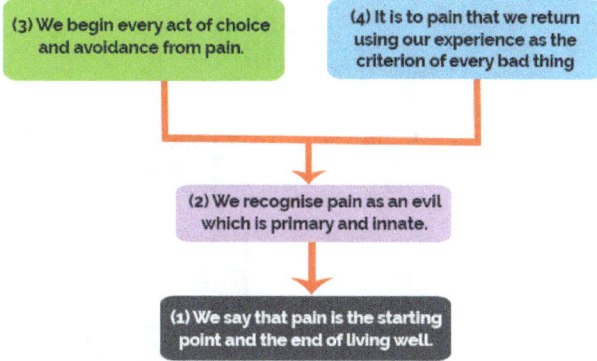

Exercise 8

(1) The doctrine of virtue is of great ethical and political significance. (2) Virtue becomes good, good becomes thought and mind stuff. (3) Human virtue is the foundation of human culture and thought.

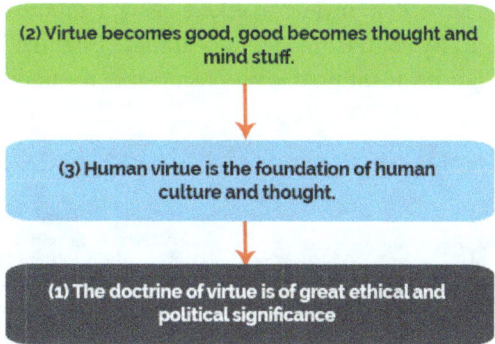

Exercise 9

(1) My spirit moves in various ways in accordance with my will, but I do not make these moves since (2) I am not aware of how they are made. (3) If I do not know how something occurs, I cannot possibly say that it is I who makes it happen.

295

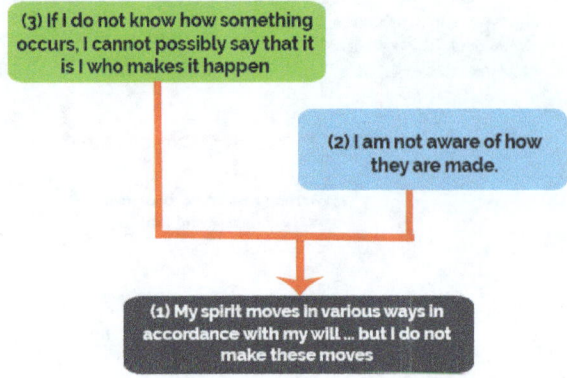

Exercise 10

(1) There is a great difference between citizenship and ethnicity, inasmuch as (2) citizenship is by its very nature always revocable, while ethnicity is utterly irrevoccable. For (3) when I consider ethnicity or myself in so far as I am merely an ethnic being, I am unable to distinguish anything unessential within myself. By contrast (4) there is nothing essential in citizenship that cannot be removed from myself or my identity; this very fact makes me understand that (5) ethnicity is essential.

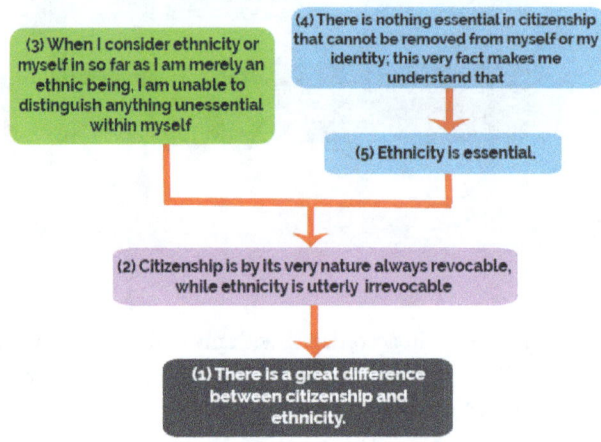

SOLUTIONS TO EXERCISES

INTRODUCTION

EXERCISES | ARGUMENTS & CRITICAL THINKING P. 17 - 21

1. Examine an inherited belief.

My parents believe in God. Should I believe in God or not?

3. Give one example in which you would use critical thinking to determine your best course of action in a given situation.

Someone comes over and tells me that if I lend him a 1000$ he can give me back a 10000$ next month. I know because I have studied economics that this type of return is either fraudulent or impossible to attain according to sound economic principles.

5. What are the building blocks of arguments?

The building blocks of arguments are premises and a conclusion or thesis.

7. What is the difference between deductive *reasoning and* inductive *reasoning?*

Deductive reasoning is based on entirely general notions and ideas. It does not require the assistance of experience in order to preserve the truth of the premises into the conclusion. Inductive reasoning is based on generalizations from a particular example or experience, so sense-experience and observation is required to conclude whether something is reasonable or not in the case of induction. Furthermore deductive reasoning is based on the concepts or notions of validity and soundness whereas an inductive argument can at best be cogent or strong or highly probable but never valid or sound.

9. What is the relationship between critical thinking and logic?

Logic shapes and supports critical thinking. Logic gives the underlying structure and form of critical thinking especially when it comes to analyzing and determining the validity and soundness of critical thinking expressed in natural language. Inductive logic also informs the structure of critical thinking when it comes to matters of judgment and reasonableness. Informal fallacies and Mill's methods give structure to inductive argumentation and the critical thinking associated with causal thinking and causal arguments.

11. Are knowledge and logic the same thing? Why or why not? Justify your answer.

No knowledge and logic are not the same thing. Logic studies the form and structure of arguments whereas knowledge or epistemology examines theories of truth and the truth claims of specific domains of knowledge (such as physics, biology, social science, economics) as well as providing a general theory of knowledge that often presupposes or is related to an ontology or metaphysics.

13. Make arguments of the following sentences. You may formulate conclusions or premises that are not present in the list.

    1. Singing is not logical.
    2. The set of all sets that are members of themselves is a member of itself.
    3. Some hard things are boring.
    4. Natural languages are easy.

SOLUTIONS TO EXERCISES

5. All logical premises are false.
6. This statement is a lie.
7. The previous statement is false.
8. The set of all sets that are members of themselves is not a member of itself.
9. The previous statement is a lie.
10. X is a set that is a member of itself.
11. Most blue birds are beautiful.
12. I am singing in the rain.
13. Formal languages are hard.
14. All beautiful objects are expensive.
15. This statement is false.

1. First argument

   Singing is not logical
   I am singing in the rain
   ─────────────────────────
   I am not doing something logical

2. Second argument (Russell's Paradox)

   The set of all sets that are members of themselves is not a member of itself
   X is a set that is a member of itself
   ───
   X is not a member of itself and X is a member of itself

3. Third argument (Liar's Paradox)

   This statement is a lie
   The previous statement is a lie
   ─────────────────────────────────

Premise 1 is both true and false at the same time, So is Premise 2 because if Premise 1 is true, it is false and if Premise 1 is true then Premise 2 is true but if Premise 1 is false, then it is false. So both premises are true and false at the same time and in their inter-relation so this is a contradiction.

4.   Formal languages are hard
      Some hard things are boring
   ─────────────────────────────
      Some formal languages are boring.

(Not there. You can add it or we can tell students to formulate independent conclusions)

5.   All beautiful objects are expensive
      Most blue birds are beautiful
   ─────────────────────────────────
      Most blue birds are expensive

CHAPTER 1 - Definition & Deduction

EXERCISES | BASIC PROPOSITIONAL LOGIC P. 31 - 33

1. Construct truth tables for the following expressions:

a) $A \leftrightarrow (B \vee C)$
b) $A \leftrightarrow (B \rightarrow C)$
c) $(A \rightarrow B) \leftrightarrow (C \wedge \neg D)$
d) $\neg (A \wedge B) \leftrightarrow (\neg A \vee \neg B)$
e) $\neg (A \vee B) \leftrightarrow (\neg A \wedge \neg B)$

a) $A \leftrightarrow (B \vee C)$

A	B	C	(B ∨ C)	A ↔ (B ∨ C)
T	T	T	T	T
T	T	F	T	T
T	F	T	T	T
T	F	F	F	F
F	T	T	T	F
F	T	F	T	F
F	F	T	T	F
F	F	F	F	T

b) $A \leftrightarrow (B \rightarrow C)$

A	B	C	(B → C)	A ↔ (B → C)
T	T	T	T	T
T	T	F	F	F
T	F	T	T	T
T	F	F	F	F
F	T	T	T	F
F	T	F	F	T
F	F	T	T	F
F	F	F	T	F

c) $(A \rightarrow B) \leftrightarrow (C \wedge \neg D)$

A	B	C	D	¬D	A → B	(C ∧ ¬D)	(A → B) ↔ (C ∧ ¬D)
T	T	T	T	F	T	F	F
T	T	T	F	T	T	T	T
T	T	F	T	F	T	F	F
T	T	F	F	T	T	F	F
T	F	T	T	F	F	F	T
T	F	T	F	T	F	T	F
T	F	F	T	F	F	F	T
T	F	F	F	T	F	F	T
F	T	T	T	F	T	F	F
F	T	T	F	T	T	T	T
F	T	F	T	F	T	F	F
F	T	F	F	T	T	F	F
F	F	T	T	F	T	F	F
F	F	T	F	T	T	T	T
F	F	F	T	F	T	F	F
F	F	F	F	T	T	F	F

d)

A	B	¬A	¬B	(A ∧ B)	¬ (A ∧ B)	¬A ∨ ¬B
T	T	F	F	T	F	F
T	F	F	T	F	T	T
F	T	T	F	F	T	T
F	F	T	T	F	T	T

e)

A	B	¬A	¬B	(A ∨ B)	¬ (A ∨ B)	¬A ∧ ¬B
T	T	F	F	T	F	F
T	F	F	T	T	F	F
F	T	T	F	T	F	F
F	F	T	T	F	T	T

1.2 The last two (iv. and v.) above are called De Morgan's Laws. Prove them using truth tables. Is there any other way of proving De Morgan's Laws?

Yes. We can prove De Morgan's laws using sets. The following is a typical way of proving it:

Proof of De Morgan's law[1]: (A ∪ B)' = A' ∩ B'

Let P = (A ∪ B)' and Q = A' ∩ B'
Let x be an arbitrary element of P then x ∈ P ⇒ x ∈ (A ∪ B)'
    ⇒ x ∉ (A ∪ B)
    ⇒ x ∉ A and x ∉ B
    ⇒ x ∈ A' and x ∈ B'
    ⇒ x ∈ A' ∩ B'
    ⇒ x ∈ Q
Therefore, P ⊂ Q .... (i)
Again, let y be an arbitrary element of Q then y ∈ Q ⇒ y ∈ A' ∩ B'
    ⇒ y ∈ A' and y ∈ B'
    ⇒ y ∉ A and y ∉ B
    ⇒ y ∉ (A ∪ B)
    ⇒ y ∈ (A ∪ B)'
    ⇒ y ∈ P
Therefore, Q ⊂ P .... (ii)
Now combine (i) and (ii) we get; P = Q i.e. (A ∪ B)' = A' ∩ B'

Proof of De Morgan's law: (A ∩ B)' = A' ∪ B'

Let M = (A ∩ B)' and N = A' ∪ B'
Let x be an arbitrary element of M then x ∈ M ⇒ x ∈ (A ∩ B)'
    ⇒ x ∉ (A ∩ B)
    ⇒ x ∉ A or x ∉ B

---

1 Source: http://www.math-only-math.com/proof-of-de-morgans-law.html

CRITICAL THINKING, WORLDVIEWS & LOGIC

⇒ x ∈ A' or x ∈ B'
⇒ x ∈ A' U B'
⇒ x ∈ N

Therefore, M ⊂ N .... (i)

Again, let y be an arbitrary element of N then y ∈ N ⇒ y ∈ A' U B'

⇒ y ∈ A' or y ∈ B'
⇒ y ∉ A or y ∉ B
⇒ y ∉ (A ∩ B)
⇒ y ∈ (A ∩ B)'
⇒ y ∈ M

Therefore, N ⊂ M .... (ii)

Now combine (i) and (ii) we get; M = N i.e. (A ∩ B)' = A' U B'

3. Let A, B, and C be three distinct atomic sentences. Decide by truth tables which of the following sentences are tautologies?

a) A ∨ B

A tautology is defined to be an expression which possesses only true truth-values in the last column of its truth table. Therefore we must make truth-tables for all the logical expressions in this exercise.

A	B	A ∨ B
T	T	T
T	F	T
F	T	T
F	F	F

This is not a tautology because the last column possesses an F truth-value.

b) A ∨ ¬A

A	¬A	A ∨ ¬A
T	F	T
T	F	T
F	T	T
F	T	T

This is a tautology.

(c) A ∨ B → B ∨ A

A	B	A ∨ B	B ∨ A	A ∨ B → B ∨ A
T	T	T	T	T
T	F	T	T	T
F	T	T	T	T
F	F	F	F	T

This is a tautology.

(d) A ∨ B → (A ∨ B) ∨ C

A	B	C	A ∨ B	A ∨ B ∨ C	A ∨ B → (A ∨ B) ∨ C
T	T	T	T	T	T
T	T	F	T	T	T
T	F	T	T	T	T
T	F	F	T	T	T
F	T	T	T	T	T
F	T	F	T	T	T
F	F	T	F	T	T
F	F	F	F	F	T

This is a tautology.

e) A → (¬A → B)

A	¬A	B	(¬A → B)	A → (¬A → B)
T	F	T	T	T
T	F	F	T	T
F	T	T	T	T
F	T	F	F	T

This is a tautology.

f) (A → B) → (C → A)

A	B	C	(A → B)	(C → A)	(A → B) → (C → A)
T	T	T	T	T	T
T	T	F	F	F	T
T	F	T	T	F	T
T	F	F	F	T	T
F	T	T	T	F	F
F	T	F	T	T	T
F	F	T	T	F	F
F	F	F	T	T	T

This is not a tautology since there are F entries in the last column which controls the whole logical expression.

g) [(A → B) ↔ B] → A

A	B	(A → B)	[(A → B) ↔ B]	[(A → B) ↔ B] → A
T	T	T	T	T
T	F	F	F	T
F	T	T	T	T
F	F	T	T	F

This is not a tautology since there are F entries in the last column which controls the whole logical expression.

h) A → [B → (B → A)]

A	B	(B → A)	[B → (B → A)]	A → [B → (B → A)]
T	T	T	T	T
T	F	T	T	T
F	T	F	F	T
F	F	T	T	T

This is a tautology.

(i) A ∧ B → A ∨ C

A	B	C	A ∧ B	A ∨ C	A ∧ B → A ∨ C
T	T	T	T	T	T
T	T	F	T	T	T
T	F	T	F	T	T
T	F	F	F	T	T
F	T	T	F	T	T
F	T	F	F	T	T
F	F	T	F	T	T
F	F	F	F	F	T

This is a tautology.

j) [A ∨ (¬A ∧ B)] ∨ (¬A ∧ ¬A)

A	B	(¬A ∧ B)	A ∨ (¬A ∧ B)	(¬A ∧ ¬A)	[A ∨ (¬A ∧ B)] ∨ (¬A ∧ ¬A)
T	T	F	T	F	T
T	F	F	T	F	T
F	T	T	T	T	T
F	F	F	F	T	T

This is a tautology.

k) [A ∧ B → (A ∧ ¬A → B ∨ ¬B)] ∧ (B → B)

A	B	(A ∧ ¬A → B ∨ ¬B)	A ∧ B	(B → B)	[A ∧ B → (A ∧ ¬A → B ∨ ¬B)] ∧ (B → B)
T	T	T	T	T	T
T	F	T	F	T	T
F	T	T	F	T	T
F	F	T	F	T	T

This is a tautology.

1.3. - Validity & Soundness

EXERCISES | VALIDITY & SOUNDNESS P. 44

1. Indicate whether or not each of the following arguments is:
    (A) valid and sound;
    (B) valid and unsound, or
    (C) invalid and unsound.

i.   If you are married, then you will have children.
       You have children.
       So, you are married.
The previous argument is invalid; it is an example of the fallacy called affirming the consequent.

ii.   Either Princess Diana was assassinated, or she was killed in an accident.
       Princess Diana was not killed in an accident.
       So, Princess Diana must have been assassinated.
The argument is valid but not sound since it instantiates the rule of inference of the disjunctive syllogism.

iii.   December 25th is Christmas.
       December 25th is this Friday.
       So, this Friday must be Christmas.
The previous argument is valid, but not sound. It may be true of a particular year, but it is not a universal truth or true in general, i.e., it is not necessarily true for all years.

iv.   It is June.
       June is in the summer.
       So, it must be summer.
The previous argument is valid but not sound, since for example in Australia, June is a Winter month.

v.   It is June.
       June is in the summer.
       So, it must very hot outside.
The previous argument is not valid because there is not enough power in the conclusion to allow us to draw it merely from the information in the premises.

vi.   Classes at McGill University start on August 20th every year.
       It is August 20th today.
       So, classes start today.
The previous argument is valid, but not sound, since it is not a universal truth that all classes start on August 20th everywhere.

vii.   Paul is an adolescent
       All adolescents are grumpy.
       Therefore, Paul is grumpy.
The previous argument is valid, but not sound, since the second premise is not universally true and the argument itself does not state a universal truth.

viii. Some Christians are fundamentalists.
       Some fundamentalists are dangerous.
       Hence, some Christians are dangerous.
The previous argument is not valid as can be verified by the method of Venn Diagrams.

ix.   All spiders are unfriendly.
        No cats are spiders.
        Therefore, no cats are unfriendly.

The previous argument is invalid. This can be verified by the method of Venn diagrams (this a case of AEE-1).

x.   Every upright person is believable.
        No woman is believable.
        Therefore, no upright person is a woman.

This argument is valid (but not sound!) because it is a case of AEE-2 which is known to be valid by the method of Venn diagrams.

3. Are deductions forms of inferences?

Yes, deductions are forms of inference. In deductive logic rules of inference are used and the concept of validity and soundness is used which guarantees that the truth is preserved when moving from premises to conclusions.

EXERCISES | TRANSLATING ENGLISH INTO LOGICAL EXPRESSIONS P.47

1. Translate the following compound sentences into symbolic notation, using letters to stand for atomic sentences.

(a) Either the indigestion was produced by beef or it was produced by noodles.

  P: Indigestion was produced by beef.
  Q: It (indigestion) was produced by noodles.
  P ∨ Q

(b) If there are more horses than zebras, then there are more bulls than goats and there are fewer wolves than horses.

  P: There are more horses than zebras.
  Q: There are more bulls than goats.
  R: There are fewer wolves than horses.
  P → (Q ∧ R)

(c) Sasquatch is a fake, and if the same is true of Santa Claus, many children are deceived.

  P: Sasquatch is a fake.
  Q: The same is true of Santa Claus (that he is a fake).
  R: Many children are deceived.
  P ∧ (Q → R)

(d) Either jobs are scarce or people like to beg, and if people do not like to beg, then jobs are scarce.

  P: Jobs are scarce.
  Q: People like to beg.
  P ∨ Q ∧ (¬P → Q)

(e) If the weather is clear, then either Henry can see the horizon or he is a nimcompoop.

    P: The weather is clear.
    Q: Henry can see the horizon.
    R: Henry is a nimpcompoop.
    P → (Q ∨ R)

(f) Either Denise is not there or Jack is, and Mark certainly is.

    P: Either Denise is not there
    Q: Jack is there
    R: Mark is there
    P ∨ Q ∧ R

(g) If Mark testifies and tells the truth, he will be found guilty; and if people do not testify, he will be found guilty.

    P: Mark testifies
    Q: Mark tells the truth-statements
    R: People will testify
    S: Mark will be found guilty
    (P → Q) ∧ (¬R → Q)

(h) If either bluejays are lovely or chickens do not have necks, then logic is confusing.

    P: Bluejays are lovely
    Q: Chickens do not have necks
    R: Logic is confusing
    P ∨ Q → R

(i) Either Jack must testify and tell the truth, or he does not have to testify.

    P: Jack must testify
    Q: Jack must tell the truth
    P ∧ Q ∨ ¬P

3. If A denotes that 'Adam wins the first prize', C that 'Chris wins the first prize', and D that 'Dan' wins the first prize, put the following compound statements into logical form:

a) If Adam and Chris both do not win first prize, then Adam and Chris do not both win first prize.
    (¬A ∧ ¬C) → ¬ (A ∧ C)

b) If Adam wins first prize, then it is not the case that either Chris or Dan wins its first game.
    A → ¬(C ∨ D)

c) If Adam wins first prize, then Chris does not win first prize but if Chris does not win first prize then Dan wins first prize.
    (A → ¬C) ∧ (¬C → D)

CRITICAL THINKING, WORLDVIEWS & LOGIC

d) Either Adam wins first prize and Chris does not win first prize or if Chris wins first prize then Dan does not win first prize.
(A ∧ ¬ C) ∨ (C → ¬D)

e) If Adam wins first prize then both Chris and Dan win first prize.
A → (C ∧ D)

1.4 Categorical or Syllogistic Logic

EXERCISES | CATEGORICAL OR SYLLOGISTIC LOGIC P. 55 - 56

1. Identify the subject and predicate terms, and name the form of each of the following propositions.

i) Some actors are extremely gifted and their acting looks like real life.
  Subject1: "Some actors"
  Predicate1: "Are extremely gifted"
  Subject 2: "Their acting"
  Predicate 2: "Looks like real life"
  Form: I-Type (Some P is M)

ii) Some members of families that are musical and literary are not men of either fame or distinction.
  Subject: "Some members of families that are musical and literary"
  Predicate: "Men of either fame or distinction"
  Form: O-Type (Some P is not M)

iii) Some politicians who could not be elected to the most minor positions and have trouble with the English language are appointed officials in our Senate today.
  Subject: "Some politicians"
  Predicate: "are appointed officials to the Senate
  Predicate: "who could not be elected to the most minor positions".
  Form: I-Type (Some S is P)

3. What can be inferred about the truth or falsehood of the remaining propositions in each of the following sets if we assume the first to be true?
If we assume it to be false?
  i) *All successful mathematicians are dupes.*
  ii) *No successful mathematicians are not dupes.*
  iii) *Some successful mathematicians are dupes.*
  iv) *Some successful mathematicians are not dupes*

If i=true ii=true iii=true iv=false

If i=false ii=false iii=false iv=true

SOLUTIONS TO EXERCISES

Base yourself on the drawing in the picture below for the justification.

TRUE:
5. i) *All successful mathematicians are dupes.*
All S is P.

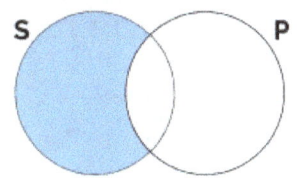

ii) *No successful mathematicians are not dupes.*
No S is not P. → All S is P.

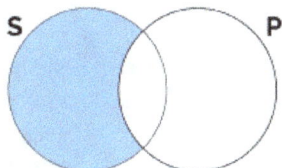

TRUE

iii) *Some successful mathematicians are dupes.*
Some S is P.

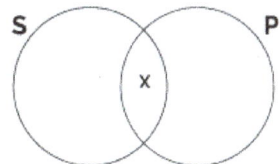

TRUE

iv) *Some successful mathematicians are not dupes*
Some S are not P.

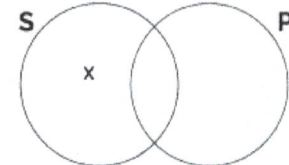

FALSE

FALSE:

5. i) *No successful mathematicians are dupes.*
No S is P.

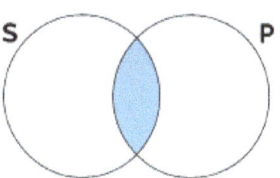

ii) *No successful mathematicians are not dupes.*
No S is not P. → All S is P.

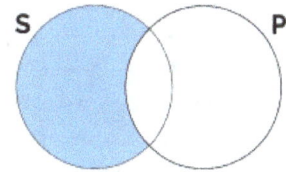

FALSE

iii) *Some successful mathematicians are dupes.*
Some S is P.

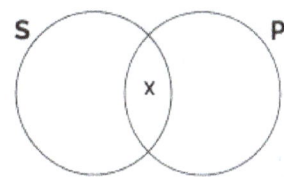

FALSE

iv) *Some successful mathematicians are not dupes*
Some S are not P.

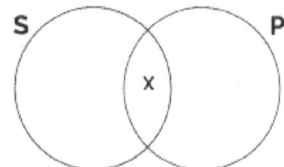

TRUE

CRITICAL THINKING, WORLDVIEWS & LOGIC

5. Rewrite each of the following syllogisms in standard form, & name its mood and figure.

(i) Some animals are objects of worship because all cows are animals, and some objects of worship are cows.

Some objects of worship are cows.	S: animals	Some P is M.
All Cows are animals.	P: objects of worship	All M is S
Therefore, some animals are objects of worship.	M: cows	Some S is P
		IAI-4

ii) All lipids are organic compounds, whence all triglycerides are lipids, as all triglycerides are organic compounds.

All triglycerides are organic compounds.	S: lipids	All M is P
All triglycerides are lipids.	M: triglycerides	All M is S
Therefore, all lipids are organic compounds.	P: organic compounds	All S is P
		AAA-3

iii) All successful individuals are well-adjusted individuals, and some successful individuals are products of stable homes, hence some well-adjusted individuals are products of stable homes.

All successful individuals are well-adjusted individuals.	S: well adjusted individuals	All M is S
Some successful individuals are products of stable homes.	P: products of stable homes	All M is P
Therefore, some well-adjusted individuals are products of stable homes.	M: successful individuals	Some S is P
		AII-3

7. Test the validity of each of the following syllogistic forms by means of a Venn diagram.

1. **AOE-1**

    All M are P
    Some S are not M
    ──────────────
    No S are P   *This syllogism is invalid.*

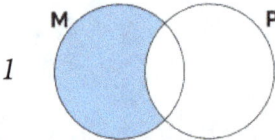

1

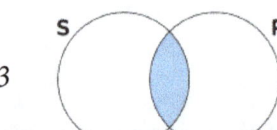

3

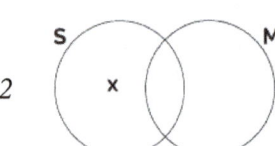

2

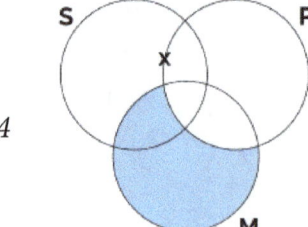

4

Contradiction/Invalid

310

SOLUTIONS TO EXERCISES

2. **AAO-2**

   All P are M
   All S are M
   ――――――――――――――
   Some S are not P   *This syllogism is invalid.*

   1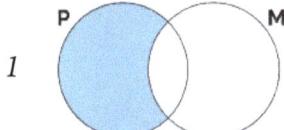

   3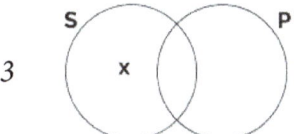

   2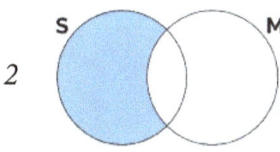

   4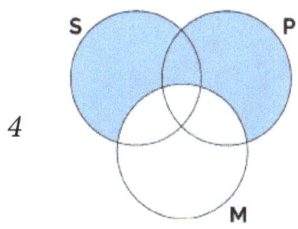

   Contradiction/Invalid

3. **AOO-4**

   All P are M
   Some M are not S
   ――――――――――――――
   Some S are not P   *This syllogism is invalid.*

   1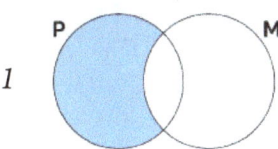

   3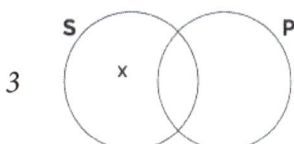

   2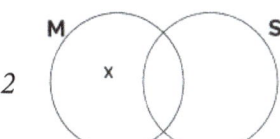

   4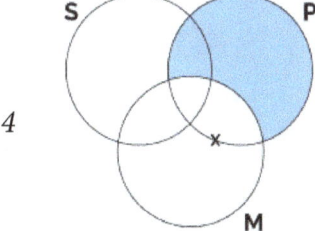

   Contradiction/Invalid

CRITICAL THINKING, WORLDVIEWS & LOGIC

4. **EEE-1**

   No M are P
   No S are M
   ─────────────
   No S are P   *The syllogism is invalid.*

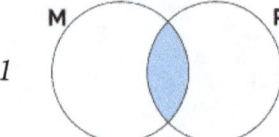

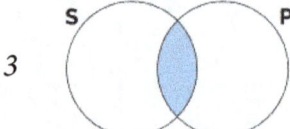

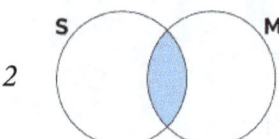

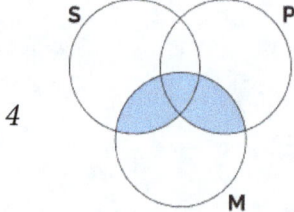

Contradiction/Invalid

5. **AAI-2**

   All P are M
   All S are M
   ─────────────
   Some S are P   *The syllogism is invalid.*

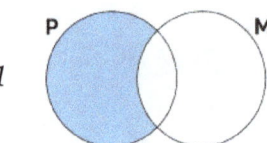

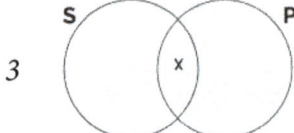

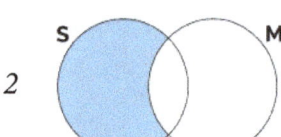

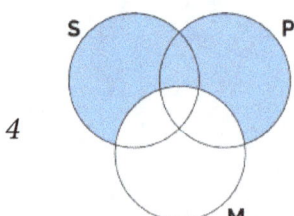

Contradiction/Invalid

6. **EEO-3**

No M are P
No M are S
―――――――――――
Some S are not P   *The syllogism is invalid.*

1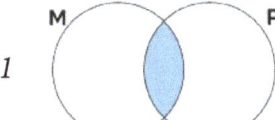

3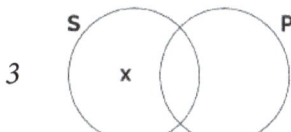

2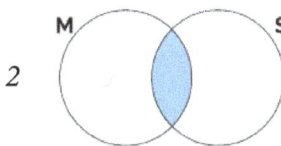

4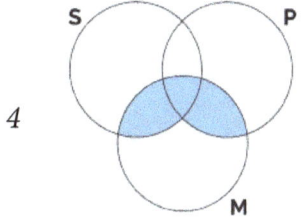

Contradiction/Invalid

7. **OOO-1**

Some M are not P
Some S are not M
―――――――――――
Some S are not P   *The syllogism is invalid.*

1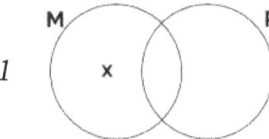

3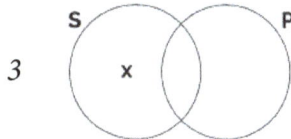

2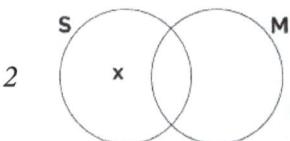

4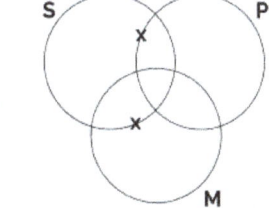

Contradiction/Invalid

CRITICAL THINKING, WORLDVIEWS & LOGIC

8. **OOI-4**

Some P are not M
Some M are not S
─────────────────────
Some S are P   *The syllogism is invalid.*

1 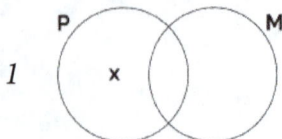   3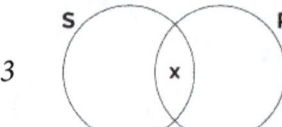

2 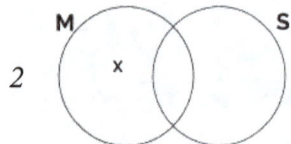   4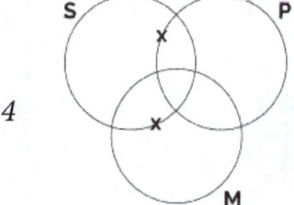

Contradiction/Invalid

9. **AAA-1**

All M are P
All S are M
─────────────────────
All S are P   *The syllogism is unconditionally valid.*

1 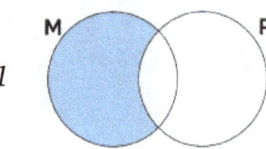   3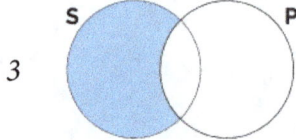

2 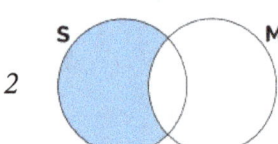   4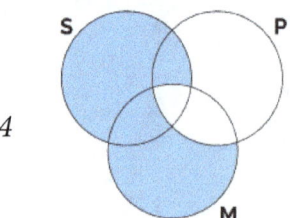

Unconditionally Valid

SOLUTIONS TO EXERCISES

10. EAE - 1

No M are P
All S are M
―――――――――――
No S are P   *The syllogism is unconditionally valid.*

Unconditionally Valid

11. AII-1

All M are P
Some S are M
―――――――――――
Some S are P   *The syllogism is unconditionally valid.*

Unconditionally Valid

12. EIO-1

No M are P
Some S are M
―――――――――――
Some S are not   *The syllogism is unconditionally valid.*

1 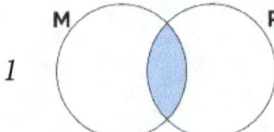   3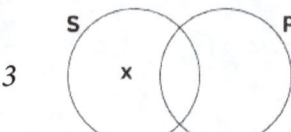

2 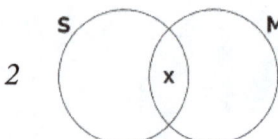   4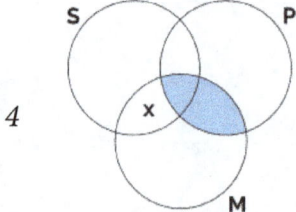

Unconditionally Valid

13. AAI-1

All M are P
All S are M
―――――――――――
Some S are P

1 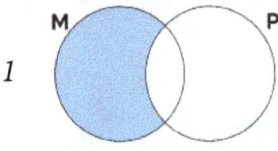   3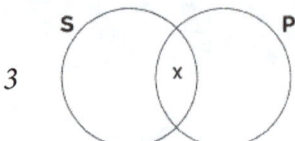

2 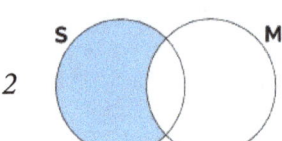   4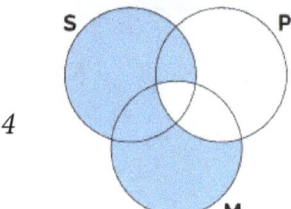

Conditionally Valid

SOLUTIONS TO EXERCISES

This syllogism is conditionally valid (see Appendix on Syllogistic Logic for notion of conditional validity) and it needs the assumption that the S class actually exists or that there is at least one logical individual in the S class in order to guarantee the validity of the syllogism. This is the case because the P class and the M class are not distributed (See Appendix on Syllogistic Logic for notion of class distribution), so we do not know what happens in the SPM sub-class unless we make the assumption that S possesses at least one logical individual within its scope.

14. EAO-1

> No M are P
> All S are M
> _____
> Some S are not P

This syllogism is conditionally valid (see Appendix on Syllogistic Logic for notion of conditional validity) and it needs the assumption that the S class actually exists or that there is at least one logical individual in the S class in order to guarantee the validity of the syllogism. This is the case because the S class is not distributed (See Appendix on Syllogistic Logic for notion of class distribution) so we do not know what happens in the SM sub-class unless we make the assumption that S possesses at least one logical individual within its scope.

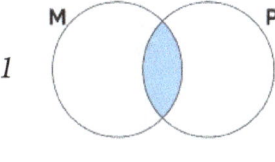

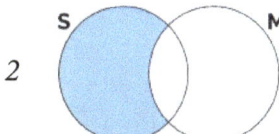

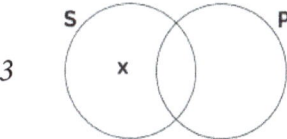

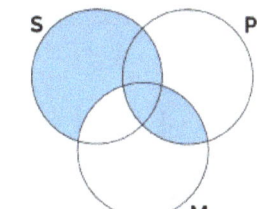

Conditionally Valid

317

15. AEE-4

All P are M
No M are S
———————————
No S are P   *This syllogism is unconditionally valid.*

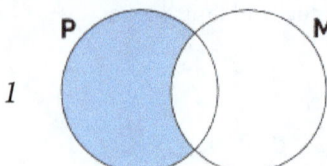
1

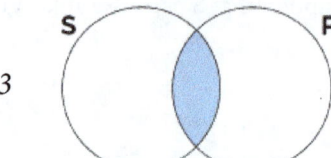
3

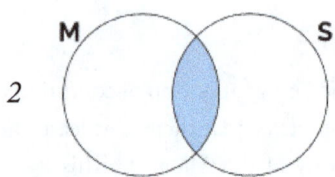
2

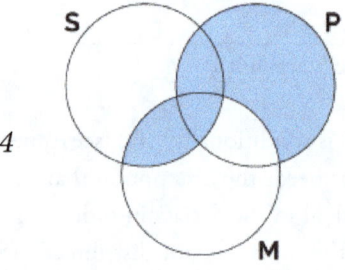
4

Unconditionally Valid

16. IAI-4

Some P are M
All M are S
———————————
Some S are P   *This syllogism is unconditionally valid.*

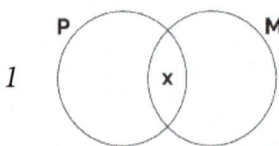
1

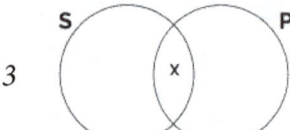
3

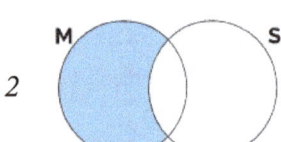
2

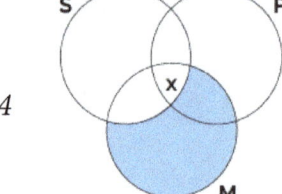
4

Unconditionally Valid

SOLUTIONS TO EXERCISES

17. EIO-4

No P are M
Some M are S
―――――――――――
Some S are not P   *This syllogism is unconditionally valid.*

1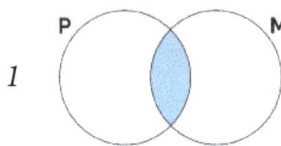

3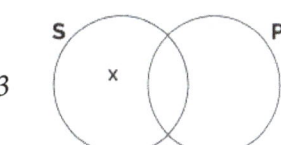

2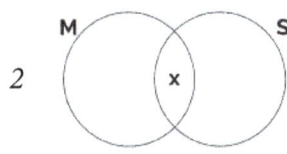

4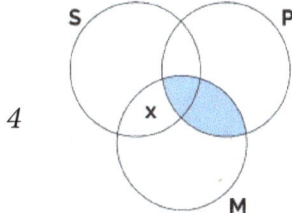

Unconditionally Valid

18. AEO-2

All P are M
No S are M
―――――――――――
Some S are not P

This syllogism is conditionally valid (see Appendix on Syllogistic Logic for notion of conditional validity) and it needs the assumption that the S class actually exists or that there is at least one logical individual in the S class in order to guarantee the validity of the syllogism. This is the case because we do not know what happens in the SM'P' sub-class unless we make the assumption that S possesses at least one logical individual within its scope.

1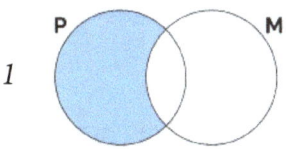

3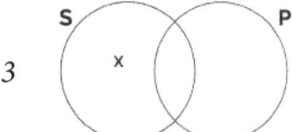

CRITICAL THINKING, WORLDVIEWS & LOGIC

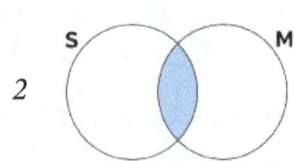

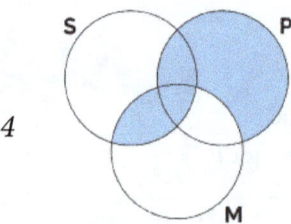

Conditionally Valid

19. EAO-3

No M are P
All M are S
Some S are not P

This syllogism is conditionally valid (see Appendix on Syllogistic Logic for notion of conditional validity) and it needs the assumption that the M class actually exists or that there is at least one logical individual in the M class in order to guarantee the validity of the syllogism. This is the case because we do not know what happens in the SMP' sub-class unless we make the assumption that M possesses at least one logical individual within its scope.

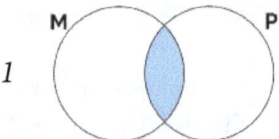

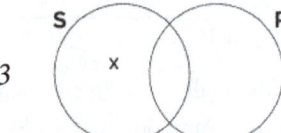

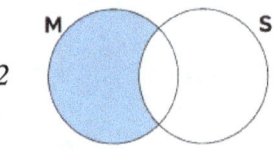

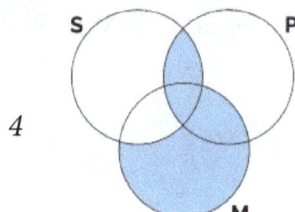

Conditionally Valid

20. AAI-4

All P are M
All M are S
Some S are P

SOLUTIONS TO EXERCISES

This syllogism is conditionally valid (see Appendix on Syllogistic Logic for notion of conditional validity) and it needs the assumption that the P class actually exists or that there is at least one logical individual in the P class in order to guarantee the validity of the syllogism. This is the case because we do not know what happens in the SMP' sub-class unless we make the assumption that P possesses at least one logical individual within its scope.

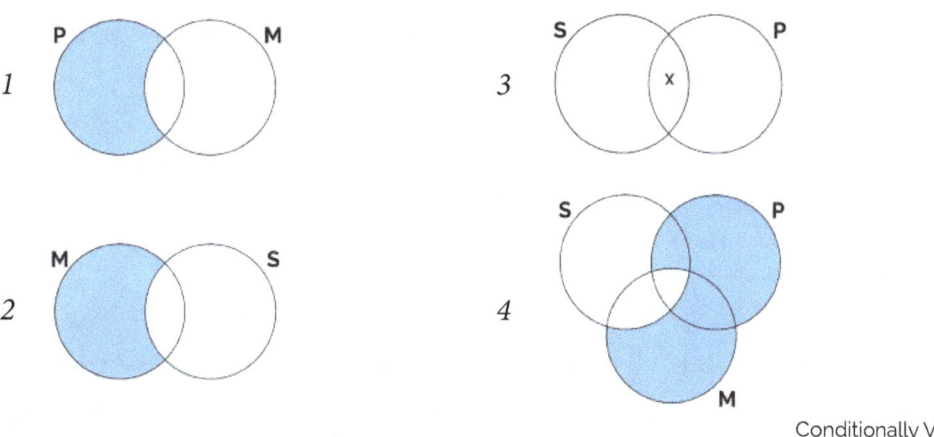

Conditionally Valid

1.5 Propositional or Sentential Logic

EXERCISES | BASIC RULES OF INFERENCE P. 64 - 65

1. State the rule of inference for each of the following arguments by which the conclusion follows from the premise or premises. It may help to symbolize the statements prior to doing so.

i) If it is sunny and I have money, then I am happy. Therefore, when it is sunny and I have money, it is sunny and I have money, and I am happy.

Hint: S: It is sunny; M: I have money; H: I am happy.
$(S \wedge M) \rightarrow H$. Therefore $(S \wedge M) \rightarrow ((S \wedge M) \wedge H)$.
This follows from the inference rule of absorption.

ii) If emery is abundant, then diamonds can be cut and diamonds can be polished; and if laser cutting technology exists, then diamonds can be cut and diamonds can be stored for later.

Emery is abundant or laser cutting technology exists, therefore the diamonds can be cut and polished or the diamonds can be cut and stored.

Hint: E: Emery is abundant, C: Diamonds can be be cut; P: Diamonds can be polished;
L: Laser technology exists; S: Diamonds can be stored for later.
$[E \rightarrow (C \wedge P)] \wedge [L \rightarrow (C \wedge S)]$
$[E \vee L]$ Therefore $(C \wedge P) \vee (C \wedge S)$
This follows from the rule of constructive dilemma.

321

iii) A → ¬ C ∧ ¬ E
      ¬ B → (D ∧ F)
      Therefore (A ∧ ¬ B) → (¬ C ∧ D)

The conclusion does not follow. This can be proven using the truth-tree method. It is left as an exercise for the student.

iv) (O ∧ M) → N

   Therefore O → M ∧ N

   The conclusion does not follow a contradiction can be built on the variable N using the truth-tree method. Left as an exercise.

EXERCISES | RULES OF REPLACEMENT P. 68 - 69

1. Consider the following sets of premises and:
   a) determine if they are 'consistent' or 'inconsistent'; and
   b) if a set is inconsistent, derive a contradiction; if it is consistent, give a 'true' sentential interpretation to prove it.
   N.B.: 'x' denotes a closed branch in the tree; 'o' denotes an open branch; 'SM' denotes a set member[2]

   A) If he is popular, then Justin will be elected. If Justin is elected Canada will not be on the right path. Either Justin will get elected or he will be out of politics. However, he will definitely be out of politics. (P, E, O)

   E: Justin will be elected
   P: Justin is popular
   O: Justin will be out of politics

   1) P → E
   2) E → ¬C
   3) E ∨ O

   4) O   We use the three methods for propositional logic.
   5) E   O   Applying tree rules for logical disjunction
   6) ¬P E   ¬P   E   From truth tree rules for 1)
      o   o   o   o

   The set is consistent since there is at least one open branch and no contradiction within the set can be provoked.

   B) If Canada bombs Iraq, then the Prime Minister will not get re-elected. In fact, Canada will bomb Iraq. If the Prime Minister does not get elected, then the leader of the Official Opposition will get elected. But it is not the case either the leader of the opposition will get elected or that Canada will bomb Iraq. (B, R, O).

   B: Canada bombs Iraq
   R: Prime Minister will get reelected

   ---
   2 We adopt this notation style from *The Logic Book* by Bergmann, Moor and Nelson.

SOLUTIONS TO EXERCISES

O: Leader of the Official opposition will get elected

1) B → ¬R
2) B
3) ¬R → O
4) ¬(O ∧ B)

5)	¬O		¬B		Truth tree rules for 4) and DeMorgan's Laws
6)	R O		R O		Truth tree rules for 3)
	o x		x o		

The set is inconsistent because some branches close, so this means that there are contradictions in the set. If all branches stay open then the set is consistent and it is possible to produce a true sentential derivation.

C)
1) (¬A ∨ B)
2) (B ∨ ¬C)
3) B → C

4)	¬A			B		∨ 1
5)	B	¬C		B	¬C	∨ 2
6)	¬B C ¬B C			¬B C ¬B C		→ 3
	x o o x			x o o x		

The set is inconsistent because there are closed branches, indicating contradictions within the logical set.

3. Prove the validity or invalidity of the following arguments:

(A)
1) $(A \land B) \to (C \to D)$
2) $\neg E \to D$
3) $\neg(\neg B \land E)$
4) $\neg(A \to C)$ Therefore $\neg C$

We use the tree method for propositional logic. You have to negate the conclusion and then check for consistency of the set. If at least one branch in the tree is open, the argument is invalid.

5)			C				
6)		E			D		2 →
7)	B	¬E	B		¬E		3 De Morgan's laws, tree rules
8)	A	x	A		A		
9)	o		¬C		¬C		4 De Morgan's laws, →, tree rules
			x		x		

One open branch exists, so the argument is invalid.

(B)
1) $F \to (G \land H)$
2) $G \to (\neg I \to J)$
3) $(\neg F \land I) \to (L \leftrightarrow M)$
4) $(\neg F \land G) \to \neg L$
5) $\neg L \to (\neg M \to J)$ Therefore J

323

We use the tree method for propositional logic. You have to negate the conclusion and then check for consistency of the set. If at least one branch in the tree is open, then the argument is invalid.

```
6)                            ¬J
7)           ¬G                           ¬I → J                    2 →
8)      I           J              I            J                   7 →
9) ¬(¬F ∧ I)    L ↔ M    x    ¬(¬F ∧ I)    L ↔ M    x               3 →
10)    F   ¬I    F   ¬I            F   ¬I    F   ¬I                 9 ∧
11)    o    x    o    x            o    x    o    x
```

Branches stay open in this tree. This means the argument is invalid. The student should work out the full tree for himself.

(C)   1) $O \rightarrow (\neg P \rightarrow Q)$
               2) $P \rightarrow (R \wedge S)$
               3) $(\neg O \wedge R) \rightarrow (T \leftrightarrow U)$
               4) $O \rightarrow (\neg P \wedge T)$
               5) $\neg T \rightarrow (\neg U \rightarrow S)$
               6) $\neg F \rightarrow (\neg G \rightarrow E)$ Therefore E

We use the tree method for propositional logic. You have to negate the conclusion and then check for consistency of the set. If at least one branch in the tree is open then the argument is invalid. Note that the only important line for us is 6) since the others do not have the same variables as E and are in fact disconnected from the arguments that entirely lies in 6)

```
7)                   ¬E
8)    F                     (¬G → E)
9)    Stays open.        G            E
                      Stays open   Closes
```

Since at least one branch stays open no contradictory counter-example can be found and the argument is invalid.

EXERCISES | TRUTH TREES WITH SENTENTIAL LOGIC p.72

1. Consistency: *Test the consistency of these sets of statements using the Tree Method.* (Note the set is consistent *if and only if* there is at least one open path through the finished tree.)

     i. $X \rightarrow Y, X \rightarrow \neg Y$;   ii) $O \rightarrow P, \neg O \rightarrow \neg P$;   iii) $M \rightarrow M$

```
i.  1)       X → Y,              SM
    2)       X → ¬Y              SM
    3)       ¬X           Y      from 1 and applying tree rules for implication
    4) ¬X      ¬Y    ¬X    ¬Y    from 2 and applying tree rules for implication
    5) branch  branch is  o   x
       closes  open
        x       o
```

Since not all branches close, this set of sentences in inconsistent.

SOLUTIONS TO EXERCISES

ii.

	1)	O	→	P		SM
	2)	¬O	→	¬P		SM

	¬O		P		1) and applying tree rules for implication
¬O	¬P	¬O	¬P		from 2) and applying tree rules for implication
o	o	o	x		

Not all branches close. The set is inconsistent. This is natural since the student will have recognized the fallacy of denying the antecedent. The student should use the method to verify the consistency of *modus tollens* and *modus ponens*.

iii.

	1)	M	→	M	
	2)	¬M		M	1) and applying tree rules for implication
		o		o	

This is a simple exercise but it is obvious that premise leading to itself is consistent. It illustrates the tree method at the simplest level and verifies our intuitions. No contradiction could come from any other proposition since we are only discussing one proposition here. So, when we cannot close even one branch, then the data set is consistent and no contradiction can be found.

3. Build a truth tree (or truth trees) for the following logical sentences and then state whether the tree shows the sentence or proposition to be a contradiction, a contingency or a tautology.

a) $(A \land \neg\neg A)$
    A
    o

The branch stays open. This is not a tautology.

b) C ∨ ¬¬C
    C   C
    o   o

The branches stay open. This is not a tautology.

c) B ∨ (D ∨ ¬D)
    B   D ∨ ¬D
    o   D   ¬D
           o   o

This is not a tautology since the branches stay open.

Exercise 3 are all tautologies (a, b and c), when all branches close we are in the presence of a **contradiction**, if a couple of branches stay open and a couple close then we are in the presence of a **contingency**, if all branches stay open we are in the presence of **tautology**.

5. Build a truth tree (or trees) for the set of propositions below and then state whether the tree shows the set of propositions to be consistent or inconsistent:

a) A → B, ¬A ∨ B

1)	A → B		SM
2)	¬A ∨ B		SM
3)	¬A	B	1 and → rules for trees
4)	¬A	B	2 and ∨ rules for trees
	o	o	

Both branches stay open. Therefore the set is consistent, as a contradiction cannot be provoked.

b) Q, ¬¬Q

1)	Q	SM
2)	¬¬Q	SM

The tree can't be developed further and a single branch does not close. Therefore the set is consistent.

c) A ↔ B, (A → B) ∧ (B → A)

1)	A ↔ B		SM
2)	(A → B) ∧ (B → A)		SM
3)	A	¬A	
4)	B	¬B	from 1 and ↔ rules for trees
5)	(A → B)	(A → B)	from 2 and ∧ rules for trees
6)	(B → A)	(B → A)	from 2 and ∧ rules for trees
7)	¬A B 5 → rules	¬B A	from 6 → rules
	¬B A 6 → rules	B x	6 → rules
	x ¬B 6 → rules	x	
	x		

All branches close. Therefore a contradiction can be recovered across at least one branch and the set is not consistent.

d) A ↔ B, A → B, B → A

1)	A ↔ B			SM
2)	A → B			SM
3)	B → A			SM
4)	A	¬A		
5)	¬B	B		from 1 and ↔ rules for trees
6)	¬A B 2 → rules	¬B	A 3→ rules	
	x ¬B 3→ rules	B 2 → rules x		
	x	x		

All branches close. Therefore a contradiction can be recovered across at least one branch and the set is not consistent.

SOLUTIONS TO EXERCISES

e) ¬ (A ∧ B), ¬ A ∨ ¬ B

    1) ¬ (A ∧ B)   SM
    2) ¬A ∨ ¬B   SM
    3)   ¬ A   ¬ B   From 2 and ∨ rules for trees
           o   o

Both branches stay open. Therefore the set is consistent.

f) ¬ (A ∨ B), ¬ A ∧ ¬B

    1) ¬ (A ∨ B)   SM
    2) ¬A ∧ ¬B   SM
    3)   ¬A   from either 1 or 2 same result
       ¬B
        o

A single branch stays open. Therefore the set is consistent.

EXERCISES | BASIC USAGE OF QUANTIFIERS P. 78

1. Rewrite the following statements in logical notation of propositional functions, and quantifiers. Use the abbreviations suggested and have each formula begin with a quantifier; not with a negation symbol.

    1. Rock stars are not always drug addicts. *(Rx: x is a rock star; Dx: x is a drug addict.)*.
        ∃x (Rx → ¬ Dx)
    2. Ebola is sometimes fatal. *(Ex: x is Ebola ; Fx: x is fatal.)*.
        ∃ x (Ex → Fx)
    3. Only citizens of Canada can vote in Canadian elections.
     (Cx: x is a citizen of Canada; Vx: x can vote in Canadian elections).
        ∀x (Vx → Cx)
    4. Not a student passed the class. *(Sx: x is a student; Px: x passed the class.)*
        ∀x (Sx → ¬Px)

3. Symbolize each of the following statements using propositional functions and quantifiers, in each case using the suggested notation.

    a) Men are humans. *(Mx: x is a man. Hx: x is a human)*
        ∀x (Mx → Hx)
    b) Only rich people have chauffeurs. *(Rx: x is rich. Cx: x has a chauffeur)*.
        ∀x (Cx → Rx)
    c) All beer and cognac are wholesome and nourishing. *(Bx: x is a beer. Cx: x is a cognac. Wx: x is wholesome, Nx: x is nourishing)*
        ∀x ((Bx ∧ Cx) → Nx)
    d) None but the courageous deserve love. *(Cx: x is courageous, Dx: x deserves love)*.
        ∀x (Dx → Cx)

CRITICAL THINKING, WORLDVIEWS & LOGIC

EXERCISES | FREE & BOUND VARIABLES P. 81

1. Count the free occurrences of variables and how many free variables there are in each of the following formulas. Which of the formulas constitute logical propositions?

a) (∃y) (∃z) (x loves y and z is their cat)
The only free variable here is x, y and z are bound by the existential quantifier.

b) (∃x)(x is a square) ∨ (∀y) (y is green and x is yellow)
x is the free variable, in the second expression where y is bound by the quantifier.

c) (∃z) (y + y = y)
Here y is the free variable.

d) (∀v)(∀w)(∀u)(v → w ∧ w → u) → (∃x) (x → x)
There are no free variables in the above expression.

e) (∃x) (∃y) (x is married to y and z is their child)
z is the free variable.

f) x + y = y + x
Both x and y are free variables.

3. Look at the formula (∀x(M(x) → N(x))) → (¬M(x) ∨ N(y)). Which variable instances are free; and which are bound?

y is a free variable and x is a bound variable in the first part of the formula preceding the implication symbol, but it is free in the expression or part of the formula following the arrow symbol.

EXERCISES | RULES OF INFERENCES FOR QUANTIFIERS P. 83

I. Write derivations corresponding to the following arguments where possible. The variables used to indicate the predicates are not necessarily the variables you should use in symbolizing the premises.

a) All philosophers are eccentrics. No eccentrics are British. Therefore no British are philosophers. (Px, Ex, Bx)

1) ∀x (P(x) → E(x))
2) ∀x (E(x) → ¬ B(x))
3) ¬ ∀x (Bx → ¬ Px)
4) ¬ (P(y) → E (y))   by 1 and universal instantiation
5) ¬ P(y)   E(y)   by 4 and → rules for trees
    o   ¬ (E(y) → ¬ B(y))   by 2 and universal instantiation
             E(y)
             B(y)

o

We may stop here because we have evidence based on the Venn diagrams that the data set on which this tree is based is consistent. The student may experiment further but it is our thesis that he will be incapable of provoking a contradiction in this set!

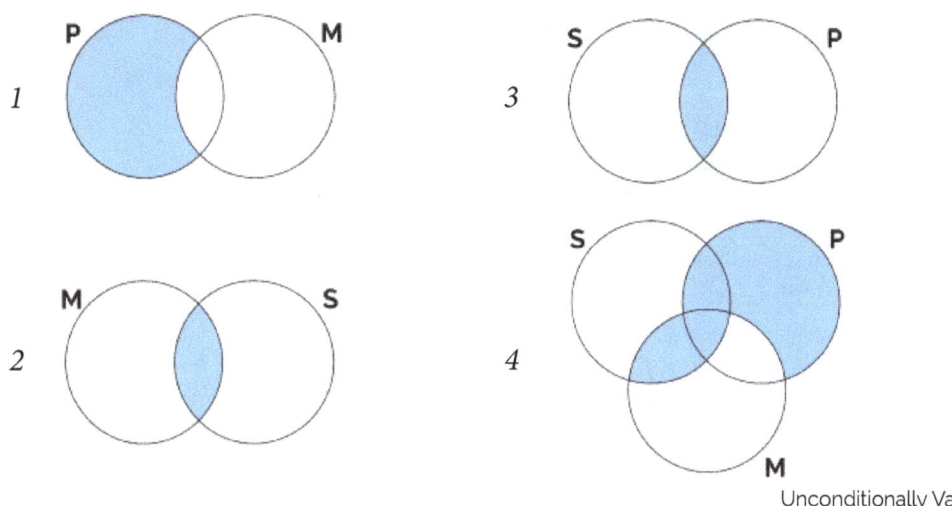

Unconditionally Valid

Philosophers: P	All P is M
British: S	No M is S
Eccentrics: M	No P is M

The student should build his own diagram and verify the validity of the class variable set.

b) *If one man is the boss of a second, then the second is not the boss of the first. Therefore no man is his own boss. (Bxy)*

So Bxy stands for x is the boss of y

1) $\forall x \forall y \ (Bxy \rightarrow \neg Byx) \rightarrow \neg Bxx$
2) $\forall x \forall y \ (Bxy \rightarrow \neg Byx)$
3) $\neg \forall x \forall y \ (Bxy \rightarrow \neg Byx)$ Always negate conclusion and verify if there is an open branch or if all branches close.
4) $\exists x \exists y \neg (Bxy \rightarrow \neg Byx)$ 3, Negation of quantifiers
5) $\exists y \neg (Bay \rightarrow \neg Bya)$ 4, Existential instantiation
6) $\neg (Bab \rightarrow \neg Bba)$ 5, Existential instantiation
7) $\neg (\neg Bab \lor \neg Bba)$
8)   Bab
9)   Bba
10) $(Bab \rightarrow \neg Bba) \rightarrow \neg Baa$ 1 and double universal instantiation
11) $\neg (\neg Bab \lor \neg Bba) \lor \neg Baa$
12)   Bab   Bba $\neg Baa$

Branches remain open so argument is invalid.

c) *The Prime Minister is a man with Canadian citizenship, and he is the boss of all Canadian citizens. Therefore he is his own boss. (p, Cx, Bxy)*

1) $\forall x \, \exists y \, (Cx \land Cy \land y = p)$
2) $\forall x \, (C(x) \rightarrow B(px))$
3) Bpp
4) $\neg Bpp$
5) $(C(a) \rightarrow B(pa))$ by 2, universal instantiation
6) $\neg C(a) \lor B(pa)$ 5, tree rules for $\rightarrow$
7) $\neg C(a)$ $B(pa)$
    o   May be closable with $\neg Bpp$

At least one branch stays open so the argument is invalid.

d) *Given: i) for any numbers x, y, z, if x = y and y = z then x = z; ii) for any number x, it is not the case that x = ~x. Therefore, for any two numbers x and y, if x = y then it is the case the y = x. (Nx, x = y)*

1) $(\exists x)(\exists y)(\exists z) \, [((x = y) \land (y = z)) \rightarrow (x = z)]$
2) $\forall x \, \neg (x = \neg x)$
3) $\neg (\forall x \, \forall y \, (x = y \rightarrow y = x))$

The tree will close because this is a valid argument. It shows a deep law of logic, namely that transitivity together with non-identity is sufficient to prove the law of commutativity.

e) *Adam is a boy who does not go to Church. Maria dates only boys who go to Church. Therefore Maria does not date Adam. (Cx, Ox, Dxy, a, m)*

1) $\neg Ca$
2) $\forall x \, (Dxm \rightarrow Cx))$
3) $\neg (\neg Dam)$
4) $\neg Dbm$ Cb 2) universal instantiation

We can assert b = a because we are doing the instantiation lower in the tree than the fixing of the Adam variable. Whenever a variable higher in the tree is fixed it can be identified with an instantiation lower in the tree as long as this is a universal instantiation and not an existential instantiation.

Therefore the tree closes on both branches and this is a valid argument.

3. Verify whether the following arguments are valid or not using the rules of inference governing of quantifiers and predicate logic. If the argument is invalid, produce an interpretation to demonstrate why the argument is not valid.

We use the simpler and more direct tree method.

a)   1) $(\exists x)(\neg Ax \lor \neg Bx) \lor Cx))$ SM

SOLUTIONS TO EXERCISES

2) $\forall x\,(\neg Bx \vee Cx)$ SM
3) Therefore $\neg\,(\forall x)\,\neg Ax$ SM Negate Conclusion
4) $\neg(\neg By \vee Cy)$ By 2 universal instantiation and rules for quantifiers
5)   By
6) $\neg Cy$ By 4 and de Morgan's rules for trees
7) $(\neg Ay \vee \neg By)$ Cy   1 Existential Instantiation
8) $\neg Ay$ $\neg By$ x
     o   x

The tree stays open. Therefore the argument is valid.

b)   1) $\forall x\,\forall y\,(\neg Ax \vee \neg By \vee \neg Cxy)$ SM
     2) $(\exists x)(Ax \wedge \neg Dx)$ SM
     3) Therefore $\neg\,\exists x\,\exists y\,(Dx \wedge Cxy)$ SM Negate Conclusion
     4) $\forall x\,\forall y\,\neg\,(Dx \wedge Cxy)$ 3, Negation of quantifiers
     5) $\neg Da \vee \neg Cab$ 4, De Morgan's Laws
     6) $\neg(\neg Aa \vee \neg Bb \vee Cab)$ $\neg(\neg Aa \vee \neg Bb \vee Cab)$
     7)   Aa
     8)   Bb
     9)   o   Cab   closes because of line 5
                               x

The set is valid because one branch stays open.

c)   1) $(\exists x)\,(Ax \wedge (\neg Cx \wedge \neg Bx))$ SM
     2) $\forall x\,(\neg Ax \vee Bx)$ SM
     3) Therefore $\neg\,(\forall x)\,\neg Cx$ SM Negate Conclusion
     4) $(Aa \wedge \neg Ca \wedge \neg Ba)$ Existential Instantiation on 1
     5) $\neg(\neg Aa \vee Ba)$ Rules for quantifiers and universal instantiation on 2
     6)   o

The unique branch stays open therefore the set is valid.

d)   1) $(\exists x)\,[Ax \leftrightarrow (Bx \vee Cx)]$ S M
        2) Therefore $\neg\forall x\,[(\neg Ax \vee \neg Bx) \wedge (\neg Ax \vee \neg Cx)]$ SM Negate Conclusion
        3) $\neg(\neg Aa \vee \neg Ba) \wedge (\neg Aa \vee \neg Ca)$
        4) $(\neg Aa \vee \neg Ca)$
        5) $\neg Aa$ $\neg Ca$
        6) Aa $Aa \leftrightarrow (Ba \vee Ca)$
        7) x   Aa $\neg Aa$
        8) $\neg(Ba \vee Ca)$ $(Ba \vee Ca)$
             o   x   because of 7 and 6

Therefore the set is valid since there is one open branch.

SOLUTIONS

CRITICAL THINKING, WORLDVIEWS & LOGIC

EXERCISES | CONSISTENCY IN PREDICATE LOGIC P. 84

1. *Determine if the following sets of expressions are consistent or inconsistent using the basic rules of inference of predicate logic (all of the rules of inference of propositional logic, the rules used to negate quantifiers, the rules of Universal and Existential Instantiation and rules of Universal and Existential Generalization if the variables are bound correctly in the expressions given).*

a)   1) $(\forall x)(\neg Mx \wedge \neg Nx)$
       2) $(\forall x)(\neg Ox \rightarrow Nx)$
       3) $(\forall x)(\neg Ox \wedge Mx)$

4)	$\neg Ma$		by Universal Instantiation on 1) We use the tree method
5)	$\neg Na$		
6)	Ob	Nb	by Universal Instantiation on 2)
	o	x	

The set is inconsistent since a contradiction can be derived. Note that since we instantiated universally the variable can be taken to be indentical which would not have been the same had this been a case of existential instantiation.

b)   1) $(\exists x)(\neg Bx \rightarrow Cx)$
       2) $(\forall x)(Cx \rightarrow Ax)$
       3) $\neg(\exists x)(\neg Ax \rightarrow Cx)$

4) Ba		Ca	Existential Instantiation on 1
5) $\neg Cb$		Ab	Universal Instantiation on 2
6) $(\forall x) \neg (\neg Ax \rightarrow Cx)$			Quantifier negation on 3
7) $(\forall x)(\neg Ax \wedge \neg Cx)$			Simplification of 6
8) $\neg Ac$			
9) $\neg Cc$			

The set is inconsistent since ¬Ac contradicts Ab since they both result from a universal instatiations, one can fix them according to one's choice. If the constant choices had been produced through existential instantiations one would have had to be more precise in the interpretation of the exercise.

c)   1) $(\exists x)(\neg Mx \rightarrow \neg Nx)$
       2) $(\forall x)(\neg Mx \wedge Ox)$
       3) $(\exists x)(\neg Ox \rightarrow \neg Nx)$

4)	Ma	$\neg Na$	Existential Instantiation on 1
5)	$\neg Mb$		
6)	Ob		Universal Instantiation on 2
7)	Oc	$\neg Nc$	Existential Instantiation on 3

I also think this set is inconsistent. ¬Mb contradicts Ma even though existential instantiation is involved. Once Ma is fixed ¬Mx can be selected appropriately and the contradiction will occur. It may not occur in all instances but all we need is that it occurs once to make the set inconsistent.

SOLUTIONS TO EXERCISES

EXERCISES | TRUTH TREES AS PROOF-METHOD IN PREDICATE LOGIC P. 86

1. Use the truth tree method to test the following arguments for validity. In each problem, state whether or not the argument is valid; if invalid, give a counterexample.

i)
    1) $Bx \to (\forall x)Mx$
    2) $(\forall x)(Bx)$
    3) $(\exists x)(Cx) \to Nx$
    _____
    4) $\neg (Ba \wedge Mb)$
    5) $\neg Ba$ $\neg Mb$ Negation of $\wedge$ in 4
    6) Ba Universal Instatiation 2
    7) x Bb Mb
                   x   x

Valid since all branches close.

ii)
    1) $(\forall x)(Nx \to Px)$
    2) $(\forall x)Bx$
    3) $Mx \wedge Cx \wedge Nx$
    _____
    4) $\neg (Na \vee Ca)$
    5) $\neg Na$
    6) $\neg Ca$ Negation of 4
    7) Cb
    8) Mb
    9) Nb
        x

Valid since single branch closes.

iii)
    1) $(\forall x)(Kx \to Ax)$
    2) $(\exists x)(Dx \wedge Gx)$
    _____
    3) $\neg (Db \to Gb)$
    4) $\neg (\neg Db \vee Gb)$ Equivalence of $\to$ and $\vee$
    5) Db
    6) Gb
        o

Invalid since the unique branch stays open and does not seem closable.

iv)
    1) $\exists x(Bx \to Cx) \vee (\forall x)Nx$
    2) $(\forall x)(Cx \wedge Nx) \to Mx$
    _____
    3) $\neg (Na \to Mb)$
    4) $\neg (\neg Na \vee Mb)$
    5) Na
    6) $\neg Mb$

The student should verify that this tree closes and thus that the argument is valid.

3. Construct, if possible, a derivation corresponding to the following arguments. If a conclusion does not follow, give an arithmetical interpretation that will prove that it does not.

a) All Quebeckers speak to anyone they know intimately. No Quebecker speaks to anyone who is not a North American. Therefore, Quebeckers know only North Americans intimately. (Qx, Sxy, Kxy, NAx)

1) $\forall x ((Qx \land Kxy) \rightarrow Sxy)$	SM
2) $\forall x \exists y ((NAy \land Qx) \rightarrow Sxy)$	SM
3) $\neg (\forall x \exists y (Qx \rightarrow Kxy))$	SM Negate conclusion

Verify that the following interpretation works:

UD (Universe of Discourse): All integers. (Note: the universe of discourse is infinite and has cardinality Aleph 0)

Qx: x is odd
Kxy: x and y are positive integers
Sxy: x is odd and y is even
NAx: x is even

We can verify that under the interpretation of the above predicates with this meaning, the premises are true since they mean: 1) $\forall x ((Qx \land Kxy) \rightarrow Sxy)$: For all x, x is odd and x and y are natural numbers implies that x is odd and y is even (1 and 2 make this interpretation true and it belongs to the universe of discourse since 1 and 2 are integers. Next 2) 2) $\forall x \exists y ((NAy \land Qx) \rightarrow Sxy)$: can also be verified to be true, for all x, x is odd and there exists a y such that x is odd and y is even (again one and 2 make this interpretation true). But 3) $\neg (\forall x \exists y (Qx \rightarrow Kxy))$, the negated conclusion is always false since the interior (for all x there exists a y such that if x is odd it implies x and y are positive integers, we propose 2 to be the value of y) is always true before the negation sign (ie 1 and 2 make the interior before the negation sign true which makes the whole expression false).

b) No intelligent person who jogs also eats to excess. Some careless persons eat to excess. Therefore, some careless persons are not intelligent. (Ix, Jx, Ex, Cx)

1) $\forall x ((Ix \land Jx) \rightarrow \neg Ex)$	SM
2) $(\exists x)(Cx \rightarrow Ex)$	SM
3) $\neg ((\exists x)(Cx \land \neg Ix))$	SM Negate conclusion
4) $((Ia \land Ja) \rightarrow \neg Ea)$	1 universal instantiation
5) $\neg (Ia \land Ja) \lor \neg Ea$	
6) $\neg Ia \lor Ja \lor \neg Ea$	
o o	

As can be seen, this tree cannot be closed. So the argument is invalid.

Make the following selection: Universe of Discourse: All numbers

Ix : x is an odd number
Jx : x is an even number
Ex : x is a number
Cx : x is 2

It is easily verified that 1) is true on this interpretation, 2) is true on this interpretation but now we come to the conclusion in its negated form ¬ (There exists an x so that x is 2 implies x is not an odd number) but then the negation of a true sentence has truth value false and we have shown we can select statements that make the premises true and the conclusion false. Therefore, this argument form is invalid.

c) Some foolish people smoke marijuana. Some students do not smoke marijuana. Therefore some students are not foolish. (Fx, Mx, Sx)

1)	$(\exists x)(Fx \wedge M(x))$	
2)	$(\exists x)(Sx \wedge \neg M(x))$	
3)	$\neg (\exists x)(Sx \wedge \neg F(x))$	SM Negate conclusion
4)	$\forall x \neg (Sx \wedge \neg F(x))$	3, Rules for negations of quantifiers
5)	$\neg (Sa \wedge \neg F(a))$	4, Universal Instantiation
6)	¬ Sa F(a)	
	o o	

Argument is invalid because branches stay open.

We make the following assignments:

UD (Universe of Discourse): Positive integers
Mx: x is an even number
Sx: x is an odd number
Fx: x is number 2

We can verify that 1) $(\exists x)(Fx \wedge M(x))$ is true since it amounts to x is number and x is an even number as for, 2) $(\exists x)(Sx \wedge \neg M(x))$ it is also true since it amounts to x is an odd number and x is not an even number. We verify the conclusion 3) $\neg (\exists x)(Sx \wedge \neg F(x))$ which amount to not (x is an odd number and x is not number 2), since the inside of the parenthesis is true, the negation is false and we have found an interpretation for which the premises are true and the conclusion is false. QED.

d) No blonde woman uses gel, but some blonde women use peroxide. Therefore, some women use peroxide and not hair gel (Bx, Wx, x, Px)

1) $\forall x ((Wx \wedge Bx) \rightarrow (\neg Hx \wedge Px))$	
2) ¬ $(\exists x) (Wx \wedge \neg Hx \wedge Px)$	Using the tree method for predicate logic.
3) ¬ (Wa ∧ Ba) (¬ Ha ∧ Pa)	Using universal instantiation on 1
4) ¬ Wa ¬Ba ¬ Ha	De Morgan's laws, Predicate disjunction
5) Pa	
6) $\forall x \neg (Wx \wedge \neg Hx \wedge Px)$	By quantifier negation laws

No matter how hard we try we will not be able to close all branches. We notice this because there is no way to get a contradiction on the Bx variable since it only appears once. Since we could develop a consistent counter-example by negating the conclusion and seeking to close all tree branches, we must conclude that the argument is valid.

Hence we cannot provide an arithmetic interpretation to show that this argument is invalid.

e) All teachers are clever. Some doctors are clever. Therefore some doctors are teachers. (Tx, Dx, Cx)

1) $\forall x \ (Tx \rightarrow Cx)$
2) $(\exists x) (Dx \land Cx)$
3) $\neg (\exists x) (Dx \land T(x))$ SM Negate conclusion; Tree method for trees in predicate logic
4) $\neg Ta \quad Ca$ 1, by Universal quantification
5) $Db \quad Cb \quad Db \quad Cb$ 2, existential quantification
6)) $\forall x \ \neg(Dx \land T(x)) \quad \forall x \ \neg (Dx \land T(x)) \quad \forall x \ \neg (Dx \land T(x)) \quad \forall x \ \neg (Dx \land T(x))$ Neg. Quant
7) $\neg Dc \quad \neg Tc \quad\quad \neg Dc \quad \neg Tc \quad\quad \neg Dc \quad \neg Tc \quad\quad \neg Dc \quad \neg Tc$

We can see that we cannot close the Cb branch no matter what we do. So we are forced to conclude that no consistent counter-example be devised to close all branches in the tree so the argument is invalid.

We can also observe that this is AII 2, by the Venn diagram method we know this argument to be invalid. The student and reader should convince himself of this by deriving the solution to this exercise using the tree method.

We also find an arithmetic interpretation to show invalidity.

    UD: All positive integers
    Tx: x is number 2
    Cx: x is an even number
    Dx: x is greater than 1

We can verify that $\neg (\exists x) (Dx \land T(x))$ is false since it amounts to not (x is number 2 and x is greater than 1) but not (true) is false. So the argument is invalid.

QUESTIONS | THE THREE LAWS OF THOUGHT P. 97

1. What is the difference between the principle of the excluded middle and logical bivalence?

The principle of excluded middle makes a claim about the nature of reality. It is a metaphysical or ontological notion. There is no middle between truth and falsity. Something is either true or false, *tertium non datur*. For bivalence a statement can be only true or false, but this is a semantic claim about the truth in our model or representational system not a truth about the universe or reality.

3. Are there logics in which the concept of bivalence does not hold but the principle of excluded middle does?

As far as I can tell, no. All logics that are minimally bivalent also satisfy excluded middle principles. To a certain extent this is misnomer since excluded middle is taken to apply to reality and bivalence applies only to a representation of reality. In theory all three valued logics that are owed originally to Lukacsiewicz are non-bivalent unless the "possible" truth-value always corresponds or is reduced to true. If "possible" is reducible to "false", then non-bivalence is guaranteed or embedded into to the three valued logic.

5. Are the principles in the above question metaphysical and logical or empirical?

The identity of indiscernibles seems to be an empirical claim about our cognitive ability to discern what Leibniz called les petites perceptions. The indiscernibility of identicals is an ontological and logical claim that is independent of our capacity to discern infinitesimally small objects.

7. Give an example of a situation in science where you would apply the identity of indiscernibles.

Some scientists do not believe the notion of logical-mathematical infinitesimals is neither reasonable nor coherent. They are using some version of this principle to ground their claims.

9. Why is logic related to ontology in Fichte's, Schelling's and Hegel's philosophical-idealist?

There is no small danger in the completeness and attempted completing of German Idealism and in its claims to absoluteness. The idealists all claimed and Hegel is the culmination of that tradition that the principle of identity is not merely logical but also ontological and metaphysical. In short they made the preposterous claim that logical and ontological identity were the same thing or a bit tautologously, identical. It is my claim that it is dangerous to assert such a total identity in the political and ethical realm that is essentially concerned with principles of limitation and with finite rights.

Critical Thinking, Informal Logic & Inductive Reasoning

2.2 Statistical Syllogisms

EXERCISES | INDUCTIVE REASONING AND INFORMAL LOGIC P. 105

Determine which of the following statistical syllogisms are weak and which are strong and justify your argument.

1. 92% of freshmen at McGill are Quebec residents. Jessica is a freshman at McGill University. Therefore, Jessica is a Quebec resident.

> *I will go through each exercise but as an excellent ex-student, Ian Wilkins, pointed out, all the examples are somewhat weak since the conclusion of each exercise should have "probably" or "most likely" in their conclusions to make the claims more prudent and to strengthen the arguments. With this preface, the first would be strong under normal conditions.*

3. Professor Horst grew up in a small mining town. Most people who grow up in small mining towns have never read Plato. So Professor Horst has never read Plato.

This is weak because it represents an atypical individual. Professors generally read more than the average population and so it is likely Horst has read Plato.

5. Most people in this town who voted (63 per cent of voters), voted for Mayor Coderre. You voted. So you supported Mayor Coderre.

The percentage is low so the argument is weak.

2.3 Formal Fallacies

EXERCISES | FORMAL FALLACIES P. 113 - 114

The first step in determining what formal fallacy we are examining is establishing the canonical or standard form of the syllogism. This can be EAO-4, AAA-1, for example. Once that form is fixed in terms of mood and figure, the major and the minor term can be ascertained clearly. The major term is the term in the first premise that is not the middle term. The minor term is the term in the second premise that is not the middle term.

1. This is a fallacy of affirming the consequent.
2. This is a fallacy of affirming a disjunct.
3. This is a fallacy of the undistributed middle.
4. This is fallacy of affirming the disjunct.
5. This a fallacy of the illicit negative.
6. This is a fallacy of four terms.
7. This is a fallacy of illicit affirmative.
8. This is a fallacy of undistributed middle.
9. This is a fallacy of illicit major.
10. This is a fallacy of affirming the consequent.
11. This is a fallacy of illicit minor.
12. This is a fallacy of illicit negative.
13. This is fallacy of denying the antecedent.
14. This is a fallacy of affirming a disjunct.
15. This is a fallacy of affirming a disjunct.
16. This is a fallacy of affirming a disjunct.
17. This is a fallacy of the illicit negative.
18. This is a fallacy of illicit minor.
19. This is a fallacy of illicit major.
20. This is a fallacy of illicit minor.
21. This is a fallacy of undistributed middle.
22. This is a fallacy of four terms.
23. This is a fallacy of illicit negative.
24. This is a fallacy of illicit affirmative.
25. This is a fallacy of illicit negative.
26. This is a fallacy of four terms.
27. This is a fallacy of undistributed middle.
28. This is a fallacy of undistributed middle.
29. This is a fallacy of illicit major.
30. This is a negation fallacy of exclusive premises.
31. This is a negation fallacy of illicit negative.
32. This is a negation fallacy of exclusive premises.
33. This is a negation fallacy of illicit affirmative.
34. This is a negation fallacy of exclusive premises.
35. This is a negation fallacy of illicit negative
36. This is a negation fallacy of exclusive premises.
37. This is a negation fallacy of illicit affirmative.
38. This is a negation fallacy of exclusive premises.
39. This is a negation fallacy of illicit negative.
40. This is a negation fallacy of exclusive premises.

SOLUTIONS TO EXERCISES

Note: The fallacies of negation were not fully introduced in the main body of the textbook. What was missing was the fallacy of exclusive premises which occurs when a syllogism has two negative premises. Exercises 30, 32, 34, 36, 38, 40 are cases of fallacies of exclusive premises.

EXERCISES | INFORMAL FALLACIES P. 131 - 132

Identify the following fallacies and group them under the categories of A) Informal Fallacies (if you are in the presence of an informal fallacy name it and classify it as 1) Linguistic Fallacies 2) Fallacies of Intrusion 3) Fallacies with Built-In Assumptions and 4) Causal Fallacies, 5) Omission Fallacies B) Formal Fallacies (also name the formal fallacy when you classify one of the fallacies as formal).

1) Criminal actions are illegal, and all murder trials are criminal actions, thus all murder trials are illegal. (Here the term "criminal actions" is used with two different meanings. Example borrowed from Copi and Cohen: 113)

This is a case of equivocation. The example is not so good: a murder trial is an action against a criminal not a criminal action.

3) Atoms are colorless. Cats are made of atoms, so cats are colorless.

Division fallacy. The parts may not have the same property as the whole.

5) Evidence of absence is absence of evidence is not solved.

This is a circular fallacy or a fallacy of begging the question.

7) Either you go to school and will get a good job or you will live in poverty for the rest of your life.

This is a case of false dilemma.

9) Donald Trump says that white people are victims of police brutality just as often as black people... but honestly, would you believe a claim made by a racist?

This is a case of attacking the person; or an Ad Hominem fallacy.

11) Everyone going shopping will increase consumer spending and will help increase our country's GDP. Everyone needs to shop because the price of oil has dropped and the global economy will soon enter into a recession.

This is a composition fallacy.

13) Socrates never existed. The only people who have ever written about him are Plato, Xenophon and Aristophanes. But they were all Sophists and wanted to deceive the people in order to create the myth of the philosopher-martyr.

This is a burden of proof fallacy.

15) There will not be a referendum in Catalonia despite public opinion being in favor of it. The people have to obey the Constitution and the Constitution will only allow a national referendum on the autonomy of one of the regions of the country. Democracy is not the rule of the people by the people it is the submission of citizens to the rule of law and to the *Rechtsstaat*.

This is an authority argument (ad verecundiam), legitimacy of a political system comes from public opinion and the consensual constitution of a political will or processes of consultation of public opinion that lead to the expression and selection of political options by a given population of citizens and individuals on a determinate and clearly defined territory.

17) Love is the natural law of all Creation. The purpose of all beings is to love each other and to live harmoniously. Even where natural beings apparently pursue their selfish goals and personal interests, the higher law of Love is the real explanation and source for their actions.

This is a fallacy of the single cause. The fallacy is also true.

19) I have been unlucky recently on the stock market. All the stocks I have bought have lost some of their value. However since the stock market as whole always increases its value in time, the next stock I buy will probably increase its net worth in the next month.

This is a case of the Gambler's fallacy.

21) There are two different words to talk about Being and existence. Ontology discusses Being while metaphysics discusses existence. Therefore Being and existence are different topics. As soon as two different words exist this means that two different realities exist that are explained and talked about by these different words.

This is an etymological fallacy but words do matter when doing philosophy and when trying to distinguish metaphysics from ontology.

23) How do you know that people at CERN (note: This is an advanced particle physics laboratory located in Geneva, Switzerland) will not create a black hole with their crazy experiments. They have to prove that their experiments will not destroy the earth or the United Nations should shut them down.

This is a fallacy of the burden of proof.

25) You have never met him in person. He is part of a government cover-up to install a world-dictatorship run by a puppet-figure.

This is a fallacy of the burden of proof.

27) The Buddha was a great man but he should not be a role model for anyone because he had trouble controlling his appetite. In fact few people know this but he actually died of an indigestion.

This is a fallacy of attacking the person. It is also historically true.

2.4 Necessary & Sufficient Conditions & Inductive Reasoning

EXERCISES | INDUCTIVE REASONING AND INFORMAL LOGIC P. 140

For the arguments 1- 10 listed below:

1. Distinguish inductive from deductive arguments.
2. Formalize or standardize each argument—that is, reduce them to their form or structure.
3. For deductive arguments, ascertain whether the argument is valid and sound;
4. For inductive arguments determine whether the argument is inductively strong or weak.

1) And it must not be imagined that in this I commit the fallacy which logicians call arguing in a circle, for since experience renders the greater part of these effects very certain, the causes from which I deduce them do not so much serve to prove their existence as to explain them; on the other hand, the causes are explained by the effects. (Descartes, *Discourse On Method,* Part VI)

> **Argument**
>
> **P1:** *for since experience renders the greater part of these effects very certain*
>
> **P2 :** *on the other hand, the causes are explained by the effects*
>
> **P3:** *the causes from which I deduce them do not so much serve to prove their existence as to explain them.*
>
> **Conclusion**: *it must not be imagined that in this I commit the fallacy which logicians call arguing in a circle.*
>
> This is an inductive argument because it requires experience for confirmation of its affirmations and seems to proceed from the particular to the general.

3) More recent philosophy, as an epistemological scepticism, is, in a concealed or open manner, anti-Christian , although (and this is said for more refined ears) in no way antireligious. Formerly, that is, people believed in "the soul," as they believed in grammar and the grammatical subject. They said "I" is the condition, "think" is the predicate and conditioned—thinking is an activity for which a subject must be thought of as cause. Now, people tried, with an admirable tenacity and trickery, to see whether they could get out of this net, whether perhaps the opposite might not be true: "think" as the condition, "I" the conditioned—thus "I" is only a synthesis which is itself created by thinking. (Friedrich Nietzsche, *Beyond Good And Evil,* Aphorism 54)

> **Partial argument**
>
> **P1:** *Formerly, that is, people believed in "the soul," as they believed in grammar and the grammatical subject.*
>
> **P2 :** *They said "I" is the condition, "think" is the predicate and conditioned - thinking is an activity for which a subject must be thought of as cause.*
>
> **P3:** *Now, people tried, with an admirable tenacity and trickery, to see whether they could get out of this net, whether perhaps the opposite might not be true: "think" as the condition, "I"the conditioned—thus "I" is only a synthesis which is itself created by thinking.*

Conclusion: *More recent philosophy, as an epistemological scepticism, is, in a concealed or open manner, anti-Christian.*

The argument seems deductive since it is a critique of the deductive cogito argument which seeks to establish the general claim that knowledge scepticism is anti-Christian.

5) It is in the empiricist development, as we know, that the new psychology, which was required as a correlate to pure natural science when the latter was separated out, is brought to its first concrete execution. Thus it is concerned with investigations of introspective psychology in the field of the soul, which has now been separated from the body, as well as with physiological and psycho-physical explanations. On the other hand, this psychology is of service to a theory of knowledge which, compared with the Cartesian one, is completely new and very differently worked out. In Locke's great work this is the actual intent from the start. It offers itself as a new attempt to accomplish precisely what Descartes's Meditations intended to accomplish: an epistemological grounding of the objectivity of the objective sciences. (Edmund Husserl, *The Crisis of the European Sciences*, 1937, Section 22)

Argument

P1: it (the new psychology, PC) is concerned with investigations of introspective psychology in the field of the soul, which has now been separated from the body, as well as with physiological and psychophysical explanations

P2 : On the other hand, this psychology is of service to a theory of knowledge which, compared with the Cartesian one, is completely new and very differently worked out.

P3: In Locke's great work this is the actual intent from the start.

P4: It offers itself as a new attempt to accomplish precisely what Descartes's Meditations intended to accomplish: an epistemological grounding of the objectivity of the objective sciences.

Conclusion: *It is in the empiricist development, as we know, that the new psychology, which was required as a correlate to pure natural science when the latter was separated off, is brought to its first concrete execution.*

This argument seems to be at best a mixture of both induction and deduction, general considerations are there, but so is a concern with the particular and the empirical and there are many historical considerations that are generally associated with induction.

7) The problem of perception presents itself to theoretical philosophy under a twofold aspect: it may be considered from a psychological and from an epistemological standpoint. Throughout the history of philosophy, the two have been in constant conflict; but the more sharply the oppositions develop, the more evident it seems that here precisely are the two poles around which the whole problem of perception must necessarily move. (Ernst Cassirer, *The Philosophy of Symbolic Forms*, Volume 3: *The Phenomenology of Knowledge*, Part I, Chapter 2).

Argument

P1: *The problem of perception presents itself to theoretical philosophy under a twofold aspect:*

P2 : *it may be considered from a psychological and from an epistemological standpoint.*

P3: *Throughout the history of philosophy, the two have been in constant conflict;*

Conclusion: *but the more sharply the oppositions develop, the more evident it seems that here precisely are the two poles around which the whole problem of perception must necessarily move.*

Perception and sense-perception is usually a matter of induction since it depends on observation of particulars.

EXERCISES | STATISTICAL SYLLOGISM P. 141

Are the following statistical syllogisms inductively cogent (i.e. strong) or weak? Why?

(1)   93% of freshmen at Concordia are from Quebec.
         Anna is a freshman at Concordia.
         Anna is from Quebec.

This is generally strong with the proviso of using "probably" and "most likely" instead of concluding categorically as is done in this exercise.

(2)   Very few employees at the Nortel Networks are from Ontario.
         Paul is an employee of Nortel Networks.
         Paul is not from Ontario.

This is a weak argument but Paul Catanu did work at Nortel Networks from 1999 to 2000!

(3)   Approximately 91% of professional philosophers are men.
         Bettina Sawyer, is a professional philosopher.
         Therefore Bettina Sawyer is a man.

It's a weak and fallacious argument. Bettina Sawyer is a great teacher and an atypical individual as the author's professor Bettina Bergo (University of Montreal) used to be.

(4)   Most of what R. Feynman has to say about the universe at the time of the Big Bang is correct.
         R. Feynman says that the universe was more highly disordered at the time of the Big Bang than it is today.
         The universe was more highly disordered at the time of the Big Bang than it is today.

This is an authority fallacy. Feynman is an expert and the science is right but it's not because he says so.

CRITICAL THINKING, WORLDVIEWS & LOGIC

SOLUTIONS

EXERCISES | ANALOGICAL INDUCTION P. 141 - 142

Analyze the following inductive analogies in terms of :

(a) The number of properties or features that the things being compared share.
(b) The relevance of the known similar properties or characteristics to the properties or characteristics inferred through the similarity in the conclusion
(c) The number and multiplicity of examples examined through the alleged or perceived analogy.

A. The universe is a living organism. It comprises processes of exchange, transportation, regulation, and equilibrium. It actuates and changes just like a living organism. Its parts are coordinated so that the part does not destroy the whole and the whole fully encompasses the part. Furthermore, like an organism the universe can birth smaller sub-worlds through the process of black wholes and of mini Big Bangs. One is forced to conclude that the universe possesses all the properties of a living organism and thus is alive. (Argument adapted and paraphrased from Plato's Timaeus).

> *The things being compared are the universe and a living organism. There are 3 aspects that are being compared: The fact that both organisms and the universe contain: I) processes of exchange, transportation, regulation and equilibrium; II) that both actuate and change; III) that its parts are coordinated so that the part does not destroy the whole and whole fully encompasses the part; and IV) a) the universe, like an organism, can birth smaller sub-worlds. b) the relevance is not always appropriate: for example when the universe breeds sub-worlds, those sub-worlds are not alive. The problem of the comparison from a scientific point of view is that the universe is known to be inorganic whereas life is organic. This is the weakness of the whole analogy. c) there is a multiplicity of examples we have listed at least four in point a).*

B. Democracy possesses many decision-making processes that are similar to that of a family. Parents often discuss with their children what they want to do and then decide what the proper course is for action. Similarly, in democracies there are large consultation processes such as focus groups and town hall meetings where leaders listen to its citizens. Like in families, these leaders then discuss among each other, just like a mother and father do, and come to the right decision as to what course the country should be set upon.

> *The things being compared are a family and the democracy of a whole country or province or city. The points of comparison are: I) the existence of discussion between parents and their children and leaders of countries who consult the people in focus groups and town hall meetings, provinces or cities; II) the coming to a decision about a proper course of action. The example smacks of paternalism. It is not clear what is*

bad that the electorate or citizenry be treated as children or that children be let to influence the decision of parents when they do not possess the maturity. In any case consultation both in families and political systems is required if the country is not to veer to utter tyranny or dictatorship. Good luck Mr Trump!

C. The universe is extremely complex and harmoniously organized. Like a clock every wheel and cog has its proper role and place. Such a perfection in design and in symmetry can only be explained through a preter-human intelligence. The clock must possess a clock-maker and the clock-maker of our universe is none other than our loving and benevolent God, our Lord. (Argument adapted and paraphrased from William Paley).

The argument from design or the teleological argument is interesting but weaker than the ontological argument for the existence of God in the opinion of this author. As Hume famously argued, there does not have to be one clock-maker, there could be a team of spirits who build up the universe. The fact that a mechanism works or a that a whole seems to subsist in reality does not guarantee that its internal parts are also constituted in the same way as the whole and have the same origin. Sometimes the argument from design is reduced a bit unjustly to a composition fallacy.

D. A beehive is like humanity on a smaller scale. There is division of labor, there is hierarchy, there are historical cycles when the queen mates and creates offspring and a new generation of bees appears. Bees like humans are highly intelligent and organized. Thus it is no wonder that Tolstoy compared the totality of humanity to a gigantic beehive in his great historical novel War and Peace.

The analogy between bees and humanity is interesting but bees lack individuality. Tolstoy's compatibilistic view of free will is not acceptable to the author. He thinks of free will in materialist and scientistic ways which reduces the problem of free will to historicistic consideration on the nature of human power. Famously for Tolstoy, it is not the officer or general Kutuzov who determines the fate of the war against Napoleon at Borodino, but the variegated and finite wills of the soldiers which coalesce in an irrational and unpredictable way. Tolstoy seems to be under the influence of Hegel's concept of the ruse of reason but ultimately his vision of human individualism is reductive and unbelievable to the eyes of this author. Dostoevsky not Tolstoy!

E. Human beings are a lot like apes. They are gregarious, can feel pain. They have alpha-males and strong females that dominate certain groups. Furthermore, the study of apes has shown that they possess an elementary communication system and can identify certain basic concepts. There is no doubt that apes and humans are related in a biological evolutionary sense. Therefore we should treat apes with compassion just as we treat human beings compassionately whenever possible.

The argument sounds cogent and reasonable to me. Pain and awareness of pain is the criterion for treating any form of life with compassion. The analogy is also convincing. Humans are forgettable and forgetful apes and simians!

CRITICAL THINKING, WORLDVIEWS & LOGIC

EXERCISES | NECESSARY & SUFFICIENT CONDITIONS P. 140

Determine whether the following statements are true or false.

1. *Being a circle is sufficient for having an infinite number of sides.*

   The assertion that a geometrical object has an infinite number of sides implies the truth or mathematical fact that this object is a circle.

3. *Hating someone is not sufficient for being hated.*

   This is true. A person who hates someone might not be hated by anyone perhaps because there are only good people in our logical world. (sic)

5. *Being selfish is both necessary and sufficient for being a great genius.*

   The statement is open to interpretation. If you heed Nietzsche, the statement is true. If you heed Christ, it is false.

7. *Being talented is sufficient for being famous.*

   The statement is false. Some talented people are cult failures and are known only after their death. Promotion and perhaps self-promotion go into it.

9. *Being a rational number is necessary for being a real number.*

   The statement is true. A real number is not necessarily rational but a rational number is necessarily real.

11. *The consequences of one's actions are sufficient for having one convicted.*

    From a juridical perspective, the statement is true.

13. *Being a complex number is necessary for being a transcendental number.*

    The statement is false. Transcendental numbers are not necessarily complex numbers. Complex numbers are algebraic. Transcendental numbers are not; they derive their nature and truth from geometry.

15. *Being either e or π is sufficient for being a transcendental number.*

    This statement is true.

SOLUTIONS TO EXERCISES

EXERCISES | NECESSARY & SUFFICIENT CONDITIONS (CON'T) P. 141

a) not being poor, being rich

>Being rich is sufficient for not being poor.

b) being an even number, being divisible by 2

>Being divisible by 2 is sufficient for being an even number.

c) being an intelligent student, being the most intelligent student

>Being the most intelligent student is sufficient for being an intelligent student.

d) having ten dollars, having more than five dollars

>Having ten dollars is sufficient for having more than five dollars.

e) giving money to another person in exchange for a favour, corruption

>Giving money to another person in exchange for a favour is not sufficient for being corrupt; the other person has to accept the money, too.

f) taking place on a weekday, not being held on Saturday

>If X takes place on a weekday it is sufficient for it not being held on Saturday.

EXERCISES | MILL'S METHOD P. 141

Classify these arguments according to Mill's classification of inductive causal arguments.

A) The ounce of gold has hit $1000 Canadian on the world market only 8 times in the last 30 years. Sometimes there were wars; sometimes there weren't. Sometimes the price of oil went up; sometimes it did not. But the price of gold always went up when the global market went into a recession.

>*This is a case of agreement. There were many different cases but always when the price of gold went up, a recession occurred. Therefore this Mill's case of agreement.*

B) Simon was sad all week, but then his mood improved remarkably. He started laughing a lot and went out to see his friends during the rest of the week. He had applied to law school and I think he received some good news this week with respect to his application.

>*This is a case of difference. As soon as Simon got some information with respect to his application his mood improved. That is the only difference with respect to his general situation and feelings that occurred that can explain the change in mood.*

C) We did a blind test with thirty customers. We gave them Coke and Pepsi in different cups. 80% of our customers preferred Pepsi without knowing what they were drinking. The only cause can be that Pepsi tastes better than Coke.

Whenever there is a case of two substances we know as established in the text book that we are in a situation of agreement and difference according to Mill's Laws.

D) The reason there had been so many terrorist attacks in the Austro-Hungarian Empire is that the Slav minority had been oppressed. Every time a large number of Slavs had been killed, persecuted or unfairly jailed there had occurred a terrorist attack in the Austro-Hungarian Empire. The last attack started the First World War.

This is a case of agreement. The situations were different in many ways but whenever the Slav minority had been unfairly oppressed there had been terrorist attacks in the Austro-Hungarian empire.

E) The risk of diabetes is related to the amount of blood sugar. The higher the blood sugar the higher the risk of diabetes. There is a direct connection between the level of blood sugar and the risk of diabetes.

This is a case of correlation or concomitant variation according to Mill's Laws. The higher the blood-sugar the higher the risk of diabetes.

F) We tested different ant exterminators over the years. Each had different methods of protecting the apartments that needed to get rid of ants. Over the years, the best exterminators all used boric acid as part of their exterminating products.

This is a case of agreement according to Mill's Laws. Different methods were used but all the good exterminators used one single substance upon which there was agreement: boric acid.

www.ingramcontent.com/pod-product-compliance
Lightning Source LLC
Chambersburg PA
CBHW080534300426
44111CB00017B/2714